Low Carbon Development

'In this student-friendly edited volume, Urban and Nordensvärd have produced the first comprehensive introduction to low carbon development. In this one volume there is an impressive focus on the economic, political and social prospects for low carbon strategies across a range of policy areas in both the rich and poor worlds.'

Dr Michael Cahill, Reader at the University of Brighton, UK

'Low carbon development is a term now widely used, often poorly understood, but increasingly central to issues both of climate change and economic development. This multi-authored textbook, the first on the subject, gives an admirably clear, comprehensive and readable introduction to the many aspects of this important new idea, and faces squarely the difficult dilemmas that low carbon development poses.'

Professor Gordon MacKerron, Director, SPRU (Science and Technology Policy Research), University of Sussex, UK

'*Low Carbon Development* is a fascinating publication about a new development paradigm. Urban and Nordensvärd paint a comprehensive picture of possible transformations needed to achieve climate compatibility. Natural scientists and social scientists both have their say. The authors analyse country cases from the OECD, Latin America, Asia and Africa and illuminate the economic, social, technological and institutional dimensions of transformation as well as strategies for realizing this goal. This publication sets standards for research on low carbon development.'

Professor Dirk Messner, Director, German Development Institute/ Deutsches Institut für Entwicklungspolitik (DIE), Germany

Low Carbon Development is the first comprehensive textbook to address the interface between international development and climate change in a carbon-constrained world. It discusses the key conceptual, empirical and policy-related issues of low carbon development and takes an international and interdisciplinary approach to the subject by drawing on insights from across the natural sciences and social sciences whilst embedding the discussion in a global context.

The first part explores the concept of low carbon development and explains the need for low carbon development in a carbon-constrained world. The book then discusses the key issues of socio-economic, political and technological nature for low carbon development, exploring topics such as the political economy, social justice, financing and carbon markets, and technologies and innovation for low carbon development. This is followed by key issues for low carbon development in policy and practice, which is presented based on cross-cutting issues such as low carbon energy, forestry, agriculture and transportation. Afterwards, practical case studies are discussed from low carbon development in low income countries in Africa, middle income countries in Asia and Latin America and high income countries in Europe and North America.

Written by an international team of leading academics and practitioners in the field of low carbon development, this book is essential reading for students, academics, professionals and policy-makers interested in the fields of low carbon development, climate change mitigation, climate policy, climate change and development, global environmental change, and environment and development.

Frauke Urban is Lecturer in Environment and Development at the Centre for Development, Environment and Policy (CeDEP) at the School of Oriental and African Studies (SOAS), UK. She specializes in the linkages between energy, climate change and development, especially low carbon development, climate change mitigation and energy policy.

Johan Nordensvärd is a Researcher specializing in the field of social policy and low carbon development, globalization, global climate governance and energy policy at the London School of Economics and Political Science (LSE), UK.

Key Issues in Environment and Sustainability

This series provides comprehensive, original and accessible texts on the core topics in environment and sustainability. The texts take an interdisciplinary and international approach to the key issues in this field.

1. Low Carbon Development: Key Issues
Edited by Frauke Urban and Johan Nordensvärd

Forthcoming title:

2. Sustainability: Key Issues
Edited by George Holmes

Low Carbon Development

Key issues

**Edited by Frauke Urban and
Johan Nordensvärd**

Routledge
Taylor & Francis Group

LONDON AND NEW YORK

earthscan
from Routledge

First published 2013
by Routledge
2 Park Square, Milton Park, Abingdon, Oxon, OX14 4RN

Simultaneously published in the USA and Canada
by Routledge
711 Third Avenue, New York, NY 10017

Routledge is an imprint of the Taylor & Francis Group, an informa business

British Library Cataloguing in Publication Data
A catalogue record for this book is available from the British Library

Library of Congress Cataloging-in-Publication Data
A catalog record has been requested for this book

ISBN13: 978-0-415-53898-5 (hbk)
ISBN13: 978-0-415-53901-2 (pbk)
ISBN13: 978-0-203-10862-8 (ebk)

Typeset in Times by
FiSH Books Ltd, Enfield

MIX
Paper from
responsible sources
FSC® C013056
www.fsc.org

Printed and bound in Great Britain by
TJ International Ltd, Padstow, Cornwall

Contents

List of figures and tables

Figures

Tables

Notes on contributors

Ewan Bloomfield is an Energy Consultant at Practical Action Consulting with 15 years' experience in international development in a number of countries, including Central and South Asia, Haiti, and East and Southern Africa. Ewan has a strong track record in international development and interdisciplinary research on all aspects of household energy access and poverty reduction, including for the Department for International Development (DfID), the World Bank, the European Union (EU) and the United Nations Development Program (UNDP). Ewan currently manages the energy delivery theme of the 5-year DfID-funded PISCES bioenergy research project, which includes the development of policy support tools for more efficiently and sustainably utilizing bioenergy resources.

Rob Byrne has been working in the sustainable energy field for more than 15 years. He is particularly experienced in energy and development in an African context, having spent a total of 5 years on renewable energy projects in a number of countries (Botswana, Tanzania and Kenya). He is a Research Fellow in Science and Technology Policy Research (SPRU) at the University of Sussex, and convenes the energy and climate domain work of the STEPS Centre. His focus is the role of science, technology and innovation in energy and development, sustainability and poverty reduction.

Blane Harvey works with the Agriculture and Environment Program at Canada's International Development Research Centre (IDRC). His research examines how knowledge on climate change is produced, validated and shared; the role of culture and technology in learning, communication and knowledge sharing; and how power dynamics shape inter-institutional cooperation. Prior to joining IDRC, he was a Research Fellow in the Institute of Development Studies' (IDS) Climate Change Team. He holds a PhD in education and international development from McGill University.

Merylyn Hedger is a Research Associate at the Overseas Development Institute (ODI). She has led research projects across both the mitigation and adaptation agendas and delivered a range of products. She has extensive experience in public sector decision-making at all scales of governance and direct responsibilities as a practitioner for policy-making on climate change, and the provision of advice on regulation. She has provided guidance, developed tools and vision for frameworks on new ways of working on the cross-cutting issue of climate change at international, national and sub-national levels. Recently she has been focusing on climate finance at national level. Dr Hedger has degrees from the LSE and Liverpool University and holds a PhD in energy policy from Imperial College, London. In 2002 she was awarded the OBE for services to climate change assessment.

Eva Heiss is an international development consultant who has been involved in projects in Bolivia, Brazil, Chile and Mexico, working for Non-Governmental Organizations (NGOs), the private sector and the United Nations (UN). She is currently working at the Inter-American Development Bank (IADB), where she contributes to the solution-seeking process of potentially affected communities through IADB-financed development projects. She holds a German Diplom (FH) in international business administration and foreign trade and an MSc in climate change and development from the Institute of Development Studies (IDS).

Rocio Hiraldo is a PhD Research Fellow at the University of East Anglia and the University of Copenhagen. Her work focuses on poverty, citizenship and environmental justice. She is also a Researcher at the Responsive Forestry Governance initiative, studying the politics of choice and the local democracy effects of forestry-related climate change interventions in Senegal, where she has worked for over a year. She holds a BA in anthropology and an MA in development studies from IDS, University of Sussex, where she did research on climate change and development policy processes. She has published two papers on the international political economy of REDD+.

Hilawe Lakew studied renewable energy and the environment at the University of Reading in the UK. He has worked on various energy technology development and renewable energy resource assessment projects including solar, wind, biomass and micro hydropower. He has worked in the energy sector for 20 years in formulating energy policy, rural energy planning and management, which involves designing, planning, monitoring and evaluation of various energy-related cross-sectoral projects. He has managed, coordinated and led teams on several local and international energy, environment and development projects related to rural and urban energy efficiency, RET development, marketing and commercialization of innovations. His regional focus is Ethiopia.

Markus Lederer is a Professor in political science with a focus on international relations at the Technical University Darmstadt in Germany. His research interests cover climate politics, in particular carbon markets, REDD+ and the role of developing/emerging economies. He received his PhD from the Ludwig-Maximilian University in Munich (2003) and has been an Assistant Professor at the University of Potsdam (2003–2011), Substitute Professor at the University of Bremen in 2010, Adjunct Professor at Universidad de Costa Rica, San José (2009) and Visiting Scholar at Columbia University in New York (1999–2000).

Matthew Lockwood is a social scientist with an interest in the political economy of climate and energy policy in both developed and developing countries. He is a Senior Research Fellow at the Energy Policy Group at the University of Exeter. He was previously Head of Climate Change at IDS, and Associate Director for Energy, Transport and Climate Change at the Institute for Public Policy Research (IPPR). He has also worked for a number of international NGOs and for the Universities of Sussex and Cambridge. He has a D.Phil from the University of Oxford.

Alexandra Mallett is an Assistant Professor, School of Public Policy and Administration (SPPA), Carleton University, Ottawa, Canada. She is also a Visiting Fellow, Sussex Energy Group (SEG), SPRU, University of Sussex. In addition, Alexandra worked for the Canadian government in the area of international energy and environmental policies. Her research focuses on the development, production, cooperation and adoption processes involved in low carbon energy technologies. She holds a PhD from the LSE, an MA from Dalhousie University, Halifax, Canada and a BA from the University of Toronto.

Napoleão Dequech Neto is an international development and partnerships specialist, who has lived and worked for several organizations in Brazil, Chile, Kenya, France, the UK and the USA. His research interests focus on identifying and analyzing development opportunities from an economic, social and environmental perspective. Mr Neto holds a BA in Law, from Unicuritiba, Brazil and an MSc in Climate change and Development from the Institute of Development Studies (IDS).'

Johan Nordensvärd is a political scientist with 10 years' experience. He currently works as Researcher in Social Policy and Development at the LSE. His work spans teaching, research and publications on social policy, welfare systems, global climate governance, climate and energy policy, education policy and citizenship. He holds a PhD in political science from the University of Oldenburg, an MA in political science and a BA in media and communication from the University of Lund. He has extensive knowledge of low carbon development and social policy. He is the editor of *Low Carbon Development: Key Issues* (Earthscan, 2013).

Andreas Oberheitmann is International Director of the Research Center for International Environmental Policy (RCIEP) and Visting Professor at the School of Environment at Tsinghua University in Beijing and Jiangnan Univerity in Wuxi, as well as Senior Research Fellow at the Rheinisch-Westfälisches Institut für Wirtschaftsforschung, Essen (Germany). The focus of work in the RCIEP is research and policy consulting on global climate change (low carbon economy in cities, post-Kyoto issues, the Clean Development Mechanism, etc.) His research results have been published in well-established and peer-reviewed journals such as *Mitigation and Adaptation Strategies for Global Change*, *Energy Policy* and the *American Journal of Climate Change*, as well as in books, partly in Chinese language. Professor Dr Oberheitmann is editor of a book on statistical analysis and empirical research in China and Member of the Editorial Board of the *American Journal of Climate Change*.

David Ockwell is a Senior Lecturer in the Geography Department at the University of Sussex, UK. He is also a Fellow of the Sussex Energy Group and the Tyndall Centre for Climate Change Research. David's research and teaching focuses on transitions to a low carbon economy with particular interest in low carbon technology transfer and development, public engagement with climate change, and reflexive climate and energy policy appraisal. He provides regular policy advice to a range of developed and developing country governments and several intergovernmental bodies.

Xiaodong Ruan is Research Assistant and PhD student at the Research Center for Eco-Environmental Science of the Chinese Academy of Sciences, Beijing. His research focuses on wastewater processing and global climate change policy (low carbon economy in cities, the Clean Development Mechanism, etc.) and the corresponding influence on the economy of China.

Jan Rosenow is currently doing a doctorate on energy efficiency policy at the Lower Carbon Futures Group of Oxford University's interdisciplinary Environmental Change Institute. Alongside his doctorate Jan works as a freelance consultant. He has more than 7 years of experience in energy and climate policy. Jan was a consultant in the London Office of

Enviros Consulting working in the Climate and Renewables Group. He also worked for Öko-Institut and the Wuppertal Institute for Climate, Environment and Energy. Jan holds two postgraduate degrees including an MSc in environmental policy and regulation from the LSE. Jan is also an active member of the Think Tank 30 of the Club of Rome.

Jennie C. Stephens is an Associate Professor of Environmental Science and Policy at Clark University in Worcester, Massachusetts. Professor Stephens' teaching, research and community engagement focuses on socio-political dimensions of energy technology innovation, renewable energy, carbon capture and storage, and climate change education/awareness. Professor Stephens received her PhD (2002) and MSc (1998) from the California Institute of Technology in environmental science and engineering, and she earned her BA (1997) from Harvard University in environmental science and public policy. Before joining the faculty at Clark, she did post-doctoral research at Harvard's Kennedy School, and she taught at Tufts, Boston University and Massachusetts Institute of Technology (MIT).

Letha Tawney is a Senior Associate in the World Resources Institute. Ms Tawney applies a decade of experience with global manufacturers and supply chains and years of research on energy policy to the challenges the renewable energy industry faces today as it matures and reaches scale. She has expertise in innovation policy, technology deployment and transfer, electricity markets and grid integration. Ms Tawney holds an MA in public administration from the Harvard Kennedy School and a BA in business from George Fox University.

Marie Blanche Ting is an interdiscplinary scientist with work experience in environmental science, energy and climate change. She is currently working as a Senior Specialist in Biotechnology and Health Innovation at the Ministry of Science and Technology, South Africa. Her academic and working experience over the past 10 years has given her expertise in bio-process engineering, biological treatment of water/effluent and waste, renewable energy, microbial kinetics and bio-catalysis research. She is now expanding her work experience to include low carbon development, policy and strategy relative to clean technologies.

Thomas Tanner is a Research Fellow at IDS specializing in climate change adaptation and its links to poverty and development. He has been engaged for 15 years with environment and development issues as a researcher, practitioner, policy-maker and negotiator on UN conventions. His work links climate change impacts and response strategies with poverty, vulnerability and social justice. Specific research interests include organizational learning and tools for mainstreaming climate change into development cooperation, child-centred approaches to disaster risk reduction and adaptation, urban climate governance and the political economy of climate change initiatives.

David Tyfield is a Lecturer at the Centre for Mobilities Research (CeMoRe), Sociology Department, Lancaster University. His research focuses on the interaction of political economy, socio-cultural change and developments in science, technology and innovation, with a particular interest in low carbon innovation in China. He was the lead researcher (2007–2010) for an Economic and Social Research Council-Advanced Institute of Management (ESRC-AIM) research-funded project examining low carbon innovation and international cooperation in China regarding agriculture, energy and transport. Recent publications include *Game-Changing China: Lessons from China about Disruptive*

Low-carbon Innovation (NESTA, 2010), a special issue of *Journal of Knowledge-based Innovation in China* on low carbon innovation in China (2010) and *The Economics of Science* (2 volumes) (Routledge, 2012).

Frauke Urban is an environmental scientist with 10 years' experience. She is a Lecturer at the Centre for Development, Environment and Policy (CeDEP) at the School of Oriental and African Studies (SOAS) at the University of London. Before joining SOAS she was a Research Fellow in Climate Change and Development at IDS at the University of Sussex, a Research Fellow at the University of Groningen in the Netherlands and a Visiting Researcher at Tsinghua University in China. Dr Urban works on the linkages between energy, climate change and development, especially low carbon development, climate change mitigation and energy and climate policy, with a regional interest in Asia, particularly China, India and Southeast Asia. She is currently the Principal Investigator for a project funded by the ESRC on Chinese hydropower dams in Africa and Asia. She is the editor of *Low Carbon Development: Key Issues* (Earthscan, 2013).

Annabel Yadoo has worked as an energy researcher and consultant for the international NGOs Practical Action and Renewable World. She has a PhD in delivery models for decentralized rural electrification from the University of Cambridge and has conducted fieldwork in Peru, Nepal, Kenya, Nicaragua and Mozambique. Annabel has published five journal and conference papers, presented at three international conferences and spent 2 months working as a researcher and assistant policy adviser in DfID's low carbon development team (part of the Climate and Environment Group). Annabel is now concentrating on building up her private sector skill set, working as a consultant for a leading management and strategy consultancy, Oliver Wyman.

Zhou Yuan is an Assistant Professor at the School of Public Policy and Management at Tsinghua University in Beijing, China. He received his PhD in technology management from the University of Cambridge in the UK in 2010. Prior to his PhD studies, he was a manager at Cascadia Capital (China) on technology commercialization transfer practice. Prior to that, he was a manager at the Nanyang Techno-entrepreneurship Centre at Nanyang Technological University (NTU) in Singapore, involved in technology entrepreneurship development activities. Joseph holds a BEng in mechanical engineering and an MSc in robotics design from NTU. He works on public policy, innovation policy and management.

Acknowledgements

We would like to thank all the contributors to this book for their valuable contributions: Ewan Bloomfield, Rob Byrne, Blane Harvey, Merylyn Hedger, Eva Heiss, Rocio Hiraldo, Hilawe Lakew, Markus Lederer, Matthew Lockwood, Alexandra Mallet, Napoleão Dequech Neto, Andreas Oberheitmann, David Ockwell, Xiaodong Ruan, Jan Rosenow, Jennie Stephens, Letha Tawney, Marie Blanche Ting, Thomas Tanner, David Tyfield, Annabel Yadoo and Zhou Yuan. We very much appreciate the time and effort you have invested in writing your chapters.

Beyond the chapter authors, we would like to thank our colleagues for stimulating discussions in the field of low carbon development, especially Hubert Schmitz, Rasmus Lema, Stephen Spratt, Lars Otto Naess, Andrew Newsham, Markus Hagemann, Niklas Höhne, Sarah Hendel-Blackford, Fatema Rajabali, Wang Yu, Shasha Wang, Yixin Dai, Ankita Narain Tilman Altenburg, Doris Fischer, Ambuj Sagar, Xue Lan, Shikha Bhasin, Ankur Chaudhary, Chen Ling and Qunhong Sheng. We would like to thank Michael Cahill for valuable discussions in the field of social policy and Giles Mohan, Sarah Cook and May Tan-Mullins for valuable discussions in the field of international development.

Thank you to institutions that have supported us throughout the book-writing process, especially SOAS, the LSE and IDS, as well as Laurence Smith, Nigel Poole, Andrew Dorward, Colin Poulton, Ben Daley and Rebecca Kent at CeDEP, SOAS. We would especially like to thank David Lewis and Tim Newburn at the LSE for their support.

Many thanks to our funders who have provided funding recently for projects in the low carbon field, including the Svenska Riksbanken Jubileumsfond and the Volkswagen Foundation, the Department for International Development (DfID), the Climate and Development Knowledge Network (CDKN) (special thanks to Natasha Grist), the Economics and Social Research Council (ESRC), the Commonwealth Secretariat and the departmental funds at SOAS.

We would like to thank Khanam Virjee, Helena Hurd and Helen Bell at Earthscan for providing editorial support and for managing the publication process. Thanks to Camille Bramall for copy-editing the book and to Mark Livermore and Karl Harrington from FiSH Books.

Finally, we would like to thank our families (especially Eva, Reinhold, Arne, Christina, Lennart, Peter and Helene) and our friends. And last, but not least, this book is dedicated to Emilie Sophie.

List of acronyms and abbreviations

AID	Alternative Indigenous Development Foundation
AIDS	Acquired Immunodeficiency Syndrome
ANC	African National Congress
AOSIS	Alliance of Small Island States
A/R	Afforestation and Reforestation
BAU	Business-As-Usual
BMVBS	Federal Ministry of Transport, Building and Urban Development
BMZ	German Federal Ministry for Economic Development Cooperation
BP	British Petroleum
BRIC	Brazil, Russia, India and China
CBRP	CO_2 Buildings Rehabilitation Programme
CCES	Centre for Climate and Energy Solutions
CCS	Carbon Capture and Storage
CCD	Climate Compatible Development
CCTV	Closed-Circuit Television
CCX	Chicago Climate Exchange
CDKN	Climate and Development Knowledge Network
CDM	Clean Development Mechanism
CeMoRe	Centre for Mobilities Research
CeDEP	Centre for Development, Environment and Policy
CER	Certified Emission Reduction credit
CERT	Carbon Emissions Reduction Target
CFL	Compact Fluorescent Lamp
CHP	Combined Heat and Power
CIF	Climate Investment Funds
CIFOR	Center for International Forestry Research
CIKOD	Center for Indigenous Knowledge and Organizational Development
CIS	Climate Innovation Centres
CMP	Meeting of the Parties
COP	Conference of the Parties
CRGE	Climate Resilient Green Economy Plan
COSATU	Congress of South African Trade Unions
CPEIR	Climate Public Expenditure and Institutional Reports
CREI	Commercializing Renewable Energy in India
CSP	Concentrated Solar Power
CTCN	Climate Technology Centre and Network

CTF	Clean Technology Fund
DECC	Department of Energy and Climate Change
DfID	Department for International Development
DG	Distributed Generation
DIIS	Danish Institute for International Studies
DOE	Designated Operating Entity
DoE	Department of Energy
DRC	Democratic Republic of the Congo
FEE	Free Energy Europe
E2W	Electric 2-Wheeler
E3W	Electric 3-Wheeler
EB	Executive Board
EC	European Commission
EEC	Energy Efficiency Commitment
EESoP	Energy Efficiency Standards of Performance
EIT	Economy in Transition
EKC	Environmental Kuznets Curve
ENB	Earth Negotiations Bulletin
EPA	Environmental Protection Agency
Eskom	Electricity Supply Commission
ESRC-AIM	Economic and Social Research Council-Advanced Institute of Management
ETC	Economic and Trade Commission
ETS	Emissions Trading System/Emission Trading Scheme
EU	European Union
EUA	EU Allowances
EU RED	European Union's Renewable Energy Directives
EV	Electric Vehicles
EVI	Economic Vulnerability Index
FAO	Food and Agriculture Organization
FDI	Foreign Direct Investment
FFV	Flex Fuel Vehicle
FYP	Five-Year Plan
G77	Group of 77
GCF	Green Climate Fund
GDP	Gross Domestic Product
GDRs	Greenhouse Development Rights
GEF	Global Environment Facility
GHG	Greenhouse Gas
GIZ	Deutsche Gesellschaft für Internationale Zusammenarbeit
GoB	Government of Brazil
GM	General Motors
GNI	Gross National Income
Gt	Gigaton
GTP	Growth and Transformation Plan
GW	Gigawatt
GWh	Gigawatt hour
GWP	Global Warming Potential
HAI	Human Assets Index

HFCs	Hydrofluorocarbons
HIV	Human Immunodeficiency Virus infection
IAA	Institute of Sugar and Alcohol
IADB	InterAmerican Development Bank
ICEs	Internal Combustion Engines
IDRC	International Development Research Centre
IDS	Institute of Development Studies
IEA	International Energy Agency
IGCC	Integrated Gasification Combined Cycle
IMF	International Monetary Fund
InfoDev	Information for Development programme
IPCC	Intergovernmental Panel on Climate Change
IPPR	Institute for Public Policy Research
IPRs	Intellectual Property Rights
IRENA	International Renewable Energy Agency
ITS	Intelligent Transport Systems
JI	Joint Implementation
JV	Joint Venture
KCJ	Kenyan Ceramic Jiko
KfW	Kreditanstalt für Wiederaufbau
KP	Kyoto Protocol
KSTF	KARADEA Solar Training Facility
kWh	Kilowatt hour
LEDS	Low Emission Development Strategies
LCA	Long term framework on Cooperative Action
LCCC	Low Carbon City China
LCD	Low Carbon Development
LCCRD	Low Carbon Climate Resilient Development
LECRED	Low Emission Climate Resilient Development Strategies
LCDP	Low Carbon Development Plans
LCDS	Low Carbon Development Strategies
LDCs	Least Developed Countries
LED	Light Emitting Diode
LPG	Liquefied Petroleum Gas
MCC	Municipal Construction Commission
MDGs	Millennium Development Goals
MDRC	Municipal Development and Reform Commission
MEC	Minerals–Energy Complex
MEM	Ministry of Energy and Minerals
MEST	Ministry of Environment, Science and Technology
MFP	Multi-Functional Platforms
MIT	Massachusetts Institute of Technology
MLP	Multi-Level Perspective
MOA	Ministry of Agriculture
MOI	Ministry of Industry
MOT	Ministry of Transport
MOST	Ministry of Science and Technology
MRFCJ	Mary Robinson Foundation for Climate Justice

MRV	Monitoring, Reporting and Verification
MSTC	Municipal Science and Technology Commission
Mt	Mega tonnes
MTB	Municipal Transport Bureaus
MW	Megawatt
MWE	Ministry of Water and Energy
MWR	Ministry of Water Resources
NAMA	Nationally Appropriate Mitigation Action
NCCPF	National Climate Change Policy Framework
NDRC	National Development and Reform Commission
NGO	Non-Governmental Organization
NHS	National Health Service
NREAP	National Renewable Energy Action Plan
NTFP	Non-Timber Forest Product
NTU	Nanyang Technological University
ODA	Overseas Development Assistance
ODI	Overseas Development Institute
OECD	Organisation for Economic Co-operation and Development
Ofgem	Office of Gas and Electricity Markets
PaMs	Policies and Measures
PASDEP	Plan for Accelerated and Sustained Development to End Poverty
ppm	Parts Per Million
PFCs	Perfluorocarbons
PES	Payments for Ecosystem Services
PMDD	Permanent Magnetic Direct Drive
PoA	Programme-of-Activity
PPP	Purchasing Power Parity
PPO	Pure Plant Oil
PV	Photovoltaic
QUELROS	Quantified Emission Limitation and Reduction Commitment
R&D	Research and Development
RCI	Responsibility and Capacity Index
RCIEP	Research Center for International Environmental Policy
REDD	Reducing Emissions from Deforestation and Forest Degradation
REEEP	Renewable Energy and Energy Efficiency Partnership
REN21	Renewable Energy Policy Network for the 21st Century
RMB	Renminbi
SHS	Solar Home System
SCF	Strategic Climate Fund
SDPRP	Sustainable Development and Poverty Reduction Programme
SE4All	Sustainable Energy for All
SEG	Sussex Energy Group
SIDS	Small Island Developing State
SNM	Strategic Niche Management
SMS	Short Message Service
SO	Supplier Obligation
SOAS	School of Oriental and African Studies
SOE	State-Owned Enterprise

SPPA	School of Public Policy and Administration
SREP	Scaling-Up Renewable Energy Programme
SPRU	Science and Technology Policy Research
SSA	Sub-Saharan Africa
SSTEC	Sino-Singapore Tianjin Eco City
TAP	Technology Action Plan
TASEA	Tanzania Solar Energy Association
TaTEDO	Tanzania Traditional Energy Development and Environment Organization
TEC	Technology Executive Committee
TEEB	The Economics of Ecosystems and Biodiversity Study
TNA	Technology Needs Assessment
TW	Terrawatt
UCS	Union of Concerned Scientists
UN	United Nations
UNECA	United Nations Economic Commission for Africa
UNAGF	United Nations Secretary General's High-level Advisory Group
UNCTAD	United Nations Conference on Trade and Development
UNDESA	United Nations Department of Economic and Social Affairs
UNDP	United Nations Development Program
UNICA	União da Indústria de Cana-de-Açúcar
UNIDO	United Nations Industrial Development Organization
UNEP	United Nations Environment Programme
UN ESCAP	United Nations Economic and Social Commission for Asia and the Pacific
UNFCCC	United Nations Framework Convention on Climate Change
UNHCR	Office of the United Nations High Commissioner for Refugees
UPB	Urban Planning Bureau
US$/USD	United States Dollar
VCM	Voluntary Carbon Market
WBCSD	World Business Council for Sustainable Development
WCED	World Commission on Environment and Development
WEC	World Energy Council
WHO	World Health Organization
Wp	Watt-peak
WRI	World Resources Institute
WWEA	World Wind Energy Association
WWF	World Wide Fund for Nature

Preface

Frauke Urban and Johan Nordensvärd

A new way of thinking is required if humankind is to survive.

Albert Einstein

Global climate change poses a serious threat to international development efforts. Developing countries – and especially the poor – have historically contributed very little to climate change. However, they are often the most vulnerable to climate change due to their limited resources and limited capacity to adapt to climate change. At the same time, developed countries are struggling to mitigate emissions that lead to climate change. To *mitigate the emissions leading to climate change* and *achieve human development*, there is a need for serious global commitment to low carbon development. Low carbon development is a new development model, which aims to achieve these two goals simultaneously.

Low Carbon Development: Key Issues fills a crucial gap by being oriented towards postgraduates, undergraduates, experts, practitioners, company representatives and policy-makers interested in the fields of climate change and development, as well as low carbon development and the low carbon economy. In addition, the interdisciplinary book bridges the divide between more technical and natural science-based books about climate change, mitigation, energy, and more social science-based books about sustainable development and international development. This book serves both as a comprehensive introduction to low carbon development and as a key reading on low carbon development concepts, policies and practices in developed and developing countries. The book presents practical solutions for how low carbon development can be achieved at the global level.

The general argument of the book is that low carbon development is essential for mitigating the emissions that lead to climate change and for enabling development in a carbon-constrained world. Low carbon development can bring opportunities and benefits for both developed and developing countries, nevertheless low carbon development can only be implemented when an adequate enabling environment is in place that addresses the political, economic, social and technological key issues. In low income and lower middle income countries, issues of social justice and poverty reduction are the key to low carbon development, while for higher middle income and high income countries, low carbon innovation and emission reductions are at the heart of implementing low carbon development.

The contributors to this book are leading academics and practitioners in the field of low carbon development. The book first elaborates the concept of low carbon development and why it important in a carbon-constrained world (Chapter 1). The book then discusses the key issues of a political (Chapters 2 and 3), socio-economic (Chapters 4 to 7) and technological nature (Chapter 8) for low carbon development, addressing issues such as the political economy, social justice, carbon markets and innovation for low carbon development. This is followed by key issues for low carbon development in policy and practice (Chapters 9 to 14), which is presented based on cross-cutting issues such as low carbon energy, forestry, agriculture and transportation. Afterwards, practical case studies are discussed from low carbon development in low income countries in Africa (Chapters 16 and 17), middle income countries in Asia and Latin America (Chapters 18 to 20) and high income countries in Europe and North America (Chapters 21 and 22).

Part 1

Introduction

Editorial for Part 1
Introduction

Frauke Urban and Johan Nordensvärd

Part 1 provides an introduction to the book. This part introduces low carbon development by discussing the origins, concepts and key issues relevant for low carbon policy and practice. This part further elaborates some of the critiques that relate to low carbon development.

Overview of Part 1

Low carbon development is crucial for mitigating emissions that lead to climate change and enabling development in a carbon constrained world. Low carbon development is being pursued by high income countries and emerging emitters to reduce emissions, increase economic growth and firm competitiveness. At the same time, low carbon development is an option for lower income countries to access modern energy, low carbon technology and to reduce poverty. Chapter 1 elaborates what low carbon development is, why it is needed, how it is defined, how it differs from other key concepts in the field of environment and development, and how to achieve low carbon development in practice.

1 Low carbon development

Origins, concepts and key issues

Frauke Urban and Johan Nordensvärd

Low carbon development is crucial for mitigating emissions that lead to climate change and for enabling development in a carbon constrained world. Low carbon development is being pursued by high income countries and emerging emitters to reduce emissions, increase economic growth and firm competitiveness. At the same time, low carbon development is an option for lower income countries to access modern energy, low carbon technology and to reduce poverty. This chapter elaborates what low carbon development is, why it is needed, how it is defined, how it differs from other key concepts in the field of environment and development and how to achieve low carbon development in practice.

Introduction

The popularity of low carbon development has rapidly increased in recent years. Low carbon development has received attention from academics, policy-makers, practitioners, the media and the wider public. Low carbon development is situated at the interface of two major fields of study: climate change mitigation and international development. Both climate change and development are two of the most important global issues of our times, but at the same time they are highly contentious and debated. This chapter aims to provide an introduction to low carbon development, its definition and origins, how to achieve low carbon development in practice, as well as a critique of low carbon development.

Global climate change

We will start this chapter by examining the role of global climate change, as mitigating climate change is one of the key goals of low carbon development. Box 1.1 then defines low carbon development.

Global climate change is considered to be one of the greatest challenges to international development efforts. It poses risks to humans, the environment and the economy (Urban, 2010). It is well documented that so-called greenhouse gas (GHG) emissions contribute to anthropogenic (or human-induced) climate change (IPCC, 2007). *Greenhouse gases* include carbon dioxide (CO_2), methane (CH_4), nitrous oxide (N_2O), hydrofluorocarbons (HFCs), perfluorocarbons (PFCs) and sulphur hexafluoride (SF_6) (UNFCCC, 1997). The most important GHG is CO_2, which is often only referred to as carbon, such as in relation to carbon emissions and low carbon development. These GHGs are emitted from the combustion of fossil fuels, from land use changes and deforestation, from industrial activity and transport

(IPCC, 2007). The effects of climate change are reported to be rising temperatures, melting glaciers, sea level rise, changes in precipitation and increases in extreme weather events like floods, droughts and cyclones (IPCC, 2007). Nevertheless impacts of climate change vary across different regions, intensities and scales. A degree of uncertainty is associated with climate change, however, there is consensus among the overwhelming majority of scientists about the anthropogenic causes of climate change, the main climatic impacts and their severity.

The Intergovernmental Panel on Climate Change (IPCC) (IPCC, 2007) reports that in terms of *climate change*, the global mean surface temperature has risen by $0.74°C \pm 0.18°C$ during the last century. This increase has been particularly significant over the last 50 years (IPCC, 2007). From a global perspective, the IPCC (2007) reports that they found high increases in heavy precipitation events, while droughts have become more frequent since the 1970s, especially in the (sub)tropics. There is also documentation about changes in the large-scale atmospheric circulation and increases in tropical cyclone activity since the 1970s (IPCC, 2007; Urban, 2009).

Global climate change is not a distant vision of a troubled future, but very much a reality of today that requires urgent action. Former United Nations (UN) Secretary General and President of the Global Humanitarian Forum, Kofi Annan, mentioned a few years ago that 'Today, millions of people are already suffering because of climate change' (Annan, 2009: i). The UN Secretary General Ban Ki-moon confirmed recently on a trip to the small Pacific nation Kiribati that 'climate change is not about tomorrow. It is lapping at our feet – quite literally in Kiribati and elsewhere' (Ban, 2011: 1). Ban further said 'I have watched the high tide impacting those villages. The high tide shows it is high time to act.' He also addressed the current development model and suggested that something is 'seriously wrong with our current model of economic development' (Ban, 2011: 1).

Increasingly, scientists agree that the possibility of staying below the 2°C threshold by 2100 between 'acceptable' and 'dangerous' climate change becomes less likely as no serious global action on climate change is taken (Tyndall Centre, 2009; Richardson *et al.*, 2009; Urban, 2009; Urban *et al.*, 2011). A rise above 2°C by 2100 is likely to lead to abrupt and irreversible changes (IPCC, 2007). These changes could cause severe societal, economic and environmental disruptions that could severely threaten international development throughout the 21st century and beyond (Richardson *et al.*, 2009; Urban, 2010; Urban *et al.*, 2011).

The need for climate change mitigation

Many climate scientists therefore call for an urgent limit to global carbon emissions. This cap on the total quantity of GHG emissions is often referred to as the carbon budget. In the late 1990s, Greenpeace calculated that a global carbon budget of about 585 Gigatons of carbon (GtC[1]) is required to achieve a stabilization at 400 to 450 parts per million (ppm) to limit global warming to 2°C by 2100 (Greenpeace, 1997). However, in the late 1990s there was still optimism that there might be a chance to limit global warming to 1°C.

Two decades later, climate scientists are less optimistic: at the global scale, the atmospheric concentration of CO_2 has increased from a pre-industrial value of approximately 280 ppm to around 380 ppm in 2005 (IPCC, 2007) and 396 ppm in 2007 (Richardson *et al.*, 2009). Climate scientists estimate that for a 50 per cent chance of achieving the 2°C target, a global atmospheric CO_2 equivalent concentration of 400 to 450 ppm needs to be achieved (Richardson *et al.*, 2009; Pye *et al.*, 2010). To limit global warming to 2°C by 2100 will require an immediate reduction in global GHG emissions and a total reduction of about

60–80 per cent of emissions by 2100 (Richardson *et al.*, 2009). This would require a peaking of global emissions by 2020 or earlier. Nevertheless, the 400 ppm target seems to have been reached recently (see the figures above from Richardson *et al.*, 2009) while emissions are still rising, which shows the urgency of needing to limit emissions now to avoid dangerous climate change.

There is thus an urgent need for serious global commitment to mitigate climate change by reducing GHG emissions and implementing low carbon development. *Climate change mitigation* is defined as 'an anthropogenic intervention to reduce the anthropogenic forcing of the climate system; it includes strategies to reduce greenhouse gas sources and emissions and enhancing greenhouse gas sinks' (IPCC, 2001: 379).

Low carbon development

Until recently, there was a predominant focus on mitigation efforts and transitions to low carbon economies in high income countries as they used to be the major GHG emitters since the Industrial Revolution about two centuries ago. Developed countries are reported to be responsible for about 75 per cent of historic or accumulated emissions (WRI, 2005). This emission balance has changed in recent years with the rise of emerging economies such as China, India, South Africa, Brazil and other large developing countries that have rapidly growing emissions and strive for *low carbon development*. Today, China alone accounts for almost 25 per cent of total global CO_2 emissions, but in per capita terms the average Chinese is responsible for about three times less CO_2 emissions than the average US citizen (IEA, 2012). In addition, some low and middle income countries increasingly seem to favour the benefits low carbon development can offer to enable development in a carbon constrained world, such as access to modern energy, low carbon technology and reducing poverty. Examples are Ethiopia, Kenya, Tanzania, Bangladesh, the Maldives, Guyana and other countries. This is despite the fact that historically, developing countries – in particular Least Developed Countries (LDCs) – have contributed very little to climate change. LDCs were reported to account for only about 4 per cent of global GHG emissions in 2005 and only 0.3 per cent of accumulated CO_2 emissions from energy use (WRI, 2005), while being at the same time the most vulnerable to the impacts of climate change (IPCC, 2007).

As climate change is a global challenge, low carbon development is of global relevance in low income, middle income and high income countries. Nevertheless its facets and characteristics can differ significantly depending on local and national priorities and concerns. Box 1.1 defines low carbon development.

Box 1.1 Defining low carbon development

There are two key definitions for low carbon development.[2] One definition is in broader development terms and the other is more specifically geared towards growth. In broader development terms, low carbon development is a development model that is based on climate-friendly low carbon energy and follows principles of sustainable development, makes a contribution to avoiding dangerous climate change and adopts patterns of low carbon consumption and production (Skea and Nishioka, 2008; Urban, 2010; Urban *et al.*, 2011).

In growth terms, low carbon development is defined as using less carbon for growth, which includes switching from fossil fuels to low carbon energy, promoting low carbon technology innovation and business models, protecting and promoting natural carbon sinks such as forests and wetlands, and formulating policies that promote low carbon practices and behaviours (DfID, 2009: 58; Urban *et al.*, 2011).

The ultimate aim of low carbon development is to mitigate emissions to avoid dangerous climate change, while at the same time achieving social and economic development (Urban, 2011). In this book, we will use the definition of low carbon development, not low carbon growth.

Low carbon development emerged primarily as a concept that was developed by donor agencies in the development field, particularly the UK Department for International Development (DfID). While it started out as a term used mainly by development aid agencies of the developed world, it has in recent years been taken up by many governments around the world, and has made its entry into the academic world.

Operationally and conceptually, low carbon development has emerged from a number of other concepts in the field of environment and development, which are outlined in Box 1.2.

Box 1.2 How does low carbon development differ from other concepts in the field of environment and development?

Low carbon development is a new concept that partly overlaps with other development concepts, such as sustainable development, green growth and climate compatible development. This textbox briefly elaborates the key similarities and differences between low carbon development and other related concepts.

> **Sustainable development** is development that meets the needs of the present without compromising the ability of future generations to meet their own needs. It contains within it two key concepts:
>
> • the concept of needs, in particular the essential needs of the world's poor, to which overriding priority should be given;
> • the idea of limitations imposed by the state of technology and social organization on the environment's ability to meet present and future needs.
>
> (WCED, 1987: 43)

Skea and Nishioka (2008: 6) indicate that actions leading to low carbon development need to follow the principles of sustainable development and 'ensuring that the development needs of all groups within society are met'. low carbon development has the goal of achieving sustainable development; nevertheless, unlike sustainable development, low carbon development does not directly address issues of environmental sustainability in broader terms beyond climate change (Urban, 2011).

Green growth focuses on sustainable consumption and production, greening business and markets, developing sustainable infrastructure, introducing green taxes and budget reforms as fiscal policies, investing in natural capital such as ecosystems, and developing and using indicators for eco-efficiency (UN ESCAP, 2009). While there are many similarities with low carbon development, there are two key differences. First, the emphasis of green growth is on achieving economic growth through stimulating green investments and green fiscal policy. Low carbon growth is a sub-set of low carbon development and low carbon development is broader and more encompassing than focusing only on growth. Key low carbon development considerations are about social justice (see Chapter 4), rather than about growth alone. Second, the term 'green' growth refers to environmentally friendly growth. This can be in line with low carbon policies; however, it can go beyond low carbon issues and include environmental sustainability in broader terms (Urban, 2011).

Climate compatible development is 'development that minimises the harm caused by climate impacts, while maximising the many human development opportunities presented by a low emissions, more resilient, future' (Mitchell and Maxwell, 2011: 1). Climate compatible development includes both low carbon development and climate resilient development and it is sometimes referred to as Low Carbon Climate Resilient Development (LCCRD). Chapter 14 discusses climate compatible development and LCCRD in detail. Low carbon development focuses on climate change mitigation by limiting or reducing emissions, whereas climate-compatible development focuses on adaptation to the effects of climate change. Adaptation is particularly relevant for countries that are especially vulnerable to climate change, such as least developed countries. Low carbon strategies will have to run alongside effective adaptation policies in these countries. Synergies between adaptation and mitigation are important, and particularly exploring the possibility of integrating both strategies, for example by ensuring that low carbon investments are consistent with adaptation investments (Urban, 2011).

Discussion: the origins of low carbon development

As mentioned before, low carbon development is a recently emerged concept that aims to mitigate emissions to avoid dangerous climate change, while at the same time achieving social and economic development in a carbon-constrained world. In simple mathematic terms, it could best be described as 'Low carbon development = climate change mitigation + development'. Figure 1.1 shows how low carbon development developed out of the synergies that exist between *mitigation* and *development*.

This section discusses the origins of low carbon development. The section first discusses the origins of low carbon development in terms of its roots within the field of climate change mitigation and then in terms of its roots within the field of international development. The section then elaborates how low carbon development emerged out of these two different fields and addresses some of the opportunities and challenges of low carbon development.

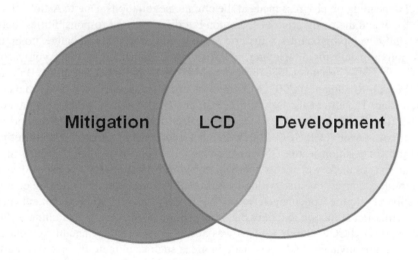

Figure 1.1 Schematic overview of low carbon development

The origins of climate change mitigation

This section discusses the origins of climate change mitigation, which is an important field in which low carbon development is rooted.

As mentioned above, climate change mitigation is defined as 'an anthropogenic intervention to reduce the anthropogenic forcing of the climate system; it includes strategies to reduce greenhouse gas sources and emissions and enhancing greenhouse gas sinks' (IPCC, 2001: 379). While the scientific community had been working on climate change for decades and the First Assessment Report on Climate Change by the IPCC dates back to 1990 (IPCC, 1990), the first highly influential report on climate change mitigation was published in 2001 by the IPCC (IPCC, 2001). The 2001 IPCC's Third Assessment Report included the so-called 'hockey stick diagram' by Mann *et al.* (1999), which showed how both CO_2 emissions and average temperatures had increased significantly throughout the 20th century, with the 1990s being the warmest decade of the millennium (IPCC, 2007). The diagram resembles the form of a hockey stick, hence its name. In the USA, a controversy developed about the statistical methods underlying the research, hence fuelling debates between climate sceptics and non-climate sceptics. This was followed by more than a dozen scientific papers that confirmed the conclusions drawn by Mann *et al.* and the IPCC that the warmest decade in 1000 years had most likely been the end of the 20th century. The urgent need for mitigating emissions leading to climate change was then acknowledged at a global level by the public.

On the climate policy side, mitigation has always played an important part. The United Nations Framework Convention on Climate Change (UNFCCC) developed an international climate treaty at the Earth Summit in Rio de Janeiro in 1992 and thereby acknowledged the role of humans in contributing to climate change. The treaty aims to prevent dangerous climate change, but makes no commitment to emission reductions yet (UNFCCC, 1992). This was followed by the Kyoto Protocol (KP) in 1997, which aims to reduce GHG emissions to avoid dangerous climate change and has binding emission reduction commitments for developed countries for the first commitment period of the Kyoto Protocol for 2008–2012. The second commitment period of the Kyoto Protocol was negotiated at the climate conference in Durban in late 2011 and is due to start in 2013 and last until 2017 or even 2020, depending on progress made at the climate negotiations. Due to Article 10 of the Kyoto Protocol and the recognition of 'common but differentiated responsibilities' between developed and developing countries' historic responsibility for climate change, no emission reduction commitments for developing countries were embedded in the Kyoto Protocol (UNFCCC, 1997: 9). Climate change mitigation also has a prominent role in the Bali Action Plan and the Bali Roadmap of 2007. Mitigation is considered one of the five pillars of the Bali Action Plan. The aim of the Bali Action Plan and the Roadmap is to develop a strategy for a post-2012 climate agreement, for the time when the first commitment period of the Kyoto Protocol is over (UNFCCC, 2007). In subsequent years, climate change mitigation took a prominent position in the UN climate change negotiations, and targets to mitigate emissions are one of the key elements over which major differences exist between developed and developing countries, but also within the group of developed and developing countries.[3] This was apparent for the Copenhagen Accord in 2009, when no binding agreement could be reached on emission reduction and only the 'strong political will to combat climate change' was mentioned (UNFCCC, 2009: 5). This was also apparent in the Cancun Agreements in 2010, where major advances had been made in areas such as climate finance (see Part 4 of this book), technology transfer (see Part 5 – Chapter 8 of this book) and REDD+ (see Chapter 11). However, only a pledge to 'reducing global greenhouse gas emissions so as to hold the increase in global average temperature below 2°C above preindustrial levels' was made (UNFCCC, 2010: 3). The climate change conference in Durban in late 2011 delivered more evidence as to how hard it is to agree on binding emission reduction targets for mitigating global climate change as it was agreed to postpone any legally binding *global* agreement – beyond those obliged by the Kyoto Protocol – until at least 2015, with implementation by 2020 (UNFCCC, 2011). This will be elaborated in more detail in Part 2 on the politics and policy processes of low carbon development. Twenty years after the first Rio Earth Summit, at Rio+20 in 2012, climate change was still a hot, however currently unsolved global issue.

While low carbon development has its roots in climate change mitigation, there are distinct differences between the two in terms of their scale, the geographic benefit, the actors, outcomes, priorities, approaches and time perspectives. Table 1.1 indicates the differences and similarities between mitigation and low carbon development.

Table 1.1 The differences and similarities between mitigation and low carbon development

	Mitigation	*Low carbon development*
Scale	Global	Global and local
Geographic benefit	Global	Global and local
Actors	Sectoral (e.g. energy, transport, forestry)	Cross-sectoral, but still limited to a few approaches
Outcomes	Measurable	More difficult to measure
Priority	The largest emitters	Emitters with development needs
Approaches	Narrow: technical approach, techno-centric	More broad: mitigation for achieving development needs (co-benefits)
Time perspective	Longer term	Medium term

Source: Adapted from Urban and Naess, 2011

This section elaborated the origins of climate change mitigation, which is an important field in which low carbon development is rooted. The following section discusses the origins of international development, which is the second important field in which low carbon development is rooted. The section on 'The emergence of low carbon development' then elaborates how low carbon development emerged out of these two fields.

The origins of international development

Humans have been concerned about economic development and social transformation for centuries. However, the concept of international development and development studies as a discipline is reported to have emerged in the late 1940s, 1950s and early 1960s. Development studies began as a post-Second World War project in support of poorer 'developing countries'. 'Development' was driven by so-called 'developed' Western/Northern countries. It has often been accused of paternalism and trusteeship (Cowen and Shenton, 1996; Urban *et al.*, 2011). Back in the 1950s, development policy was dominated by the goal of achieving modernity, by an optimistic worldview, by expecting the state to play an active, positive role and by focusing on national development (Humphrey, 2007; Urban *et al.*, 2011).

There are various definitions for development and, despite its universal use, there is no universally agreed definition. Some scholars such as Chambers simply define development as 'good change' (Chambers, 1995: 174), others make a distinction between formal development, such as development aid, and development as a deeper process of change, such as capitalism (Urban *et al.*, 2011). Hart (2001: 650) distinguishes between D and d development whereby "'big D" Development (is) defined as a post-Second World War project of intervention in the "third world" that emerged in the context of decolonisation and the cold war, and "little d" development or the development of capitalism as a geographically uneven and contradictory set of historical processes' (Urban *et al.*, 2011: 6–7).

There are various approaches to Western development thinking, including rights-based approaches, which focus on human rights and/or increasing the voice of marginalized groups (Mohan and Holland 2001; Hickey and Mohan 2005; Urban *et al.*, 2011); human development approaches, which incorporate broader development objectives than economic ones and aim to expand human choices and strengthen human capabilities related to education, health and income (Jolly, 2003; Urban *et al.*, 2011); approaches that are based on concerns for the poorest 'bottom billion' (Collier, 2007; Urban *et al.*, 2011) (see Part 3 for more detail on social dimensions). There are also approaches that come from different disciplines such as anthropology, economics, political science and different perspectives such as gender, globalization and the environment. In other parts of the world, such as in China, different streams of non-Western development thinking prevail that are more related to these countries' own experiences, cultures and philosophies of development (Urban *et al.*, 2011).

While development studies started with optimism after the Second World War, the concept of development and development studies as a discipline has had to endure criticism in recent years (Urban *et al.*, 2011). This is linked to ongoing problems such as widespread poverty in many parts of the world, global neo-liberalism, which sees states as part of the problem rather than part of the solution (Humphrey, 2007), as well as the occurrence of various transboundary phenomena. Challenges like the global financial crisis, terrorism and large-scale environmental problems such as climate change and resource depletion are seen to require international and multilateral solutions (Urban *et al.*, 2011). One other major shift in development policy is due to the so-called 'Rising Powers': the rise of countries like China, India, Brazil, South Africa and states of the Middle East (Urban *et al.*, 2011). This involves a questioning of dominant 'Western' approaches to development (Humphrey, 2007). Unfortunately, the optimism of earlier decades has been replaced by some pessimism, including when development was declared dead in the 1990s by both the political right and the political left (Hart, 2001; Urban *et al.*, 2011). Fifteen years later, Rist argued that development as practised and imposed by the West is 'toxic' (Rist, 2007; Urban *et al.*, 2011). The notion of 'Reimagining Development' is therefore prevailing within the discipline of development studies to rethink what development policy and practice means today, who is driving it and for whom, particularly with a view of what will happen post-2015 after the Millennium Development Goals (MDGs) (Urban *et al.*, 2011). In relation to climate change, low carbon development is a new and emerging concept that can help with reimaging development and responding to new global challenges such as climate change.

The emergence of low carbon development

Many issues addressing low carbon considerations have been hot topics since the 1970s and 1980s, such as technology transfer for low carbon technologies, innovation for low carbon energy, and their relevance and importance has continued until today (see Part 5, Chapter 8 for a discussion of low carbon innovation and technology transfer). However, back then these technologies were not called low carbon, but rather they were called renewable energy or clean energy technologies. Nevertheless, the issue of mitigating GHG emissions only achieved momentum in the late 1990s to early 2000s, when the UN climate policy process began to fully develop. Many long-established fields addressing low carbon considerations, such as hydropower and forestry, have seen a renaissance due to climate change and the emergence of low carbon development. While the academic community and practitioners worked on renewable energy, technology transfer and innovation as separate issues and disciplines for decades, in the late 2000s the donor community – and particularly DfID – first coined the term low carbon development to merge all these disparate issues and disciplines under one roof (see DfID, 2009). Low carbon development was hence first developed by donors as a response to the immediate needs of developing countries to address climate change by mitigating emissions while ensuring development needs. The academic community has been relatively slow in responding to the emerging field of low carbon development. While there are a growing number of projects, activities, networks and publications by bilateral and multilateral donors on low carbon development, there is a lack of more academic and in-depth work in this field. This textbook – which is the first textbook on low carbon development – therefore aims to bring together academic debates relating to a wide range of key issues for low carbon development.

The next section elaborates the benefits and opportunities of low carbon development, which will then be followed by a discussion of some of the challenges of achieving low carbon development.

The benefits and opportunities of low carbon development

Low carbon development can bring opportunities and benefits for both developed and developing countries. Nevertheless low carbon development can only be implemented when an adequate enabling environment is in place, which addresses the political, economic, social and technological key issues. In low income and lower middle income countries, issues of social justice and poverty reduction are the key to low carbon development, while for higher middle income and high income countries, low carbon innovation and emission reductions are at the heart of implementing low carbon development.

It is often assumed that the main benefits and opportunities for low carbon development rest with emerging emitters, many of which are middle income countries with booming economies such as China, India, Brazil, South Africa, Mexico and the Middle East. Nevertheless, the Danish Institute for International Studies (DIIS) affirms that 'there are real and sustained benefits to be had for [poorer countries] from engaging in approaches and practices that mitigate future emissions and at the same time support poverty alleviation and economic development' (DIIS, 2009: 1).

Low carbon development can be beneficial to poorer countries and their people as it can provide access to climate-friendly modern energy, such as electricity or biogas, for lighting, cooking, heating and other basic needs, as an alternative to traditional fuels and fossil fuels (see Chapter 9). At the same time, low carbon development can also provide low carbon energy for income-generating activities and educational purposes. Examples are solar-powered electricity for running a mobile phone-charging business or wind-powered electricity for lighting a school. Further energy-related benefits are to increase energy security and energy access. Low carbon development can further lead to social benefits, such as improved health, for example through reduced indoor air pollution when switching from fuelwood to modern energy options. Other social benefits include an opportunity for green job creation, such as jobs in the renewable energy sector. More economic and competitiveness-related opportunities of low carbon development include access to low carbon technology and innovation (see Part 5, Chapter 8), an opportunity to attract green investments, the possibility of reducing the costs of carbon liability and increasing low carbon competitiveness. Low carbon development also avoids carbon lock-in, which means avoiding investments and infrastructure being locked into high carbon pathways for decades. In terms of political opportunities, low carbon development has the potential to create political support for the climate change negotiations and other diplomatic issues (see Chapters 2 and 3). In addition, low carbon development offers an opportunity to promote the sustainable use of forest and land resources and thereby improve environmental quality (see Chapters 11 and 12). Finally, low carbon development provides an opportunity to promote climate resilience in view of future climate impacts (see Chapter 14) (DIIS, 2009; Urban, 2011).

This section elaborated the benefits and opportunities of low carbon development. The following section discusses how low carbon development can be achieved in practice and elaborates some of the challenges of achieving low carbon development.

How to achieve low carbon development in practice – the role of decoupling growth from emissions and the Environmental Kuznets Curve

This section discusses two crucial issues for achieving low carbon development in practice and overcoming major challenges in its implementation: the decoupling of economic growth from carbon emissions and the Environmental Kuznets Curve (EKC).

Achieving low carbon development, and particularly low carbon growth, in practice requires **decoupling economic growth from carbon emissions**, so that at some point in time the emission growth rate is lower than the Gross Domestic Product (GDP) growth rate. **Absolute decoupling** requires an absolute cut in emissions. However, no absolute decoupling has so far been observed in relation to climate change (Sustainable Development Commission, 2009). Instead, there is a clear link between economic growth and GHG emissions. Both have strongly increased over the last 100 years (IPCC, 2007), which shows that absolute decoupling has not happened (Urban, 2010).

Relative decoupling means that more economic activity is possible with lower emissions. This is measured for example in carbon intensity or energy intensity, which is the amount of carbon emissions or energy used per unit of GDP. Relative decoupling in terms of carbon and energy intensity has been observed in a number of countries during the last few years. China and India for example have rapidly decreasing carbon and energy intensities (Van Ruijven *et al.*, 2008; Urban, 2010).

The issue of decoupling is fiercely debated. Some advocate that decoupling growth from energy use and emissions is only possible to some extent due to physical limits (Ockwell, 2008) and that instead the structure of market economies has to be changed to achieve deep cuts in emissions (Sustainable Development Commission, 2009; Urban, 2010). The UK Sustainable Development Commission even talks about the 'myth' of decoupling (2009: 8; 46 onwards). Others advocate that decoupling is possible when low carbon and energy-efficient technology is used (Barrett, 2008), however this does not take into account the emissions from deforestation and land use changes (Urban, 2010). While there are discussions about the limits of decoupling growth from emissions, many case studies argue that low carbon growth is possible, for example, for China (IEA, 2007), India (World Bank, 2008), South Africa (Government of South Africa, 2008) and Mexico (Project Catalyst, 2008) (Urban, 2010). Data from countries within the Organisation for Economic Co-operation and Development (OECD) suggest that relative decoupling has indeed happened, for example in France by a large-scale introduction of nuclear energy or in Sweden by a large-scale introduction of hydropower (IEA, 2012). Figure 1.2 shows the *relative* decoupling of economic growth from emissions for the 34 OECD member states between 1980 and 2008. Figure 1.3, however, indicates that *absolute* decoupling of growth from emissions has not happened for OECD countries (IEA, 2012).

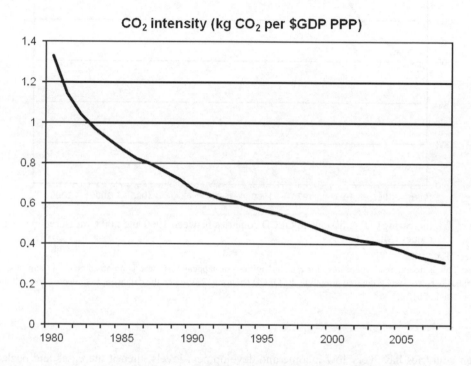

CO_2 intensity (kg CO_2 per \$GDP PPP)

Figure 1.2 Decreasing CO_2 intensity in OECD countries between 1980 and 2008, measured as the CO_2 emissions in kg per \$ of GDP purchasing power parity (PPP)

Source: IEA, 2012

Notes: This is an example of *relative decoupling*, as the emission growth rate is lower than the GDP growth rate over time. There has been constant economic growth in the OECD between 1971, when the data were first recorded, and 2008. An exception was 2009, when economic growth was negative for the first time in nearly four decades due to the global financial crisis; nevertheless by 2010 economic growth prevailed again (World Bank, 2012).

The second issue that is important for achieving low carbon development in practice and overcoming major challenges in its implementation relates to environmental pollution throughout the development process. This is exemplified in the so-called Environmental Kuznets Curve (EKC).

The *EKC* is a concept that makes a correlation between environmental pollution and economic development. The EKC has the shape of an inverted U-curve, similar to the income inequality curve described by Kuznet in the 1950s (Kuznets, 1955; Van Ruijven *et al.*, 2008). The hypothesis behind the EKC is that environmental pollution is at a low level

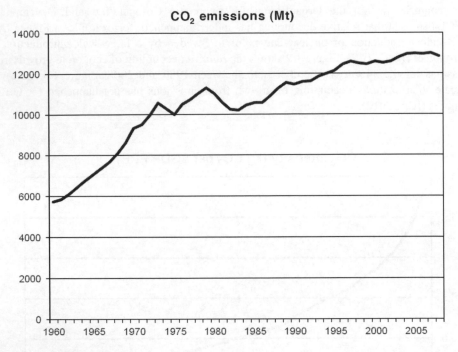

CO₂ emissions (Mt)

Figure 1.3 Increasing CO₂ emissions in OECD countries between 1960 and 2008, measured in mega tonnes (Mt)

Source: IEA, 2012
Notes: This is an example where *absolute decoupling* has not happened as there is no absolute cut in emissions. There has been constant economic growth in the OECD between 1971, when the data were first recorded, and 2008 (World Bank, 2012).

when countries have very low income and development levels, then it increases and peaks when mid levels of incomes and development are reached and pollution levels decrease again when income and development levels increase (Beckerman, 1992; Van Ruijven *et al.*, 2008). This is based on the assumption that pollution levels will increase when developing countries industrialize; however, pollution levels will decrease again when countries become more prosperous and can afford to invest in pollution control technologies. Figure 1.4 shows a stylized example of the EKC.

Some of the controversies of the EKC are related to whether the EKC can be observed in practice and how it can be measured, as various approaches to units and measurements exist. Nevertheless, the EKC has been historically observed in many countries for pollutants such as sulphur dioxide (SO₂), where end-of-pipe technologies are relatively inexpensive and easy to add. However, for carbon emissions, the EKC has not been observed (Van Ruijven *et al.*, 2008). It has rather been observed that carbon emissions increase with increasing levels of income and development and then either still continue to increase, such as in the case of the USA, Australia, Canada and most European countries, or level off, such as in the case of Sweden (IEA, 2012). Essentially, achieving the EKC requires a decoupling of economic growth from emissions (see discussion on decoupling above). To achieve low carbon development in the long-run a decrease in emissions is needed, however this proves to be difficult

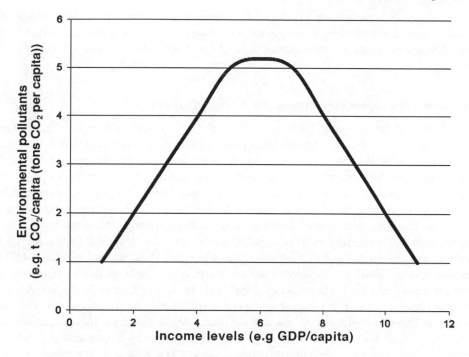

Figure 1.4 Stylized example of the Environmental Kuznets Curve

as the experience of the EKC and absolute decoupling of economic growth from emissions suggest.

The section above discussed two crucial issues for achieving low carbon development in practice and overcoming major challenges in its implementation: the decoupling of economic growth from carbon emissions and implementing the EKC.

This chapter elaborated what low carbon development is, why it is needed, how it is defined, how it differs from other key concepts in the field of environment and development and how to achieve low carbon development in practice. The next section discusses the challenges and barriers to low carbon development in the form of a critique of the concept.

The challenges and barriers to low carbon development: a critique

After discussing the opportunities and benefits of low carbon development, this section serves as the 'devil's advocate' by discussing fundamental critiques of low carbon development.

DIIS mentions that 'not all low carbon development is pro-poor, and some options offer far better benefits for the poor than others' (DIIS, 2009: 1). There are several key challenges and barriers to low carbon development, which will be briefly explained here. First, there is often an emphasis on low carbon growth rather than an emphasis on low carbon development. Low carbon growth requires decoupling economic growth from carbon emissions, which in itself is problematic as discussed above. Second, many poor countries already have unintentional 'low carbon economies' and face a number of trade-offs in relation to low carbon development, particularly in relation to hydropower and biofuels. Third, a range of political, social, economic and technological key issues have to be addressed before low carbon development can be implemented at a global scale. These issues are elaborated below.

First critique: low carbon development and the role of growth

Growth is crucial for achieving development; hence most experts would agree that growth plays an important role for low carbon development. Collier mentions that growth is vital for the poor 'bottom billion', the one billion people worldwide who are the poorest (Collier, 2007). At the same time, development is broader than growth. Growth can be a sub-set of low carbon development, while at the same time the low carbon development debate also needs to incorporate other key issues such as social development and environmental sustainability. The limits to decoupling economic growth from carbon emissions have been discussed above in the section on 'How to achieve low carbon development in practice' and it has been pointed out that some countries such as China and India, as well as many OECD countries, have achieved relative decoupling of growth from emissions due to increases in energy efficiency and the replacement of fossil fuels by low carbon technologies. At the same time, absolute decoupling – an absolute cut in emissions – has not been observed yet (Sustainable Development Commission, 2009; Urban, 2010). However, this is required to achieve low carbon development in the long term. While there may be physical and technical limits to decoupling growth from emissions, it is clear that growth will continue to play a crucial role for the poorest to eliminate poverty, but growth needs to be equally distributed so that the poor can also benefit in relation to low carbon development (Urban, 2010).

Second critique: low carbon development and its trade-offs

Many poorer countries already have unintentional 'low carbon economies', such as countries with low energy use and low emissions. This is not due to a transition from a high carbon to a low carbon economy, but due to their low income levels and pre-industrialized economies. Many low income countries, particularly the least developed countries, depend primarily on agriculture, often subsistence farming or small-holder farming, while the industrial and service sectors are yet to be developed (World Bank, 2012). Many people in low income countries do not have access to electricity or other forms of modern energy and are therefore dependent on cooking and heating with traditional biomass, such as fuelwood, dung and agricultural residues. It is estimated that 1.4 billion people worldwide do not have access to electricity; that is 20 per cent of the global population (IEA, 2010). It is further estimated that 2.7 billion people rely on traditional biomass; this is 40 per cent of the global population. In Sub-Saharan Africa about 70 per cent of the population is reported not to have access to electricity and 80 per cent of them rely on traditional biomass (IEA, 2010) (see Chapter 9). Hence, many poor people around the world do not have access to fossil fuels for basic human needs and lead an involuntary and unintended 'low carbon lifestyle'.

At the same time, poor people and countries are often the most vulnerable to climatic changes and, most ironically, to the trade-offs created by low carbon development. Two key trade-offs related to low carbon development are the trade-offs of heavy reliance on hydropower and biofuels, both sources of low carbon energy. Many poorer countries are heavily reliant on hydropower as a main source of electricity. In some climatic areas, high dependence on hydropower can make a country's energy supply very vulnerable to drought, water stress and other climatic changes. An example is Ghana where more than 80 per cent of the country's electricity came from hydropower in 2005 and more than 50 per cent in 2007 (IEA, 2012; World Bank, 2012). Climate change has become a serious threat to Ghana's economy and a threat to people's livelihoods. Droughts pose a serious risk to energy provision as not enough water is available to generate electricity from hydropower. Load shedding and fluctuating voltage temporarily stops or slows down electricity generation from hydropower and thereby stops or slows down economic activities. Other trade-offs are related to the resettlement of the local population for large hydropower projects such as for the Three Gorges Dam in China, as well as the high environmental impacts of large dams.

Another key trade-off is the increasing investment in biofuels. Many countries are increasingly investing in biofuels for the production of low carbon fuels for transport, such as bioethanol and biodiesel. This development may sometimes be driven by large energy companies that invest in biofuel production. Unfortunately it has been reported that some of these developments can threaten food security. The food security issue arises due to the fact that land used for biofuel production cannot be used for food production; hence there is a conflict between land for biofuels and land for food production. To make things worse some biofuel crops, such as sweet potato or cassava, are also food crops (Rathmann *et al.*, 2010; Murphy *et al.*, 2011). At the same time, there are allegations that some biofuel operations, including by wealthy corporations, have evicted poor people in developing countries from their lands to gain access to land for growing biofuels. Hence some biofuel developments are reported to be associated with so-called land grabs (Neville and Dauvergne, 2012; Oxfam, 2012).

Third critique: political, social, economic and technological barriers to low carbon development

A range of political, social, economic and technological barriers have to be overcome before low carbon development can be implemented at a global scale.

From a political perspective, tackling climate change has received much attention, and many promises and pledges have been made by politicians and governments, but the practical implementation has often been sluggish or even at a standstill. The global financial crisis, widespread unemployment, continuing debt, regional conflicts as well as continued widespread poverty are some of the reasons why tackling climate change has not been a key priority in many countries in recent years. Nevertheless, tackling climate change and implementing low carbon development cannot wait as delays will lead to dangerous and irreversible climate change. Overcoming political barriers and particularly political opposition to change are therefore key priorities for being able to achieve low carbon development.

From a social perspective, the public seems to be aware of the urgency of climate change. Social movements have emerged recently, particularly around the Copenhagen climate conference, to pressurize policy-makers into tackling climate change. However, widespread political inaction has resulted in frustration and even resignation among some groups. Others are critical of the social impacts that low carbon development can have. Ironically, there is a risk that low carbon development might be implemented at the expense of the poorest people in society. This can be the poor in developed countries, who may face higher energy bills and fuel poverty due to utility companies that pass on the costs of renewable energy investments to customers. This can be the poor in developing countries, who may be faced with higher food prices due to limited availability of land due to extensive biofuel developments or who might even be evicted from their land due to biofuel developments or large dam building and who face a desolate future. Low carbon development therefore needs to be achieved in a way that promotes social and economic benefits for all social strata of society, particularly for the poorest.

From an economic perspective, it is often argued that investments in low carbon energy, such as in wind turbines and solar parks, require a high up-front investment. This is correct, however, the discussion often omits that most low carbon energy options, particularly renewable energy, usually have very low operation and maintenance costs and even lower (or no) fuel costs compared with fossil fuels. While high up-front investment costs are required, running costs are usually much cheaper than for fossil fuels. In addition, the costs for renewable energy have decreased rapidly in recent decades. For example, the price of solar photovoltaic (PV) panels has decreased from about US$60 per Watt in 1979 to only about $2 per Watt in 2009 (IEA, 2010). Experience shows that the doubling of the cumulative volume sold decreases the price of PV panels by 22 per cent (IEA, 2010). Economic criticism of low carbon energy options is therefore often linked to political unwillingness to make a transition to a different development pathway.

From a technological perspective, low carbon technologies, particularly renewable energy technologies like wind, solar and hydropower, have been commercialized for several decades and are mature technologies. Technologies such as electric cars or carbon capture and storage (CCS) power plants are still in an as yet uncommercialized stage, which requires further research and development (R&D). They have the potential to become mature technologies in the future, however, there are still major technological and economic issues to be overcome. One problem with low carbon technologies is that they often require a paradigm change, hence a change in the dominant supply and demand models and a rethinking of infrastructure models. For example, electric vehicles require charging stations, which are currently hardly available. A large-scale introduction of wind energy and solar energy requires decentralized distribution – such as smart-grids – rather than centralized distribution by the national grid. While many of these low carbon technologies are readily available at cost-effective prices, their large-scale introduction requires a rethinking of our economies and our lifestyles. This is the major barrier to achieving a transition to low carbon development in the long run.

These are some of the most problematic and fiercely debated aspects related to low carbon development. It is therefore important to recognize that not all interventions that have a 'low carbon' label are necessarily good or will be successful, and they might involve complex ethical questions. The political, social, economic and technological key issues of low carbon development will be discussed in the following chapters of this book.

Conclusion

Global climate change poses a serious threat to international development efforts. Developing countries – and especially the poor – have historically contributed very little to climate change. However, they are often the most vulnerable to climate change due to their limited resources and limited capacity to adapt to climate change. At the same time, developed countries are struggling to mitigate emissions that lead to climate change. To mitigate the emissions leading to climate change there is a need for serious global commitment to low carbon development.

Low carbon development is essential for mitigating the emissions leading to climate change and for enabling development in a carbon constrained world. Low carbon development can bring opportunities and benefits for both developed and developing countries, nevertheless low carbon development can only be implemented when an adequate enabling environment is in place that addresses the political, economic, social and technological key issues. In low income and lower middle income countries, issues of social justice and poverty reduction are the key to low carbon development, while for higher middle income and high income countries low carbon innovation and emission reductions are at the heart of implementing low carbon development.

References

Annan, K. (2009) The anatomy of a silent crisis. Human Impact Report – Climate Change. Geneva: Global Humanitarian Forum.

Ban, K.-M. (2011) Climate change lapping Pacific shores: Ban Ki-moon. TVNZ. Available at: http://tvnz.co.nz/national-news/climate-change-lapping-pacific-shores-ban-ki-moon-4387638 (accessed 18 October 2012).

Barrett, M., Lowe, R., Oreszczyn, T. and Steadman, P. (2008) How to support growth with less energy. *Energy Policy*, 36(12), 4592–9.

Beckerman, W. (1992) Economic growth and the environment: whose growth? Whose environment? *World Development*, 20(4), 481–96.

Chambers, R. (1995) Poverty and livelihoods: whose reality counts? *Environment and Urbanization*, 7(1), 173–204.

Collier, P. (2007) *The Bottom Billion: Why the Poorest Countries are Failing and What Can Be Done About It.* Oxford: Oxford University Press.

Cowen, M. and Shenton, R. (1996) *Doctrines of Development.* London: Routledge.

Department for International Development (DfID) (2009) Eliminating world poverty: building our common future. DfID White Paper. London: DfID.

Danish Institute for International Studies (DIIS) (2009) Reducing poverty through low carbon development. Recommendations for development cooperation in least developed countries. Available at: http://www.diis.dk/graphics/Publications/PolicyBriefs2009/PB2009_nov_Reducing_poverty_low_carbon_development.pdf (accessed 18 October 2012).

Economic and Social Commission for Asia and the Pacific (UN ESCAP) (2009) Green growth. Available at: www.greengrowth.org (accessed 18 October 2012).

Government of South Africa (2008) South Africa long-term mitigation scenarios. Available at: http://www.environment.gov.za (accessed 18 October 2012).

Greenpeace (1997) Fossil fuels and climate protection: the carbon logic. Available at: http://archive.greenpeace.org/climate/science/reports/carbon/clfull-5.html (accessed 18 October 2012).

Hart, G. (2001) Development critiques in the 1990s: *cul de sac* and promising paths. *Progress in Human Geography*, 25(4), 649–58.

Hickey, S. and Mohan, G. (2005) Relocating participation within a radical politics of development. *Development and Change*, 36(2), 237–62.

Humphrey, J. (2007) Forty years of development research: transformations and reformations. *IDS Bulletin*, 38, 14–19.

International Energy Agency (IEA) (2007) *World Energy Outlook 2007.* IEA/OECD, Paris.

IEA (2010) *World Energy Outlook 2010.* Paris: IEA/OECD.

IEA (2012) Statistics of the International Energy Agency. Available at:http://www.iea.org/stats/index.asp (accessed 18 October 2012).

Intergovernmental Panel on Climate Change (IPCC) (1990) Climate change 1990. Overview Chapter. First Assessment Report of the Intergovernmental Panel on Climate Change. Cambridge: Cambridge University Press.

IPCC (2001) Climate change 2001. Working Group III: Mitigation. Third Assessment Report of the Intergovernmental Panel on Climate Change. Cambridge: Cambridge University Press.

IPCC (2007) Climate change 2007. Synthesis report. Fourth Assessment Report of the Intergovernmental Panel on Climate Change. Cambridge: Cambridge University Press.

Jolly, R. (2003) Human development and neo-liberalism: paradigms compared, in: Kukudar-Parr, S. and Shiva Kumar, A. K. (eds) *Readings in Human Development*. New Delhi: Oxford University Press.

Kuznets, S. (1955) Economic growth and income inequality. *The American Economic Review*, 45(1), 1–28.

Mann, M. E., Bradley, R. S. and Hughes, M. K. (1999) Northern hemisphere temperatures during the past millennium: inferences, uncertainties, and limitations. *Geophysical Research Letters*, 26(6), 759–62.

Mitchell, T. and Maxwell, S. (2011) Defining climate compatible development. Available at: http://www.southsouthnorth.org/wp-content/uploads/CDKN_Defining-climate-compatible-development_Final.pdf (accessed 18 October 2012).

Mohan, G. and Holland, J. (2001) Human rights and development in Africa: moral intrusion or empowering opportunity. *Review of African Political Economy*, 88, 177–96.

Murphy, R., Woods, J., Black, M. and McManus, M. (2011) Global developments in the competition for land and biofuels. *Food Policy*, 36(1), 52–61.

Neville, K. J. and Dauvergne, P. (2012) Biofuels and the politics of mapmaking. *Political Geography*, in press, doi.org/10.1016/j.polgeo.2012.03.006.

Ockwell, D.G. (2008) Energy and economic growth: grounding our understanding in physical Reality. *Energy Policy*, 36(12), 4600–4.

Oxfam (2012) Land grabs. http://www.oxfam.org.nz/what-we-do/issues/grow/land-grabs

Project Catalyst (2008) Low-carbon growth: a potential path for Mexico. Centro Mario Molina, Delegación Cuajimalpa de Morelos, Mexico.

Pye, S., Watkiss, P., Savage, M. and Blyth, W. (2010) The economics of low carbon, climate resilient patterns of growth in developing countries: a review of the evidence. Available at:http://sei-international.org/mediamanager/documents/Publications/Climate/economics_low_carbon_growth_report.pdf (accessed 18 October 2012).

Rathmann, R., Szklo, A. and Schaeffer, R. (2010) Land use competition for production of food and liquid biofuels: an analysis of the arguments in the current debate. *Renewable Energy*, 35(1), 14–22.

Richardson, K., Steffen,W., Schellnhuber, H. J., Alcamo, J., Barker, T., Kammen, D. M., Leemans, R., Liverman, D., Munasinghe, M., Osman-Elasha, B., Stern, N. and Wæver, O. (2009) Climate change. Global risks, challenges and decisions. Synthesis Report. Available at:http://climate-congress.ku.dk/ pdf/synthesisreport/ (accessed 18 October 2012).

Rist, G. (2007) Development as a buzzword. *Development in Practice* 17(4–5), 485–91.

Skea, J. and Nishioka, S. (2008) Policies and practices for a low-carbon society. *Climate Policy, Supplement Modelling Long-Term Scenarios for Low-Carbon Societies* 8, 5–16.

Sustainable Development Commission (2009) Prosperity without growth. Available at: http://www.sd-commission.org.uk/data/files/publications/prosperity_without_growth_report.pdf (accessed 18 October 2012.

Tyndall Centre (2009) Climate change in a myopic world, Tyndall Briefing Note No. 36. Available at: http://www.tyndall.ac.uk/Tyndall-Publications/Briefing-Notes/2009/Climate-change-myopic-world (accessed 18 October 2012).

United Nations Framework Convention on Climate Change (UNFCCC) (1992) The United Nations Framework Convention on Climate Change. Available at: http://unfccc.int/resource/docs/convkp/conveng.pdf (accessed 18 October 2012).

UNFCCC (1997) The Kyoto Protocol. Available at: http://unfccc.int/resource/docs/convkp/kpeng.pdf (accessed 18 October 2012).

UNFCCC (2007) Bali Action Plan. Available at: http://unfccc.int/resource/docs/2007/cop13/eng/06a01.pdf#page=3 (accessed 18 October 2012).

UNFCCC (2009) Copenhagen Accord. Available at: http://unfccc.int/resource/docs/2009/cop15/eng/11a01.pdf (accessed 18 October 2012).

UNFCCC (2010) Cancun Agreements. Available at: http://unfccc.int/resource/docs/2010/cop16/eng/07a01.pdf#page=2 (accessed 18 October 2012).

UNFCCC (2011) Durban platform for enhanced action. Available at: http://unfccc.int/files/meetings/durban_nov_2011/decisions/application/pdf/cop17_durbanplatform.pdf (accessed 18 October 2012).

Urban, F. (2009) Sustainable energy for developing countries – modelling transition to renewable and clean energy in rapidly developing countries. PhD Thesis. Groningen: University of Groningen.

Urban, F. (2010) Pro-poor low carbon development and the role of growth. *International Journal of Green Economics*, 4(1), 82–93.

Urban, F. (2011) *Technology, Trade and Climate Policy: the Pursuit of Low Carbon Development in Least Developed Countries, Vulnerable Economies and Small Island Developing States*. London: Commonwealth Secretariat.

Urban, F. and Naess, L. O. (2011) The differences and similarities between mitigation and low carbon development. Brighton: University of Sussex/IDS.

Urban, F., Mitchell, T. and Silva Villanueva, P. (2011) Issues at the interface of disaster risk management and low-carbon development. *Climate and Development*, 3(3), 259–279.

Urban, F., Mohan, G. and Zhang, Y. (2011) The understanding and practice of development in China and the European Union. IDS Working Paper, Vol 372.

Van Ruijven, B., Urban, F., Benders, R. M. J., Moll, H. C, Van der Sluijs, J., De Vries, B. and Van Vuuren, D. P. (2008) Modeling energy and development: an evaluation of models and concepts. *World Development*, 36(12), 2801–21.

World Bank (2012) World Bank Data. Available at: http://data.worldbank.org/ (accessed 18 October 2012).

World Bank (2008) *Low Carbon Growth in India*. Washington, DC: World Bank.

World Commission on Environment and Development (WCED) (1987) *Our Common Future*. Oxford: Oxford University Press.

World Resources Institute (WRI) (2005) Navigating the numbers: greenhouse gas data and international climate policy. Chapter on cumulative emissions. Available at: http://pdf.wri.org/navigating_numbers_chapter6.pdf (accessed 18 October 2012).

Further reading

Danish Institute for International Studies (DIIS) (2009) Reducing poverty through low carbon development. Recommendations for development cooperation in least developed countries. Available at: http://www.diis.dk/graphics/Publications/PolicyBriefs2009/PB2009_nov_Reducing_poverty_low_carbon_development.pdf (accessed 18 October 2012).

Mulugetta, Y. and Urban, F. (2010) Deliberating on low carbon development. *Energy Policy*, 38(12), 7546–9.

Skea, J. and Nishioka, S. (2008) Policies and practices for a low-carbon society. *Climate Policy, Supplement Modelling Long-Term Scenarios for Low-Carbon Societies*, 8, 5–16.

Sustainable Development Commission (2009) Prosperity without growth. Available at: http://www.sd-commission.org.uk/data/files/publications/prosperity_without_growth_report.pdf (accessed 18 October 2012).

Urban, F. (2010) Pro-poor low carbon development and the role of growth. *International Journal of Green Economics*, 4(1), 82–93.

Notes

1   1 tonne (t) Carbon (C) = 3.67 t Carbon Dioxide (CO_2).
2   Despite the fact that 'low carbon development' is commonly used, no internationally agreed definition for low carbon development exists so far.
3   For example, there are major differences in opinions within the developed countries, the so-called

Annex I countries, particularly between the member states of the European Union –which are mostly for stringent emission reduction commitments – and countries like Canada, Japan, Russia and the USA who have either not ratified the Kyoto Protocol (US) or withdrawn from its second commitment period in 2011/2012 (Canada, Japan, Russia). There are also major differences in opinions within the group of the developing countries, the so-called non-Annex I countries, particularly between emerging emitters such as China and India – who would like to delay legally binding emission reduction targets for developing countries – and the Small Island Developing States and many African states – who would like to see stringent and immediate mitigation actions at a global level.

Part 2

The politics of low carbon development

Editorial for Part 2

The politics of low carbon development

Frauke Urban and Johan Nordensvärd

Part 2 discusses the politics of low carbon development. Low carbon development is often discussed from a rather technical and/or economic perspective, and the political dimensions behind many decisions relating to low carbon development are often neglected. Nevertheless tackling climate change and implementing low carbon development requires understanding the politics and policy processes behind it. This part therefore acknowledges that low carbon development is inherently a political issue. The chapters in this part hence address the political economy of low carbon development and the climate change policy process related to low carbon development.

Overview of Part 2

Chapter 2 discusses the political economy of low carbon development. Low carbon development cannot be treated as a depoliticized neutral approach that escapes the influence of politics and the economy. Instead, low carbon development needs to be treated as an approach that is influenced, shaped and often driven by political and economic stances. The pursuit and the implementation of low carbon development depend on political will, governance and financial and political deals just as much as they depend on the technicalities of emission reductions. This chapter therefore elaborates some of the key issues of a political economy approach to low carbon development.

Chapter 3 elaborates the climate change policy process and low carbon development. Policy processes can be characterized as a dynamic outcome of: knowledge and narratives; actors and networks; and politics and interest. This chapter explains the role of the United Nations Framework Convention on Climate Change (UNFCCC) in generating the development of low carbon policy. The complex framework of emerging incentives and policy mechanisms is explored, which reflects balances negotiated between developed and developing country governments at international level, which are then mediated within national frameworks. The chapter further discusses some of the recent challenges related to low carbon policy processes.

2 The political economy of low carbon development

Matthew Lockwood

This chapter discusses the political economy of low carbon development. Often the politics and the political economy behind action on tackling climate change are neglected. Low carbon development cannot be treated as a depoliticized neutral approach that escapes the influence of politics and the economy. Instead, low carbon development needs to be treated as an approach that is influenced, shaped and often driven by political and economic stances. The pursuit and the implementation of low carbon development depend on political will, governance and financial and political deals just as much as they depend on the technicalities of emission reductions. This chapter therefore elaborates some of the key issues of a political economy approach to low carbon development. This chapter further discusses examples from South Africa, China and Indonesia.

Introduction: why political economy?

The challenge of low carbon development is often seen in technical terms, for example as transferring and providing renewable energy technologies, or setting up the right financial mechanisms to prevent deforestation. However, low carbon development is in fact a profoundly political process, just like development more widely.

Politics has been defined as the 'constrained use of social power' (Goodin and Klingemann, 1996: 5). This definition focuses attention on the more powerful actors in a society. These are often political elites, who control state resources and can wield state force, in some developing countries often with less accountability and transparency than in the mature democracies of the developed world. But they may also include private sector companies (both national and multinational), social movements, religious groups or trade unions. In some cases, a fundamental problem for low carbon development is that several powerful actors are aligned in protecting a high carbon development path.

A closely related concept is that of 'political economy', which places particular emphasis on the interplay between political power and economic power. A political economy approach is important for understanding the transition to a low carbon growth path in both developing and developed counties, because such a transition will always involve a restructuring of the economy and therefore challenges to powerful vested interests.

But the political context is also important for other external actors, including banks and companies wanting to buy carbon offsets, or potential investors in low carbon energy projects. They will be concerned with the effectiveness and stability of institutions in a country, and about the credibility of policies on which their investments will depend

(Helm *et al*, 2003). The politics of a country will bear heavily on both, and indeed political risk is a significant barrier to low carbon investments in many countries (Brown and Jacobs, 2011).

The central argument of this chapter is that the barriers to and opportunities for low carbon development in a country are heavily determined by the interaction of ideas, interests and the nature of political and economic institutions. This interaction can be changed by factors ranging from international political pressure, a new political regime or shifts in energy prices, but the political difficulties of moving countries onto a low carbon development path should not be underestimated.

In the next section I elaborate on the political drivers for and barriers to low carbon development, including material and political interests, narratives or ideologies of development and institutional incentives. The section on 'The political economy of low carbon development' then applies some of these ideas to case studies from South Africa, China and Indonesia. Finally, in the Conclusion, I consider some of the implications of a political economy approach to low carbon development for the international negotiations at the UNFCCC.

A framework for understanding the political economy of low carbon development

Box 2.1 first discusses the key concepts and terms relevant for this chapter.

Box 2.1 Definition of key concepts and terms

Politics – Defined by Goodin and Klingemann (1996: 5) as the 'constrained use of social power'. At its core, politics is about the resolution of opposing interests or views without open conflict or violence.

Political economy – Places particular emphasis on the relationships between political power and interests on the one hand, and economic power and interests on the other. There are several different schools of political economy, ranging from neo-Marxist analysts (e.g. Arrighi, 2001) to approaches rooted in institutional economics (e.g. Acemoglu *et al.*, 2005)

Power – Lukes (1974) argues that power can be understood in three dimensions: (i) the ability to make decisions according to one's own interests or desires; (ii) the ability to make other people take decisions, through influence or force; and (iii) the ability to make people take decisions (including to acquiesce in their own subjugation willingly) through shaping the way they think through ideology. Power is wielded through political and economic institutions, but these can be both formal (such as political parties) and informal (such as networks of personal patronage).

Ideas – Narratives or evidence that shape political options.

Vested interests – actors with a material (or political) interest in the maintenance of an existing system or institution (often in the form of physical or financial assets).

Institutions – The 'rules of the game' (North, 1990): formal or informal arrangements that evolve to lower the costs of interactions with others, by reducing uncertainty and building trust, and to solve collective action problems. These can be economic institutions or political institutions.

Within a given political setting, there are a number of potential drivers for and barriers to the emergence of a low carbon development agenda. These can be usefully be thought of in terms of the frequently used political science typology of the 'three i's': ideas, interests and institutions (Harrison and Sundstrom, 2010).

The first of these, *ideas*, would include climate science itself as a driver, along with evidence of near-term climate change impacts. This kind of driver may increasingly be playing a role in some emerging economies such as Indonesia, India (Dubash, 2011) and China, where concerns about drought and water scarcity have been growing for some time. However, other ideas may play a more dominant role, and one of the big challenges for low carbon development is how to engage political leaders whose ways of thinking about development have little place for environmental issues. For example, many developmental states will have powerful narratives about economic growth and national strength, so that even if there is some concern about climate change impacts, low carbon development policies will have to fit into a high growth paradigm. This is partly why the language of 'green growth' often appeals more to developing country governments than 'low carbon', and why the former term appears in their strategies. For example Ethiopia, one of the more developmental states in Africa, has recently launched a Climate Resilient Green Economy Strategy (Federal Democratic Republic of Ethiopia, 2011), while Vietnam is developing a green growth strategy.[1]

A second set of potential drivers and barriers for low carbon development are *interests*, especially those of powerful actors, including elites, and large national and multinational companies, but also trade unions and social movements. The interests of political leaders are mainly to stay in power (or for opposition leaders, to gain power), and this is often the lens through which they will view low carbon policies or investments.

The logic of interest can represent a barrier, as in the case of fossil fuel subsidies, which are effectively negative carbon prices. Removing or reforming such subsidies would in many cases both reduce carbon emissions and free up resources for spending on services for poor people (World Bank, 2010). For example, in some Indian states, as much as 50 per cent of the budget goes on subsidies to electricity (Joseph, 2010). Moreover, most of the benefits from fuel subsidies are captured by the middle class rather than the poor. For example, the International Energy Agency (IEA) estimates that of US$22.5 billion spent by India on fossil fuel subsidies in 2010, less than $2 billion benefited the poorest 20 per cent of the population (IEA, 2011: 40). However, attempts to remove subsidies typically meet strong opposition, often from poorer urban populations. This is partly because poor people are proportionately more affected by subsidy removal. But it is also because there is little confidence that money saved by reduced subsidies will be spent on pro-poor provision of public goods in what are often highly corrupt countries. In the face of such opposition it is politically risky for regimes to cut subsidies. Reform can be rapidly dropped, as was the case in Nigeria where the government removed petrol subsidies on 1 January 2012 but partially reversed this decision by 16 January following a week of rioting in major cities. Only carefully prepared reform programmes that offer credible alternative benefits are likely to succeed (Victor, 2009).

Other political interests can work the other way, helping drive economies towards certain kinds of low carbon technologies or investments. One example is better energy security, which is particularly important for developmental state leaders seeking to maintain high economic growth. This issue makes political leaders and some business leaders interested in and supportive of improving energy efficiency[2] and investing in renewable energy. Another example is the prospect that investing in the capacity to produce and innovate in low carbon technologies can itself be a driver of growth, especially growth in exports into a rapidly growing world market for such technologies. The most obvious case here is China's wind industry, which is discussed briefly below and in more depth in Chapter 20 of this book.

Political elites also have incentives to pay attention to large, powerful private sector actors in strategic parts of their economies, which of course will have their own interests. These can include both multinational corporations and key domestic firms, whose owners and managers often have close links with the political world. Given that most existing development is high carbon, these vested interests will tend to oppose major moves towards a low carbon economy. One clear example is the coal industries in major economies like South Africa, India, Indonesia and China. Corporate interests can also distort low carbon development policies themselves. Biofuels production is a prime example. Where biofuel crops displace rainforest or peat forest, they are actually high carbon not low carbon (e.g. Fargione *et al.*, 2008), and where they displace smallholder farmers (Matondi *et al.*, 2011) they cannot be said to be unambiguously developmental in a pro-poor sense. But in both cases, short-term returns are the primary interest of the companies involved, and for local and national politicians controlling access to land, there are gains to be made by allowing those companies to pursue their interests.

The third important area for understanding the political economy of low carbon development is *institutions*. These can include informal institutions, for example, customary rights to use forest resources, as well as formal institutions, for example, carbon markets. Some institutions can be hybrids that have both formal and informal elements. In many developing countries, fewer institutions are formalized, and some of the most important decisions are taken through informal mechanisms or relationships that are often invisible in the discourse of official development aid. The shape and function of institutions in a country will be heavily influenced by the nature of the wider political context, and especially the nature of the state and political leadership. These factors can have a major impact on opportunities for low carbon development.

One important example is the electricity system. Even where a government is supportive of low carbon electricity generation and where subsidies to cover additional capital costs are available, institutional arrangements for electricity can still be a barrier (Mitchell, 2010). Electricity grids and markets are designed for existing high carbon sources, with power that can be despatched with very short notice, in controllable ways, as opposed to renewable sources, especially wind, which is intermittent. The best wind resource is often not in the same place as grid infrastructure, and a large penalty may have to be paid for this. In liberalized markets, wholesale electricity prices are usually set by the dominant, high carbon fuel (coal, or gas), which increases the revenue risk for alternatives, whether renewables or nuclear (Gross *et al.*, 2007). This is why electricity institutions, with their long lasting infrastructure, are path-dependent and prone to high carbon 'lock-in' in both developed and developing countries (Unruh, 2000, 2006). The dominant technology firms can easily marginalize new technologies through institutional arrangements.

However, the politics of electricity in particular settings can also open up spaces for new technologies. In India, the power sector has been dominated by state-owned companies for many years. Electricity pricing has been used for political purposes, with richer farmers typically receiving free or very cheap power for irrigation, especially in states where politics was primarily driven by patronage (Tongia, 2006; Joseph, 2010). The consequence was that electricity companies were usually loss making, and lacked funds to maintain or expand their networks and capacity, meaning that electricity supply was unreliable for industry and unavailable to the rural poor. Despite heavy pressure from the World Bank and bilateral donors, reform has been only partial, with most state-owned providers remaining in place and markets only partially liberalized. However, in 2003, the possibility for outsiders to invest in generation capacity was opened up. Many factories rushed to invest in their own on-site supply, called 'captive' power, which by the late 2000s was approaching 20 per cent of total electricity generation. Much of this capacity was high carbon coal and diesel.

But, the captive power boom also allowed the development of India's wind industry, with the turbine manufacturer and developer Suzlon cleverly marketing wind as the answer to independence from both the unreliable grid and volatile diesel prices. At the same time, the 2003 Electricity Act completely deregulated off-grid electricity, which has allowed the development of mini-grids, some of which now rely on the gasification of biomass.

The political economy of low carbon development: some examples

In this section, the ideas developed in the last section are illustrated in some particular cases where attempts at low carbon development – some more successful than others – have been made in a number of different countries.

South Africa – political constraints to the expansion of renewable energy

South Africa has an excellent renewable solar energy resource, with solar irradiation more than double that in Europe, and some wind potential on the west coast (Edkins *et al.*, 2010). It is estimated that a little over 1 per cent of the high solar resource potential in the north west of the country alone could meet projected 2020 generation needs (Pegels, 2010: 4948). Recognizing this potential, the Department of Minerals and Energy published a Renewable Energy White Paper in 2003, setting a generation target for renewable power of 10,000 gigawatt hour (GWh) by 2013. However, by 2009 only 3 per cent of this target had been realized (Pegels, 2010: 4948).

The main technical barriers to an expansion of renewable power are fairly clear. The main technologies, such as concentrated solar power (CSP), are more costly than coal-fired generation, and the grid is not well located for CSP or wind (Pegels, 2010). Support from the Clean Technology Fund of $500 million will help overcome some of those barriers, bringing on-line 300 MW of CSP and wind capacity (CIF, 2009). But even if the technical and cost barriers can be surmounted, the main thrust of South Africa's investment in electricity generation is likely to continue to be in coal-fired capacity. For example, a World Bank loan of $3.75 billion is helping to build what will be the world's largest coal-fired plant at Medupi, with a capacity of 4.8 gigawatt (GW), adding over 13 per cent to the country's capacity in one single investment.[3]

To understand why it will be so hard for South Africa to switch away from its high dependence on coal, one needs to grasp the inter-locking set of political and commercial interests at work in South Africa's 'minerals–energy complex' (MEC) (Fine and Rustomjee, 1996), as well as the political driver of expanding energy access.

A primary political driver for the government is expanding access to electricity in the post-apartheid context, where until the early 1990s large parts of the majority black population had been unserved. Despite an ambitious electrification programme in the 1990s (Winkler and Marquard, 2009) only 55 per cent of the rural population has access (Bekker *et al.*, 2008). At the same time, South Africa has an unusually energy-intensive and energy-inefficient industrial sector. Demand is already exceeding supply, and there is an urgent need to expand capacity now and into the future, with an expected 4 per cent annual growth in demand to 2020 (Bekker *et al.*, 2008).

There are a series of close relationships between the dominant electricity supplier, the coal industry, other heavy industries, the trade unions and the ruling party in South Africa (Winkler and Marquand, 2009). For South African coal companies, the electricity market is their most important customer, making up about 40 per cent of the total and well over half of domestic use. This market is dominated by the state-owned power company Electricity Supply Commission (Eskom), which is essentially the sole, monopoly supplier of electricity in the country. The ruling African National Congress (ANC) party has ensured that Eskom provides electricity to both the residential and the industrial sector at some of the lowest prices in the world, but one consequence has been a lack of investment funds and increasingly tight margins leading to rolling black-outs. Eskom is now investing in new capacity, especially the large new coal-fired plant at Medupi as noted above. The investment wing of the ANC is reported to own shares in firms that will construct the Medupi plant.[4] The ANC is also closely linked to the mining industry through the unions. South Africa's Congress of South African Trade Unions (COSATU) is politically influential and close to the ANC. Its single largest affiliated union is the mine workers union, with 300,000 members (Buhlungu, 2010). Such an interlocking group of powerful interests make the development of low carbon forms of energy at scale very difficult in South Africa (Hallding *et al.*, 2011: 50–52; Stockholm Environment Institute, 2010).

China – balancing objectives in an authoritarian state

China became the world's largest emitter of greenhouse gases in 2006, and now accounts for almost a quarter of global emissions (IEA, 2011). The huge rise in its emissions is linked to rapid economic growth fuelled mainly by coal, which provides around 70 per cent of primary energy supply (Heggelund *et al.*, 2010).

However, despite its high carbon emissions and economic growth targets, China has also adopted and achieved clear targets on energy use and emissions intensity. The 11th Five-Year Plan (2005–2010) achieved a reduction of 19 per cent in the energy intensity of GDP (Climate Policy Initiative, 2011). The 12th Five-Year Plan (EUCTP, 2011), covering the period 2011–2015, gives unprecedented attention to environmental concerns. It sets a number of national targets, including reducing carbon intensity per unit of GDP by 17 per cent and increasing renewable energy to 15 per cent of total primary energy consumption. Five provinces and eight cities have been selected to act as low carbon pilots, and a trial carbon market has already started.

China's performance in areas like wind energy is also very striking, with a near doubling in installed capacity *every year* between 2006 and 2010, to reach over 42 GW.[5] In 2003, the top ten largest turbine manufacturers by global market share were all from Europe, the USA and Japan, by 2010, Chinese firms had taken four of the top ten places (Lema *et al.*, 2011).

China's politics are very different from South Africa's; the country is led by a small elite within the ruling Communist Party, and political dissent is tightly controlled. However, this does not mean that the elite faces no domestic political incentives. These come not in the form of electoral competition, but rather in the need to avoid widespread social unrest. Such unrest has in recent years been driven by a range of factors, including unemployment when economic growth has slowed, land grabbing in areas of rapid industrial and commercial development, and local water and air pollution problems. The government thus has an incentive to try to manage a development path that produces rapid economic growth but at the same time is responsive to local concerns about the negative spillovers from industrial development (Heggelund *et al.*, 2010). This in turn points to a number of specific political drivers of Chinese climate policy.

Energy policy has been the main driver of domestic climate policy so far, because it is so closely linked to economic growth. Domestic oil production is falling off even as demand skyrockets. In 2007 there were 31 million vehicles on the roads; by 2030 the total is expected to reach 150 million (Heggelund *et al.*, 2010: 234) and imports are expected to make up 80 per cent of oil demand by the late 2020s (Hallding *et al.*, 2011). China does have domestic coal reserves, but these are below the per capita world average, and domestic production could peak as early as the 2020s. In last 5 years the country has turned from a net exporter of coal into a net importer.

The importance of energy security as a driver can be seen in the design of policy, with a heavy emphasis on energy efficiency since 2006. In coal-fired power generation, most of the reduction in emissions intensity has come from the closure of over 60 GW of old, small inefficient plants and their replacement by modern high efficiency power stations (Climate Policy Initative, 2011: 2). By contrast, China has to date shown little interest in developing carbon capture and storage (CCS) technology (Reiner and Liang, 2012), which imposes quite a heavy penalty in terms of extra energy (and therefore extra coal) required.

Along with energy security, some observers argue that low carbon development is increasingly being driven by environmental concerns (Hallding *et al.* (2011) China has now become such a large emitter of greenhouse gases that it faces increasing international pressure to be more active both in the search for international agreement and taking domestic action. The long-term impacts of climate change *within* China are also a growing concern, and in the Chinese political system, where leaders are able to take a long view, climate science is a more powerful driver than it might be elsewhere. Attention is focused on the increasing frequency of severe droughts and water shortages in the north of the country, and extreme flooding in the south. As noted, there is also widespread local concern (and increasingly vocal protest) about air and water pollution linked to heavy industry and coal-fired power generation. These local environmental pressures are only to a degree overlapping with carbon emissions, but are politically important and reinforce the wider idea of the need for a cleaner economy.

A final factor in the politics of China's low carbon development is an interest in capturing a share of global markets in low carbon goods and services, a strategy coordinated by government. This driver fits very well with China's growth model based on export-oriented production. The experience with wind energy can be seen in this perspective, where policy has prioritised the development of manufacturing capacity over renewable electricity generation *per se* (Lema *et al.*, 2011).

Overall, China's policies on low carbon development are pulled in two different directions. Economic growth remains paramount as a political and policy goal, and this requires affordable energy supply, which continues to drive the construction of coal-fired power capacity, which despite the growth in wind, will continue to dominate China's electricity generation for the foreseeable future. Energy security, environmental concerns and low carbon exports all pull the other way. The government has to balance these forces, as well as dealing with other long term problems, such as the need to reduce domestic savings and manage an ageing population. There is no guarantee that the system will be able to do this, but at the same time, a developmental state with centralized political control and the ability to take a longer-term perspective may succeed.

Indonesia – corruption as a barrier to ending deforestation

Indonesia has the third largest expanse of forest in the world, after Brazil and the Democratic Republic of the Congo (DRC). Timber from Indonesian forests has particularly high commercial value, and land cleared is also used for palm oil plantations. Palm oil demand for traditional products is strong, and since the early 2000s has been further bolstered by the emergence of the global market for biofuels (Waltermann and Streubel, 2010; REN21, 2011: 31).

Deforestation in Indonesia started in a major way in the 1970s and intensified in the 1990s. Since 1990 one-fifth of the forest area in Indonesia has been lost, and by 2010, only 52 per cent of the total land area was forested (FAO, 2010), down from over 80 per cent in 1900. The high rate of deforestation in Indonesia makes it the third largest emitter of greenhouse gases after China and the USA, once land use change is taken into account. This is in part due to the special role of peat forest in Indonesia, which is a particularly concentrated store of carbon.

Indonesia's push to develop a biofuels industry based on palm oil and japhotra may look like a low carbon development strategy, but in some circumstances producing biofuels can actually create far more carbon emissions than it saves by displacing petrol or diesel, creating a carbon 'debt'. In the case of biofuels from crops grown on land that was previously tropical rainforest and peat forest, the carbon emissions created can be hundreds of times greater those abated (e.g. King, 2007; Fargione *et al.*, 2008).

There is increasing concern about climate change in Indonesia, partly because the country is vulnerable to sea-level rise in the long term and to food security threats in the shorter term. In September 2011, the Prime Minister of Indonesia, S. B. Yudhoyono pledged to dedicate his remaining 3 years in office to protecting Indonesia's forests (*Jakarta Globe*, 27 September 2011). At the same time, many of the large multinational companies involved in the palm oil and biofuels trade have formed groups with environmental organizations, aimed at more sustainable production.

However, in practice such initiatives are likely to have limited impacts for the foreseeable future, because of the nature of Indonesian politics. The core issue is that, in the words of Smith *et al.* (2003: 293), 'illegal logging is rampant and corruption is entrenched'. For many years under President Suharto's rule, corruption was centrally controlled and linked to politics.. Suharto used natural resources for political patronage, giving out concessions for logging and plantations on a discretionary basis to family, business partners, and members of the political and military elite (Ascher, 1998; MacIntyre, 2000; Smith *et al.*, 2003,). Payments for concessions were supposed to be paid into a Reforestation Fund, but many of these resources were siphoned off for other politically strategic investments.

The Suharto regime fell in 1998, and the new state was weak, fragmented and politically unstable (Smith *et al.*, 2003). Indonesia had three heads of state within 3 years. New decentralization policies were brought in, aimed at devolving more authority to local administrations to improve management and ensuring that more revenue from resource extraction stayed in producing areas (Human Rights Watch, 2009).

However, these reforms simply decentralized corruption, and accountability if anything decreased, producing a boom in illegal logging in the late 1990s. Despite attempts to bring forests back under central control, many local administrations continue to issue permits anyway due to lack of enforcement capacity in the ministry in Jakarta. Many local authorities do not publish data on logging, without facing any sanction from provincial or national authorities, and there are no incentives for local forest officers to improve data collection (Human Rights Watch, 2009: 12–13). Corruption has moved from being tolerated but controlled to being decentralized and largely beyond the reach of central government (Smith *et al.*, 2003: 294–5).[6]

The issue of deforestation in Indonesia gives an illustration of how the interplay between interests and institutions can be a major block to low carbon development, despite increasing concern about climate impacts. Any realistic strategy for getting Indonesia on to a low carbon development path will have to engage with the corruption issue at the heart of the deforestation issue, either by changing the incentives to exploit the forest resource, or by transforming the institutions for enforcing control over exploitation. These changes could be brought about by the Indonesian government, or possibly by the large international corporations involved in timber, palm oil or biofuels, but currently neither of these actors have a strong interest in making such changes.

Box 2.2 discusses the key issues in the political economy of low carbon development.

Box 2.2 Key issues in the political economy of low carbon development

Policies for low carbon development that make overall economic sense may nevertheless be politically hard to deliver. **Fossil fuel subsidy reforms** are an example of this, where people do not understand the hidden costs of policies and do not trust governments to protect them from the costs of transition.

In many developing countries, **electricity** generation is a major source of emissions, but electricity markets are highly politicized and resistant to reform. However, where the rural poor are neglected, this can open up space for alternatives, such as off-grid or mini-grid renewables.

Where **political and commercial interests are enmeshed** – as in coal-fired power generation in South Africa, or concessions to develop land in tropical rainforest areas in Indonesia – the barriers to low carbon development are especially powerful.

Low carbon development can be driven by **concerns about climate change**, but it can also be the **outcome of other factors**, including energy security and low carbon industrial policy. All of these drivers appear to be present in China.

Interests always work in the context of **political and economic institutions**, and affect the outcomes that result. A central edict by the President to stop deforestation in Indonesia might well have been effective under the centralized rule of Suharto, but following the decentralization of power it is much less likely to make a difference.

International pressures and rules do have some effect on national politics, but **national politics have a much more powerful impact on international negotiations**. The current failure to reach an international agreement to mitigate climate change is rooted in the national political barriers to low carbon development.

Conclusion

Low carbon development brings two kinds of problem together. One is how to develop – how to manage a process of economic growth and diversification, and investment in education and health, while avoiding social conflict and environmental degradation. The other is how to go low carbon – how to undertake major shifts in energy systems and land use to reduce emissions against business-as-usual growth.

In many cases, countries suffer from regimes that are completely failing to solve the first problem, and it is unrealistic to expect them to make much headway in tackling the second. In other cases, countries have experienced complete transformations in their economies and societies, and movement onto a lower carbon development pathway may be a feasible option. However, the low carbon imperative does not arrive into a vacuum, but into a development trajectory that is path-dependent and the result of a political process. Energy systems and land use institutions develop a form that reflects the ideas and interests of the dominant actors, as the cases of South Africa and Indonesia illustrate. Change will be resisted, and so if it is to happen it requires some powerful drivers, as the case of China suggests.

All of these examples demonstrate the importance of looking beyond approaches that simply identify an ideal set of policies or technologies for low carbon development. There is a need to learn from the large literature on politics, institutions and development the lesson that 'best practice' is often politically unfeasible, and that what is needed is the best fit in a second-best world (Rodrik, 2008). Leaders may be strongly influenced by climate science and the need to move to a lower carbon development path, but they also have limited political capital, and need to use that as effectively as they can.

The political economy of low carbon development is primarily national, although sometimes involving subnational actors (for example local government) or multinational actors (such as large corporations). But it also has implications for global processes. It is now clear that avoiding dangerous climate change will require carbon emission reductions not only in the developed world, but also in developing countries, especially the larger emerging economies (Hepburn and Ward, 2010). This implies that any effective global agreement on climate change mitigation will depend crucially on domestic politics in those countries (Harrison and Sundstrom, 2010). As Barrett (2003) notes, effective international environmental agreements depend both on making participation attractive and on ensuring compliance, and both elements have to be sellable to governments' domestic constituencies.

The low carbon development agenda is still relatively new, but it is already clear that political economy factors play a crucial role. A better understanding of their dynamics is crucial if that agenda is to progress.

References

Acemoglu, D., Johnson, S. and Robinson, J. (2005) Institutions as the fundamental cause of long-run growth, in P. Aghion and S. Durlauf (eds) *Handbook of Economic Growth*. North Holland: Elsevier.

Arrighi, G. (2001) Global capitalism and the persistence of the North-South divide. *Science and Society*, 65(4), 469–76.

Ascher, W. (1998) From oil to timber: the political economy of off-budget development financing in Indonesia. *Indonesia*, 65, 37–61.

Barrett S. (2003) *Environment and Statecraft*. Oxford: Oxford University Press.

Bekker, B., Eberhard, A., Gaunt, T. and Marquand, A. (2008) South Africa's rapid electrification programme: policy, institutional, planning, financing and technical innovations. *Energy Policy*, 36, 3125–37.

Brown, J. and Jacobs, M. (2011) Leveraging private investment: the role of public sector climate finance. Background Note. London: Overseas Development Institute.

Buhlungu, S. (2010) *A Paradox of Victory: COSATU and the Democratic Transformation in South Africa*. Durban: University of KwaZulu-Natal Press.

Climate Investment Funds (CIF) (2009) Clean Technology Fund: revised investment plan for South Africa. Available at: http://www.climateinvestmentfunds.org/cifnet/sites/default/files/South%20 Africa%20CTF%20Investment%20Plan%20-%20Endorsed.pdf (accessed 22 October 2012).

Climate Policy Initiative (2011) Review of low carbon development in China: 2010 report. CPI, Beijing, Available at: http://climatepolicyinitiative.org/beijing/files/2011/02/Review-of-LCD-in-China-2010.pdf (accessed 22 October 2012).

Dubash, N. (2011) Toward a progressive Indian and global climate politics, in Dubash, N. (ed.) *Handbook of Climate Change in India*. London: Earthscan.

Edkins, M., Marquand, A. and Winkler, H. (2010) South Africa's renewable energy policy roadmaps. Report for the United Nations Environment Programme Research Project Enhancing information for renewable energy technology deployment in Brazil, China and South Africa.

EU China Trade Project (2011) *12th Five-Year Plan of the Peoples' Republic of China* (English translation). Available at: http://www.euctp.org/index.php/component/jdownloads/finish/42-china-s-

12th-five-year-plan/193-translation-of-the-12th-five-year-plan.html?Itemid=19 (accessed 18 October 2012).

Fargione, J., Hill, J., Tilman, D., Polasky, S. and Hawthorne, P. (2008) Land clearing and the biofuel carbon debt. *Science*, 319(5867), 1235–8.

Federal Democratic Republic of Ethiopia (2011) Ethiopia's climate resilient green economy: green economy strategy. Available at: http://www.epa.gov.et/Download/Climate/Ethiopia's%20Climate-Resilient%20Green%20economy%20strategy.pdf (accessed 18 October 2012).

Food and Agriculture Organization (FAO) (2010) Global forest assessment report. Rome: FAO.

Fine, B. and Rustomjee, Z. (1996) *The Political Economy of South Africa: from Minerals–Energy Complex to Industrialisation.* Boulder, CO: Westview Press.

Goodin, R. and Klingemann H.-D. (1995) *A New Handbook of Political Science.* Oxford: Oxford University Press.

Gross, R., Heptonstall, P. and Blyth W. (2007) Investment in electricity generation: the role of costs, incentives and risks. London: UK Energy Research Council.

Hallding, K, Olsson, M., Atteridge, A., Vihma, A., Carson, M. and Román, M. (2011) Together Alone: BASIC countries and the climate change conundrum. Nordic Council of Ministers, Copenhagen. Available at: http://www.norden.org/en/publications/publikationer/2011-530 (accessed 18 October 2012).

Harrison, K. and Sundstrom, L. (2010) Introduction: global commons, domestic decisions, in Harrison, K. and Sundstrom, L. (eds) *Global Commons, Domestic Decisions: the Comparative Politics of Climate Change.* Cambridge, MA: MIT Press.

Heggelund, G., Andresen, S. and Buan, I. (2010) Chinese climate policy: domestic priorities, foreign policy and emerging implementation, in Harrison, K. and Sundstrom, L. (eds) (2010) *Global Commons, Domestic Decisions: the Comparative Politics of Climate Change.* Cambridge, MA: MIT Press.

Helm, D., Hepburn, C. and Mash, R. (2003) Credible carbon policy. *Oxford Review of Economic Policy*, 19, 438–50.

Hepburn, C. and Ward, J. (2010) Should emerging market economies act on climate change, or wait? Paper presented at a Forum on Emerging Markets, October 2010. Available at: http://www.emerging-marketsforum.org/wp-content/uploads/pdf/2010_EMF_Global_Hepburn_Ward_Climate_Change.pdf (accessed 22 October 2012).

Human Rights Watch (2009) *Wild Money: The Human Rights Consequences of Illegal Logging and Corruption in Indonesia's Forestry Sector.* Human Rights Watch, New York. Available at: http://www.hrw.org/sites/default/files/reports/indonesia1209webwcover.pdf (18 October 2012).

International Energy Agency (IEA) (2011) *Energy for All – Financing Access for the Poor*, Special excerpt of the World Energy Outlook 2011. Geneva: IEA.

Joseph, K. (2010) The politics of power: electricity reform in India. *Energy Policy*, 38, 503–11.

King, J. (2007) The King Review of low-carbon cars: Part I: the potential for CO_2 reduction HM Treasury, London. Available at: http://www.hm-treasury.gov.uk/d/pbr_csr07_king840.pdf (accessed 18 October 2012).

Lema, R., Berger, A., Schmitz, H. and Hong, S. (2011) Competition and cooperation between Europe and China in the wind power sector IDS Working Paper 377. Brighton: IDS.

Lukes, S. (1974) *Power: a Radical View.* London: Macmillan.

MacIntyre, A. (2000) Funny money: fiscal policy, rent-seeking and economic performance in Indonesia, in Khan, M. and Jomo, K. S. (eds) *Rents, Rent-seeking and Economic Development: Theory and Evidence in Asia.* Cambridge: Cambridge University Press.

Matondi, P., Havnevik, K. and Beyene, A. (eds) (2011) *Biofuels, Land Grabbing and Food Security in Africa.* London: Zed Books.

Mitchell, C. (2010) *The Political Economy of Sustainable Energy.* Basingstoke: Palgrave Macmillan.

North, D. (1990) *Institutions, Institutional Change and Economic Performance.* Cambridge: Cambridge University Press.

Pegels, A. (2010) Renewable energy in South Africa: potentials, barriers and options for support. *Energy Policy*, 38, 4945–54.

Reiner, D. and Liang, X. (2012) Stakeholder views on financing carbon capture and storage demonstration projects in China. *Environmental Science & Technology*, 46(2), 643–51.

Renewable Energy Policy Network for the 21st Century (REN21) (2011) *Renewables 2011: Global Status Report.* Paris: REN21 Secretariat.

Rodrik, D. (2008) Second best institutions. *American Economic Review*, 98(2) 100–4.

Smith, J., Obidzinski, K., Subarudi, S and Suramenggala, I. (2003) Illegal logging, collusive corruption and fragmented governments in Kalimantan, Indonesia. *International Forestry Review*, 5(3), 293–302.

Sorrell, S. (2007) *The Rebound Effect: an Assessment of the Evidence for Economy-wide Energy Savings from Improved Energy Efficiency.* London: UK Energy Research Council.

Stockholm Environment Institute (2010) Multiple identities: behind South Africa's approach to climate change. Available at: http://sei-international.org/mediamanager/documents/Publications/Climate-mitigation-adaptation/sei_policy_brief_atteridge_southafrica.pdf (accessed 22 October 2012).

Tongia, R. (2006) The political economy of Indian power sector reforms, in Victor, D. and Heller, T. (eds) *The Political Economy of Power Sector Reform.* Cambridge: Cambridge University Press.

Transparency International (2011) Forest governance integrity in Asia Pacific, TI, Berlin. Available at: http://www.illegal-logging.info/uploads/ProjectPaper012011PoliticalCorruption28February2011.pdf (accessed 22 October 2012).

Unruh, G. (2000) Understanding carbon lock-in. *Energy Policy*, 28, 817–3.

Unruh, G. (2006) Globalizing carbon lock-in. *Energy Policy*, 34, 1185–97.

Victor, D. (2009) The politics of fossil fuel subsidies. Global Subsidies Initiative, International Institute for Sustainable Development. Available at: http://www.globalsubsidies.org/files/assets/politics_ffs.pdf (accessed 22 October 2012).

Waltermann, B. and Streubel, H. (2010) Bright future for biodiesel in Indonesia. *The Jakarta Post*, 4 April 2012.

Winkler, H. and Marquand, A. (2009) Changing development paths: from an energy-intensive to low-carbon economy in South Africa. *Climate and Development*, 1, 47–65.

World Bank (2010) Subsidies in the energy sector: an overview. World Bank, Washington DC. Available at: http://siteresources.worldbank.org/EXTESC/Resources/Subsidy_background_paper.pdf (accessed 22 October 2012).

World Wind Energy Association (WWEA) (2011) *World Wind Energy Report 2010.* Bonn: World Wind Energy Association.

Further reading

Ascher, W. (1998) From oil to timber: the political economy of off-budget development financing in Indonesia. *Indonesia*, 65, 37–61.

Harrison, K. and Sundstrom, L. (2010) Introduction: global commons, domestic decisions, in Harrison, K. and Sundstrom, L. (eds) (2010) *Global Commons, Domestic Decisions: the Comparative Politics of Climate Change.* Cambridge, MA: MIT Press.

Joseph, K. (2010) The politics of power: electricity reform in India. *Energy Policy*, 38, 503–11.

Notes

1   http://dsi.mpi.gov.vn/en/1/16.html.
2   It should be noted that the net effect of energy efficiency improvements may be smaller than expected because the money saved will generally be spent on something else. This is the so-called 'rebound effect' (Sorrell, 2007).
3   http://siteresources.worldbank.org/INTSOUTHAFRICA/Resources/Eskom_Power_Investment_Support_Project_Fact_Sheet.pdf.

4   http://mg.co.za/article/2010-04-03-zille-says-anc-stands-to-make-r1bn-from-medupi.
5   However, many wind farms are not connected to the grid, due to high connection costs. The WWEA (2011) reports that in 2010 only 31 GW out of the total capacity of 45 GW was connected to the grid; this means that 31 per cent of the installed capacity was standing idle.
6   For a typical recent case see the account in Transparency International (2011).

3 The climate change policy process and low carbon development

Merylyn Hedger

Climate change policy processes on low carbon development are emerging in all countries, stimulated by the international political framework. Policy processes can be characterized as a dynamic outcome of: knowledge and narratives; actors and networks; and politics and interests. This chapter explains the role of the UNFCCC in generating the development of low carbon policy. The complex framework of emerging incentives and policy mechanisms is explored, which reflects balances negotiated between developed and developing country governments at international level, which are then mediated within national frameworks. Enormous challenges remain related to contested issues on responsibilities between developed countries and major emerging economies, and the provision of resources for low carbon development policy pathways especially for the poorer countries.

Introduction

Climate change policy can be identified since the UNFCCC became operational in 1992. Policy is, however, a result of a dynamic process, and operates at different scales. Key components of policy processes are explained in Box 3.1. This chapter focuses on the role of the UNFCCC in generating the development of low carbon policy through mechanisms and agreed processes that operate at international, national and local levels. The chapter adopts a narrow focus on low carbon development, and not adaptation to climate change, to make the bigger connections between the international and national levels, and explain the complexities. First the main features of the UNFCCC are explored with the development of its mitigation agenda: the implications for developing and developed countries are explained together with some outcomes. Basically the trend is to scale up project-based approaches, to programmes and national strategies, and indeed legislation in some cases. Finally future challenges are considered.

Climate change encompasses two main spheres of policy activity: **adaptation** to the unavoidable impacts of climate change to which we are already committed, and the reduction of reducing emissions of GHGs to **mitigate** concentrations in the atmosphere. Policy development and implementation is consolidating: climate policy on adaptation to impacts becomes embedded or mainstreamed in various sectors such as water and agriculture and links to disaster risk reduction are strengthened. Within the mitigation sphere 'low carbon' policy is an emerging area with various formulations (see Chapter 1) and is generally undertaken in entirely separate frameworks from adaptation. Climate change policy at international level is driven by the UNFCCC (see Chapter 1) and linked to the science

---

Box 3.1 Policy processes

Policy processes can be characterized as a dynamic outcome of: knowledge and narratives; actors and networks; and politics and interests (IDS, 2006). Some points about how this framework relates to climate change are listed below.

Knowledge and narratives: how the problem gets framed and becomes visible is critical as to how it may get addressed. In the case of climate change, scientific knowledge, mediated by the Inter-Governmental Panel on Climate Change (IPCC) was the catalyst for the creation of policy space and led to the establishment of the UNFCCC. This chapter outlines how the UNFCCC has worked within this policy space.

Actors and networks: at all scales, governments play a crucial role, to agree the policy framework at an international level and to implement interventions at national and subnational levels. For this reason civil society organizations campaign within this policy space to reinforce the scientific narratives, create an enabling environment and also undertake actions themselves. Increasingly since the UNFCCC came into force in 1992, business opportunities have been perceived around the low carbon agenda and it has become organized at a collective level (Newell and Paterson, 2010).

Politics and interests: despite an increasing evidence base about the need to act, governments have not fully responded and implemented a route-way to economies based on low carbon development, because of perceptions about short-term economic damage and lack of competitiveness. Environmentally focused civil society organizations campaign in support of low carbon development and increasingly an emerging low carbon business community. Some scientific knowledge has been contested in relation to urgency of action, with alternative narratives suggested, supported by vested interests that have influenced formal democratic structures in the case of the USA-based on fossil fuel businesses (UCS, 2007).

---

outputs of the IPCC.[1] In the past three to five years a broad range of countries have started to prepare climate strategies and policies with low carbon elements, a significant move forward. Two countries, the UK (2008) and Mexico (2012), now have formal legislative frameworks for a low carbon economy – a result of national government leadership, enabled by policy space supported by civil society organizations. At national level there are strong policy connections with energy security, economic growth and environmental management, altogether a complex framework, and which has often been running for some time.

There are different narratives within low carbon strategies, which create different policy challenges: in developed economies decarbonization is needed particularly in the power and transport sectors, and so the energy efficiency agenda is a core element (IEA, 2011). Technology switches are also needed: the key reason to develop and deploy advanced energy technologies is to control the cost of stabilizing GHG concentrations (Edmonds *et al.*, 2007). Some strands have been running for a considerable time: in India for example, programmes and institutions to promote energy efficiency, energy conservation and renewable energy technologies were initiated over two decades ago (GoI, 2012). In China concerns about environmental pollution and international competitiveness have framed policy development. Of the 118 countries that had renewable energy targets in 2012, over half were developing countries (REN21, 2012).

The United Nations Framework Convention on Climate Change (UNFCCC)

Overall policy context

Overall, the main driver for low carbon policy development has been the UNFCCC (UNFCCC, 1992). Since 1992 this framework convention, through a highly contested geo-political policy process has set out a framework for action aimed at stabilizing atmospheric concentrations of GHG at a level that would prevent dangerous human interference with the climate system, based on scientific knowledge; and in so doing created policy space at national level.[2] In the Convention it is recognized that the largest share of historical and current global emissions had originated in developed countries and that per capita emissions in developing countries were relatively low and that the share of emissions in developing countries would grow to meet their social and development needs. From this the principle of 'common but differentiated responsibilities' was derived, reflecting a political balance. Common but differentiated responsibilities means the following: Climate change is a global problem. However, developed countries have the historic responsibility for contributing to climate change and are legally obliged to cut their emissions. Developing countries on the other hand have very little historic responsibility for contributing to climate change and are currently not legally obliged to cut their emissions. Some actions applied to all parties, others chiefly relating to emission cuts, and the provision of finance and technology applied to developed country parties and were listed. Developed countries therefore became the so-called Annex I parties.

The Annex I countries agreed to adopt policies and measures on the mitigation of climate change, with the aim of reducing individually or jointly anthropogenic emissions of GHGs to 1990 levels (UNFCCC, 1992, Article 4.2 and b). The developed countries recognized they had historic responsibilities to take the lead and agreed to provide technology transfer and financial resources to developing countries on the basis of common and differentiated responsibilities. The treaty, however, recognized that measures should be integrated with national development programmes, taking into account that economic development is essential for adopting measures to address climate change, and these terms were used within the framework of promoting sustainable development (UNFCCC, 1992, Art. 4.4).[3]

But, emissions have continued to rise unabated since 1992, and the Kyoto Protocol (see Box 3.2), which introduced clear obligations when it came into effect in 2005, has made little impact on GHG emission reductions, with a key player – the USA – walking away, and despite efforts in the European Union (EU). Moreover, financial resources and technology transfer were not committed on the scale needed to have an impact to reduce concentrations of GHGs in the atmosphere. Narratives based on scientific understanding have not been sufficient to introduce major policy shifts.

One of the problems has been that 1990 is the base year for emissions, the cornerstone of the UNFCCC. This is right: carbon dioxide has a long lifetime in the atmosphere, so the problem is accumulation of emissions, not the annual balance, and thus the early industrializers have left a historic burden. However, going forward, the new emerging economies such as China, India, South Africa and Brazil will produce substantial emissions, and this is already evident from data. Since the Kyoto Conference in 1997, the US Congress has effectively blocked any serious engagement in the international process with legal obligations, on the basis that US economic interest would be adversely affected unless all countries were involved – an issue relating in particular to the USA–China relationship. Meanwhile, while emissions have continued to rise in the emerging emitters notably China, these countries have refused to adopt constraints on emission reductions imposed under the Convention until

---

Box 3.2 The International Climate Change Negotiation Process since 1992

The Convention, signed in 1992 and which entered into force on 21 March 1994, now has 195 parties. On-going negotiations take place annually for the Conferences of the Carties (COPs) and the Meetings of the Parties (CMPs) and for subsidiary bodies established to examine specific technical issues, twice or even four times a year.

Kyoto Protocol: within the Convention there are provisions to review the adequacy of commitments. The Kyoto Protocol agreed in 1997 was the product of the First Review of the IPCC where Annex I Parties agreed to reduce their overall emissions of six major GHGs by an average of 5 per cent below 1990 levels between 2008 and 2012, the first commitment period. It became operational in 2005.

At Montreal in (COP12) in 2005, it was decided to establish two processes to examine further commitments under the Protocol, which mandates consideration of Annex I Parties' further commitments at least seven years before the end of the first commitment period of the Kyoto Protocol. In Bali, in 2007 (COP13, the Bali Roadmap was established, with long-term issues with the Ad hoc Work Group on Long term Cooperative Action exploring mitigation, finance, technology and the shared vision for long-term cooperative action. There was significant progress on the finance side arising from Copenhagen in 2009 (COP15). In Cancun (COP16) in 2010, new institutions and processes were established including the Green Climate Fund. In Durban (COP17) in 2011 a new negotiation process – the Durban Platform for Enhanced Action – was established to develop a new outcome applicable to all parties with a process scheduled to end in 2015. This effectively recognizes global economic change since 2012, but as intermediary talks in Bonn 2012 showed, this is likely to be a difficult negotiation as some industrialized parties such as the USA still have to deliver on their 1992 climate commitments.

---

the 'developed' countries fulfil their obligations. Eventually at the Bali Conference of the Parties (COP) in 2007, agreement was reached on a process to lead to a new 'Long term framework on Cooperative Action' (LCA) after a late concession by the Bush Presidency. But after Copenhagen in 2009 and Cancun in 2010, there was still no new long-term legally binding deal in prospect from this process. However, at Durban in 2011, there was a global political re-alignment with the EU, the Small Island States and the Least Developed Countries (LDCs), effectively breaking up the Group of 77 (G77) and China negotiating group. While India talked of a 'right to development', Grenada (a Small Island State) pointed out 'whilst they develop we die in the process' (Sterk *et al.*, 2012: 8). The EU agreed to take forward the Kyoto Protocol process to a second commitment period, with Norway, Switzerland and the Ukraine effectively alone, after Canada, Japan and Russia joined the USA in walking away (UNDP, 2012). In return a mandate was agreed to launch negotiations on a new comprehensive climate agreement that will be implemented from 2020. This development is regarded as major progress – for the first time the USA, China and India signed up to a global agreement – albeit not for another decade (UNDP, 2012: 32). After the June 2012 Bonn talks, it seems that this is not likely to be accomplished easily.

Development of the mitigation agenda within the UNFCCC

Within the formal Convention process, the term low carbon development is not used. As indicated the main expression used is 'measures on the mitigation of climate change'. The Kyoto Protocol to the Convention where 37 States (Annex I industrialized parties), consisting of highly industrialized countries and countries undergoing the process of transition to a market economy, have legally binding emission 'quantified emission limitation and reduction commitments' (usually known as QUELROS) in order to promote sustainable development. These commitments cover a wide range of policies and measures including: energy efficiency; renewable energy; protection of carbon sinks and reservoirs; sustainable forms of agriculture; research on innovative environmentally sound technologies; removal of subsidies and phasing out of market imperfections; regulatory reforms; transport policies; methane management in waste and energy production; bunker fuels and trade policy.[4]

Pressures for an increased emphasis on mitigation have risen in the past few years. Recent advances in science have generated more strident narratives about the need to tackle climate change and reduce GHG emissions (UNEP, 2010; den Elzen *et al.*, 2012). Second, the rapid pace of the growth emissions in the major emerging economies such as China, India and South Africa is projected to add to the accumulated emissions of the industrialized countries. Within the formal Convention process, whilst major emitters, notably the USA, have themselves been increasing rather than reducing emissions, the political space has been limited to tackle the agenda. A pull factor for governments and their business lobbies has been the possibility of financing from the UNFCCC framework though various mechanisms outlined below; for example, the offsetting device – cheaper reductions to achieve EU targets in developing countries through the Clean Development Mechanism (CDM).

Clean Development Mechanism (CDM)

Developed countries implement projects leading to emission reductions in developing countries. Developing countries gain access to climate-friendly technology, while developed countries gain emission reduction credits to offset their emissions, seemingly a neat political balance. The CDM was operationalized under the Kyoto Protocol, as an offsetting mechanism – a way for developed countries to achieve cuts by investing in developing countries. But it has created an important nexus of operational activity around the UNFCCC. China, for example, created its own CDM fund. As the sustainable development dimension was intended as the main driver for developing country interest in participating in CDM projects, the uneven distribution of registered CDM projects has been a source of contention.[5] This pattern has also occurred despite recognition at the outset in the design of the CDM that private investment tends to gravitate towards a handful of the larger developing countries that have relatively good infrastructure and stable governance systems and a specific obligation in Article 12-6 of the Kyoto Protocol, which states that Parties to the Kyoto Protocol (Meeting of the Parties, CMP) have an explicit need to review the regional distributions of projects with a view to identifying systematic barriers to their equitable distribution (Yamin and Depledge, 2004). Brazil, China, India and Mexico still currently host around 80 per cent of all CDM projects.[6] The EU have said that in the absence of an ambitious international agreement, only credits from new CDM projects in Least Developed Countries (LDCs) will be eligible for the Emissions Trading Scheme (ETS) (EC, 2009: 16). And there are still major challenges in building capacity for CDM in Sub-Saharan Africa (SSA) countries with a poor record in attracting any private sector investments.

The CDM has been subjected to a 'withering crossfire of criticism' for a number of reasons to do with its lack of impact on real emissions reductions, its governance and the scale at which it operates (Streck, 2009: 68). A key governance recommendation has been the need for strong and effective institutions from local to international level and the need for active donor management (GCD, 2011).

Reducing Emissions from Deforestation and Forest Degradation (REDD) and REDD+ (including conservation and sustainable management of forests)

Through this mechanism developing countries can be paid for climate-friendly forest and land use management, while developed countries can gain emission reduction credits to offset their emission obligations. These schemes with the possibility of financial flows are incentivizing activity in many countries (and the World Bank's Forest Carbon Partnership Facility and Investment Program is targeted for those with significant forest resources) and possibly soil sequestration as well, which is being pushed by FAO. Brazil, Cameroon, DRC, Indonesia, Guyana, Malaysia and Papua New Guinea are the major rainforest nations. UN-REDD is supporting national programmes in 13 countries, to provide capacity for monitoring systems, improvement of governance systems, engagement of civil society, indigenous peoples and local communities (UN-REDD, 2011). The proposed REDD mechanisms are very contentious for many NGOs, indigenous peoples' organizations and social movements in developing countries because of adverse environmental and social impacts.[7] At Durban a process was agreed for countries to participate according to national circumstances and most countries are currently preparing national strategies or action plans, devising reference levels and undertaking capacity-building and demonstration projects (CIFOR, 2012).

Technology Needs Assessments (TNAs)

TNAs were intended to get the key negotiation issue process of technology transfer started and emerged in 1998 when developing countries were urged to submit their prioritized technology needs (UNFCCC, 1999, decision 4/CP4), and the Global Environment Facility (GEF) as the financial mechanism was directed to provide funding for them (UNFCCC, 1999, decision 2/CP4). Since then the GEF has financed 92 TNAs. Most effort since then within the UNFCCC has been invested in technology transfer on TNAs (Hedger, 2012). Finally the TNA process itself has been found to be deficient in providing clear road maps and integration with national planning, so National Technology Action Plans are now being developed within the context of updating and developing TNAs. As many as 36 countries are involved in this current initiative, funded through the GEF, and several countries have submitted Technology Action Plans (TAPS) (including Costa Rica, Cote d'Ivoire, Indonesia, Mali and Thailand) (UNFCCC, 2012). Needs assessments (TNAs) of LDCs show that agriculture, water, forestry and household energy needs are priorities, yet these are not being given specific attention within the UNFCCC in relation to technology transfer (Hedger, 2012). For more details see Chapter 11.

Nationally Appropriate Mitigation Actions (NAMAs)

The purpose of NAMAs is to outline national mitigation options in developing countries that are in line with domestic policies and that are 'supported and enabled by technology, financing and capacity building' (IEA/OECD, 2009: 7). NAMAs are capturing the attention of climate policy negotiators and practitioners. But, whilst there has been a significant uptake of NAMA activities, few NAMAs have reached the implementation stage (Tilburg *et al.*, 2012). They emerged in legal text for the first time in the Bali Action Plan and were formally established as a voluntary mechanism in the Cancun Agreement (UNFCCC, 2011a). NAMAs will outline national mitigation options in line with domestic policies. Different tiers of action are likely to be established contingent on the level of external finance and technology available for developing countries. There is no clear definition of NAMAs. The concept remains vague and includes any nationally prioritized, voluntary action that contributes to sustainable development, aims at achieving a deviation in emissions relative to business-as-usual emissions in 2020 and meets the applicable measurement, reporting and verification requirements. Lacking international guidance, developing countries have chosen different approaches to identify NAMAs.

NAMAs have been described as a new instrument that is being defined and ground-tested in parallel (Tilburg *et al.*, 2012). In the best case, the NAMAs communicated to the UNFCCC are the result of a national process of policy evaluation and assessment, take into account stakeholder consultation and are embedded in national low carbon strategies. However, in many cases the NAMAs communicated to the UNFCCC seem to be mere declarations of intent, which still have to be vetted and analysed in the context of national policy development (Streck and Guimaraes, 2011). At the end of May 2012, over 50 countries had made submissions covering energy supply, industry, transport, buildings, waste, agriculture and forestry – with most actions proposed for the energy and forestry sectors. Some countries did not formulate NAMAs for specific sectors but for national emissions targets, such as China and India. In a few cases, countries such as Ethiopia, Morocco and Mongolia, identified concrete measures and specific investment projects. Others stressed the importance of policy reforms and the establishment of enabling policy frameworks (e.g. Argentina, Botswana).[8] Currently the NAMA database shows 54 NAMAs in 25 countries (Ecofys, 2012).[9]

Low carbon development: the climate mitigation agenda from a developing country perspective

A critical challenge ahead for low carbon development policy is to deliver energy for development. The LDCs currently present a low carbon profile, due to their low levels of carbon emissions. As their economies rely on natural capital (agriculture, forest resources, biodiversity, tourism, mineral extraction) there exists a large potential for renewable energies. Further, refocusing policies and investments that are most relevant to the livelihoods of the poor would be more conducive to inclusive growth and jobs, and would make a significant contribution to the MDGs (UNEP *et al.*, 2011). The argument is that international sources of funding are needed to support clean energy technology adoption and trade-related capacity to catalyse and sustain LDCs' transition to a green economy, and they are well suited to benefit from this integrated approach. There are known technology and institutional packages that can help delivery in key sectors such as Climate Smart Agriculture (Wolemberg *et al.*, 2011) and Integrated Water Resources Management.

Within the UNFCCC negotiations, the issue of low carbon development for developing countries is contentious and contested and approached carefully by most developed countries due to their role as the polluting Annex I countries. However, operating as donors there is a different game in town. From a development perspective, donors have continued and remodelled the energy access agenda running since the 1980s to overcome the dependency of now around 3 billion poor people on traditional biofuels for cooking and heating with 1.5 billion having no access to electricity (UNDP and WHO, 2009). However, the expansion in energy services has been impeded in part because the vast majority of the population is too poor to enjoy these without some form of subsidy (UNDESA, 2009). A bewildering number of global and regional initiatives have been established, all seemingly looking at clean energy, sustainable and renewable energy and their technology dimensions, and achieving very little.[10,11] The UNFCCC has not delivered and has failed to create notable measures to provide for technology transfer or low carbon development in the LDCs (UNFCCC, 2011b). This is despite the fact that the LDCs generally receive special treatment under the UNFCCC – in Article 4 Paragraph 9 (UNFCCC, 1992).

Around the dynamic low carbon agenda, various types of integrated plans and more strategic national planning processes are also being promoted by UN agencies, some governments and policy institutes: Low Emission Development Strategies (LEDS – the OECD countries and USA), Low Carbon Development Strategies (LCDS – EU), Low Carbon Development Plans (LCDPs – Project Catalyst); Low Emission Climate Resilient Development Strategies (LECREDs – UNDP); Low Carbon Growth Strategies (included in Copenhagen Accord text of 2009); Low Carbon, Climate Resilient Development Programmes (LCCREDs – UK); and Low Carbon Development (DFID, UK). These also cover support for the preparation of NAMAs. These softer, less divisive approaches have been seen as alternatives to obligatory target reductions (WRI, 2005, Tilburg *et al.*, 2011). However, questions are already emerging about what will be the relationship between the TNAs and NAMAs, LEDS, LCDs and national policy processes (UNFCCC, 2011c; Der Gaast, 2012). Clearly, this plethora of effort is confusing when capacities within countries are limited, and could also work against the integration of climate change into national development planning processes.

These new initiatives have been driven by the prospect of new and additional finance for climate change under the Green Climate Fund, which was launched at Durban – under the Durban COP 17. The naming of the Fund ties in with the development of the green growth agenda – the subject of the Rio +20 conference in 2012.[12] The finance features of the Copenhagen Accord – short-term (US$30 billion 'fast track' 2010–2012) and medium-term finance ($100 billion annually by 2020) were formalized in the Cancun Agreements, and the Green Climate Fund was launched in Durban in 2010. The UN Secretary General's High-level Advisory Group (UNAGF) had identified that it was challenging, but feasible, to meet the goal of mobilizing $100 billion a year by 2020 to meet the needs of the developing countries (UNAGF, 2010). Despite the launch of the Green Climate Fund at Durban, there was failure to provide clear signals on how long-term finance will be raised and mobilized for the period 2013–2020 after the Fast Start Funds (see Chapter 6).

The allocation of the Green Climate Fund's (GCF) resources is to be balanced between mitigation and adaptation activities. One stumbling block on development of this fund has always been the sourcing of the new and additional funds required. Developing countries have frequently emphasized that the new and additional climate finance should be from developed country public finances. Developed countries think that it will be innovative funding, linked to the private sector, which delivers over the long term. One new idea that has been developed by the World Bank, OECD and Regional Development Banks has been to put a price on carbon fuels from aviation and shipping, the so-called bunker fuels. Reference to these bunker fuels was included in draft text in Durban. But a group of larger developing countries opposed endeavours to raise this international carbon tax in the absence of compensation (including India, China, Brazil and Saudi Arabia) (Sterk *et al.*, 2012).

Low carbon development: the climate mitigation agenda from a developed country perspective

Under the provisions of the UNFCCC, all countries are required to publish and regularly update programmes containing measures to mitigate climate change. In practice, the developed countries have undertaken these National Communications more frequently. The UNFCCC Secretariat publishes syntheses and reviews of these. A useful summary is reported here from the fifth round in 2011 (UNFCCC, 2011d).

All developed countries have adopted and keep updating national climate change strategies, action plans and programmes with Policies and Measures (PaMs) to reduce GHG emissions. The policies and measures are applied at all levels of governmental jurisdiction – regional, national, state/provincial and municipal – and involve a wide range of actors and institutions in many activities. Parties to the Kyoto Protocol made substantial changes to their strategies with a greater use of broad carbon-pricing frameworks based on emission trading schemes and stronger mandatory regulations. The UNFCCC reports that, despite diversity and complexity, eight general trends are apparent (UNFCCC, 2011d):

1 Most developed countries now treat climate change mitigation as a core top-level issue in the national policy agenda and have developed greater policy capacity as well as legal and institutional frameworks including top-level inter-ministerial coordinating groups to reduce emissions.
2 Parties are making great use of multilevel governance across multiple scales of government (e.g. local to regional) and non-governmental actors on climate change issues.
3 Parties, in the context of the global economic crisis and shifts in global economic and energy flows, are looking for climate change PaMs that can align the goals of emission reductions, energy security, job creation and economic competitiveness, as well as air and water quality. To that end integrated energy and climate packages have been developed by several Parties and emphasis is put on R&D of new technologies and innovative solutions, such as CCS.
4 Some Parties have progressed through one or more policy cycles, and are now implementing second- and third-generation policy strategies and PaMs, which reflect lessons learned and are likely to be more effective in reducing emissions than previous efforts.
5 Many Parties have established or are planning multi-sector (cross-cutting) ETSs as a foundation element upon which climate change mitigation strategies are based.
6 Many Parties are changing voluntary programmes with mandatory regulations, including mandatory ETSs, in the key emissions sectors of electricity generation, emissions-intensive industry, transport energy supply and road vehicle transportation.
7 Parties are continuing to make great use of the relatively low-cost options of mitigating non-CO_2 (i.e. CH_4, N_2O, PFCs, HFCs and SF_6) emissions in industrial processes and waste, but there is little remaining room for further emission reductions in these areas.
8 Several Parties are developing long-term strategies, with corresponding R&D programmes, for decoupling of GHG emissions and economic growth and establishing low carbon societies.

(UNFCCC, 2011d)

From the base year (1990) to 2008 total aggregate GHG emissions excluding land use, land use change and forestry for all Annex I parties (industrialized countries) decreased by 18.5 per cent in large part due to the steep decline in emissions in economies in transition, such as countries of the former Soviet Union. Overall reductions are likely to exceed the 5 per cent target of the first Kyoto commitment period. But apart from the EU, few parties have committed to targets for the post-2012 period (UNFCCC, 2011d).

Moving forwards

As explained above, developed countries have established new institutions and ways of working that are focused specifically on climate change actions. Developing countries have tentatively started policy changes but implementation of low carbon development is still largely dependent on the provision of additional support, apart from in the major developing economies, notably in the group formed of Brazil, South Africa, India and China – the BASIC group. These countries have clear climate change strategies and policies and significant institutional structures, according to national circumstance. Brazil, for example has pledged to keep its emissions 36 per cent below projected levels from 1990 by 2020 and has announced targets to reduce GHGs in heavy industry, mining and transport sectors, with the intention that these targets will drive reductions in emissions from Amazonian deforestation through offset projects (GoB, 2010).

China has rapidly emerged as the country with the largest emissions, but not on a per capita basis. With the recent growth, and experience of some extreme weather events – an indication of the possible future – it has also developed a complex and ambitious low carbon development agenda based on resource limits, economic growth, competitiveness and the international climate agenda (The Climate Group, 2011). The Chinese Premier asserted that it will never seek economic growth at the expense of its ecological environment and public health (Xinhuanet, 2012). The 12th Five-Year Plan (FYP) adopted by the Chinese government in March 2011 devotes considerable attention to energy and climate change and establishes a new set of targets and policies for 2011–2015. While some of the targets are largely in line with the status quo, other aspects of the plan represent more dramatic moves to reduce fossil energy consumption, promote low carbon energy sources and restructure China's economy. Among the goals is to 'gradually establish a carbon trade market'. Key targets between 2011 and 2015 include:

* a 16 per cent reduction in energy intensity (energy consumption per unit of GDP);
* increasing non-fossil energy to 11.4 per cent of total energy use;
* a 17 per cent reduction in carbon intensity (carbon emissions per unit of GDP).

(CCES, 2012: 1)

China's approach to its low carbon strategy is diverse and includes taxes and quotas, industrial and equipment standards, energy taxes and financial incentives and penalties (Seligson *et al.*, 2009). Other countries are less well advanced. Various ways of supporting engagement are now underway: the EU-UNDP Low Emission Capacity Building Programme is a collaborative initiative between the European Commission (EC), the Governments of Germany and Australia and the UNDP. The programme now covers a 25-wide range of middle income countries and some LDCs (Argentina, Bhutan, China, Colombia, Costa Rica, DRC, Ecuador, Egypt, Ghana, Indonesia, Kenya, Lebanon, Mexico, Moldova, Morocco, Peru, the Philippines, Tanzania, Thailand, Trinidad and Tobago, Uganda, Vietnam and Zambia), and is aiming to strengthen institutional and technical capacities to: develop national GHG inventory systems; identify and formulate NAMAs; prepare low-emission development strategies; facilitate the design and adoption of mitigation action plans by industries; and design systems of measuring, reporting and verification of proposed mitigation actions (EU-UNDP, 2012).

As the move from projects to programmes and national planning gets underway, gaps in capacities for implementation at all scales are revealed, for example, in Nepal, Ghana and Bolivia (Hedger *et al*, 2011). There is evidence that this is beginning to lead to new initiatives for formal subnational plans (e.g. India), where state planning is being encouraged by the national government and at the same time the states can see advantages for action (Hedger and Sharma, 2011). Probably the most critical function at national level is the coordination and technical leadership function, although this needs to be operational at all critical governance points through a country. The importance of the national level has been reinforced by the decision of the Green Climate Fund that clarifies the role and voice of national designated authorities in approval of funding proposals so as to ensure consistency with national strategies and plans, in response to pressures from developing countries. Externally supplied finance for climate change has yet to dwarf countries' own resources, so many developing country governments are using existing budgets, policies and institutions to address the climate change issue.[13]

There is often a gap in effective mechanisms and links to interface the national level and the subnational and local levels: there are rarely active dialogues about learning. Whilst an international framework for climate change remains a critical ingredient of coordinated action, it is often at a lower governance level that behaviour is most influenced (Burch, 2009). An OECD assessment of cities and climate change found that city and regional governments are increasingly initiating action on climate change, but to date these efforts have been largely decoupled from national policy frameworks (Corfee-Morlot *et al.*, 2011). However, working at a subnational level does not necessarily mean implementation is easier. Barriers (structural/operational, regulatory/legislative, cultural/behavioural and contextual) remain, together with ever evolving advice on science (Burch, 2009). One conclusion that can be drawn is that subregional actions need a clear and supportive framework at national level that is maintained over time. Even in the UK, which has been a global leader on low carbon policy, its Climate Change Committee has identified that additional funding and/or a statutory duty is required for local authorities to implement low carbon plans, and that this local authority action was vital for UK targets (Planning, 2012).

Challenges

According to the World Business Council for Sustainable Development, to meet the needs of the 9 billion people living on the planet in 2050 will require substantial changes in the global energy system, while substantially reducing emissions to avoid dangerous climate change. This will require a radical departure from historical energy and carbon pathways and will require government policy intervention at a level not seen in the past (WBCSD, 2012).

The world today is very different from 1992 when the solutions to climate change were framed in Rio, with the division of the world into two groups – industrialized and developing countries. With the emergence of China, and the other major emerging economies such as Brazil, South Africa and India, a third category of emerging developing countries needs to be factored into the mix. New alignments are visible, following from Durban, and Bonn 2012 in the UNFCCC and also in the Rio +20[14] (ENB, 2012). But the on-going needs of the poorer countries mean that, 'Unless poor countries get adequate funds from the major polluter nations, it won't be possible for them to green their economy', according to the main Bangladesh negotiator at Rio +20 (Reuters, 2012: 1).

Conclusions

Within new policy spaces created by scientific knowledge, climate change policy and low carbon development policy is developing at international level, and driving developments at national level. New mechanisms have been created to provide incentives for action at national level arising from a negotiated balance of interests between the developing and developing countries. This is not a homogenous process: this process is strongest for developed countries and emerging economies where low carbon development policy tends to absorb existing sectoral strategies at national level including energy security policy and development policy, and generally includes some innovatory activities on low carbon. At the same time, the policy implementation for all countries is constrained currently by the lack of priority given to low carbon pathways by governments.

References

Burch, S. (2009) In pursuit of resilient, low carbon communities: an examination of barriers to action in three Canadian cities. *Energy Policy*, 38(12), 7575–85. Centre for Climate and Energy Solutions (CCES), 2012. Energy and climate goals of China's 12th Five-Year Plan. Available at http://www.c2es.org/policy/international/key-country-policies/china (accessed 22 October 2012).

Center for International Forestry Research (CIFOR) (2012) A step-wise framework for setting REDD+ forest reference emission levels and forest reference levels. CIFOR Brief written by Herold, M., Verchot, V., Maniatis, D. and Bauch, S. available at: www.cifor.org (accessed 22 October 2012).

Corfee-Morlot, J., Kamal-Chaoui, L. Donovan, M. G., Cochran, I., Robert, A. and Teasdale, P.-J. (2011) Cities, climate change and multilevel governance. OECD Environmental Working papers 14. Paris: OECD Publishing.

Den Elzen, M., Roefsema, M., Hof, A., Bottcher, H. and Grassi, G. (2012) Analysing the emission gap between pledged emission reductions under the Cancun Agreement and the 2 degree climate target. The Hague/Bilthoven: PBL Netherlands Environmental Assessment Agency (PBL).

Der Gaast, W. van (2012) Opportunities for co-ordinating and harmonising TNA and LEDS processes. JI Network (JIN), JT Groningen.

EC (2009) Supporting a climate for change: the EU and developing countries working together. Luxemburg Publications Office of the European Union, 32pp. doi: 10.2773/82318.

Ecofys (2012) NAMA database. Available at: www.namadatabase.org (accessed 22 October 2012).

Edmonds, J. A., Wise, M. A., Dooley, J. J., Kim, S. H., Smith, S. J., Runcie, P. J., Clarke, L. E., Malone, E. L. and Stokes, G. M. (2007) Global Energy Technology Strategy: addressing climate change. Global Energy Technology Strategy Program. Joint Global Change Research Institute, Battelle, MD, 7.

Earth Negotiations Bulletin (ENB) (2012) *Earth Negotiations Bulletin*, 12(546), 25. Available at: http://www.iisd.ca/download/pdf/enb12546e.pdf (accessed 22 October 2012).

EU-UNDP (2011) Low emission capacity building programme: a global initiative to support mitigation actions. UNDP, New York. Available at: www.lowemissiondevelopment.org (accessed 22 October 2012).

Government of Brazil (GoB) (2010) New decree details Brazil's national policy on climate change. 10 December. Available at: www.brasil.gov.by (accessed 22 October 2012).

Government of India (GoI) (2012) Second National Communication to the UNFCCC. Executive Summary. Delhi: Ministry of Environment and Forests.

Governing Clean Development (GCD) (2011) Governing clean development: what have we learnt? Briefing 03. The Governance of Clean Development Project. Brighton: UEA and University of Sussex.

Hedger, M. (2012) Stagnation or regeneration: technology transfer in the UNFCCC, in Ockwell, D. and Mallett, A. (eds) *Low Carbon Technology Transfer: from Rhetoric to Reality.* Abingdon: Earthscan, pp. 211–30.

Hedger, M. and Sharma, V. (2010) Moving ahead on climate change planning: lessons from Orissa. CDKN Policy briefing. Brighton: CDKN and IDS.

Hedger, M, Moench, M., Dixit, A., Kaur, N. and Anderson, S. (2011) Approaches to planning for climate change: bridging concepts and practise for low carbon resilient development. Learning Hub. Brighton: IDS and DFID.

IDS (2006) Understanding policy processes: a review of IDS research on the environment. Knowledge, Technology and Society, IDS, Brighton. Available at: http://www.dfid.gov.uk/r4d/pdf/thematicsummaries/understanding_policy_processes.pdf (accessed 22 October 2012).

IEA (2011) Energy efficiency policy and carbon pricing. Information paper. Energy Efficiency Series. Paris: IEA.

IEA/OECD (2009) Linking mitigation actions in developing countries with mitigation support: a conceptual framework. Available at: http://www.oecd.org/dataoecd/27/24/42474721.pdf (accessed 22 October 2012).

International Emissions Trading Association (IETA) (2012) IETA response to the AW LCA call for input regarding new market-based mechanism, 5 March. Geneva: IETA.

Newell, P. and Paterson, M. *Climate Capitalism: Global Warming and the Transformation of the Global Economy*. Cambridge: Cambridge University Press.

Mulgetta, Y. and Urban, F. (2010) Deliberating on low carbon development. *Energy Policy*, 38(12), 7546–9.

Planning (2012) Call for council carbon duty. *Planning magazine*, 1 June.

Ren21 (2012) Renewables 2012 – Global Status Report. Paris: Ren21.

Reuters (2012) Bangladesh wary of 'green economy' agenda at Rio+20. 18 June. Available at: http://www.trust.org/alertnet/news/bangladesh-wary-of-green-economy-agenda-at-rio20/ (accessed 22 October 2012.

Seligson, D., Heilmayr, R., Tan, X. and Weisher, L. (2009) China, the US and the climate change challenge. Washington, DC: World Resources Institute.

Sterk, W., Arens, C., Mersmann, F., Wang-Helmreich, H. and Wehnert, T. (2011) On the road again: progressive countries score a realpolitik victory in Durban while real climate change continues to heat up. Wuppertal: Wuppertal Institute.

Streck, C. (2009) Expectations and reality of the Clean Development Mechanism, in Stewart, R. B., Kingsbury, B. and Rydyk, B. (eds) Climate Finance: Regulatory and Funding Strategies for Climate Change and Global Development. New York University.

Streck, C. and Guimaraes, L. (2011) Nationally appropriate mitigation actions in developing countries: emerging opportunities for private sector engagement. Washington, DC: Climate Focus.

Tilburg, X. van, Roser, F., Hansel, H., Cameron, L. and Escalente, D. (2012) Status report on nationally Appropriate Mitigation Actions (NAMAs). Mid-year update, May 2012. ECN and ECOFYS.

The Climate Group (TCG) (2011) Delivering low carbon growth: a guide to Chinas' 12th Five Year Plan. London: TCG.

Union of Concerned Scientists (UCS) (2007) Smoke, mirrors and hot air: how ExxonMobil uses big tobacco tactics to 'manufacture uncertainty on climate change'. Available at: http://www.ucsusa.org/global_warming/science_and_impacts/global_warming_contrarians/exxonmobil-report-smoke.html (accessed 22 October 2012).

UNAGF (2010) Report of UN Secretary General's High level Advisory Group on Climate Change Financing, 5 November. Available at: http://www.un.org/wcm/content/site/climatechange/pages/financeadvisorygroup/pid/13300 (accessed 22 October 2012).

United Nations Department of Economic and Social Affairs (UNDESA) (2009) Climate change and the policy challenge UNDESA Policy Brief No 24. Washington, DC: UNDESA.

United Nations Development Programme (UNDP) (2012) Taking stock of Durban: review of key outcomes and the road ahead. C. Carpenter. UNDP Environment and Energy Group. April 2012. New York: UNDP.

UNDP and World Health Organization (WHO) (2009) The energy access situation in developing countries. Sustainable Energy Programme Environment and Energy Group Report. New York: UNDP.

United Nations Environment Programme (UNEP) (2010) The emissions gap report: are the Copenhagen accord pledges sufficient to limit global warming to 2. Nairobi: UNEP.

UNEP, United Nations Conference on Trade and Development (UNCTAD) and UN-OHRLLS (2011)

Why a green economy matters for the Least Developed Countries. Available at: http://www.unctad.org/en/docs/unep_unctad_un-ohrlls_en.pdf (accessed 22 October 2012).

United Nations Framework Convention on Climate Change (UNFCCC) (1992) United Nations Framework Convention on Climate Change. UNFCCC Secretariat, Bonn. Available at: http://unfccc.int/resource/docs/convkp/conveng.pdf (accessed 22 October 2012).

UNFCCC (1999) Report of the Conference of the Parties on its Fourth session, Buenos Aires 2–14 November 1998. Addendum. Part two: Action taken by the Conference of the Parties at its fourth session. Available at: http://maindb.unfccc.int/library/view_pdf.pl?url=http://unfccc.int/resource/docs/cop4/16a01.pdf (accessed 22 October 2012).

UNFCCC (2008) Report of the Conference of the Parties on its thirteenth session, held in Bali, 3–15 December 2007. FCCC/CP/2007/6/Add.1*14 March 2008, Addendum Part Two. Decisions adopted. Page 3 Decision 1/CP.13 Bali Action Plan and Decision 3/CP.13. Development and transfer of technologies under the Subsidiary Body for Scientific and Technological Advice, p. 12. UNFCCC Secretariat, Bonn. Available at: http://unfccc.int/resource/docs/2007/cop13/eng/06a01.pdf#page=3 (accessed 22 October 2012).

UNFCCC (2011a) March Report of the Conference, held in Cancun, 29 November – 10 December 2010, Addendum Part Two: Action taken by the Conference of the Parties at its sixteenth session, Decisions adopted by the Conference of the Parties. Bonn: UNFCCC Secretariat. Available at: http://unfccc.int/resource/docs/2010/cop16/eng/07a01.pdf#page=2 (accessed 22 October 2012).

UNFCCC (2011b) The LDCs. Reducing vulnerability to climate change, climate variability and extremes, land degradation and loss of biodiversity. Contribution to Fourth UN Conference on LDCs. May 2011. Bonn: UNFCCC Secretariat.

UNFCCC (2011c) Interlinkages between technology needs assessments and national and international climate policy making processes. Background Paper III. UNFCCC Workshop on Technology Needs Assessments, Wissenschaftszentrum, Bonn, Germany, 1–2 June 2011. Available at: http://unfccc.int/ttclear/jsp/TrnDetails.jsp?EN=TNAWshpBonn (accessed 22 October 2012).

UNFCCC (2011d) Compilation and synthesis of fifth national communications. Executive Summary Note by the Secretariat FCCC/SB/2011/INF.1. Bonn: UNFCCC Secretariat.

UNFCCC (2012) Report of the GEF on the progress made in carrying out the Poznan strategic programme on technology transfer. FCCC/SBI/2012/9. Bonn: UNFCCC Secretariat.

United Nations Collaborative Programme on Reducing Emissions from Deforestation and Forest Degradation (UN-REDD) (2011) UN-REDD programme 2011 year in review. UN-REDD Programme. Available at: www.un-redd.org (accessed 22 October 2012).

Wolemberg, E., Campbell, B. M., Holmgren, P., Seymour, F., Sibanda, L. and von Braun, J. (2011) Actions needed to halt deforestation and promote climate-smart agriculture. CCAFS Policy Brief no 4 CGIAR Research Program on Climate Change, Agriculture and Food Security. CCAFS, Copenhagen. Available at: www.ccafs.cgiar.org (accessed 22 October 2012).

World Business Council for Sustainable Development (WBCSD) (2012) The energy mix: low carbon pathways to 205. Available at: www.wbcsd.org (accessed 22 October 2012).

World Resources Institute (WRI) (2005) Growing in the Greenhouse: Protecting the Climate by Putting Development First. Bradley, R. and Baumert, K. (eds). Washington, DC: WRI.

Xinhuanet (2012) China explores possibilities of low carbon future. Available at: http://news.xinhuanet.com/english/china/2012-03/13/c_131464710.htm (accessed 22 October 2012).

Yamin, F. and Depledge, J. 2004. *The International Climate Change Regime: A Guide to Rules, Institutions and Procedures*. Cambridge: Cambridge University Press.

Further reading

UNDP (2012) Taking stock of Durban: review of key outcomes and the road ahead. C. Carpenter. UNDP Environment and Energy Group. April 2012. New York: UNDP.

World Business Council for Sustainable Development (2012) The energy mix; low carbon pathways to 2050. Available at: www.wbcsd.org (accessed 22 October 2012).

Notes

1   One of the main IPCC activities is the preparation of comprehensive assessment reports about the state of scientific, technical and socio-economic knowledge on climate change, its causes, potential impacts and response strategies. Since its inception in 1988 the IPCC has prepared four multivolume assessment reports that are submitted to the UNFCCC.

2   For an account of the negotiations at each stage since 1995, see Earth Negotiations Bulletin reports http://www.iisd.ca/process/climate_atm.htm.

3   The critical Article 4.5 enshrined in the 1992 Convention text obliges the developed country Parties, to 'take all practical steps to promote, facilitate and finance, as appropriate the transfer of, or access to, environmentally sound technologies and know-how to other parties, particularly developing country Parties, to enable them to implement the provisions of the Convention, (its core objective being the avoidance of dangerous climate change) including enhancement of endogenous capacities and technologies of developing countries'.

4   Further details on QUELROs, under the Durban Platform for the second commitment period were due to be submitted by May 2012.

5   The focus on HFC23 projects is also a major problem for those concerned.

6   www.cdmpipeline.org.

7   For example, see www.globalforestcoalition.org.

8   On the forestry side, there has been a concern that NAMAs could get round the robust reporting that is being established through REDD.

9   Also monitoring changes in forest stocks and carbon sequestration and losses in soils is very complex – so consistency with NAMAs is difficult (FCCC/SBSTA/2012/MISC.1).

10   Such as, the Forum on Sustainable Energy, the International Renewable Energy Conference, the Global Renewable Energy Forum, the Vienna Energy Conference, the World Future Energy Summit series, the Global Energy Assessment, the Global Green Growth Forum, the International Renewable Energy Agency (IRENA), the Renewable Energy Policy Network for the 21st Century (REN21) and also the Renewable Energy and Energy Efficiency Partnership (REEEP).

11   Over 30 years ago, in 1981, the UN hosted a major conference on renewable energy in the wake of the 1980s oil price hikes, and their adverse effects on developing countries.

12   The Rio +20 Conference ended with vague commitments on the green economy and failed to agree timetables for sustainability.

13   See the Climate Public Expenditure and Institutional Reports (CPEIR) reports undertaken by the overseas Development Institute (ODI) and UNDP in Nepal, Bangladesh, Thailand, Cambodia and Samoa.

14   In the COP Durban, 2011, the EU and the LDCs and the Alliance of Small Island States (AOSIS) joined up. In Bonn too, the LDC/AOSIS independent line was continuingly visible, with the support of some Latin American countries, all looking for action on mitigation from developed and developing countries to be incentivized for all countries.

Part 3
The social dimensions of low carbon development

Editorial for Part 3

The social dimensions of low carbon development

Frauke Urban and Johan Nordensvärd

Part 3 discusses the social dimensions of low carbon development. While it is widely recognized that climate change affects people – especially the poor and vulnerable – both directly and indirectly, the social dimensions of climate change are often neglected. The social dimensions of low carbon development receive even less attention. This part therefore aims to address the social dimensions of low carbon development by discussing social justice and equity issues as well as elaborating the complex links between low carbon development and social policy.

Overview of Part 3

Chapter 4 explores some of the different dimensions and interpretations of equity and social justice in the context of climate change and development, with a particular focus on low carbon development. The chapter examines the dominant application of social justice through the lens of equity within global mitigation agreements. Using examples drawn from Ghana's low carbon development planning processes, the chapter then demonstrates how greater attention is required to the consideration of social justice in decision making and implementation of low carbon development at national level.

Chapter 5 discusses how to link social policy with low carbon development. The chapter outlines some of the challenges to make social policy comply with low carbon development on one side and to support low carbon development on the other. It aims to discuss the main approaches to the welfare state, the market and climate change. The main argument of the chapter is that there needs to be a fundamental societal change such as reforming capitalism and world governance before social policy can really become low carbon.

4 Social justice and low carbon development

Thomas Tanner and Blane Harvey

The shift to low carbon development implies winners and losers. This chapter explores some of the different dimensions and interpretations of equity and social justice in the context of climate change and development. It initially examines the dominant application of social justice through the lens of equity within global mitigation agreements. Using examples drawn from Ghana's low carbon development planning processes, the chapter then demonstrates how greater attention is required to the consideration of social justice in decision making and implementation of low carbon development at national level.

Introduction

Social justice generally refers to a societal value or institution that is based on the principles of equality (the egalitarian belief that all people ought to be treated equally) and fairness (referred to here as equity). In this chapter, we relate social justice to equity in both process and outcome, known as *procedural equity and distributive equity* (see Box 4.1). It is important to recognize the multiple interpretations or 'framings' for equity and social justice. These create very different 'takes' on equitable low carbon development issues. For example, there are fundamentally different approaches to regulating the use of the planetary resources. Some focus on living humans, such as utilitarian views that are usually characterized as calling for 'the greatest happiness for the greatest number' (Bentham, 1962). Others focus on equity between generations (Page, 2006) or extend equity considerations by allocating rights to other living creatures or even the non-living world (Pepper, 1993).

Climate change represents a global collective action problem with causes and effects unevenly distributed geographically and across generations. This implies differentiated responsibilities for action and a central role for ethics and social justice in determining responses (Barker *et al.*, 2008). This chapter seeks to examine social justice as a critical component of low carbon development across scales. To date, most attention in this regard has been at the international scale, particularly under the UNFCCC. We extend this focus to demonstrate that justice and equity considerations also need to be made more explicit in low carbon development policy and decision making at national and subnational levels.

After introducing social justice concepts and framings, the chapter examines the equity considerations of the international climate agreements under the UNFCCC, before exploring issues at national scale using Ghana as a country case study. Throughout, we stress the existence of different and contested visions of social justice at different scales that generate different policy decisions from those in international fora. Box 4.1 discusses the key concepts and terms.

Box 4.1 Key concepts and terms: social justice and equity

Social justice, equity, morality and ethics are often used interchangeably. Social justice is most commonly used to refer to *equity* in society, which refers to the state, quality or ideal of being just, impartial and fair. This is underpinned by *morality*; judgements about right and wrong that people hold and act upon in their daily lives. It is informed by our understanding of *ethics*, which concerns the systematic evaluation of such beliefs.

Social justice and equity refer to the perception of fairness in both process and outcome. Analysis of social justice is therefore generally split into aspects of:

Procedural equity: Concerned with the position of people and groups in the processes of decision making. Includes whether their competing ideas and interests are recognized, their ability to participate and the distribution of power in decision making.
Distributive equity: Concerned with the way that costs and benefits should be distributed among people and groups with competing claims. This involves both specifying people's entitlements (for example to welfare or income) and the obligations of others to respect these entitlements.

(Adapted from Page, 2006)

Low carbon social justice across scales

Putting social justice considerations at the heart of low carbon development responses is important for two main reasons. First, there is an instrumental rationale for mitigating climate change as a core part of development policy. If we are to make further widespread improvements in human welfare, these must be combined with efforts to ensure the sustainability of the planetary system on which development is founded (UNDP, 2007; World Bank, 2010). This includes avoiding dangerous interference with the climate system that would impose an inequitable burden of impacts on those least responsible for the problem (Adger *et al.*, 2006). There is also potential to implement low carbon development that specifically tackles poverty, inequality and equity, such as health benefits gained from widening access to clean energy or providing payments to incentivize forest protection among indigenous peoples (Haines *et al.*, 2007; Kok *et al.*, 2008; Angelsen *et al.*, 2012).

Second, there are moral and ethical issues around developing a low carbon development approach that seeks to impose greenhouse gas mitigation on developing countries that have historically done little to cause the climate change problem (Najam, 2005; Page, 2006; Barker *et al.*, 2008; Roberts and Parks, 2006). This is particularly the case for low income countries that not only have a legacy of low emissions but are also unlikely to make a major contribution to global emissions rises in the near future (UNDP, 2007). In addition, these countries are often in a less powerful position in terms of the international negotiations on tackling climate change, providing a barrier to distributive equity through procedural inequity (Najam, 2005). As a consequence:

> The problem of equity (across social groups living today and across generations) raised by climate change, and the need for urgent and deep mitigation, are ethical problems, and should be informed by moral philosophy (drawing on scientific findings with respect to climate change impacts) and not just by economics in isolation.
>
> (Barker *et al.*, 2008: 317–18)

Box 4.2 discusses the key issues relating to social justice and low carbon development.

Box 4.2 Key issues

There is no single definition of social justice. It is interpreted differently within climate change by different groups depending on their interests and values (Ikeme, 2003). Developing a common normative framework for balancing low carbon objectives with those of development objectives, equality and fairness remains a key challenge. A process of deliberation and negotiation among stakeholders on a common vision for socially just, low carbon development is therefore itself an important goal (Barker *et al.*, 2008).

Social justice considerations are crucial for low carbon development both because of:

• The instrumental rationale of promoting sustainability and climate stability in order to make progress on improving human welfare.
• The ethics of imposing greenhouse gas mitigation on poorer countries, who have historically done little to cause the climate change problem.

For low carbon development, most attention to social justice has been on burden sharing for global mitigation agreements. By contrast, there is more limited understanding of the implications of internationally driven climate policy actions at national and subnational levels (Thomas and Twyman, 2006; Tanner and Allouche, 2011).

Social justice considerations highlight the trade-offs and tensions between climate change objectives and development objectives. In developed countries, policy may focus on energy security goals or emissions reductions targets at the expense of the consequences for poor households and their well-being (Gough, 2011). For many developing countries, the overriding concern is with enhancing economic growth and employment opportunities (Kok *et al.*, 2008). Low carbon development is often therefore focused on fitting with this paradigm rather than on social justice issues at national level.

At the global level, a tension exists between efficiency and equity. On the one hand, climate change must be tackled as an urgent problem, so focus should be on reducing emissions wherever it is quickest and most efficient. The cheapest emissions reductions economically are often found in developing countries (Stern, 2007; World Bank, 2010). But demanding that developing countries take an uncertain development pathway and forego their own fossil fuel resources as an economic driver may not be seen as equitable given that the problem was caused by richer nations in the process of becoming rich (Roberts and Parks, 2006).

At national and subnational levels the impacts of climate change are unevenly distributed across communities, social groups or classes and demographics. This is often, although not always, in line with other forms of marginalization or vulnerability such as lack of political representation or poverty (Tanner and Mitchell, 2008). As such, questions of procedural and distributive equity remain crucial to responding to the costs and opportunities presented by climate change, but take on somewhat different features.

Procedural considerations, for example, may centre around questions of who determines how strategies for responding to climate change (including low carbon development) are set and resources are allocated, and how. The high degree of variability in transparency and participation in policy-setting from one country to another, and the absence of a standard model of practice between and within nations, means procedural justice is less easily scrutinized than in international forums such as the UNFCCC. Distributive considerations, on the other hand, may interrogate the extent to which the costs and benefits for responding to climate change are equitable with respect to need and responsibility. Gough (2011) suggests that, for countries in the global North, the distributional consequences of climate mitigation programmes' action will create new social injustices and impose new demands on the welfare state. The same is likely to apply for developing countries where service provision and social safety nets are often limited in both availability and coverage.

Low carbon development and international social justice

While the UNFCCC reflects a cosmopolitan approach to creating binding decisions based on an international vision of equity, communitarian perspectives on equity and justice are also reflected in the different positions taken in the negotiations (Roberts and Parks, 2007). Distributional equity issues have been crucial in determining both the nature of, and progress on, international collective action on climate change. The Convention and Kyoto Protocol differentiate commitments between countries based largely on a binary distinction between two groups of countries (Annex I and non-Annex I). There have historically been contrasting views regarding equity among these groups (Najam *et al.*, 2003; Roberts and Parks, 2009):

Industrialized countries of the OECD and former Soviet Union (Annex I) have regarded equity primarily in terms of 'meaningful participation' of other countries to ensure fairness in sharing the costs of mitigation efforts, especially given the growing emissions contribution and international trade competition from large, rapidly industrializing countries such as Brazil, India and China (Richards, 2003). They argue that this is consistent with the 'polluter-pays' principle underpinning the Convention.

'Developing countries' (non-Annex I) on the other hand regard equity in terms of the need for those with historic responsibility (Annex I countries) to take action first, consistent with the principle of 'common but differentiated responsibilities' enshrined in the Convention. Equity is then used to lobby for redistribution and resource transfers for both mitigation and adaptation on the basis that these countries contributed least to its causes and are likely to suffer most from its consequences (Barker *et al.*, 2008; Roberts and Parks, 2009).

With the emergence of rapidly growing middle income economies, however, this binary distinction may need to evolve into new forms of differentiation (Bodansky, 2011). Negotiations for a post-2020 climate agreement are taking place in a global context that is radically different from that when the Kyoto Protocol was agreed in 1997. The Protocol has not delivered reductions at a large scale, due to both poor performance against targets and the absence of major emitters such as the USA. At the same time, developed countries no longer account for the majority of greenhouse gas emissions, with non-Annex I countries, particularly emerging economies such as China and India, now contributing over half of CO_2 emissions and making up seven of the largest 15 emitters (World Bank, 2010).

Nevertheless, the historic and current contribution to global emissions by low income countries remains small, even including the influence of land-use change. As a consequence, negotiations for a post-2020 regime are providing an evolving vision for equity that begins to distinguish between existing Annex I countries, higher emitting developing countries, and the poorest developing countries, who have little historic responsibility and little prospect of significant emissions growth in the near future (La Viña *et al.*, 2012)..

As a normative proposal for international climate equity, the *Greenhouse Rights Development Framework* developed by Paul Baer and colleagues linked a population-based emissions allocation with a GDP-based proxy for the ability to pay for actions (Baer *et al.*, 2009). What makes this approach innovative is that it examines distributional equity *within* as well as between countries (see Box 4.3). The result is that under this proposal, almost all countries of the world have some allocated responsibility to mitigate emissions and pay for adaptation, based on the wealthier and higher emitting members of their societies. This idea is central to creating more nuanced definition than the current binary divide between 'rich' and 'poor' countries when allocating commitments in the international regime.

In line with these social justice considerations, Box 4.3 elaborates the greenhouse rights development framework.

Box 4.3 The Greenhouse Rights Development Framework

The 'Greenhouse Development Rights' (GDRs) framework combines a per capita approach to global emissions distribution with arguments that costs should be borne by those most able to afford them. In doing so, it allocates obligations to pay for climate policies (both mitigation and adaptation) on the basis of capacity (ability to pay) and responsibility (contribution to the problem).

Both aspects include a 'right to development' by excluding the income and emissions of individuals below a 'development threshold' (set at $7500 per capita per year, purchasing power parity adjusted) from the calculation of responsibility and capacity. Capacity is derived from aggregate incomes above this threshold, while responsibility assumes that emissions are linearly proportional to income within a country and derived by aggregating total CO_2 emissions of a country since 1990 that are above the development threshold, while the rest is excluded.

In doing so, it examines the distribution of income *within* countries and treats people of equal wealth similarly, whatever country they live in. Thus even poor countries have some obligations, proportional to the size and wealth of their middle and upper classes. The result is a global distribution that places very limited obligations on low income countries, a limited but growing burden on middle income countries and a large but declining burden on high income countries. This demonstrates the considerable differentiation that is masked by the Annex I/non-Annex I countries under the UNFCCC, which groups the low and middle income countries together. Table 4.1 shows the responsibility and capacity index for various countries for climate change.

Table 4.1 Responsibility and capacity index for climate change

| | Responsibility and capacity index for climate change (% of global accumulated emissions total)[1] | |
	2020	2030
High income countries	69	61
Middle income countries	30	38
Low income countries	0.3	0.5

1 The single 'responsibility and capacity index' (RCI) is derived as a percentage of the global total of accumulated emissions using a simple weighted sum: RCI = aR + bC, where a and b are weightings that can be applied to the index. Baer *et al.* use equal weightings of 0.5 and 0.5.
Source: Baer *et al.*, 2009

Notions of social justice and equity have been central to many of the global climate change advocacy campaigns driven by pressure groups, especially those with an international development dimension (Pettit, 2004). These have commonly attempted to emphasize the need for richer nations to step up and take action in light of the distributive inequity of climate causes and effects. For example, the Mary Robinson Foundation for Climate Justice (MRFCJ) was founded on the basis of a set principles of climate justice that include the need to:

> Respect and protect human rights; Support the right to development; Share benefits and burdens equitably; Ensure that decisions on climate change are participatory, transparent and accountable; Harness the transformative power of education for climate stewardship; and to use effective partnerships to secure climate justice.
>
> (MRFCJ, n.d.)

However, much of the programming, analysis and advocacy for climate justice is focused on the international scale, with much more limited attention to national and subnational scales (Thomas and Twyman, 2006; Tanner and Allouche, 2011). In the following section, we examine how issues of equity are embedded in discussions around national low carbon development planning. In doing so, we suggest that creating common, deliberated visions for low carbon social justice are vital at the national level in a similar way to those at international level.

Low carbon social justice at national and subnational scales

Debates over social justice at the international scale have highlighted issues of procedural and distributional equity between major emitters and countries who bear less current or historical responsibility for the current unsustainable level of GHG emissions. At national and subnational scales similar debates remain equally relevant, where decisions on low carbon development pathways or adaptation strategies will bring about different costs and benefits to differently situated groups of people. The debates may ultimately be more complex at smaller scales given the lack of a common definition of socially just low carbon development within communities, and the frequent absence of forums for deliberating the tensions between these interpretations. Research from the UK, for example, suggests that 'while general principles of climate justice for low carbon communities can be identified [...] multiple, sometimes overlapping forms of just low carbon community responses exist in practice.' (Bulkeley and Fuller, 2012: 14).

The social differentiation of climate impacts has been explored in considerable depth in terms of policies and practices aimed at helping those who are most vulnerable adapt to climate impacts from national, to subnational and even household levels (Stern, 2007; Tanner and Mitchell, 2008). However, considerably less attention has been paid to differentiation at these scales in the context of articulating, selecting and pursuing low carbon development pathways. This gap is particularly significant in considering how the balance of emphasis is decided between low carbon development strategies that place greater or lesser emphasis on emissions reduction potential or development and poverty alleviation. Without consideration of how concerns about procedural and distributional justice are addressed, the assumed benefits of low carbon development may either reduce or reinforce national or subnational inequalities in terms of poverty and development. While particularly relevant in the context of development, this gap is also relevant to developing countries, where the distributional impacts of action on climate change may engage and impact the poor differently than other socio-economic groups (Gough, 2011).

There are a number of reasons that social justice considerations – or spaces for debating such considerations – may be absent in these contexts. First, the distributive benefits of low carbon transitions may be assumed to be pro-poor, but may not be the product of open deliberation over how particular options that would yield greater benefits to some groups or regions than others. For example, the competing interests between developing small scale hydro-electrical installations which may feed an existing power grid that leaves particular segments of a country's population under-served on one hand, or solar panel installations which may bring electrification to new households but not offer significant new benefits to more developed areas of a country may be seen more as question of cost–benefit analysis than of distributive justice in some contexts (see Byrne *et al.*, 2011). As with other cases of access to or allocation of resources for development at community scales, these benefits may be allocated depending on who has a voice and access to decision making processes rather than by who could derive the greatest benefit (Kumar and Corbridge, 2002).

A second related issue is that low carbon development remains, in the eyes of many, a predominantly technical process focused upon the identification and implementation of feasible and cost-effective strategies identified by specialists in the fields of energy, finance and planning, many of whom are often external consultants (see case study in Box 4.4 below). Even in those cases where opportunities for participation are present, the technical and expert-oriented nature of these discussions may preclude meaningful participation among communities and interest groups whose development pathways are at stake.

Box 4.4 Case study: social justice in Ghana's low carbon development strategy

Ghana, a fast-developing lower middle-income West African country, offers a useful study in the complexities and contrasting interests that may shape national low carbon development strategies. Ghana is rich in natural resources, many of which (forestry, agriculture, fisheries and hydro-electricity, for example) are exposed to current and future impacts of climate change and variability, as well as an emerging oil industry that promises to change the national political and economic landscape. It is also marked by high levels of inequality and income disparity, with rural and northern populations being both poorest and most directly exposed to climate impacts, with widely recognized adaptation needs. Long considered a 'model' of good governance and inclusive development in Africa, a look at Ghana's actions towards low carbon growth reveals that even in such a context decision making has paid scant attention to the considerations outlined in this chapter.

While Ghana's total GHG emissions represent a minute contribution to global totals, it has pursued a low carbon agenda through its proposed 'National Climate Change Policy Framework' (NCCPF) (MEST, 2010), which has *low carbon growth* as the first of its three objectives, alongside adaptation and social development. The NCCPF's discussion document states the key motivations for pursuing the low carbon growth agenda are to make longer-term development more robust and less carbon intensive, access business opportunities and cost savings in the near term through low carbon strategies, and access international funding such as those around REDD+ (Angelsen *et al.*, 2012; MEST, 2010). Early steps towards implementing this strategy have been shaped by a donor-funded technical assistance package that proposes using Ghana's 55 existing NAMAs as a starting point for prioritizing action (Tilburg and Würtenberger, 2010). Civil society organizations, however, have criticized the strategy for relying primarily on these market-based schemes – which rarely benefit the poorest most – and for a lack of meaningful integration of gender and equity concerns (Social Watch, 2012). Elsewhere concerns have been raised that insufficient transparency and coordination between existing initiatives will hamper attempts at a more cohesive framework approach (Würtenberger *et al.*, 2011).

A review of climate change initiatives in Ghana from 1995 to 2010 reveals that of a total US$240 million of funding over this period, $126.4 million has been directed towards low carbon growth initiatives and $28.5 million (or less than 12 per cent) towards adaptation activities (Würtenberger *et al.*, 2011). Major low carbon initiatives highlighted in this review focus on *energy efficiency* (including the distribution of 6 million compact fluorescent light bulbs and promoting energy-efficient refrigerators); *renewable energy* (both integrating renewables into the grid and increasing off-grid access); *transportation* (public transportation and infrastructure); and *forestry* (primarily REDD+ readiness). In this light the government's position that adaptation is expected to be Ghana's main priority in addressing climate change (MEST, 2010) is striking given that the $15 million investment into compact fluorescent light bulbs alone represents over 50 per cent of the total investment into adaptation programming.

Returning to the factors that may lead to an absence of social justice considerations in national and subnational low carbon development strategies noted above, we can find many of these features playing out in the case of Ghana. There is little evidence of a systematic assessment of the distributional benefits of the various low carbon initiatives, or of a deliberative process in collectively assessing these. In the case of REDD+, for example, even basic awareness of this mechanism is limited to a small subset of stakeholders, who are largely technical experts, making open deliberation a major challenge (see Figure 4.1).

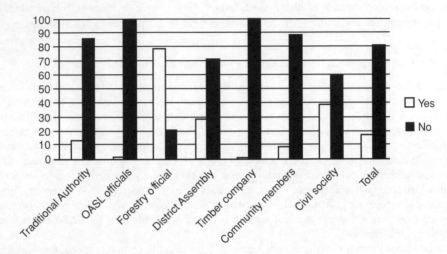

Figure 4.1 Awareness of REDD among stakeholders in Ghana
Source: CIKOD, 2011[1]

Reports point to a lack of data and capacity for assessing the impacts that various initiatives would offer, suggesting an insufficient understanding of the potential negative impacts of initiatives on the poorest. Further, while the NCCPF process involves a discussion document aimed at collecting feedback, the development and implementation is heavily reliant on outside expertise and there information sharing among stakeholders and experts is notably limited (Würtenberger *et al.*, 2011). Finally, perhaps the most widely documented justification for Ghana's pursuit of low carbon strategies is to capitalize on international incentive structures – while work on the most frequently cited of these, REDD+, has been problematized for undermining social justice concerns and lacking in transparency and informed debate (Friends of the Earth – Ghana, n.d.; CIKOD, 2011). More broadly, specific mention of social justice is almost entirely absent from existing documentation outlining proposed actions or strategies – though the concept of equity features in the NCCPF discussion document.

The case of Ghana reveals how, even in a country with a strong tradition of open governance processes, concerns of procedural and distributional equity in low carbon development rarely feature in the shaping of low carbon development strategies. Consequently, there is limited scope for those who are often excluded from decision making processes (non-experts, marginalized communities, etc.) to provide input into how decisions should be made, on the balance of emphasis in low carbon strategies, or on the extent to which low carbon development should be prioritized over other actions on climate change. This calls into question who will bear the costs, and reap the rewards of these initiatives.

Finally, both the distributive and procedural dimensions of developing and selecting low carbon strategies, particularly in LDCs may be shaped more fundamentally by the international incentives and instruments developed to support low carbon development (REDD, technology transfer, CDM, etc.) than by national or subnational agenda-setting. This is high-lighted by Byrne *et al.* who argue that the dominant technical and economic framing of low carbon development strategies articulated through international instruments 'actually fails to address how communities can develop greater control over their own low carbon pathways' (Byrne *et al.*, 2011: 17).

Conclusion

This chapter has outlined the reasons for and challenges of viewing low carbon development through a social justice lens. We argue that it is important to understand how the negotiation of interests and priorities plays out in the process of identifying and implementing low carbon development strategies. Questions of procedural and distributive justice will have an important bearing on how these strategies are developed, whose priorities they reflect, where the benefits will be felt the most and whether the balance of emphasis in these strategies prioritizes emissions reductions or development dividends (or a 'development first' approach).

The case from Ghana sheds light on a number of important issues, including the role of government and governance in dictating distributional and procedural outcomes. Governance and institutional architecture, from international to subnational and local scales, have a significant bearing on how equity issues arising from low carbon development options and actions are tackled in different countries. Highly centralized or autocratic regimes are less likely to engage in public consultation or public debate over the nature, costs and benefits of low carbon development options, and where capacity levels are limited and concentrated within a small number of actors the potential for meaningful engagement is significantly weakened.

Further, poor people's ability to derive direct benefits from international instruments within the climate change regime is often predicated on their ability to establish or draw upon effective multi-stakeholder structures or alliances that can advocate for their interests (Perez *et al.*, 2008). As such, the development benefits of international low carbon develop-ment instruments for those who are most vulnerable may depend on how well support mechanisms can enable their access to deliberative spaces at national or subnational levels. Similar to the evolution of adaptation thinking, which emerged as predominantly 'hard' responses to climate impacts (through technical and engineering-orientated interventions) and later grew to enshrine participatory process into standard models of practice such as the National Adaptation Programmes of Action (NAPAs), low carbon development may require the emergence of more participatory models of planning and implementation to support procedural justice.

The case from Ghana also highlights that the social justice dimensions of low carbon development should not be considered independently of the other range of actions that might otherwise be taken to address climate change. Across all scales, the allocation of funding towards low carbon development activities may come at the expense of other climate initia-tives such as adaptation, which could have a significantly greater impact on the poverty and vulnerability levels of marginalized groups. As such, social justice considerations should look at the distribution of resources and outcomes both *within* the low carbon development agenda, as well as at the interfaces between low carbon development and other climate and development priorities.

References

Adger, W. N., Paavola, Y., Huq, S. and Mace, M. J. (eds) (2006) *Fairness in Adaptation to Climate Change*. Cambridge, MA: MIT Press.

Angelsen, A., Brockhaus, M., Sunderlin, W. D. and Verchot, L. V. (eds) (2012) Analysing REDD+ challenges and choices. Bogor: CIFOR.

Baer, P., Athanasiou, T., Kartha, S. and Kemp-Benedict, E. (2009) The Greenhouse Development Rights Framework: the right to development in a climate constrained world. 2nd edition. Heinrich-Böll-Stiftung, Berlin. Available at: www.ecoequity.org/docs/TheGDRsFramework.pdf (accessed 23 October 2012).

Barker T., Scrieciu, S. and Taylor, D. (2008) Climate change, social justice and development. *Development: Journal of the Society for International Development*, 51(3), 317–24.

Bentham, J. (1962) An introduction to the principles of morals and legislation, in Warnock, M. (ed.) *Utilitarianism*. London: Fontana.

Bodansky, D. (2011) W[h]ither the Kyoto Protocol? Durban and beyond. Viewpoints – Harvard Project on Climate Agreements. Cambridge, MA: Harvard University.

Bulkeley, H. and Fuller, S. (2012) 'Low carbon communities and social justice', Joseph Rowntree Foundation Viewpoint, 16pp.

Byrne, R., Smith, A., Watson, J. and Ockwell, D. (2011) Energy pathways in low-carbon development: from technology transfer to socio-technical transformation, STEPS Working Paper 46. Brighton: STEPS Centre.

Centre for Indigenous Knowledge and Organisational Development (CIKOD) (2011) Making the forest sector transparent – annual transparency report card 2010 Ghana. Available at: http://www.cikod.org/Products.html (accessed 23 October 2012).

Friends of the Earth – Ghana (n.d.) REDD in Ghana: an independent monitoring report by Friends of the Earth – Ghana, available at: http://www.ug.edu.gh/fos/vbrp/climate/REDD_in_Ghana.pdf (accessed 23 October 2012).

Gough, I. (2011) Climate change, double injustice and social policy: a case study of the United Kingdom. UNRISD Occasional Paper 1: Social Dimensions of Green Economy and Sustainable Development. Geneva: United Nations Research Institute for Social Development.

Haines, A., Smith K. R., Anderson D., Epstein P. R., McMichael A. J., Roberts I., Wilkinson P. *et al.* (2007) Policies for accelerating access to clean energy, improving health, advancing development, and mitigating climate change, *Lancet*, 370(9594), 1264–81.

Ikeme, J. (2003) Equity, environmental justice and sustainability: incomplete approaches in climate change politics. *Global Environmental Change*, 13(3), 195–206.

Kok, M., Metz, B., Verhagen, J. and Van Rooijen, S. (2008) Integrating development and climate policies: national and international benefit. *Climate Policy*, 8(2), 103–18.

Kumar, S. and Corbridge, S. (2002) Programmed to fail? Development projects and the politics of participation. *Journal of Development Studies*, 39(2), 73–103.

La Viña, A. G. M., Ang, L. G., De Leon, A. and Roxas, M. (2012) The UNFCCC after Durban: Recognizing limitations and calling for a multi-track approach to climate multilateralism and action. Working paper. London: Foundation for International Environmental Law and Development (FIELD).

MRFCJ (Mary Robinson Foundation) (n.d.) Climate Justice. Available at: http://www.mrfcj.org/about (accessed 23 October 2012).

Ministry of Environment, Science and Technology (MEST) Ghana (2010) Ghana goes for Green Growth – national engagement on climate change, discussion document, November. Accra: MEST.

Najam, A. (2005) Developing Countries and Global Environmental Governance: From Contestation to Participation to Engagement. International Environmental Agreements, *International Environmental Agreements: Politics, Law and Economics*, 5(3), 303–21.

Najam, A., Huq, S. and Sokona Y. (2003) Climate negotiations beyond Kyoto: developing countries concerns and interests. *Climate Policy*, 3(3), 221–31.

Page, E. (2006) *Climate Change and Future Generations*. Cheltenham: Edward Elgar.

Pepper, D. (1993) *Eco-socialism: from Deep Ecology to Social Justice*. London: Routledge.

Perez, C., Roncoli, C., Neely, C. and Steiner, J. L. (2007) Can carbon sequestration markets benefit low-income producers in semi-arid Africa? Potentials and challenges. *Agricultural Systems*, 94(1), 2–12.

Pettit, J. (2004) Climate justice: a new social movement for atmospheric rights, *IDS Bulletin*, 35(3), 102–6.

Richards, M. (2003) Poverty reduction, equity and climate change: global governance synergies or contradictions? Globalisation and Poverty Programme. London: Overseas Development Institute.

Roberts, J. T. and Parks B. C. (2006) *A Climate of Injustice: Global Inequality, North-South Politics and Climate Policy*. Cambridge, MA: MIT Press.

Social Watch (2012) Social Watch report 2012: the right to a future, Social Watch, 116–17. Available at: http://www.socialwatch.org/annualReport (accessed 23 October 2012).

Stern, N. (2007) *The Economics of Climate Change: The Stern Review*. Cambridge: Cambridge University Press.

Tanner, T. M. and Allouche, J. (2011) Towards a new political economy of climate change. *IDS Bulletin*, 43(3), 1–14.

Tanner, T. M. and Mitchell, T. (2008) Entrenchment or enhancement: could climate change adaptation help to reduce chronic poverty? *IDS Bulletin*, 39(4), 6–15.

Thomas, D. and Twyman, C. (2006) Equity in resource management amongst natural resource dependent societies: implications for equity in adaptation to climate change, in Adger, W. N., Paavola, Y., Huq, S. and Mace, M. J. (eds) *Fairness in Adaptation to Climate Change*. Cambridge, MA: MIT Press.

Tilburg, X. van and Würtenberger, L. C. (2010) Technical Assistance Outline: supporting low carbon growth in Ghana. Amsterdam: ECN.

United Nations Development Programme (UNDP) (2007) Human development report 2007/2008 fighting climate change: human solidarity in a divided world. New York: United Nations Development Programme.

World Bank (2010) World development report 2010: development and climate change. Washington DC: World Bank.

Würtenberger, L., Bunzeck I. G. and Tilburg, X. van (2011) Initiatives related to climate change in Ghana: towards coordinating efforts. ECN Policy Studies, Amsterdam. Available at: http://www.ecn.nl/publications/ECN-E—11-010 (accessed 23 October 2012).

Yamin, F. and Depledge, J. (2004) *The International Climate Change regime: a Guide to Rules, Institutions and Procedures*. Cambridge: Cambridge University Press.

Further reading

Baer, P., Athanasiou, T., Kartha, S. and Kemp-Benedict, E. (2009) The Greenhouse Development Rights Framework: the right to development in a climate constrained world. 2nd edition. Heinrich-Böll-Stiftung, Berlin. Available at: www.ecoequity.org/docs/TheGDRsFramework.pdf (accessed 23 October 2012).Page, E. (2006) *Climate Change and Future Generations*. Cheltenham: Edward Elgar.

Roberts, J. T. and Parks B. C. (2007) *A Climate of Injustice: Global Inequality, North-South Politics and Climate Policy*. Cambridge, MA: MIT Press.

Note

1   This figure was first published by Center for Indigenous Knowledge and Organizational Development (CIKOD) (2011) Making the Forest Sector Transparent – Annual Transparency Report Card 2010 Ghana. Available at: http://www.cikod.org/Products.html.

5 Social policy and low carbon development

Johan Nordensvärd

This chapter discusses how to link social policy with low carbon development. The chapter outlines some of the challenges to make social policy comply with low carbon development on one side and to support low carbon development on the other. It aims to discuss the main approaches on the welfare state, the market and climate change. This chapter aims to address issues from both developed and developing countries. The main argument of the chapter is that there needs to be a fundamental societal change such as reforming capitalism and world governance before social policy can really become low carbon.

Introduction

Climate change has become one of the most debated and feared global issues of the 21st century. Stern argues that climate change is a big, global, long-term, persistent und uncertain risk (Stern, 2007: 25). There is an ironic (and very social) twist in the fact that climate change hits the poorest the hardest and often the poorest in the world are the ones who are the least responsible for CO_2 emissions and contributing to climate change (UNDP, 2007; Opschoor, 2008; Battisti and Naylor, 2009; Stern, 2009). Low carbon development is often seen as a possible answer to the question of how humanity is going to cope with its excessive CO_2 emissions. In general, low carbon development is a development model that is based on climate-friendly low carbon energy and follows principles of sustainable development, makes a contribution to avoiding dangerous climate change and adopts patterns of low carbon consumption and production (Skea and and Nishioka, 2008; Urban, 2010).

Despite the strong link between social well-being and environmental well-being, social policy in general and the welfare state in particular have until recently never had an overt focus on the environment. As the terms social policy and welfare state might suggest, the focus is on humans and their well-being. Social policy is often seen as actions to promote human well-being and the study of it (Alcock, 1997). Social policy could also be defined as the academic study of social services and the welfare state (Spicker, 1995). Social policy as both a welfare state activity and as an academic subject is often centred in and around the developed countries (such as Sweden, UK, Germany and the USA) which possess government policies and institutions that implement social welfare. In addition, social policy is considered as being the public management of social risks (Esping-Andersen, 1999: 36), whereas environmental risks, such as climate change also have an affect on social risks. There is therefore a strong rationale for addressing environmental issues when it comes to social policy (Huby, 1998; George and Wilding, 1999; Cahill, 2001).

Low carbon development could add a second and maybe also rival focus for social policy. This chapter aims to describe the challenges that social policy faces in becoming in tune with or even supporting low carbon development. Developed welfare states such as in Europe for example will not only have to be able to adapt to become more low carbon in their day-to-day activities; they will also need to help the global society and the economy to reconstruct themselves as low carbon societies/economies on a global scale. In developing countries the challenges are even more severe since most of the countries lack formal welfare states and they are often dependent on social services/resources from kinship, charities and/or foreign aid.

The main argument of this chapter is that implementing low carbon development within a social policy framework will demand drastic changes in how we perceive social services and living standards on a global level. This chapter will answer the following questions: How can social services and the welfare state transform when faced by climate change and reduce their emissions to become low carbon? How can social policy help achieve low carbon development?

Box 5.1 elaborates some critical thinking on the de-commodification of humans and nature, followed by box 5.2, which discusses the challenges of social policy in relation to low carbon development.

Box 5.1 De-commodification of nature?

Social policy has often been discussed as a counter-movement to some of the more destructive aspects of capitalism. One of the greatest social threats has been the (ab)use of labour and workers as mere commodities. Some social policy scholars have debated this view of humans as being dependent on the market for survival. Karl Polanyi discussed labour as a 'fictitious commodity' since it is not produced for sale and it cannot be detached from the rest of a human's life (Polanyi, 1944: 72). De-commodification has often been linked to being a citizen in a welfare state and thereby linked to both duties and rights towards the state. The first conception of de-commodification as discussed by Polanyi 'protected citizens from major social risks and insulated their living standards from dependence on wage payments' and the counter-movement that pressed for social reforms led to the creation of a welfare state dependent on public services paid for by taxes and social contributions' (Gough, 2010: 62). Such a perspective has often been seen as human-centric and usually did not include the environment.

Still Polanyi did point out the importance of adding environment to the analysis. He argues that there are two other 'fictitious commodities': money and land. Land is considered by Polanyi as 'another name for nature, which is not produced by man' (1944: 72). He argues that the commodification of land, natural resources, the oceans, and so on will generate collective 'bads'. This will need a collective response from society. Polanyi argued for a more active role of the state in regulating the land and protecting natural resources from market forces: '[T]he commodity fiction disregarded the fact that leaving the fate of soil and people to the market would be tantamount to annihilating them' (Polanyi, 1944: 73). In line with this thinking, there needs to be a critical debate as to whether natural resources and the environment are mere human resources or commodities.

Box 5.2 discusses the challenges of social policy in relation to low carbon development.

Box 5.2 The challenges of social policy in relation to low carbon development

Social policy is predominantly understood through a social discourse that often relies on a notion of social citizenship. Marshall used a social citizenship discourse to describe European welfare state developments in the middle of the 20th century. During this time, 'rights' developed to grant working people a modicum of economic welfare, social security and 'the right to participate in full in the heritage and economic wealth of society' (Wagner, 2004: 280). This was partially to guarantee the working class a certain living standard independent of the market. Social rights should offer some protection for workers against particular aspects and outcomes of the market such as unemployment (Wagner, 2004: 280). Some of the major challenges of social policy might involve aspects where the individuals' and corporations' rights might be limited. Two of the major challenges to low carbon development are directly linked to the conception of rights and freedom of choice prevailing in the developed world.

The developed world is predominantly responsible for the overconsumption of this planet's natural resources. A social-liberal perspective on consumption has been an underlying assumption in our perception of social citizenship. In Marshall's classical conception, the citizens were 'first and foremost private individuals and consumers whose freedom of choice had to be protected against government interference' (Wagner, 2004: 280). It is no secret that the consumption of wealthy developed countries caused by this freedom of choice is posing an environmental problem. At the Rio Summit in 1992 consumption patterns in the wealthy developed world were identified as a problem in the move to a more sustainable society (Michaelis, 2000). A few years later the World Wide Fund for Nature (WWF) argued that people 'put pressure on forest, freshwater and marine ecosystems through the production and consumption of resources such as grain, fish, wood, and freshwater, and the emission of pollutants such as carbon dioxide' (WWF, 1998: 1). Today the main problem is the excessive consumption of CO_2 emissions and energy use, particularly in developed countries. For example, the average Bangladeshi consumed 0.3 tonnes CO_2/capita in 2008, whereas the average US American consumed 18 tonnes CO_2/capita in 2008, which is about 60 times higher (World Bank, 2012). Two decades later, the Rio +20 Summit in 2012 highlighted the need to mitigate climate change and reduce the consumption of natural resources.

The state has historically been able to implement very strict social measures when it comes to family policies such as negative eugenics in the developed world and the Chinese 'One Child Policy', whereas the state has been much more careful with limiting consumption of natural resources. Limiting consumption will also mean limiting choice, limiting the free market and in the end it will mean an increase of the power of the state over the market. Excessive consumption of natural resources, particularly in developed countries and emerging economies, coupled with a rapidly growing global population, poses global challenges both for social policy and low carbon development. Jackson therefore suggests that 'There is no credible, socially-just, ecologically-sustainable scenario of continually growing incomes for a world of nine billion people' (Jackson, 2009: 57). The conflict is that we have rich countries that consume far too many resources on one side and the rest of the world dreams of modernizing, which means to consume as much as the developed countries. Barber expresses this ambivalence: 'Yet this ecological consciousness has meant not only greater awareness but also greater inequality, as modernized nations try to slam the door behind them, saying to developing nations, "The world cannot afford your modernization; ours has wrung it dry"' (Barber, 1992). One could therefore argue that social policy should aim to protect both humans and the environment; however, this would require reducing overconsumption of natural resources while trying to limit excessive population growth. However, these are highly provocative issues from a human right perspective, which aims to protect the rights of the individual.

Discussion

The discussion is divided into two parts based on the questions asked in the introduction: How can social services and the welfare state transform when faced by climate change and reduce their emissions to become low carbon? How can social policy help achieve low carbon development?

Transforming social services and the welfare state to become low carbon

The first part of this section addresses the question of how social services and the welfare state can transform when faced by climate change and reduce their emissions to become low carbon. The classic answer is to reduce the carbon emissions of these services. This is being attempted by many states, such as the member states of the European Union, which aim to reduce their greenhouse gas emissions by 20 per cent by 2020 in comparison to 1990 and by 80 per cent in 2050 (EC, 2010a, b). This has led to a position where many countries' welfare service providers produce both research and strategies for reducing their carbon footprints. National social policy will have to adapt to these European goals. The UK for example has a legally binding commitment to 'reduce emissions of greenhouse gases by 80 per cent by 2050, compared with the base year of 1990' (Gough, 2011: iii), which is in line with European Union targets. To give an example from the UK welfare state, the National Health Service (NHS) carbon footprint represents 25 per cent of England's public sector emissions. In the NHS carbon reduction strategy it indicates that the 'NHS has a carbon footprint of 18 million tonnes CO_2 per year' (NHS, 2009: 8) and that this is composed of energy (22%), travel (18%) and procurement (60%). Even though the NHS has become more energy and carbon efficient in recent years, it has 'increased its carbon footprint by 40% since 1990' (NHS, 2008: 8). The NHS as an organization faces challenges that span from becoming more reliant on low carbon energy to upgrading their building to become more energy efficient. The NHS estimates that 'NHS buildings consume over £410 million worth of energy and produce 3.7 million tonnes of CO_2 every year which is 22% of the total NHS carbon footprint' (NHS, 2008:8:41). An example of a low carbon innovation could be the following example at the Pilgrim Hospital in Lincolnshire where the introduction of a biomass boiler could reduce the estate's carbon footprint by up to 50 per cent (NHS, 2008: 8, 42). Transformations of social services and the welfare state are therefore required to become low carbon.

In the 1970s, Titmuss defined the UK's and Swedish welfare states as institutional, combining the principles of comprehensive social provision with egalitarianism and guaranteed benefits to all citizens or residents (Titmuss, 1974). The institutional model has often relied on financing and providing the majority of the healthcare services in the country. Many European healthcare systems are state-funded, either directly as in the UK or indirectly as in Germany (Wadam and Hütt, 2004); while healthcare in the US is mostly financed by private health insurance. These different approaches to healthcare are likely to have an influence on the way climate change and resource scarcity are addressed and decarbonization strategies are developed and implemented. An example is the American healthcare system, which, according to Chung's and Meltzer's estimations including upstream supply-chain activities, emits 546 million Mt CO_2 of which 254 million Mt CO_2 are a consequence of direct healthcare activities, of which the hospitals and prescription drug sectors are the largest emitters (Chung and Meltzer, 2009). These studies conclude that the US healthcare system is responsible for 8 per cent of total CO_2 emissions, whereas in the UK the NHS is reported to be accountable for 3 per cent of total emissions (Chung and Meltzer, 2009). One could argue that a free market and insurance-based healthcare system as in the US might struggle to reach lower levels of CO_2 emissions such as in the UK. Either way, reducing the carbon footprint of the welfare state will not be enough for either system. Gough and Meadowcroft even argue that the welfare state would need to decarbonize (Gough and Meadowcroft, 2010).

The role of social policy for achieving low carbon development

The second part of this section addresses the role of social policy for achieving low carbon development. While there are increasing numbers of studies about emission reductions and low carbon efforts in the welfare systems, the far less researched topic of welfare systems and their role for achieving low carbon development will be elaborated below.

While the question of how to make the welfare state achieve a lower carbon footprint is often a technical question, the role of social policy and the welfare state in supporting a low carbon society is much more debatable and in the end ideological. Some liberal scholars argue that low carbon development and capping CO_2 emissions is something that should be taken care of by the free market. An economic stand point on climate change can be found in the Stern Review where climate change is described as an externality (Stern, 2007). Scholars such as Duncan Foley argue that it is about making the market work for the environment and adjusting the prices (Foley, 2006). William Nordhaus argues that there is a need to allocate a full set of property rights to the atmosphere where carbon emissions get a price. This will force the external cost of CO_2 emissions on to the corporations and consumers (Nordhaus, 2007: 689). 'The belief is that economic incentives, self-interest and market mechanisms will achieve an efficient, least-cost solution to the climate crisis, regardless of how the target of atmospheric CO_2eq stabilization is set' (Storm, 2009: 1017). This view is shared by organizations such as IEA, the International Monetary Fund (IMF), the World Bank and the European Union who all support a common belief that carbon markets are the way to achieve a low carbon economy and low carbon development (Storm, 2009: 1018). The Stern Review argues that '[e]missions trading schemes can deliver least cost emissions reductions by allowing reductions to occur wherever they are cheapest' (Stern, 2007: 326). Such a perspective will not involve social policy more than trying to help people to cope with climate change adaption and in some cases mitigation.

Market-based social policy mechanisms

Examples of this market-based mechanism would be to implement market-based social policy mechanisms, such as Reducing Emissions from Deforestation and Forest Degradation (REDD), which could be interpreted as a form of social protection mechanism, if implemented correctly. REDD has been embedded in the Copenhagen Accord and Cancun Agreements and is a mechanism that aims to pay developing countries for climate-friendly forest management and afforestation. In return, developed countries who invest in REDD in developing countries could gain emission reduction credits to offset their emission obligations. Nevertheless, it is unclear yet how REDD will affect people in developing countries, particularly indigenous people who depend on forest resources, and how their welfare will be secured through mechanisms like REDD.

Economic growth, social policy and low carbon development

To expand the discussion on market-based social policy mechanisms for low carbon development, one must acknowledge that most of the discussion on low carbon development still implies that both growth and capitalism is possible for achieving low carbon development. Low carbon development addresses mitigation and development, which requires an increased use of low carbon energy and energy efficiency technology, protecting natural resources that store carbon such as forests, and implementing policies and incentives that discourage carbon intensive practices and behaviours (DfID, 2009). The dominant perception is that growth and low carbon development are not mutually excusive.

A second approach is proposed by scholars who argue for a green Keynesian approach where low carbon development is included in the development of a green welfare state and a green economy. The economist John Maynard Keynes argued for a stronger intervention of the state and public spending in the economy. This is exemplified by the quote below:

> In the traditional Keynesian macroeconomic model, growth theory maintains that public spending, particularly of a recurrent nature, contributes positively to economic growth. For instance, a high level of government consumption is likely to increase employment, profitability and private investment through the multiplier effect on aggregate output. Government spending raises aggregate demand, leading to an increase in output, depending on the size and effectiveness of the expenditure multiplier.
>
> (Nketiah-Amponsah, 2009: 486)

Jeffrey Sachs argues that for a green economy 'we will need large-scale public funding of research, development and demonstration projects; intellectual property rights to promote rapid dissemination to poor countries; and the promotion of public debate and acceptance of new options' (Sachs, 2008: 40). Hence, the state needs to fund education and research, which will kick-start low carbon development. Green Keynesian approaches could also go one step further and argue for a global carbon tax instead of carbon trading. This could be linked up with direct regulations and redistribution through a global welfare state (Bello and George, 2009). Such an approach does not abolish the market, but regulates it and it assumes that nation states at national and international level will coax the markets and firms to invest in a low carbon economy and low carbon development (Rezai *et al.*, 2009). There is a preference to finance this through global carbon taxes and/or Tobin taxes on international financial transactions. A Tobin tax means a tax on 'short term, cross-border foreign exchange transactions' (Wagner, 2004: 285). It could also be financed through payments of developed industrial countries' carbon debts to developing countries (Bello and George, 2009).

A practical example of this could be the study of the Green Fiscal Commission in the UK that researched the effect of raising green taxes to 20 per cent of total tax revenues, which would be offset by lower employer social security contributions and an extra 10 per cent funds for retrofitting houses and eco-innovation. The Commission suggests that this alone would achieve the UK's commitment to reduce GHGs by 34 per cent by 2020. The study indicates further that a positive side effect could be a potential rise in employment due to lower employment cost (Green Fiscal Commission, 2009). A major issue is that high green taxes or high carbon taxes can be regressive since lower income households tend to spend a higher share of their income on energy. Regressive means here that costs will be disproportionately high for people with lower incomes whereas people with higher incomes can cope with these costs in a better way. This is amplified by the fact that many people with lower incomes tend to live in fuel inefficient houses, which cause higher energy costs. Hills argues that carbon taxation requires complementary social policies for investing on the one hand in low-emission housing, transport, communities and on the other to protect low income citizens who have high carbon consumption (Hills, 2009). Some even go further and discuss a

Green New Deal that outlines a transformational programme to reduce the carbon emissions and in the process handle the decline in demand caused by the global financial crisis (nef, 2008).

A third and more radical approach would go further, and argues that we need to change the global system of governance. Scholars such as Lohman (2009), Galbraith (2008) and Speth (2008) argue not only for higher global carbon taxes and higher investment in low carbon development, specifically low carbon energy and low carbon technology, but in addition they suggest that there is a need to replace the market; 'by alternative democratic co-ordination and decision-making mechanisms' (Storm, 2009: 1026). One could therefore go one step further and suggest that a low carbon society can only be sustained by low growth, no growth or, for Western developed countries, even de-growth. The discourse around de-growth argues that endless economic growth is impossible to sustain. It questions the possibility of globally decoupling economic activity and emissions. The famous book by Meadows *et al. The Limits to Growth* argues that exponential growth in population and material output threatens the well-being of all and that it could lead to an uncontrolled global decline (Meadows *et al.*, 1972). More recently, Tim Jackson (2009) and the Sustainable Development Commission (2009) argue for 'prosperity without growth' or prosperity within the ecological limits of our finite planet. Still the concept of growth and consumption is ingrained in the way we perceive our world. 'Someone once said that it is easier to imagine the end of the world than to imagine the end of capitalism' (Jameson, 2003: 76). A de-growth approach would focus more on well-being and quality of life, which could be decoupled from growing GDP or increased economic activity. This would imply a new macroeconomic approach, which could mean for example a reduction in working hours (Victor, 2008). However, the state would need to ensure that economic resources are more evenly distributed so that the poor would not be disproportionally affected. This might imply sharing some of the wealth of nations more equally, such as by taxing the richer groups of society more to ensure that the poorer groups of society are well off despite a de-growth or reducing the excessive pay of top firm executives and creating employment opportunities with the available funding. This would also give social policy and the state a greater role vis-à-vis firms and the economy. Understandably, in our current economic climate these are controversial ideas that are rarely well received by the powerful and wealthy.

There is therefore a larger need to reform capitalism's institutions, governing corporations, employment, income formation, technology and knowledge processes, and the way trade and finance work. This should be done to share resources in a more equitable way. Some scholars go even further and argue that capitalism's search for growth and profit is not compatible with ecological sustainability. Max Weber discusses in his famous book *The Protestant Ethic: The Spirit of Capitalism* that the capitalist economic world order will proceed until 'the last ton of fossilized coal is burnt' (Weber, 1953: 181). Scholars such as Bello (2008) and Speth (2008) argue that we are heading towards either a collapse of the present capitalist system or a collapse of our global climate.

An alternative, though radical, scenario for global governance would be that natural resources are collectively owned and cooperatively managed and that the use of natural resources is subject to decentralized democratic decision-making. It would be dependent on people and governments being willing to accept a model of lower consumption, lower growth, more distribution of resources and higher social equality that would result 'in an improved welfare, a better quality of life and greater democratic control of production and (renewable) resources' (Storm, 2009: 1026). This would need a complete reconfiguration of our understanding of welfare states, global social policy and the global market.

The following section presents a critique to discuss the role of social policy for low carbon development in developing countries (see Box 5.3).

Box 5.3 Critique: the role of social policy for low carbon development in developing countries

Western developed countries offer their citizens formal welfare rights, but most developing countries cannot offer comprehensive or even basic welfare services. Many developing countries have an informal welfare system that relies more on informal communities and informal social services. Gough and Woods discuss the nature of informal security arrangements where rights and duties are often informal and people rely heavily 'upon community and family relationships to meet their security needs' (Gough and Wood, 2006: 1699–700). This means that the role of social policy and its support of low carbon development are often dependent on international aid, charities and NGOs. It can be upsetting and difficult to accept that developing countries have the least social security in the form of a welfare state, have caused the least CO_2 emissions in historical or cumulative terms and are still suffering the most from the effects of global climate change.

The dominant development discourse assumes that there is a possible compromise between capitalist growth and development on one side and poverty alleviation and low carbon development on the other side. This could be summed up for example in the concept around green jobs, which involves:

> the implementation of measures that reduce carbon emissions or help realise alternative sources of energy use…[to] align poverty reduction and employment creation in developing countries with a broader set of investments in environmental conservation and rehabilitation to also preserve biodiversity.
>
> (UNDP, 2009: 2, 23–36)

The aim is often for the relevant global, national and local actors to alleviate poverty through growth and development, as well as achieve this through low carbon efforts. One of the major priorities is to provide access to electricity or other modern energy sources to all citizens. In this way it becomes a priority to link up access to electricity or modern energy with low carbon energy sources. In this context, the Solar Cooker Project by the Office of the United Nations High Commissioner for Refugees (UNHCR), the Dutch foundation KoZon and CARE International, which provides solar cookers to Darfuri refugee women and girls in refugee camps in Chad as an alternative to fuel wood, is an example of how low carbon energy can help improve people's lives as well as reduce pressure on the environment in a context of instability. Instead of letting women and girls leave the safety of their refugee camps in Chad and risk being assaulted in their pursuit of fuel wood the solar cookers reduce (or even eliminate) the need for fuel wood and thereby allow women and girls to stay safely in the camp. The cookers are easy to use and maintain, reduce pressure on forests and woodland and are a climate-friendly low carbon way of providing energy for cooking (Urban and Lind, 2011).

There are some negative aspects of the predominant low carbon development discourse when it comes to developing countries. The cynical aspect is that social policy in developing countries is far less about de-commodification of its citizens and its land and far more about poverty alleviation through economic growth and development. The main problem is that the current discourses neglect the destructive and wasteful aspects of capitalism and how these are linked to climate change and social inequalities.

Conclusion

One of the most dominant interpretations of social policy and low carbon development is to discuss how social policy services could cause less CO_2 emissions. This question is therefore first and foremost a Western developed country issue (and a very technical issue) since the welfare state's services are more comprehensive in developed countries. Decarbonizing the welfare state has become a hot issue since it involves aspects such as using less energy for services. This means for example switching from fossil fuel energy sources to renewable energy sources and technologies. However, this requires substantial investment in sectors such as the health sector or other social sectors that consume large amounts of energy, such as public transport. It is also about improving energy efficiency of housing stock and public buildings like hospitals and schools, and so on.

The more overarching goal to turn global society in general and the nation state specifically to becoming low carbon is far more difficult. The main question mark is whether the current system of capitalism can support low carbon development or even worse, can sustain our environment. There is a sneaking suspicion that unless technological improvement increases rapidly and the profits of capitalism trickle down more efficiently we are bound to continue to deplete our resources and increase inequality at the same time.

This chapter has discussed three disparate answers to these questions: more market-led social policy options such as carbon trading (e.g. REDD) to alleviate both poverty and climate change, a green new deal to kick-start both environmental protection and the economy, and a whole change of our global capitalist system to become a more democratic, more equitable and environmentally friendly global society.

The greatest challenge is that global low carbon development and global poverty are not exclusive questions for nation states. Climate change is a quintessential 'global public bad' since CO_2 emissions in one place will have consequences for all other places. Climate change can only be halted by global collective action to prevent carbon leakage and free-riding (Arrow, 2007; Roberts and Parks, 2007; Stern, 2007). At the same time, poverty is a global issue that goes beyond the nation state. There is a problem and this problem is that development comes at an environmental cost and environmental protection comes at a social cost. Huby argues that:

> The problem is that, used alone, policies to promote social welfare carry long term costs to both society and the environment, while policies for long-term environmental protection tend to produce distributional effects that work to the detriment of vulnerable groups of people in the shorter term.
>
> (Huby, 2001: 521–2)

The definition of Western welfare states and the understanding of well-being could not be implemented on a global scale taking the current consumption of natural resources into account. If the rest of the world aspired to Western development and well-being it would lead to drastic increases in CO_2 emissions. 'In First World countries, industry's promise of unlimited consumerism has led to disproportionate levels of energy and water use, emission of greenhouse gasses and the conversion of natural habitats' (Ho, 2006: 4). On the other hand, the West cannot keep its protected position forever, so it will have to cut down its consumption and its emissions in the long run. This will of course be a challenge for some countries such as the USA, where most of its infrastructure is built around cars, aeroplanes and fossil fuel power. Urban sprawl has created an increasing dependence on cars and as long as vehicle technology remains high carbon, the US will be struggling to rebuild its infrastructure. This could result in enormous costs compared to countries that have just recently started to invest in more low carbon transport. Still, the greatest overarching problem lies in our perception of development. 'Development implies industrialization, urbanization and the intensification of resource use, the costs of which have often been externalized at the expense of the environment' (Ho, 2006: 4). Key questions for future global development are therefore uncomfortable and controversial, but necessary for saving the global climate and natural resources: Are high consuming countries such as the USA or European countries ready for a de-growth? Is the USA or European society ready to give up its way of life of excessive consumption and production? These questions could be extended to other developed countries and even emerging economies with high emissions. The question is whether the world aspires for something else other than economic development, production and, in the end, consumption, or do all countries in the world need to continue to strive for a Western life-style, Western development and a Western capitalist system with high resource depletion and social inequalities.

References

Alcock, P. (1997) The subject of social policy, in Alcock, P., Erskinem, A. and May, M. (eds) *The Student's Companion to Social Policy*. Chichester: Wiley-Blackwell.

Arrow, K. (2007) global climate change: a challenge to policy. *Economists' Voice*, June, 1–5.

Battisti, D. S. and Naylor, R. L. (2009) Historical warnings of future food insecurity with unprecedented historical heat. *Science*, 323 (9 January), 240–4.

Barber, B. (1992) Jihad vs McWorld. *Atlantic Monthly*, March. Available at: http://www.theatlantic.com/magazine/archive/1992/03/jihad-vs-mcworld/303882/ (24 October 2012).

Bello, W. (2008) Will capitalism survive climate change?. Available at: http://www.zmag.org/znet/viewArticle/17095 (accessed 24 October 2012).

Bello, W. and George, S. (2009) A new, green, democratic deal. *New Internationalist* 419. Available at: http://www.tni.org/detail_page.phtml?act_id=19499&username=guest@tni.org&password=9999&publish=Y (accessed 24 October 2012).

Cahill, M. (2001) *The Environment and Social Policy*. London: Routledge.

Chung, J and Meltzer, D. (2009) Estimate of the carbon footprint of the US health care sector. *Journal of American Medical Association*, 18, 1970–2.

Department for International Development (DfID) (2009) Eliminating world poverty: building our common future. DfID White Paper. London: DfID.

Esping-Andersen, G. (1999) *Social Foundations of Postindustrial Economies*. Oxford: Oxford University Press.

European Commission (EC) (2010a) EU energy and climate package. Available at: http://ec.europa.eu/clima/policies/package/index_en.htm (accessed 24 October 2012).

EC (2010b) Roadmap for moving European Commission to a low carbon economy in 2050. Available at: http://ec.europa.eu/clima/policies/roadmap/index_en.htm (accessed 24 October 2012).

Foley, D. (2006) *Adam's Fallacy. a Guide to Economic Theology*. Cambridge, MA: The Belknap Press.

Galbraith, J. K. (2008) *The Predator State. How Conservatives Abandoned the Free Market and Why Liberals Should Too*. New York: Free Press.

George, V. and Wilding, P. (1999) *British Society and Social Welfare: Towards a Sustainable Society*. Basingstoke: Macmillan.

Gough, I. (2010) Economic crisis, climate change and the future of welfare states. *21st Century Society*, 5(1), 51–64.

Gough, I. (2011) Climate change, double injustice and social policy: a case study of the United Kingdom. Geneva: United Nations Research Institute for Social Development (UNRISD).

Gough, I. and Meadowcroft, J. (2010) Decarbonising the welfare state, in Dryzek, J. S., Norgaard, R. B. and Schlosberg, D. (eds) *Oxford Handbook of Climate Change and Society*. Oxford: Oxford University Press

Gough, I. and Wood, G. (2006) A comparative welfare regime approach to global social policy. *World Development*, 34(10), 1696–712.

Green Fiscal Commission (2009) *The Case for Green Fiscal Reform*. London: GFC.

Hills, J. (2009) Future pressures: intergenerational links, wealth, demography and sustainability, in Hills, J., Sefton T. and Stewart, K. (eds) *Towards a More Equal Society? Poverty, Inequality and Policy since 1997*. Bristol: Policy Press, 319–39.

Ho, P. (2006) Trajectories for greening in China: theory and practice. *Development and Change*, 37(1), 3–28.

Huby, M. (1998) *Social Policy and the Environment*. Buckingham: Open University Press.

Huby, M. (2001) The sustainable use of resources on a global scale. *Social Policy and Administration*, 35(5), 521–37.

Jackson, T. (2009) *Prosperity without Growth*. Abingdon: Earthscan.

Jameson, F. (2003) Future city. *New Left Review*, 21 (May–June), 65–79.

Lohmann, L. (2009) Climate as investment. *Development and Change* 40(6): 1063–83.

Meadows, D. H., Meadows, D. L., Randers, J. and Behrens III, W. W. (1972) *The Limits to Growth: a Report to the Club of Rome*. New York: Universe Books.

Michaelis, L. (2000) Sustainable consumption and production in Dodds, F. (ed.) *Earth Summit 2002*. Abingdon: Earthscan.

nef (2008) *A Green New Deal*. London: nef.

NHS (2009) Saving carbon, improving health, NHS carbon reduction strategy for England, Sustainable Development Unit. London: NHS.

Nketiah-Amponsah, E. (2009) Public spending and economic growth: evidence from Ghana (1970–2004). *Development Southern Africa*, 26(3), 477–97.

Nordhaus, W. D. (2007) A review of The Stern Review on the Economics of Climate Change. *Journal of Economic Literature*, 45(3), 686–702.

Opschoor, J. (2008) Fighting climate change: human solidarity in a divided world. *Development and Change*, 39(6), 1193–202.

Polanyi, K. (1944) *The Great Transformation*. Boston, MA: Beacon Press.

Rezai, A., Foley, D. K. and Taylor, L. (2009) Global warming and externalities. SCEPA Working Paper 2009–3. New York: New School University.

Roberts, J. T. and Parks, B. C. (2007) *A Climate of Injustice. Global Inequality, North–South Politics, and Climate Policy*. Cambridge, MA: MIT Press.

Sachs, J. (2008) Technological keys to climate protection. *Scientific American*, 298(4), 40.

Skea, J. and Nishioka, S. (2008) Policies and practices for a low carbon society. *Climate Policy, Supplement Modelling Long-Term Scenarios for Low Carbon Societies*, 8, 5–16.

Speth, J. G. (2008) *The Bridge at the Edge of the World. Capitalism, the Environment and Crossing from Crisis to Sustainability*. New Haven, CT and London: Yale University Press.

Spicker, P. (1995) *Social Policy: Themes and Approaches*. Upper Saddle River, NJ: Prentice Hall.

Stern, N. H. (2007) *The Economics of Climate Change: The Stern Review*. Cambridge: Cambridge University Press.

Stern, N. (2009) *A Blueprint for a Safer Planet: How to Manage Climate Change and Create a New Era of Progress and Prosperity*. London: Bodley Head.

Storm, S. (2009) Capitalism and climate change: can the invisible hand adjust the natural thermostat? *Development and Change*, 40, 6, 1011–38.

Sustainable Development Commission (SDC) (2009) *Prosperity without Growth*. London: SDC.

Titmuss, R. (1974) *Social Policy*. London: Allen and Unwin.

United Nations Development Programme (UNDP) (2007) *Human Development Report 2007/8*. New York: Palgrave Macmillan.

UNDP (2009) Green jobs for the poor: a public employment approach, Poverty Reduction Discussion Paper PG/2009/002. Available at: http://www.undp.org.gy/documents/bk/PG-2009-002-discussion-paper-green-jobs.pdf (accessed 24 October 2012).

Urban, F. (2011) *Technology, Trade and Climate Policy: The Pursuit of Low Carbon Development in Least Developed Countries, Vulnerable Economies and Small Island Developing States*. London: Commonwealth Secretariat.

Urban, F. and Lind, J. (2011) Low carbon energy and conflict: a new agenda. *Boiling Point*, 59, 26–7.

Victor, P. (2008) *Managing Without Growth: Slower by Design, not Disaster*. Cheltenham: Edward Elgar.

Wadam, R. and Hütt, R. (2004) The need for a new go-to-market strategy in Europe: how to survive and thrive in the new more complex healthcare marketplace. *Journal of International Medical Marketing*, 4, 154–62.

Wagner, A. (2004) Redefining citizenship for the 21st century: from the National Welfare State to the UN Global Compact. *International Journal of Social Welfare*, 13, 278–86.

Weber, M., 1953. *The Protestant Ethic and the Spirit of Capitalism*. New York: Scribner.

World Bank (2012) World Bank data. Available at: http://data.worldbank.org (accessed 24 October 2012).

World Wide Fund for Nature (WWF) (1998) Living planet report. Godalming: World Wide Fund for Nature.

Further reading

Cahill, M. (2001) *The Environment and Social Policy*. London: Routledge.

Gough. I. (2010) Economic crisis, climate change and the future of welfare states. *21st Century Society*, 5(1), 51–64.

Gough, I. (2011) Climate change, double injustice and social policy: a case study of the United Kingdom. Geneva: United Nations Research Institute for Social Development (UNRISD).

Gough, I. and Meadowcroft, J. (2010) Decarbonising the welfare state, in Dryzek, J. S., Norgaard, R. B. and Schlosberg, D. (eds) *Oxford Handbook of Climate Change and Society*. Oxford: Oxford University Press.

Jackson, T. (2009) *Prosperity without Growth*. Abingdon: Earthscan.

Part 4

The economics of low carbon development

Editorial for Part 4

The economics of low carbon development

Frauke Urban and Johan Nordensvärd

Part 4 explores the economics of low carbon development. Economic approaches to climate change and low carbon development have become well established in recent years, not least due to the influential Stern Review on the economics of climate change. This part elaborates the key issues related to the economics of low carbon development, it also addresses the issue of carbon markets and provides some criticism of the key issues.

Overview of Part 4

Chapter 6 discusses first the economics of low carbon development and then discusses options for financing the transition to a low carbon economy. The chapter addresses the economic impact of climate change, the costs of stabilizing GHG emissions and the financial options for moving towards a low carbon economy. The chapter makes reference to the Stern Review on the economics of climate change, which suggests that deep cuts in emissions will be required to mitigate climate change, whereas the costs will be significant but manageable. Nevertheless, the Stern Review is highly disputed for various reasons, which are explored in this chapter to provide an understanding of the economics of climate change and the assumptions behind these prominent figures. Furthermore the chapter explores more wide-ranging criticism of economics and low carbon development.

Chapter 7 elaborates the current status and the future of carbon markets. The chapter describes how the idea of using market instruments in the field of climate change developed, why it became popular and what kind of markets exist. Individual carbon markets, including the European ETS and the CDM, are analysed and debated. The argument of the chapter is that carbon markets share many characteristics of other financial markets, but they are also different in some important and potentially beneficial ways.

6 Climate change economics

Financing low carbon development

Frauke Urban and Johan Nordensvärd

This chapter discusses first the economics of low carbon development and then discusses options for financing the transition to a low carbon economy. The chapter addresses the economic impact of climate change, the costs of stabilizing GHG emissions and the financial options for moving towards a low carbon economy. The chapter makes reference to the Stern Review on the economics of climate change, which suggests that deep cuts in emissions will be required to mitigate climate change, whereas the costs will be significant but manageable. Nevertheless the Stern Review is highly disputed for various reasons, which are explored and evaluated here to provide an understanding of the economics of climate change and the assumptions behind these prominent figures. Furthermore the chapter explores more wide-ranging criticism of economics and low carbon development.

Introduction

Climate change is inherently a political issue; nevertheless the causes of climate change and solutions for tackling climate change involve an economic dimension. Climate change and GHG emissions are linked to economic development. 'Development implies industrialization, urbanization and the intensification of resource use, the costs of which have often been externalized at the expense of the environment' (Ho, 2006: 4). Moreover, the use and over-use of natural resources has been linked by scholars such as Max Weber to the capitalist economic system. Max Weber suggests in his famous book *The Protestant Ethic and the Spirit of Capitalism* that the capitalist economic world order would proceed until 'the last ton of fossilized coal is burnt' (Weber, 1953: 181). The economic rise of developed countries in the Western world has played a major role in the historic rise in GHG emissions. It is therefore not surprising that there is a scholarly debate about how the economy and development are both part of the problem of climate change as well as part of the solution.

The most influential, but also most debated report on the economics of climate change is the Stern Review, which was commissioned by the Treasury of the UK Government (Stern, 2006, 2007). The report discusses the economic impacts of climate change and the costs of stabilizing GHG emissions. The Stern Review considers climate change as 'the greatest and widest-ranging market failure ever seen' (Stern, 2006: 1). This is due to the fact that those who caused the majority of the emissions – namely developed countries – do not pay for their damage and are not even the worst affected. Hence, the Polluter Pays Principle is not working in this case, despite the important, but financially only marginal attempts made by mechanisms such as the Clean Development Mechanism (CDM) and climate finance (which will be discussed later in this chapter).

The Stern Review suggests that 'stabilising at or below 550[1] ppm CO_2 equivalent would require global emissions to peak in the next 10–20 years … By 2050, global emissions would need to be around 25% below current levels' (Stern, 2006: xi). The Review reveals that 'achieving these deep cuts in emissions will have a cost. The Review estimates the annual costs of stabilisation at 500–550 ppm CO_2 equivalent to be around 1% of GDP by 2050 – a level that is significant but manageable' (Stern, 2006: xii). Other studies suggest that delaying global action on climate change mitigation until 2020 or later could increase the costs by at least half (Jakob *et al.*, 2011). In addition, the Stern Review argues that 'emissions trading schemes can deliver least cost emissions reductions by allowing reductions to occur wherever they are cheapest' (Stern, 2007: 326). Introducing a price on carbon emissions is hence hailed by many scholars and organizations as the most cost-effective way of mitigating emissions that lead to climate change.

This chapter will discuss the economics of climate change mitigation and low carbon development, paying particular attention to issues related to carbon markets as well as investments and overseas development assistance for low carbon development.

Box 6.1 elaborates the key definitions relevant for this chapter, followed by Box 6.2, which briefly addresses the key points of the Stern Review on the economics of climate change.

Box 6.1 Definitions of key concepts and terms

Economics is a discipline that deals with the production, distribution and consumption of goods and services and their management. Economics helps us understand the material well-being of society.

Market failure is defined as an inefficient allocation of resources within a free market. The market has hence failed to produce results that are advantageous (win–win situations). For climate change this means that economic activities – such as powering industries that produce goods and services – lead to inefficient, negative results – such as greenhouse gas emissions leading to climate change. These negative results are often referred to as externalities.

Externalities are non-monetary by-products of economic processes and they usually affect a party who did not have a choice or whose interests were not considered. There can be both positive and negative externalities, although in the field of climate change externalities are usually negative. Climate change as such is considered an externality as it is a non-monetary by-product of economic growth and industrialization, however, it affects poor people in developing countries disproportionally who have not caused the problem and who were not consulted on its impacts.

The **Polluter Pays Principle** is an environmental policy principle, which indicates that those who caused the pollution should bear the costs of cleaning it up. For example, industries that cause water pollution should pay the costs for waste water treatment and water protection. With regard to climate change, the Polluter Pays Principle is not working as there are a plethora of sources of GHG emissions at a global level and – despite overwhelming scientific evidence – political difficulties exist in agreeing who is responsible and to what extent. Hence, climate change is considered a market failure.

Box 6.2 presents a brief overview of the findings of the Stern Review, which is the most well known study on the economics of climate change and which changed the common perceptions about climate change and its costs.

Box 6.2 Key findings of the Stern Review on the economics of climate change

There is solid scientific evidence that a business-as-usual (BAU) emissions pathway is likely to lead to dangerous and irreversible climate change. Therefore climate change mitigation is urgently needed. While all countries are affected by climate change, the climatic impacts are not evenly distributed. The poorest countries and people are disproportionally affected by climate change (Stern, 2006).

Early action on climate change is expected to outweigh the costs of climate change. The Stern Review estimates that unmitigated climate change could cost at least 5 per cent of global GDP per year, and up to 20 per cent of global GDP if more extreme climate predictions become reality (Stern, 2006). To stabilize global CO_2 equivalent emissions at 550 ppm, the Stern Review estimates the annual costs for climate change mitigation could be as low as 1 per cent of global GDP by 2050. The Review considers 1 per cent of global GDP per year as significant costs, however, they are manageable (Stern, 2006). The Review estimates that each emitted tonne of CO_2 causes damage of about US$85, such as damage associated with sea-level rise, extreme weather events, rising temperatures, and so on. In comparison, Stern suggests that emissions can be cut at a cost of less than $25 per tonne (Stern, 2006).

The transition to a low carbon economy is therefore urgently needed to stabilize GHG concentrations in the atmosphere. A low carbon economy poses challenges, but also offers opportunities for growth and competitiveness. Nevertheless, the transition to a low carbon economy is only possible when effective policies and financial arrangements are in place, particularly for facilitating low carbon transitions in developing countries. The Stern Review suggests that a global low carbon transition could eventually benefit the global economy by $2.5 trillion per year. The review further projects that by 2050, markets for low carbon technologies could be worth at least $500 billion (Stern, 2006).

While mitigation is crucial, adaptation is also urgently needed to deal with unavoidable climatic impacts. Particularly adaptation efforts in developing countries need to be accelerated and supported, including through overseas development assistance (ODA) (Stern, 2006, 2007).

The figures in the Stern Review however have to be addressed with caution due to scientific uncertainty around climate change and its economic costs, and therefore the Review indicates a range of figures with low and high estimates, rather than one specific figure. Also, these figures are estimates and describe potential events, they are however not predictions. The Stern Review used economic models, of macro-economic nature and integrated assessment models, as well as disaggregated approaches and compared the current cost level and potential future cost levels associated with climate change and greenhouse gas abatement costs. However, the Stern Review is heavily criticized for various reasons as the section on 'Low carbon economies and finance: a critique' indicates.

More recent reports on the economics of climate change mitigation, such as by the OECD in 2009 and Ackerman and Stanton in 2011, build on the findings of the Stern Review (OECD, 2009). Ackerman and Stanton (2011) represent a report on the state of the art of climate economics in late 2011, which assesses the latest climate science, analyses the economic methodologies and assumptions used in climate economics, and reiterates the warning messages on early action presented by the Stern Review. However, no new figures are presented (Ackerman and Stanton, 2011). Similar assessments to the Stern Review have been done on a regional basis for Southeast Asia (ADB, 2009) and Kenya (SEI, 2009).

The next section discusses the key ideas of the economics of the environment and low carbon development, followed by a discussion about options for financing the transition to a low carbon economy.

Discussion

The economics of the environment and low carbon development

The mainstream discourse on climate change mitigation and low carbon development has often been portrayed in market terms. DfID defines low carbon development as using 'less carbon for growth' (DfID, 2009: 58), which implies that economic growth is important and achievable, but needs to be low carbon.[2] Other recent influential studies such as 'The economics of ecosystems and biodiversity study' (TEEB, 2010) and the United Nations' 'Towards a green economy' report and initiative (UNEP, 2011) portray environmental problems framed in economic terms. The core argument in these studies is that the environment in general and CO_2 emissions in particular are to be understood in market terms and that a price needs to be attached to CO_2 emissions and environmental goods and services. The idea that the environment is only valued by people, governments and firms if a price is attached to it became popular in the fields of ecological economics and environmental economics due to thinkers such as Constanza *et al.* (1997). This thinking is based on the idea that nature provides environmental goods and services for free, such as clean air, clean water, clean soils and access to food, minerals and energy. As no price is attached to these goods and services, their value is often understated or non-existent. Environmental destruction and degradation, such as air pollution, water pollution, soil contamination, climate change, natural resource depletion and biodiversity loss, have a 'zero' price tag and thereby lead to negative trade-offs and to a relationship of (self-) destructiveness that people have with nature (TEEB, 2010). This understanding of not valuing nature has changed in recent years, since ecosystem services, nature conservation and even CO_2 emissions are part of economic considerations and today often have a price tag.

However, valuating nature in economic terms has also resulted in neo-liberal economic arrangements, such as carbon markets and low carbon growth. Scholars such as Foley and Nordhaus argue that the market should be used to protect the environment through pricing. This means that CO_2 emissions have a price attached to them that is paid by corporations and consumers (Foley, 2006; Nordhaus, 2007). There is a belief among scholars from a market discourse perspective that 'economic incentives, self-interest and market mechanisms will achieve an efficient, least-cost solution to the climate crisis, regardless of how the target of atmospheric CO_2 eq stabilization is set' (Storm, 2009: 1017). This approach is shared by organizations such as the IEA, the IMF, the World Bank and the EU who support a common belief that carbon markets are an effective option for achieving a low carbon economy and low carbon development (Storm, 2009: 1018). Often this boils down to introducing carbon market schemes, which are briefly elaborated in the next section and in more detail in Chapter 7.

Financing the transition to a low carbon economy: carbon markets

This section briefly outlines some key mechanisms for financing the transition to a low carbon economy, with a focus on carbon markets. This section briefly introduces the key concepts and mechanisms, whereas Chapter 7 discusses in more details the current status of carbon markets and their future.[3]

The **Clean Development Mechanism (CDM)** is a system that enables developed countries to finance projects leading to emission reductions in developing countries. Developing countries gain access to climate-friendly technology, such as renewable energy, while developed countries gain certified emission reduction credits (CERs) to offset their emissions. In early 2012, 3742 projects had been registered and another 7500 were in the pipeline (UNEP, 2012a, see Chapter 7). The large majority of CDM projects are located in emerging economies, most of which are in China and India. The CDM is currently being reformed to enable LDCs to benefit from the mechanism, as poor countries – particularly in Sub-Saharan Africa – have in the past hardly attracted any funding through the CDM. Another key criticism of the CDM is that it is an offsetting mechanism. This means that rather than reducing emissions, countries and firms invest in low carbon projects in poorer countries. This could be described as a modern form of selling of indulgences.

The **Emissions Trading System (ETS)** is another quasi-market mechanism that sets a cap on GHG emissions and introduces a trading system. Once emission allowances are exceeded, emission credits must be bought from those who have emitted less. Emissions trading is currently in place for developed countries only, with the European Emissions Trading System (EU ETS) being the world's biggest, although a more international ETS might be extended to other countries in the future (see Chapter 7). It is estimated that annually 6.5 Gt of CO_2 emissions are traded (EU Commission, 2005; Skjaerseth and Wettestad, 2008). The EU ETS has a value of about US$120 billion annually and thereby represents about 97% of all global carbon trading (see Chapter 7).

Joint implementation (JI) is a third scheme in which developed countries can invest in certified emission reduction projects in other developed countries as an alternative to reducing emissions domestically. JI is currently in place for developed countries only. For example, Eastern European countries, where carbon emissions have declined after the fall of the Soviet Union, can reduce their emissions jointly with other countries that have growing emissions, for example Japan. Most of the JI projects are implemented in the sectors energy efficiency and methane reduction. In early 2012, a total of 305 projects with 143,438 emission reduction units had been recorded (UNEP, 2012b).

Reducing Emissions from Deforestation and Forest Degradation (REDD+) was introduced as a new mechanism in the Copenhagen Accord (UNFCCC, 2009) and the Cancun Agreements aimed to operationalize REDD+ (UNFCCC, 2010). The key principle is that developing countries can be paid for climate-friendly forest management, conservation and enhancement of forest carbon stocks, while developed countries can gain emission reduction credits to offset their emission obligations. Major initiatives include the Forest Investment Programme, the Forest Carbon Partnership Facility and the UN-REDD Programme. The UN-REDD programmes estimates that between $30 and 100 billion per year can be brought to developing countries as payments for REDD+ (UN-REDD, 2010, 2012). Recipients of REDD+ payments are developing countries with tropical forests, including countries that have high deforestation rates such as Brazil, the Democratic Republic of Congo (DRC) and Indonesia (see Chapter 11 for a more detailed discussion of REDD+).

Financing the transition to a low carbon economy: investments and ODA for low carbon finance

The previous section briefly outlined some key mechanisms for financing the transition to a low carbon economy, with a focus on carbon markets (for more detail, see Chapter 7). This section briefly introduces other low carbon finance options related to investments and ODA, both within the UNFCCC and outside of the UNFCCC.

For achieving a global low carbon economy to mitigate climate change, the IEA estimates that $45 trillion of investments are required between 2010 and 2050 to reduce global carbon emissions by 50 per cent – of which a significant amount will be needed for restructuring energy systems and moving to low carbon energy (IEA, 2010). A large share of this funding is expected to come from the private sector, although public finance – such as through ODA – also plays a role, as well as private–public partnerships.

An important part of climate finance and low carbon finance is to invest in low carbon technology and innovation. Key features of recent UNFCCC climate finance arrangements were first discussed in Copenhagen in 2009 and then formalized in the Cancun Agreements in 2010. As a result, the *Green Climate Fund* was launched at the Conference of the Parties (COP17) in Durban in late 2011. The UNFCCC climate finance includes short-term finance from developed countries to developing countries, namely $30 billion 'fast track' finance for the period 2010–2012, and medium-term finance, namely $100 billion annually by 2020 (see Chapter 3). This funding should be 'new and additional' to existing ODA[4] and is dedicated to the LDCs, African countries and Small Island Developing State (SIDS). Emerging economies such as China or India are not eligible for funding from the Green Climate Fund. The Green Climate Fund aims to finance projects and programmes in developing countries in the fields of mitigation (including REDD), adaptation, capacity building and technology transfer and technology development. The fund is directly accountable to the UNFCCC and is governed by a board of representatives from Asia-Pacific, Africa, Latin America and the Caribbean, SIDS and LDCs (UNFCCC, 2011). Despite the operational set up of the Green Climate Fund and the pledges by developed countries, there is concern that the actual funding is not being met. The World Resources Institute (WRI) attempts to keep track of financial pledges made by donor countries and the actual budget allocation and payments made. WRI reports that by 2011, the actual amount that has been allocated by donor countries to the Green Climate Fund was roughly $12 billion, which is obviously far below the pledged $30 billion (WRI, 2011). Similar situations have been observed in recent years with adaptation funding pledged by developed countries, such as for the Adaptation Fund and the Least Developed Country Fund, which are chronically under-funded.

Other main low carbon finance options include funding from donor countries that are administrated by the multilateral organization the *World Bank*, such as the Climate Investment Fund (CIF) programmes which include the Clean Technology Fund (CTF) and the Scaling-Up Renewable Energy Programme (SREP) in low income countries. The *Global Environmental Facility (GEF)* is further administrating a large source of low carbon finance for renewable energy and energy efficiency projects. However, the external funding – particularly the World Bank funding – has not been particularly well received by the G77 (the group of 77 powerful developing countries) and is seen as potentially undermining the legitimacy of the UNFCCC in tackling climate change. The G77 has argued over recent years that all climate funding should be under the control of the UNFCCC, hence the UNFCCC's Green Climate Fund is of outmost importance. Nevertheless, the following section will briefly discuss the World Bank funding.

The **Climate Investment Fund (CIF)**: The World Bank currently administrates the CIF, which receives funding from various donors such as Australia, France, Germany, Japan, the Netherlands, Norway, Sweden, Switzerland, the UK and the USA. The CIF emphasizes the need to support the poor and vulnerable, particularly in LDCs. The CIF therefore includes programmes with a total funding of $6.1 billion.

The aim of the fund is low carbon development and developing a climate resilient economy. The World Bank administrates the CIF and its funding; however, other multilateral development banks are also involved in the CIF. The CIF is divided into the Clean Technology Fund (CTF) and the Strategic Climate Fund (SCF), which will be briefly elaborated below (World Bank, 2009a).

The **Clean Technology Fund** provides additional funding to finance the demonstration, deployment and transfer of low carbon technologies for mitigation. The main emphasis is on the power sector, the transport sector and energy efficiency. The World Bank advocates that the private sector will be mainly targeted in this approach, while the public sector will need to be reformed to allow more private sector action. The goal is to integrate the funded actions into national plans and policies in developing countries. The World Bank uses concessional financing instruments, like grants and concessional loans, and risk mitigation instruments for funding these technologies (World Bank, 2008a).

The **Strategic Climate Fund** is also administrated by the World Bank under the CIF. It funds pilot projects for new approaches, such as sectoral approaches to climate change and technology transfer. Its overall objectives are to provide financing for pilot approaches, provide lessons, encourage international cooperation, scale up action for climate change mitigation and adaptation, support sustainable development, sustainable forestry and to focus on highly vulnerable countries. Key pilots are in the fields of renewable energy, forestry and climate resilience (World Bank 2008b, c). Eligibility for funding under the CIF are for developing countries which (1) qualify for ODA; and (2) have a lending programme and/or policy dialogue with the World Bank or other multilateral development banks.

In addition to the CIF, three programmes on climate change have been established under the Strategic Framework on Climate Change and Development of the World Bank: the Scaling-up Renewable Energy Programme (SREP), which specifically targets low income countries; the Pilot Programme for Climate Resilience (PPCR); and the Forest Investment Program (FIP) (World Bank, 2009a).

The **Scaling-Up Renewable Energy Program (SREP)** for LDCs is of particular interest for low carbon development. SREP has a budget of $250 million from various donors, which is available for low carbon development in low income countries. It is often argued that the greatest barriers and challenges to tapping the high renewable energy potential in developing countries is a lack of access to capital, the need to engage the private sector to increase investments in renewable energy, a lack of affordability of current technologies and weak enabling environments. The objective of the SREP is therefore to facilitate the transformation to low carbon energy pathways in low income countries and to tap their renewable energy potential as an alternative to fossil fuels. Other goals of SREP are to scale up the deployment of renewable energy in target countries, encourage improved energy provision, increase access to modern forms of energy – particularly electricity, achieve a high leverage of SREP funding and mainstream renewable energy in national energy provision. The fund focuses both on providing access to electricity for the poor and promoting income-generating activities. Small-scale renewable energy technology is being promoted such as biomass energy technology, solar, hydro, wind and geothermal energy technology, with an average capacity of below 10 MW. Both off-grid and grid-connected applications are being promoted for electricity generation to households and industries. Thermal renewable energy for industry, agriculture, commerce and households are also promoted. Financing is achieved through aid, grants, loans and credit enhancement (World Bank 2009b, c).

In addition to these public and public–private funding options, there are a wide range of private funding options for low carbon development. Of the estimated $45 trillion required for investing in low carbon technologies to halve global emissions by 2050, a large share will have to come from the private sector (IEA, 2010). **Private firms**, such as energy firms and transport firms, play a pivotal role in levering finance for low carbon development, investing in low carbon technologies and carrying out research, development and deployment of low carbon technologies and innovation. Key firms are for example wind energy and solar energy firms and producers of electric and hybrid vehicles. Chapter 8 elaborates in more detail the role that firms play for low carbon innovation and technology transfer.

The discussion section elaborated key issues relevant for understanding the ideas of environmental economics and the economics of low carbon development. This was followed by an overview of the finance options for achieving the transition to a low carbon economy, with a focus on carbon markets as well as investments and ODA. The next section presents a critique of low carbon economics and finance.

Low carbon economics and finance: a critique

There are many critical issues concerning the attempt to integrate climate change mitigation into a distinct market framework.

Let us start with the Stern Review. The Stern Review was praised and criticized at the same time. The criticism came particularly from various economists who question the methodological approaches of the study. The main criticism is that the figures for the financial damage of climate change could be estimated too high, while the figures for the cost of mitigation could be estimated too low. Other well-known studies suggest that the financial damage of climate change is in the range of +1 to −5 per cent of global GDP each year (compared to −5–20 per cent of global GDP advocated by the Stern Review) and the cost of mitigation is estimated in the range of 0 to −7.5 per cent of global GDP (compared to +1 to nearly −4 per cent of global GDP suggested by the Stern Review) (Dasgupta, 2006; Dietz *et al.*, 2007; Helm and Hepburn, 2009; Mendelsohn, 2007; OECD, 2009; Tol, 2006; Tol and Yohe, 2006; Weitzman, 2007). In addition, the Review's methodology was criticized as it works with existing predictions of climate impacts and existing cost estimates. The study does not calculate new figures from scratch, but uses existing figures from earlier studies.

Also, the financial damage from climate change impacts seems very high. Some economists claim that there is a risk of double-counting in these figures and that the Review uses a discount rate that is very low. The discount rate suggests that a given sum of money today is generally considered more valuable than the same amount of money in the future. This is based on the facts that (1) future generations are assumed to be richer than today's generation due to economic growth; (2) people value money higher if it is given to them today rather than in the future. This has the following implications. (1) A high discount rate therefore assumes that economic growth will increase substantially in the future. This assumption might have been correct before the financial crisis in 2008, however due to the continuing recession in many parts of the developed world a lower discount rate might be more sensible as it implies lower economic growth. (2) The Stern Review does not value the welfare of current generations differently than the welfare of future generations, hence implying an element of inter-generational justice in relation to climate change. Both assumptions were criticized by other studies (see e.g. Giddens, 2009; Helm and Hepburn, 2009; Weitzman, 2007).

In addition, it has been criticized that the damage estimates in the analysis do not take adaptation into account. Adapting to climatic impacts can be a way of living with climate change and reducing some of its negative impacts. In general, it can be assumed that the financial losses are higher when people and countries do not adapt to climate change. On the other hand, the financial losses can be lower when people and countries adapt to climate change and thereby reduce some of the risks associated with climate change. Other methodological criticisms are related to the low per capita growth rate of the economy, hence assuming weaker and less resilient economies and the short time horizon of the study, which does not enable longer-term projections. Despite this criticism, the time projections for the scenarios in the Stern Review are for 2100, which is in line with the scenarios of the IPCC (Dasgupta, 2006; Dietz *et al.*, 2007; Helm and Hepburn, 2009; Mendelsohn, 2007; Tol, 2006; Tol and Yohe, 2006).

Despite this criticism of the methodological approach and the ranges of specific figures, there is strong support from climate scientists and climate economics with regard to the findings and the message of the Stern Review. The Stern Review remains the most important and most cited report on the economics of climate change and it is commonly accepted nowadays that actions that delay mitigation will not only risk dangerous climate change, but also entail costs that will be higher in the long run than the costs for mitigating climate change.

The second criticism goes beyond the Stern Review and relates more broadly to the market approach for low carbon development. Some scholars question whether market solutions can be effective in mitigating climate change and achieving low carbon development. Storm brings up the problematic issue that many neo-liberal scholars and organizations believe that capitalism can easily correct its fundamental ecological flaws through what is known as the 'invisible hand' of the market[5] (Storm, 2009). This is, however, questionable and heavily criticized by scholars such as Storm and Foster *et al.* Foster *et al.* (2009:1085) argue that the global capitalist economy is the primary driving force of climate change and that the current capitalist system needs to be replaced by a system focused on 'meeting human needs in a sustainable way' to mitigate climate change and achieve low carbon development. Alternatives to market approaches are therefore vividly discussed, such as global carbon taxes or taxes on financial transactions. Investments in low carbon technologies could also be financed through compensation payments of developed countries that pay off their carbon debt to developing countries (Bello and George, 2009). Scholars such as Lohman (2009), Galbraith (2008) and Speth (2008) argue not only for higher global carbon taxes and higher investment in low carbon energy technology, but that there is a need to replace the market 'by alternative democratic co-ordination and decision-making mechanisms' for achieving low carbon development (Storm, 2009: 1026). One could even go one step further and argue that low carbon development can only be sustained by low growth, no growth or even a contraction of growth in developed countries. This is in line with the discussion on 'prosperity without growth' brought up by Tim Jackson (2009) and the Sustainable Development Commission (2009), which argues for prosperity within the ecological limits of a finite planet. This reflects earlier ideas of key thinkers of ecological economics, such as Herman Daly who argued there are no restrictions to human well-being, but there are limits to economic growth (Daly, 1997) as well as Meadows *et al.* who discuss the limits to growth from an environmental perspective (Meadows *et al.*, 1972, 2004). Nevertheless four decades after these ideas of a more sustainable economy were first developed, mainstream economics and the current global order is still struggling to find more sustainable approaches to economics, development and progress. During these four decades climate change has however become a pressing global challenge that requires urgent action.

Conclusion

This chapter discussed the economics of climate change mitigation and a low carbon economy. Based on the findings of the Stern Review and other recent studies, the chapter concludes that early mitigation actions are likely to outweigh the costs of climate change (Dasgupta, 2006; Stern, 2006; Tol, 2006; Tol and Yohe, 2006; Weitzman, 2007; Dietz *et al.*, 2007; Mendelsohn, 2007; Helm and Hepburn, 2009; OECD, 2009; Jakob *et al.*, 2011).

However, urgent action is required, as the likelihood of avoiding dangerous climate change is becoming less likely the longer we wait (Richardson *et al.*, 2009). Delaying global action on climate change mitigation until 2020 or later could increase the costs by at least half (Jakob *et al.*, 2011). The chapter further discussed a range of options for financing low carbon development, particularly carbon markets and mechanisms such as the CDM, emissions trading and REDD+, as well as investments and ODA for enabling the transition to a low carbon economy, such as the UNFCCC Green Climate Fund, and financing by multilateral organizations such as the World Bank and the private sector.

The chapter then discussed the main criticisms of the Stern Review, which are particularly related to the choice of methodological approaches and the ranges of specific figures, such as the financial damage of climate change and the cost of mitigation. Despite these criticisms, there is strong support from climate scientists and climate economics with regard to the findings and the message of the Stern Review. The Stern Review remains the most important and most cited report on the economics of climate change and it is commonly accepted nowadays that actions that delay mitigation will not only risk dangerous climate change, but also entail costs that will be higher in the long run than the costs for mitigating climate change. Finally, the chapter discussed some broader issues relating to economic growth and the fact that development and growth are both part of the solution for tackling climate change, but also its cause.

References

Ackerman, F. and Stanton, E. A. (2011) *Climate Economics: The State of the Art*. Somerville: Stockholm Environmental Institute.

Asian Development Bank (ADB) (2009) *The Economics of Climate Change in Southeast Asia: a Regional Review*. Manila: ADB.

Bello, W. and George, S. (2009) A new, green, democratic deal. *New Internationalist*, 419. Available at: http://www.tni.org/detail_page.phtml?act_id=19499&username=guest@tni.org&password=9999&publish=Y (accessed 24 October 2012).

Constanza, R., d'Arge, R., de Groot, R., Farber, S., Grasso, M., Hannon, B. *et al.* (1997) The value of the world's ecosystem services and natural capital. *Nature*, 387, 253–60.

Daly, H. (1991) *Toward a Steady-state Economy*. Washington, DC: Island Press.

Daly, H. (1997) *Beyond Growth: The Economics of Sustainable Development*. Boston, MA: Beacon Press.

Dasgupta, P. (2006) Comments on the Stern Review's economics of climate change. Available at: http://econ.tau.ac.il/papers/research/Partha%20Dasgupta%20on%20Stern%20Review.pdf (accessed 24 October 2012)

Department for International Development (DfID) (2009) Eliminating world poverty: building our common future. DfID White Paper. London: DfID.

Dietz, S., Hope, C. and Patmore, N. (2007) Some economics of 'dangerous' climate change: reflections on the Stern Review. *Global Environmental Change*, 17(3–4), 311–25.

EU Commission (2005) MEMO/05/84 questions & answers on emissions trading and national allocation plans. Brussels: EU Commission.

Foley, D. (2006) *Adam's Fallacy. A Guide to Economic Theology*. Cambridge: The Belknap Press.

Foster, J. B., Clark, B. and York, R. (2009) The Midas effect: a critique of climate change economics. *Development and Change*, 40(6), 1085–97.

Galbraith, J. K. (2008) *The Predator State. How Conservatives Abandoned the Free Market and Why Liberals Should Too*. New York: Free Press.

Giddens, A. (2009) *The Politics of Climate Change*. Cambridge: Polity Press.

Helm, D. and Hepburn, C. (2009) *The Economics and Politics of Climate Change*. Oxford: Oxford University Press.

Ho, P. (2006) Trajectories for greening in China: theory and practice. *Development and Change*, 37(1), 3–28.

International Energy Agency (IEA) (2010) Energy poverty: how to make modern energy access universal? Special early excerpt of the World Energy Outlook 2010 for the UN General Assembly on the Millennium Development Goals. IEA, Paris. Available at: http://www.unido.org/fileadmin/user_media/Services/Energy_and_Climate_Change/Renewable_Energy/Publications/weo2010_poverty.pdf (accessed 24 October 2012).

Jackson, T. (2009) *Prosperity Without Growth*. Abingdon: Earthscan.

Jakob, M., Luderer, G., Steckel, J., Tavoni, M. and Monjon, S. (2011) Time to act now? Assessing the costs of delaying climate measures and benefits of early action. *Climatic Change*, 114, 79–99.

Meadows, D. H., Meadows, D. and Randers, J. (1972) *Limits to Growth*. Universe Books, New York.

Meadows, D.H., Randers, J. and Meadows, D. (2004) *Limits to Growth: the 30-Year Update*. White River Junction, VT: Chelsea Green Publishing Company.

Mendelsohn, R. O. (2007) A critique of the Stern Report. *Regulation*, 29(4), 42–6.

Nordhaus, W. D. (2007) A Review of The Stern Review on the economics of climate change. *Journal of Economic Literature*, 45(3), 686–702.

Organisation for Economic Cooperation and Development (OECD) (2009) The economics of climate change mitigation. Policies and options for global action beyond 2012. Paris: OECD.

Pye, S., Watkiss, P., Savage, M. and Blyth, W. (2010) The economics of low carbon, climate resilient patterns of growth in developing countries: a review of the evidence. Available at: http://sei-international.org/mediamanager/documents/Publications/Climate/economics_low_carbon_growth_report.pdf (accessed 18 October 2012).

Richardson, K., Steffen, W., Schellnhuber, H. J., Alcamo, J., Barker, T., Kammen, D. M., Leemans, R., Liverman, D., Munasinghe, M., Osman-Elasha, B., Stern, N. and Wæver, O. (2009) Climate change. Global risks, challenges and decisions. Synthesis Report. Available at: http://climate-congress.ku.dk/pdf/synthesisreport/ (accessed 24 October 2012).

Skjaerseth, J. B. and Wettestad, J. (2008) *EU Emissions Trading. Initiation, Decision-Making and Implementation*. Ashgate, Aldershot.

Speth, J. G. (2008) *The Bridge at the Edge of the World. Capitalism, the Environment and Crossing from Crisis to Sustainability*. New Haven, CT and London: Yale University Press.

Stern, N. (2006) Stern Review: the economics of climate change. Executive Summary. Available at: http://www.hm-treasury.gov.uk/d/Executive_Summary.pdf (accessed 24 October 2012).

Stern, N. (2007) *The Economics of Climate Change. The Stern Review*. Cambridge: Cambridge University Press.

Stockholm Environmental Institute (SEI) (2009) *The Economics of Climate Change: Kenya*. Oxford: SEI.

Storm, S. (2009) Capitalism and climate change: can the invisible hand adjust the natural thermostat? *Development and Change*, 40(6), 1011–38.

Sustainable Development Commission (SDC) (2009) *Prosperity without Growth*. London: SDC.

The Economics of Ecosystems and Biodiversity Study (TEEB) (2010) The Economics of Ecosystems and Biodiversity. Mainstreaming the economics of nature: a synthesis of the approach, conclusions and recommendations of TEEB. Available at: http://data.iucn.org/dbtw-wpd/edocs/2010-051.pdf (accessed 24 October 2012).

Tol, R. (2006) The Stern Review of the economics of climate change: a comment. *Energy and Environment*, 17(6), 977–81.

Tol, R. and Yohe, G. (2006) A review of the Stern Review. Available at: http://www.fnu.zmaw.de/fileadmin/fnu-files/publication/tol/RM551.pdf (accessed 24 October 2012).

UN-REDD (2010) MRV and monitoring for REDD+ implementation. Available at: http://www.un-redd.org/Newsletter10/MRV_and_Monitoring/tabid/4864/language/en-US/Default.aspx (accessed 24 October 2012).

UN-REDD (2012) About REDD+. Available at: http://www.un-redd.org/AboutREDD/tabid/582/Default.aspx (accessed 24 October 2012).

United Nations Environmental Programme (UNEP) (2011) *Towards a Green Economy. Pathways to Sustainable Development and Poverty Reduction.* Nairobi: UNEP.

UNEP (2012a) UNEP Risoe CDM pipeline analysis and database. Available at: http://www.cdmpipeline.org/overview.htm (accessed 24 October 2012).

UNEP (2012b) UNEP Risoe JI pipeline analysis and database. Available at: http://www.cdmpipeline.org/ji-projects.htm (accessed 24 October 2012).

United Nations Framework Convention on Climate Change (UNFCCC) (2009) Copenhagen Accord. Available at: http://unfccc.int/resource/docs/2009/cop15/eng/11a01.pdf (accessed 24 October 2012).

UNFCCC (2010) Cancun Agreements. Available at: http://unfccc.int/resource/docs/2010/cop16/eng/07a01.pdf#page=2 (accessed 24 October 2012).

UNFCCC (2011) Green Climate Fund – report of the Transitional Committee. Draft decision -/CP.17. Available at: http://unfccc.int/files/meetings/durban_nov_2011/decisions/application/pdf/cop17_gcf.pdf (accessed 24 October 2012).

Weber, M. (1953) *The Protestant Ethic and The Spirit of Capitalism.* New York: Scribner.

Weitzman, M. L. (2007) A review of the Stern Review on the economics of climate change. *Journal of Economic Literature,* 45(3), 703–24.

World Bank (2008a) The Clean Technology Fund. Washington, DC: World Bank.

World Bank (2008b) Strategic Climate Fund SCF. Available at: http://siteresources.worldbank.org/INTCC/Resources/Strategic_Climate_Fund_final.pdf (accessed 24 October 2012).

World Bank (2008c) Governance Framework for the Strategic Climate Fund. Washington, DC: World Bank.

World Bank (2008d) Development and Climate Change: A Strategic Framework for the World Bank Group. Available at: http://siteresources.worldbank.org/DEVCOMMINT/Documentation/21928837/DC2008-0009(E)ClimateChange.pdf (accessed 24 October 2012).

World Bank (2009a) Strategic Climate Fund Program SCF for Scaling-up Renewable Energy in Low Income Countries (SREP). Preliminary design document. Climate Investment Funds. CIF/SREPWG/2. Washington, DC: World Bank.

World Bank (2009b) Preliminary Design Document. SCF Program for Scaling-Up Renewable Energy in Low Income Countries (SREP). CIF/SREPWG/2. Washington, DC: World Bank.

World Resources Institute (WRI) (2011) Have countries delivered fast start climate finance? Available at: http://www.wri.org/stories/2011/05/have-countries-delivered-fast-start-climate-finance (accessed 24 October 2012).

Further reading

Ackerman, F. and Stanton, E. A. (2011) *Climate Economics: The State of the Art.* Somerville: Stockholm Environmental Institute.

Dietz, S., Hope, C. and Patmore, N. (2007) Some economics of 'dangerous' climate change: reflections on the Stern Review. *Global Environmental Change,* 17(3–4), 311–25.

Foster, J. B., Clark, B. and York, R. (2009) The Midas effect: a critique of climate change economics. *Development and Change,* 40(6), 1085–97.

Helm, D. and Hepburn, C. (2009) *The Economics and Politics of Climate Change.* Oxford: Oxford University Press.

Stern, N. (2006) Stern Review: the economics of climate change. Executive Summary. Available at: http://www.hm-treasury.gov.uk/d/Executive_Summary.pdf (accessed 24 October 2012).

Notes

1   Note that climate scientists estimate that for a 50 per cent chance of achieving the 2°C target to avoid dangerous climate change, a global atmospheric CO_2 equivalent concentration of 400–450 ppm needs to be achieved by 2100 (Richardson *et al.*, 2009; Pye *et al.*, 2010). Nevertheless the

Stern Review refers to the costs for stabilizing CO_2 equivalent concentration at 550 ppm, which is more likely to result in a 3°C warming, rather than a 2°C warming, according to recent scientific studies.

2   The difficulty in decoupling economic growth from GHG emissions has been discussed in Chapter 1.

3   There is a plethora of financial options and mechanisms for mitigation and low carbon development, however not all can be discussed here. This chapter is therefore limited to the most important and most well-known financial options.

4   The prerequisite for 'new and additional' finance in relation to existing ODA means that existing development assistance for other sectors, such as for education and health, should not be reduced at the expense of financial assistance for tackling climate change. Nevertheless this is difficult to enforce and some governments have indicated that their climate finance might come from existing ODA budgets, rather than new and additional budgets.

5   The 'invisible hand' is a term that was coined by the economist Adam Smith, who lived in the 18th century, to describe the self-regulating nature of the marketplace. It is a theory that assumes that a free market regulates itself so that demand and supply are in balance and efficient levels of production, consumption and distribution of goods in society is achieved. Today mainstream economics, such as neo-liberal economics, builds on the theory of the 'invisible hand'.

7 The future of carbon markets

Carbon trading, the clean development mechanism and beyond

Markus Lederer

Carbon markets have become one of the pillars of climate politics. The chapter describes how the idea of using market instruments in the field of climate change developed, why it became popular and what kind of markets exist. In a second step individual markets (the EU ETS, national and subnational approaches, the CDM and voluntary markets) are analysed and their pros and cons are compared. Finally, the chapter provides a short overview of recent developments towards sectoral approaches. The argument of the chapter is that carbon markets share many characteristics of other financial markets but they also are different in some important and potentially beneficial ways.

Introduction

Carbon markets are a crucial part in the attempt to tackle dangerous climate change. The idea of including market mechanisms for mitigation purposes is, however, highly controversial and has led to various controversies about the pros and cons of using market mechanisms.[1] This chapter, therefore, provides an overview of what carbon markets are, of how they have developed and whether they might contribute to low carbon development in the future.

The idea of internalizing negative environmental externalities through market mechanisms goes back to the US American economist Coase (1960) and was worked out in detail by the Canadian Dales (1968). First practical instances of setting up such markets were in the field of pollution control in the US in the 1970s and later in the US Acid Rain Program in the early 1990s. In the same decade Shell and British Petroleum (BP), as well as the UK and Denmark also set up small trading schemes and internationally the Montreal Protocol for the first time made use of an ETS in order to reduce ozone depleting substances. Ever since, economists, politicians as well as bureaucrats working on climate change, hail the use of financial instruments as one of most promising ways to stop the increase of GHG emissions efficiently and effectively (two of the strongest advocates for using market instruments are Stern, 2007; Eliasch, 2008). With the Kyoto Protocol signed in 1997, state as well as non-state actors realized that various carbon markets could soon become a reality and started to engage in setting up and preparing for the trade of carbon. In this context it is important to understand that carbon markets can come about in two ways (see Box 7.1).

Box 7.1 Cap-and-trade and baseline-and-credit systems

Cap-and-trade systems combine a political decision of how much a particular sector (or country in the case of the EU) is allowed to emit (= the cap) and the possibility to trade saved emission rights in the forms of certificates or carbon credits. An ETS thus limits the quantity of possible emissions, but it does not directly affect the price, as an emission tax would do. The European Emission Trading System (EU ETS; see below for details) as well as the Kyoto Protocol's International Emission Trading (which never really took off and is thus not covered in this article) are both cap-and-trade systems. In *baseline-and-credit systems* companies reduce their emissions against a specific baseline (most likely a BAU projection) and can then sell the saved emissions to firms who emit more than they are allowed to by their baseline. The Kyoto Protocol's CDM and JI are both baseline-and-credit systems and they can be linked to cap-and-trade systems as it is done through the linking directive of the EU, which allows CERs issued under the CDM rulebook to be transferred into the EU ETS. Again, however, without scarcity no market can develop as there will be no incentive to 'produce' emission rights and thus to deviate from a BAU baseline.

There are several reasons for the popularity of using carbon markets ranging from (1) successful attempts in national markets, in particular the US market for sulphur dioxide, that provide positive examples (for a good overview of the development, see Voß, 2007); (2) an ideological hegemony of 'liberal environmentalism' (Bernstein, 2002); (3) a culture of commodification (Levin and Espeland, 2002); (4) the development of a winning coalition of public and private actors (Paterson, 2011); to (5) the simple fact that a strong lobby has developed in the City of London and in other financial centres that tries to profit from such new markets (Spash, 2009). Thus today carbon markets are well established and can be seen as the very representation of 'climate capitalism' (Newell and Paterson, 2010) in which one can even claim that the business of climate has now become more important than the politics of climate (Bernstein *et al.*, 2010).

Current practices for carbon markets

Today we do not have one common global carbon market, but rather a highly fragmented field of carbon market practices evolving in various places. In a recent overview, Betsill and Hoffman counted 33 instances of emissions trading taking place or being planned (Betsill and Hoffmann, 2011). Carbon markets are not only proliferating, but they are also becoming bigger. Thus from 2005 to 2008 carbon assets were one of the fastest growing financial asset classes that were traded by more than 80 investment companies in 2008 (Lohmann, 2009a). In the same year, the overall size of all carbon markets – primary project-based transactions, secondary market and allowance markets – reached an astonishing US$135 billion, doubling from 2007, when the market was worth 'only' $76 billion (Capoor and Ambrosi, 2009: 1). Since the end of 2008, the market has, however, been growing much more slowly, primarily due to the repercussions of the financial crisis. In 2009, the overall market only grew marginally to $143.7 billion and in 2010 it shrank for the first time to $141.9 billion (World Bank, 2011: 9). Some have, therefore, claimed that carbon has become the world's worst performing commodity (Journalist Gerard Wynn, quoted in Friends of the Earth, 2011: 3), but this seems to be a great exaggeration for the market as a whole as well as for individual carbon market segments.

The European Emission Trading System (EU ETS)[2]

The EU ETS is the biggest cap-and-trade system initially covering some 11,500 facilities (in 2005) with a total of 6.5 Gt of CO_2 emissions per year (EU Commission, 2005; Skjaerseth and Wettestad, 2008). It is a regional market, but due to its size – generating almost \$120 billion in 2009 and the same amount in 2010 – it dominates all other markets and in 2010 has a share of about 97 per cent of all carbon trading. The idea of setting up such a system came after it became evident that no carbon tax could be established within the European Community. Due to strong pressure from individual member states but also corporate entities, the European Commission pushed for a market instrument in order to get the Kyoto Protocol off the ground (Gupta and Ringius, 2001; Schreurs and Tiberghien, 2007).

The EU ETS' first phase ran until 2008 and was considered by everyone to be a test phase in preparation for the 'real market' and a symbol for the EU's commitment in international climate politics (Lindenthal, 2009; Oberthür and Pallemaerts, 2010: 42). It was thus no surprise that some design flaws, like a decentralized over-allocation of allowances that generated massive windfall profits particularly for power companies, were present. However, in the second phase, the Member States set more stringent caps and the European Commission pushed hard to reduce Member States' allocation proposals even more (Ellerman *et al.*, 2010; Egenhofer, 2011). Similarly, for the third phase from 2013 onwards, a new common and ever-decreasing level will be established (linear decrease of 1.74 per cent annually), and gradually all allowances at least for the power sector will be auctioned off (Skjaerseth and Wettestad, 2010; Egenhofer, 2011). Half of all revenues generated from future auctions shall be reinvested into domestic or developing countries' efforts to tackle climate change. The system will also be extended to cover more sectors like aluminium and chemical productions as well as more types of gases (e.g. nitrous oxide from fertilizers). Finally, the EU ETS will be less open to inflows from credits from other markets, particularly from the CDM, as it will only accept credits generated in LDCs. This is partially due to a given oversupply of emission credits within the EUT ETS, but also due to political considerations that many CDM credits are considered to be neither additional nor initiating sustainable development practices in their host countries (see below for details).

The jury is still out as to whether or not the system has been effective, as CO_2 emissions are increasing in most European countries, although the EU ETS is certainly a functioning allowance market. This increase in emissions can be witnessed even in those sectors that are under the cap, although the growth is less dramatic here than in those sectors that are outside the cap, and this can be seen as a small achievement by the scheme. It would, nevertheless, be exaggerating to claim that the EU ETS has led Europe onto a low carbon development path, but neither can the argument be upheld that the use of market instruments has been completely ineffective. The market is still quite unstable and has problems regarding its transparency, as the multi-billion-carousel value-added-tax (VAT) fraud scheme in 2009 showed (World Bank, 2010b). Similarly, various cyber-thefts of EU allowances in national registries in 2010–11 did not raise confidence in the system (World Bank, 2011). The biggest problem of the EU ETS is, however, the low price for EU Allowances (EUA) due to reduced demand from crisis-hit industries (Egenhofer, 2011). This also hinders any progressive development of global carbon markets, as the last thing that the biggest single carbon market needs at the very moment is an increase in supply. Possible solutions like the introduction of floor prices or the set up of a European Carbon Bank are currently only speculative.

National and subnational markets and market initiatives

Other regional or national ETS are already operating or are being launched in New Zealand, Australia, Switzerland, Canada and Japan. But also non-Annex I countries are active (for an overview, see Sterk and Mersmann, 2011). For example, South Korea is currently setting up a voluntary trading scheme that is supposed to evolve into a full-fledged cap-and-trade system by 2015. Also China has declared its willingness to use trading mechanisms at the provincial and city level. Developing countries have also used other financial instruments like subsidies or feed-in tariffs in order to support mitigation initiatives. Prominent examples are Brazil's ethanol programme or China's push towards wind energy, which both can be qualified as successful attempts at green industrial policies (Buen and Castro, 2012).

On a subnational scale, we primarily witness a fragmentation of trading systems in the USA like the Regional Greenhouse Gas Initiative that started in 2008, California's carbon trading scheme set up by former governor Arnold Schwarzenegger, and the Midwestern Regional Greenhouse Gas Accord, which all developed simultaneously (Flachsland *et al.*, 2008: 2; Schreurs, 2008). Paterson argues that these regional trading schemes put some pressure on the national level and thus could lead to the set up of a national system (Paterson, 2011), but one can of course also argue that the more or less successful schemes at the subnational level allow the federal government to stay inactive.

The CDM

The CDM is one of the three flexible mechanisms of the Kyoto Protocol (JI and emission trading being the other two), allowing Annex I parties (industrialized countries) to implement emission reduction or sequestration projects in non-Annex I countries (developing countries). The emission reductions that are achieved can be used as offsets that count towards the emission targets of Annex I entities (countries and companies). The CDM is of particular interest as it is (1) the largest project-based market with about 3742 projects registered and more than 7500 more in the pipeline (UNEP, 2012); (2) the strongest link between developing and developed countries in the climate change regime (Grubb *et al.*, 1999; Fuhr and Lederer, 2009); (3) linked to the EU ETS and thus a credit of the CDM (= CER) can be exchanged for an emission allowance in the EU; and (4) the most criticized form of carbon governance (see below). The working of the CDM is explained in Figure 7.1.

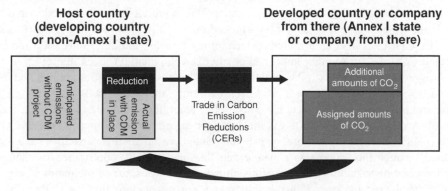

Figure 7.1 How the CDM works

The aims of the CDM are first to provide flexibility as well as cost efficiency, and second to initiate sustainable development practices in non-Annex I countries. It evolved from a public–private partnership scheme into a highly efficient market mechanism (Benecke *et al.*, 2008) that is now being hosted in 80 countries, although China, India, Brazil and South Korea take up the lion's share of about 90 per cent of issued CERs (Michaelowa and Buen, 2012: 24). The CDM is primarily governed by the UNFCCC, but as the secretariat cannot handle the monitoring, verification and registration of the mechanism, a regulatory agency – labelled the Executive Board – has been set up. The Executive Board is again supported by various panels and working groups, as well as by private entities that have been accredited for verification and validation exercises (Designated Operating Entities, DOEs). The process from setting up an individual project to the issuance of the first credits is a highly bureaucratic one.

The effectiveness of the CDM – in terms of actually allowing a cost-efficient and real reduction of GHGS – is highly controversial. Some argue that, particularly in emerging economies and in some sectors (e.g. industrial gases), very high efficiency gains have been made and various new renewable energy projects have been supported (Carbon Trust, 2009). Others claim that issues of non-additionality, underperformance, fraud, inequity and inefficiency abound (see also Box 7.2).[3]

Box 7.2 Critique of the CDM

The CDM has been criticized for various aspects. The following is just a selection of the most important issues:

1   Offsetting emission reductions in developing countries is similar to selling indulgences in the Middle Ages – an easy way out, without any change of lifestyle.
2   CDM projects are often non-additional, e.g. they would have happened anyhow as the amount of revenues generated is generally too low to initiate investments.
3   The CDM does not initiate low carbon development, as host countries – who are in charge of doing so – do not really control whether projects are leading to sustainable development.
4   The CDM does not promote development, as it is regionally biased towards emerging economies.
5   Transaction costs are too high and the projects are too small to really bring about significant change.

Nevertheless, the market has delivered low cost options in producing emission reductions on a significant scale, although it has not only picked the so-called low-hanging fruits (Castro, 2011). The CDM has also contributed to technology transfer, although only on a modest scale (UNFCCC, 2010). Another important positive development has been the set-up of so-called Programs-of-activities (PoAs) in which various small-scale activities are bundled into larger ones so that transaction costs are lower. Currently, there are 706 PoAs in the CDM pipeline and although most projects are again set in emerging economies like China, India and South Africa, the share of LDCs is much higher regarding PoAs than 'classical' CDM projects (UNEP, 2012). Furthermore, one should not underestimate that capacities have been developed through the process as a whole and this has partially contributed to changed perceptions and understanding of dangerous climate change in some of the major emerging economies (Fuhr and Lederer, 2009). It thus seems fair to conclude that the CDM worked much better than most optimists hoped for and that state as well as non-state actors learned a lot from setting up such an instrument, although it certainly is not a perfect mechanism.

The future of the CDM after COP17 in Durban is open: on the one hand, the prolongation of the Kyoto Protocol and the agreement to set up a new legally binding mechanism until 2015 allow the CDM or a CDM-like mechanism (see below) to continue. Furthermore, some minor reforms of the CDM were established, for example, it will in the future be possible to include CCS projects in the CDM, although civil society pressure against such projects has been rather high. More questionable is, however, where future demand will come from, as the EU ETS will only accept credits from low-income countries after 2012 and most national ETS that are being set up do not have provisions for including CERs.

The voluntary carbon market (VCM)

Voluntary emission reduction schemes and the use of voluntary offsets have been in use for at least 20 years (Hamilton *et al.*, 2008). In the beginning, offsets were primarily generated in the forestry sector, but later diversified into a high variety of projects on a global scale. It was only during the last five to ten years that the market developed rapidly, however – compared to the market segments discussed above – its size is still very small, with a turnover of $424 million in 2010 (Peters-Stanley *et al.*, 2011: iv).

For a long time, the voluntary market lacked any central regulatory oversight and was referred to as the 'Wild West' of offset trading (Fahrenthold and Mufson, 2007). In the meantime, various regulatory institutions were set up, and the time of 'anything goes' is over (Bumpus and Liverman, 2008; Newell and Paterson, 2010). Thus, various certification schemes have been developed, although the quality of the generated offsets and their environmental effectiveness can still be questioned (for a good overview, see Lovell, 2010). The developing regulatory structures all resemble private governance mechanisms, which function outside of the classical shadow of hierarchy provided by national legislation or international contracts. There is, however, a certain convergence towards the requirements of the CDM and the regulatory oversight of the voluntary market is parasitic to the compliance market (Lovell, 2010: 357).

The current market sends out partially contradictory signals. On the hand the voluntary carbon market (VCM) expanded by almost 30 per cent in comparison to 2009 primarily due to an increase in new forestry activities. The increase was generated by the hope that forestry credits could eventually enter new international or regional (California) compliance markets (World Bank, 2011: 54). On the other hand, the Chicago Climate Exchange (CCX) stopped trading at the end of 2010, partially due to the political failure to bring about any serious climate legislation in the US Congress (Peters-Stanley *et al.*, 2011: iii). For the future, it thus seems most realistic that voluntary markets will stay as niche markets.

Just another financial market?

Carbon markets have lots in common with financial markets: First, both markets are highly volatile and experience ups, downs and cyclical movements. For example the price for allowances on the EU ETS dropped an astonishing 75 per cent within 8 months from July 2008 to February 2009, but transactions for CERs also fell by 30 per cent from 2007 to 2008 (Capoor and Ambrosi, 2009: 2–6). Second, and for most commentators one of the most worrying parallels, is the dominance of derivative trading. As most existing carbon derivatives – like all other derivatives – are not traded on regular exchanges but rather over-the-counter and are thus under almost no regulatory oversight, there is fear that 'subprime carbon' and a 'carbon bubble' are developing (Chan, 2009: 3f). Third, delegation of regulatory authority to private agents is strong in both markets. An example are DOEs, whose duty is to validate and verify CDM projects. The institutional safeguards that are supposed to ensure that a conflict of interest between a DOE and a project developer does not come up are judged to be insufficient by almost all observers (de Sepibus, 2009: 14; Lund, 2010). So, similarly to rating agencies, there is a certain incentive not to rate your client too negatively, because otherwise one will never be allowed to do the job again (Chan, 2009: 6). Another parallel between the financial and carbon markets is that carbon markets like any other market can be captured be private interests. These similarities are striking and provide a strong back up for those who believe that carbon markets are, in the end, just another financial market with lots of problems to materialize (Böhm and Dabhi, 2009; Lohmann, 2009b).

There are, however, also some important and neglected differences between 'normal' financial markets and the carbon market: first and already mentioned, demand in the carbon market is completely artificial. Without government regulation that sets up a stringent cap on GHG emissions, there is neither demand for CERs nor for EUAs. As long as governments take up reduction commitments, the demand curve should therefore be stable and thus the volatility of the business cycle should be smaller. A second difference concerns regulation and the rather top-down mode in which at least the EU ETS and CDM have been governed. In the EU ETS, the European Commission influenced not only the set up but also the day-to-day business of the market. In the CDM, the Executive Board has evolved from a gentleman's club to a supervisory agency or, as Buen and Michaelowa claim, if carbon markets are the Wild West, the Executive Board is the sheriff (Michaelowa and Buen, 2012: 18). Carbon markets are therefore subject to a more hierarchical and bureaucratic oversight than other markets and although this increases transaction costs, it induces some stability into the system. The current state of carbon markets is thus less frightening than many commentators claim and particularly the strong role of international governance mechanisms has proven a strong asset that any future developments should build on.

The future of carbon markets? Scaling up!

One important issue for the future of carbon markets is how to scale up existing markets. Particularly, the idea of upgrading the CDM so that it becomes less bureaucratic, encompasses more than one project and thus delivers more credits that hopefully also initiate more sustainability has been around for more than 10 years (Sterk, 2011). It is also something that those states that never benefited from the CDM like low-income countries that have neither the kind of entrepreneurs nor the necessary financial basis for setting up projects have asked for.

Currently, three kind of approaches are discussed (see also Buen and Castro, 2012; Sterk, 2011: 116f): First, sectoral crediting, which would be based on absolute or intensity-based emissions thresholds on the sectoral level. If a developing country were then to keep its emissions within the agreed range, it would be compensated. If it fails to do so, it would not face penalties so that the thresholds are also labelled 'no-lose targets'. The idea is that developing countries are incentivized to reap potential low-hanging mitigation options fast and wholeheartedly. Second, sectoral trading based on a mandatory reduction target (a cap) that a developing country would have the legal obligation to fulfil. In the case of overperformance the country could again sell its credits, but contrary to sectoral crediting, it would have to buy missing credits in the case it underperforms. This could eventually lead into a global cap-and-trade system. Finally, crediting of NAMAs (see Box 7.3) taken up by developing countries for which they would receive financial contributions from industrialized countries (NAMA crediting) (Hayashi and Wehner, 2012).

Box 7.3 What is a NAMA?

NAMAs are policies that developing countries undertake in order to prevent dangerous climate change. These planned actions are communicated to a registry established at the UNFCCC secretariat and can thus be supported by Annex I countries or the international community. The concept of NAMAs was introduced in the Bali Action Plan in 2007 and has been reiterated as a major contribution of the developing world at every COP ever since. NAMAs on the one hand reflect the global South's insistence on sovereign decisions on how to cope with environmental issues and on the other hand, the international community has agreed that particularly least developed countries will need and will get support from Annex I states in order to fulfil their NAMAs. An independent NAMA registry can be found at http://namadatabase.org/.

All of these ideas have been discussed but so far no procedures have been established (Buen and Castro, 2012: 149), although COP17 agreed that 'new market mechanisms' should become part of the new legally binding agreement from 2015 onwards. We thus can expect quite controversial discussions during the next years on these mechanisms, in particular regarding monitoring, reporting and verification (MRV) as developing countries emphasize their sovereign right to define what an 'appropriate action' should be. The compromise that seems to develop at the negotiations states that domestic MRV are appropriate for unilateral NAMAs, whereas supported NAMAs, for example through revenues from carbon markets, require international MRV (Hayashi and Wehner, 2012: 169). Another potential point of contestation could be the relationship of NAMAs and the CDM, as it could happen that industrialized countries pay twice (once in a CDM project and once by supporting a NAMA) for the same emission reduction (Hayashi and Wehner, 2012: 175f).

One particularly interesting sectoral approach would be the introduction of REDD+ credits into the carbon market(s). REDD+ stands for Reducing Emissions from Degradation and Deforestation and is possibly a potentially highly effective and, at the same time, cost-efficient mitigation option, and has evolved into one of the pillars of the evolving international climate regime (for overviews of the debate around REDD+, see Angelsen, 2009; Corbera and Schroeder, 2011; Lederer, 2012a). It is, however, highly contentious whether any market mechanism should be established in this policy field. On the one hand, some argue that only through eventually linking REDD+ to markets could enough money be raised (Eliasch, 2008). But on the other hand, many are highly sceptical that markets could work in tropical forestry as the science is uncertain, the practical obstacles are too high and governance problems, particularly in many tropical forest countries, abound.[4]

Particularly the EU pushed at COP17 in Durban for the introduction of a sectoral approach, but the resistance of developing countries is still rather high, as they are afraid that sectoral approaches would ultimately lead to legally binding emission reduction targets also for emerging and developing countries. Much discussion was centred on how such a new market mechanism could lead to more 'sustainable practices', but as sectoral baselines are rather complicated, it remains open whether any new market mechanism is being introduced soon. Thus, any kind of sectoral approach will most likely not develop into the silver bullet that brings about radical change, as many of the difficulties that underlie the CDM will most likely stay. The same discussions about additionality, problematic baselines and potential fraud will thus reappear. Furthermore, it will be difficult to incentivize the private sector to engage in any sectoral scheme as strong incentives to free-ride are apparent (Buen and Castro, 2012: 155). Sectoral approaches will also be more state-centred than the CDM, as only developing countries' governments are able to take the responsibility of transforming a whole sector (Buen and Castro, 2012; Sterk, 2011). Finally, the question of who would finance NAMAs or buy the generated credits is no minor issue, as currently demand, particularly within the EU ETS, is very low. Without stringent caps in Annex I countries, neither sectoral approaches nor the classical CDM will make much of a difference.

Conclusion

Carbon markets are highly fragmented and there is not much of a chance that one global market for emissions will evolve in the near future. Although fragmented climate policies can in theory lead to innovation or the development of frontrunners (Biermann *et al.*, 2009; Zelli, 2011), most observers of carbon markets make a convincing claim that markets need a minimum amount of centralized coordination to work (Michaelowa, 2011). Furthermore, carbon markets need lots of skills in the bureaucratic process as well as entrepreneurs willing to take risks, and both need time to develop. Michaelowa's claim that in the near future the best we can expect is therefore a 'co-existence of project-based mechanisms, sectoral crediting and crediting of policies' (Michaelowa, 2011: 22) thus seems justified.

It also seems rather unrealistic to propagate new market mechanisms in other subfields of climate politics. Some have, for example, discussed the possibility of a market mechanism for adaptation (Michaelowa *et al.*, 2012, nicely describe challenges and chances of such a market), in particular as the future need for adaptation finance, particularly in developing countries, will be immense (World Bank, 2010a). Adaptation aid has been growing (Michaelowa and Michaelowa, 2012), but as long as there is no consensus on a basic 'adaptation unit' that would allow valid comparisons, trading and markets will not play a major role in this policy field. Similarly, the study on The Economics of Ecosystems and Biodiversity (TEEB) has raised discussions about an internalization of biodiversity costs (TEEB, 2010), but again the establishment of market mechanisms seems rather unlikely at this moment.

Have carbon markets thus already surpassed their high point and become an endangered species? Various current efforts to fund adaptation and mitigation projects, particularly in developing countries, are summarized under the label of 'climate finance' and thus do not explicitly rely on market-based instruments (Glemarec, 2011; Streck and Chagas, 2011). In the public debate climate finance is often juxtaposed to carbon markets, particularly by critical NGOs (Friends of the Earth, 2010). This does, however, underrate what carbon markets, particularly the EU ETS and the CDM have achieved in some sectors. It, furthermore, neglects that carbon markets have evolved into a significant source of carbon finance. Examples are the levy on CDM projects that flow into the adaptation fund or revenues from auctions of emission rights in the EU ETS that support climate change mitigation and adaptation projects also in developing countries.[5] Finally, both public finance and markets do need good governance to work and without stringent regulation as well as oversight neither form of financing the fight against dangerous climate change will be successful. Furthermore, all instruments towards low carbon development – market-based or not – completely depend on the political will that needs to be organized locally, nationally and internationally. Carbon market proponents as well as critics should thus be more modest about the role markets can play in avoiding or bringing about dangerous climate change. As Adam Smith knew markets are only means, never ends and it is thus up to the political process to define that the means get us to the ends.

References

Angelsen, A. (2009) Realising REDD+. Bogor: National Strategy and Policy Options.

Benecke, G., Friberg, L., Lederer, M. and Schröder, M. (2008) from public-private partnership to market. The Clean Development Mechanism (CDM) as a new form of governance in climate protection. SFB Governance Working Paper Series 10. Berlin: SFB.

Bernstein, S. (2002) Liberal environmentalism and global environmental governance. *Global Environmental Politics*, 2(3), 1–16.

Bernstein, S., Betsill, M. M., Hoffmann, M. and Paterson, M. (2010) A tale of two Copenhagens: carbon markets and climate governance. *Millennium*, 39(1), 161–73.

Betsill, M. M. and Hoffmann, M. J. (2011) The contours of 'cap and trade': the evolution of emissions trading systems for greenhouse gases. *Review of Policy Research*, 28(1), 83–106.

Biermann, F., Pattberg, P., van Asselt, H. and Zelli, F. (2009) The fragmentation of global governance architectures: a framework for analysis. *Global Environmenal Politics*, 9(4), 14–40.

Böhm, S. and Dabhi, S. (2009) *Upsetting the Offset. The Political Economy of Carbon Markets*. London: MayFlyBooks.

Boyd, E., Hultman, N. E., Roberts, T. J., Corbera, E., Ebeling, J., Liverman, D. M., Brown, K. *et al.* (2007) The Clean Development Mechanism: an assessment of current practice and future approaches for policy (Tyndall Working Paper 114). Norwich: Tyndall Centre for Climate Change Research.

Buen, J. and Castro, P. (2012) How Brazil and China have financed industry development and energy security initiatives that support mitigation objectives, in Michaelowa, A. (ed.) *Carbon Markets or Climate Finance? Low Carbon and Adaptation Investment Choices for the Developing World*. London: Routledge, pp. 53–91.

Bumpus, A. and Liverman, D. (2008) Accumulation by decarbonization and the governance of carbon offsets. *Economic Geography*, 84(2), 127–155.

Capoor, K. and Ambrosi, P. (2009) *State and Trends of the Carbon Market 2009*. Washington, DC: World Bank.

Carbon Trust (2009) *Global Carbon Mechanisms. Emerging Lessons and Implications*. London: Carbon Trust.

Castro, P. (2011) Does the CDM discourage emission reduction targets in advanced developing countries? *Climate Policy*, 12(2), 198–218.

Chan, M. (2009) *Subprime Carbon? Re-thinking the World's Largest New Derivative Market*. Washington, DC: Friends of the Earth.

Coase, R. H. (1960) The problem of social cost. *Journal of Law and Economics* 3, (1–44).

Corbera, E. and Schroeder, H. (2011) Governing and implementing REDD+. *Environmental Science and Policy*, 14(2), 89–99.

Dales, J. H. (1968) *Pollution, Property and Prices, an Essay in Policy-making and Economics*. Toronto: Toronto University Press.

de Sepibus, J. (2009) The environmental integrity of the CDM mechanism – a legal analysis of its institutional and procedural shortcomings. Bern: NCCR Working Paper 2009/24.

Egenhofer, C. (2011) Perspectives on the EU carbon market, in Lütken, S. and Olsen, K. H. (eds) Progressing towards post-2012 carbon markets. Perspectives Series 2011. Roskilde: UNEP Riso Centre, pp. 25–35.

Eliasch, J. (2008) *Eliasch Review: Climate Change: Financing Global Forests*. London: Office of the Prime Minister.

Ellerman, A. D., Convery, F. J. and Perthuis, C. D. (2010) *Pricing Carbon. The European Union Emission Trading System*. Cambridge: Cambridge University Press.

EU Commission (2005) MEMO/05/84 questions & answers on emissions trading and national allocation plans. Brussels: EU Commission.

Fahrenthold, D. and Mufson, S. (2007) Cost of saving the climate meets real-world hurdles. *Washington Post*, 16 August, p. A01.

Flachsland, C., Marschinski, R. and Edenhofer, O. (2008) *Global Trading versus Linking: Architectures for International Emissions Trading*. Potsdam: Potsdam Institute for Climate Impact Research.

Friends of the Earth (2010) *Clearing the Air. Moving on From Carbon Trading to Real Climate Solutions*. London: Friends of the Earth.

Friends of the Earth (2011) State of the forest carbon market: a critical perspective. Washington, DC: Friends of the Earth.

Fuhr, H. and Lederer, M. (2009) Varieties of carbon governance. *Journal of Environment and Development*, 18(4), 327–45.

Glemarec, Y. (2011) *Catalysing Climate Finance. A Guidebook on Policy and Financing Options to Support Green, Low-Emission and Climate-Resilient Development*. New York: UNDP.

Grubb, M., Vrolijk, C. and Brack, D. (1999) *The Kyoto Protocol: A Guide and Assessment*. London: Royal Institute of International Affairs.

Gupta, J. and Ringius, L. (2001) Climate leadership: reconciling ambition and reality. *International Environmental Agreements*, 1(2), 281–99.

Hamilton, K., Sjardin, M., Marcello, T. and Xu, G. (2008) *Forging a Frontier. State of the Voluntary Carbon Markets 2008*. Washington DC: Ecosystem Marketplace.

Hayashi, D. and Wehner, S. (2012) Mobilizing mitigation policies in the south through a financing mix, in Michaelowa, A. (ed.) *Carbon Markets or Climate Finance? Low Carbon and Adaptation Investment Choices for the Developing World*. London: Routledge, pp. 168–87.

Lederer, M. (2012a) REDD+ governance. *Wiley Interdisciplinary Reviews: Climate Change*, 3(1), 107–13.

Lederer, M. (2012b) Market making via regulation: the role of the state in carbon markets. *Regulation and Governance*, early view at: http://onlinelibrary.wiley.com/doi/10.1111/j.1748-5991.2012.01145.x/abstract.

Levin, P. and Espeland, W. N. (2002) Pollution futures: commensuration, commodification, and the market for air, in Hoffman, A., Ventresca, M. (eds) *Organizations, Policy and the Natural Environment: Institutional and Strategic Perspectives*. Stanford, CA: Stanford University Press, pp. 119–147.

Lindenthal, A. (2009) *Leadership im Klimaschutz. Die Rolle der Europäischen Union in der internationalen Umweltpolitik*. Campus, Frankfurt.

Lohmann, L. (2009a) Neoliberalism and the calculable world: the rise of the carbon trading, in Böhm, S. and Dabhi, S. (eds) *Upsetting the Offset. The Political Economy of Carbon Markets*. London: MayFlyBooks, pp. 25–40.

Lohmann, L. (2009b) Regulatory challenges for financial and carbon markets. *Carbon & Climate Law Review*, 3(2), 161–71.

Lovell, H. C. (2010) Governing the carbon offset market. Wires Climate Change. *Wiley's Interdisciplinary Reviews*, 1, 353–62.

Lund, E. (2010) Dysfunctional delegation: why the design of the Clean Development Mechanism's supervisory system is fundamentally flawed. *Climate Policy*, 10(3), 277–88.

Michaelowa, A. (2011) Fragmentation of international climate policy – doom or boon for carbon markets?, in Lütken, S. and Olsen, K. H. (eds) Progressing towards post-2012 carbon markets. Perspectives Series 2011. Roskilde: UNEP Riso Centre, pp. 13–23.

Michaelowa, A. and Buen, J. (2012) The Clean Development Mechanism gold rush, in Michaelowa, A. (ed.) *Carbon Markets or Climate Finance? Low Carbon and Adaptation Investment Choices for the Developing World*. London: Routledge, pp. 1–38.

Michaelowa, K. and Michaelowa, A. (2012) Development cooperation and climate change. Political-economic determinants of adaptation aid, in Michaelowa, A. (ed.) *Carbon Markets or Climate Finance? Low Carbon and Adaptation Investment Choices for the Developing World*. London: Routledge, pp. 39–52.

Michaelowa, A., Köhler, M. and Butzengeiger, S. (2012) Market mechanisms for adaptation. An aberration or a key source of finance?, in Michaelowa, A. (ed.) *Carbon Markets or Climate Finance?*

Low Carbon and Adaptation Investment Choices for Developing Countries. London: Routledge, pp. 188–208.

Newell, P. and Paterson, M. (2010) *Climate Capitalism. Global Warming and the Transformation of the Global Economy*. Cambridge: Cambridge University Press.

Oberthür, S. and Pallemaerts, M. (2010) The EU's internal and external climate policies: an historical overview, in Oberthür, S. and Pallemaerts, M. (eds) *The New Climate Policies of the European Union: Internal Legislation and Climate Diplomacy*. Brussels: VUB Press, pp. 27–63.

Paterson, M. (2011) Who and what are carbon markets for? Politics and the development of climate policy. *Climate Policy*, 12(1), 82–97.

Peters-Stanley, M., Hamilton, K., Marcello, T. and Sjardin, M. (2011) Back to the future. State of the voluntary carbon markets 2011. Washington, DC: Ecosystem Marketplace.

Schreurs, M. A. (2008) From the bottom up: local and subnational climate change politics. *Journal of Environment and Development*, 17(4), 343–55.

Schreurs, M. A. and Tiberghien, Y. (2007) Multi-level reinforcement: explaining European Union leadership in climate change mitigation. *Global Environmental Politics*, 7(4), 19–46.

Skjaerseth, J. B. and Wettestad, J. (2008) *EU Emissions Trading. Initiation, Decision-Making and Implementation*. Aldershot: Ashgate.

Skjaerseth, J. B. and Wettestad, J. (2010) Making the EU Emissions Trading System: the European Commission as an entrepreneurial epistemic leader. *Global Environmental Change*, 20(2), 314–21.

Spash, C. (2009) The brave new world of carbon trading. Munich: MPRA.

Sterk, W. (2011) Sectoral approaches as a way forward for the carbon market, in Lütken, S., Olsen, K. H. (eds) Progressing towards post-2012 carbon markets. Perpectives Series 2011. Roskilde: UNEP Riso Centre, pp. 113–25.

Sterk, W. and Mersmann, F. (2011) Domestic Emission Trading Systems in developing countries – state of play and future prospects. JIKO Policy Paper 2/2011. Wuppertal: JIKO.

Further reading

Michaelowa, A. (ed.) (2012) *Carbon Markets or Climate Finance? Low Carbon and Adaptation Investment Choices for the Developing World*. London: Routledge.

Newell, P. and/ Paterson, M. (2010) *Climate Capitalism. Global Warming and the Transformation of the Global Economy*. Cambridge: Cambridge University Press.

Lohmann, L. (2009) When markets are poison. Learning about climate policy from the financial crisis. Briefing 40. Dorset: The Corner House.

Stern, N. (2007) *The Economics of Climate Change. The Stern Review*. Cambridge: Cambridge University Press.

Stern, N. (2009) *A Blueprint for a Safer Planet. How to Manage Climate Change and Create a New Era of Progress and Prosperity*. London: The Bodley Head.

Sterk, W. and Mersmann, F. (2011) Domestic emission trading systems in developing countries – state of play and future prospects. Wuppertal: JIKO Policy Paper 2/2011.

Streck, C. and Chagas, T. (2011) Developments in climate finance from Rio to Cancun. *World Bank Legal Review* 3, 345–62.

TEEB (2010) The Economics of Ecosystems and Biodiversity: Mainstreaming the economics of nature: a synthesis of the approach, conclusions and recommendations of TEEB. Gland: TEEB.

UNEP (2012) UNEP Risoe CDM/ JI Pipeline Analysis and Database. Risoe: UNEP.

UNFCCC (2010) The contribution of the CDM under the Kyoto Protcol to technology transfer. Bonn: UNFCCC.

Voigt, C. (2008) Is the Clean Development Mechanism sustainable? Some critical aspects. *Sustainable Development Law & Policy* 7(2), 15–21.

Voß, J.-P. (2007) Innovation processes in governance: the development of emissions trading as a new policy instrument. *Science and Public Policy* 34(5), 329–43.

Wara, M. W. and Victor, D. G. (2008) A realistic policy on international carbon offsets. Program on

Energy and Sustainable Development Working Paper 74. Stanford, CA: Stanford University.

World Bank (2010a) Economics of adaptation to climate change. a synthesis report. Washington, DC: World Bank.

World Bank (2010b) World development report 2010: Development and climate change. Washington, DC: World Bank.

World Bank (2011) State and trends of the carbon market 2011. Washington, DC: World Bank.

Zelli, F. (2011) The fragmentation of the global climate governance architecture. *Wiley Interdisciplinary Reviews: Climate Change* 2(2), 255–70.

Notes

1   The reader is advised to shortly browse two webpages in order to get a feeling for how politicized carbon markets are. First, you might want to have a look at Point Carbon's webpage (http://www.pointcarbon.com/) to understand how a company has successfully developed a business case on commodifying carbon. Second, the NGO Carbon Trade Watch (http://www.carbontradewatch.org/) might be a good first starting point for analysing critical perspectives.

2   The following descriptions partially draw on Lederer (2012b).

3   Critical perspectives on the CDM are *inter alia* offered by Boyd *et al.* (2007), de Sepibus (2009), Voigt (2008), Wara and Victor (2008) and Böhm and Dabhbi (2009). Many current issues can also be found on http://www.cdm-watch.org/. For an excellent discussion and a differentiated defence of the CDM, see Michaelowa and Buen (2012).

4   For highly critical comments on REDD+ and carbon markets in general, see the discussions on http://www.redd-monitor.org/.

5   Examples from the German government's International Climate Initiative, which channels some of the revenues generated from auctions into mitigation and adaptation projects can be found at http://www.bmu-klimaschutzinitiative.de/en/news.

Part 5

Technology and innovation for low carbon development

Editorial for Part 5

Technology and innovation for low carbon development

Frauke Urban and Johan Nordensvärd

Part 5 explores the key issues related to technology, innovation and technology transfer for low carbon development. Low carbon development can only be implemented when access to low carbon technologies are provided. Key low carbon technologies are for example renewable energy, such as wind turbines and solar panels, and energy efficient technology. Access to these technologies is predominantly limited to high income countries and partly to emerging emitters (e.g. China), whereas lower income countries often lack access to these technologies. The transfer of these technologies from richer to poorer countries is therefore one of the key elements that is needed for a global low carbon transition.

Overview of Part 5

Chapter 8 explores the fact that low carbon technology transfer is considered to be a fundamental pillar in realizing effective low carbon development. At the same time, the general view is that current efforts aimed at eliciting low carbon technology transfer – focusing on financing equipment or 'hardware' – have largely been ineffective. Chapter 8 therefore discusses how a more systemic approach is warranted, given the complex nature of the phenomenon. Specifically, there is a need to build innovation capacity and to align low carbon technologies with the needs and peculiarities of their social environs. The chapter concludes with some emerging ideas, such as engaging local stakeholders and innovation centres, as potential ways in which to facilitate effective technology transfer, and ultimately low carbon development.

8 Low carbon innovation and technology transfer

David Ockwell and Alexandra Mallett

Low carbon technology transfer is considered to be a fundamental pillar in realizing effective low carbon development. At the same time, the general view is that current efforts aimed at eliciting low carbon technology transfer – focusing on financing equipment or 'hardware' – have largely been ineffective. We suggest that a more systemic approach is warranted, given the complex nature of the phenomenon. Specifically, there is a need to build innovation capacity and to align low carbon technologies with the needs and peculiarities of their social environs. We conclude with some emerging ideas, such as engaging local stakeholders and innovation centres, as potential ways to facilitate effective technology transfer, and ultimately low carbon development.

Introduction

It is widely recognized that technology will play a central role in mitigating and adapting to climate change (Stern, 2006; IPCC, 2007) and for achieving low carbon development. While many industrialized nations are likely to struggle with the major efforts involved in unlocking themselves from the high carbon infrastructure around which they have developed, developing nations could potentially choose instead to develop around lower carbon[1] technologies, defined here as technologies that are lower carbon than conventional technologies, including renewable energy, energy efficiency and lower carbon fossil technologies. This could enable developing nations to develop along lower GHG emissions trajectories resulting in lower aggregate emissions over time. This chapter engages with two inter-linked issues that are critical to realizing low carbon development, namely 'low carbon technology transfer' and 'low carbon innovation'.

The transfer and uptake of low carbon technologies in developing nations has long been of interest from a policy perspective and forms a key commitment under international climate regulations (see discussion further below). Nevertheless, it is also a key area where policy (whether at the international, national and/or subnational level) is viewed as having been unsuccessful. In this chapter we seek to demonstrate how this ineffectiveness is, to a large extent, related to the failure to understand low carbon technology transfer and low carbon innovation as intricately linked processes. Without the low carbon innovation capacities (defined further below), a country is less likely to be able to attract, adopt and work with flows of low carbon technologies imported from elsewhere. Critically, without low carbon innovation capacities they are also unlikely to be able to adapt and incrementally change these technologies (both processes of innovation) in order to sustain low carbon development trajectories in the long term. Indeed, the development of these capacities has led to the significant flows of low carbon technologies and related funding (e.g. under the CDM) to the BRICs (Brazil, Russia, India, China).

Hence, we suggest that it is impossible to understand how low carbon technology transfer might be pursued as part of a broader process of low carbon development without also understanding low carbon innovation (and related ideas such as low carbon innovation capacities and low carbon innovation systems). In this chapter we present an introduction to these core concepts, using low carbon technology transfer to tie our narrative together, but with the aim of using this approach to introduce readers to low carbon innovation as an intricately related concept.

The chapter begins by discussing why low carbon technology transfer is unique from conventional technology transfer before moving on to introduce the international policy context relating to low carbon technology transfer. The chapter then moves on to unpack the intricate relationship between low carbon technology transfer and low carbon innovation. This requires understanding technology as more than just hardware, but also as qualitatively different types of knowledge. This includes the knowledge necessary to develop low carbon innovation capacities. Here the chapter goes into more depth as to what is meant by innovation in this context, who innovators might be and the importance of innovation systems. This exploration of the relationship between low carbon innovation and technology transfer enables the chapter to pause and consider why existing, hardware financing-oriented policy mechanisms are largely failing to facilitate low carbon technology transfer and uptake, particularly in poorer developing countries. Before concluding by introducing some promising new policy initiatives that are currently emerging, the chapter first pauses to introduce one final, critical consideration, namely the need to ensure that low carbon technologies are carefully matched to the context-specific circumstances within which they are expected to contribute to low carbon development, and the self-defined needs (including poverty reduction) of the communities that use them.

Our aim in writing this chapter is to introduce the central ideas and issues and provide pointers towards relevant resources for further reading. For a more comprehensive treatment of these issues readers are encouraged in particular to consult the various contributions to Ockwell and Mallett (2012).

Box 8.1 outlines the key terms and concepts relevant for this chapter.

Box 8.1   Key terms and concepts

Horizontal technology transfer: the transfer of technologies from one geographic setting to another (see Figure 8.1).

Vertical technology transfer: the transfer of technologies along the innovation chain (from the research and development (R&D) stage, demonstration, revision and commercial deployment) (see Figure 8.2).

Low carbon technologies: technologies that produce less carbon emissions than their conventional counterparts (e.g. using renewable energy sources versus fossil fuels to generate electricity).

Intellectual Property Rights (IPRs): are legal rights over ideas, creative processes and products. They include copyrights, trademarks, and patents – where holders can prevent the use of these technologies.

Research and Development (R&D): distinguished between basic (knowledge for knowledge's sake) and applied (knowledge with a goal/application in mind) research and experimental design, it can be thought of as 'creative work done on a systematic basis, to increase knowledge (including knowledge of people, culture and society) and to use this knowledge to devise new applications' (OECD, 2002; Frascati Manual: 30).

Valley of death: a term used to reflect the fact that public funding is often available at a technology's experimental stage (e.g. university lab), and private funding available later on, once technologies have been proven (referred to as almost commercial) but that limited funding exists for the critical middle stage (demonstration, revision) (see Figure 8.3).

Radical (often referred to as 'new to the world' – a process, product, way of doing things new to all markets/industries), **incremental** (gradual changes, over time) and **adaptive** (adapting existing practices, equipment, etc. to improve performance in new contexts) innovation.

Technological leapfrogging: the idea that developing countries can skip certain 'dirty' stages associated with development, at a macro level through development pathways, through skipping stages of industrial development and/or through the use of low carbon technologies.

Low carbon innovation capacities: the capacity to adopt, adapt, develop, deploy and operate low carbon technologies effectively.

Low carbon innovation systems: the coordination and connection of the available skills, knowledge, institutions and so on that aggregate innovation capacity.

Socio-technical transitions: the concept that technologies are embedded interdependently in existing social practices and so more adoption is likely to occur when technologies' form and function are 'aligned' with dominant social practices, or offer opportunities to realize new practices that are attractive in particular social and geographical settings.

Sources: taken from some of our previous work (see Ockwell and Mallett references below), unless noted above.

Why is low carbon technology transfer unique?

International and domestic technology transfer can be considered essential parts of technology development and uptake, especially in developing countries. It is an important channel in which technologies are acquired in the developing world. This can be pursued in order to obtain technology directly, to obtain components and/or to encourage domestic innovation through absorption and adaptation to the local environment. In the past, technology transfer referred to the movement of 'nuts and bolts' (equipment, or 'hardware') from one location to another. Later, the concept evolved to include the 'know-how' or skills involved in operating and maintaining physical equipment. More recent renditions attempt to capture the notion that technologies also include knowledge – to not only operate them, but to understand the principles behind the technologies (sometimes referred to as 'know-why') (Bell, 1990; Lall, 1995). These facets (processes and knowledge) are often referred to as 'software'. These different conceptions of hardware and software flows and their relevance are discussed further below in relation to Figure 8.1.

Technology transfer in developing countries is characterized by a number of features. It can be integrated, where the originating body (e.g. multinational corporation, large domestic firm, academic institution) maintains the ownership of the technology. Or, it can be less integrated, where the actor in the local context can own and/or manufacture the technology (Forsyth, 1999). Technology transfer can also be short term, or longer term. Moreover, technology transfer can be internal, where one firm shares technology with a subsidiary company or through a Joint Venture (JV), or external, where one entity sells the technology and/or issues a license for others to use the technology. It can be formal (e.g. agreements, Memoranda of Understanding) or informal (e.g. personnel movement, publications, conferences, network discussions) (Pietrobelli, 2000), or contain a mixture of both. It can be in the public or private domains (UNFCCC, 1992). Finally, it can be through commercial (e.g. Foreign Direct Investment (FDI), joint ventures) or non-commercial (e.g. scientific exchanges, foreign aid) mechanisms (Able-Thomas, 1996).

Interest in technology transfer and its role in the development of firms and industries and countries' technological bases is long-standing. Technology transfer from one country or firm to another occurs within and/or between sectors (e.g. firms in the private sector, a university and an NGO, etc.), and scholars in fields such as innovation studies and economic geography have been researching this process for decades. But low carbon technologies have a number of characteristics that make the issues pertaining to their transfer and uptake in developing countries unique from conventional technology – these are explored in turn below.

Public good nature of low carbon technology

First, low carbon technologies are of interest for the purposes of delivering a global public good,[2] that is, the mitigation of climate change (Mowery *et al.*, 2010). This public good is unlikely to be optimally provided by the market as the full social costs (future impacts of climate change from GHG emissions) and benefits (mitigating GHGs) of private sector activities are external to the market. So when a firm conducts cost–benefit analysis to help them determine decisions, generally speaking they do not include aspects that lack a monetary value (Clayton *et al.*, 1999; Renewables, 2004). Low carbon technology-producing firms are therefore unable, without policy intervention, to capture the full value of the benefit their technologies provide to society. There is thus a clear incentive for policy intervention to facilitate their transfer and uptake, which may not be the case for conventional technologies. If these factors were to be captured in the cost of producing electricity, for instance, the price of producing power from fossil fuels would be significantly higher.

Transfer under conditions of urgency

The second unique characteristic of low carbon technologies is temporal. Low carbon technology transfer is of interest in relation to climate change. It therefore needs to be achieved as quickly as possible if it is to be effective for either mitigation or adaptation. Conventional technology transfer, on the other hand, occurs over unspecified timescales. Knowledge is therefore necessary to determine how policy might intervene to facilitate low carbon technology transfer over short timescales.

Different stages of technological maturity

Conventional technologies are often transferred as a result of commercial opportunities for their use in new markets; in this case their application in emerging markets in developing countries. This often means these technologies are already technologically mature and commercially viable. Many low carbon technologies are, however, at earlier stages of development. This could be anywhere along the innovation chain from the early R&D stage, through demonstration, revision to supported commercial. A distinction can therefore be drawn between 'horizontal' technology transfer, which refers to the conventional definition of transferring technology from one place to another, and 'vertical' technology transfer, which refers to the transfer of technologies along the innovation chain, from R&D through to the point where they become commercially viable. This is illustrated in Figures 8.1 and 8.2.

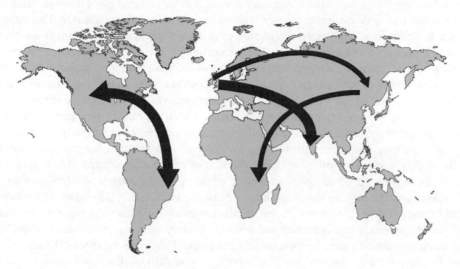

Figure 8.1 Horizontal technology transfer

Horizontal technology transfer refers to the transfer of technologies from one place to another. This is the more traditional notion of technology transfer. Increasingly, as Brewer (2008) notes, flows of low carbon technology transfer include south–south and even south–north transfers as opposed to just north–south, developed–developing country transfers.

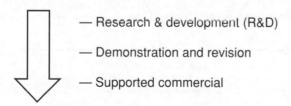

Figure 8.2 Vertical technology transfer

Vertical technology transfer refers to the transfer of technologies along the innovation chain, from early R&D, through demonstration, revision and commercial deployment. Many low carbon technologies require both horizontal and vertical transfer, raising a range of difficult challenges, especially with technologies at earlier stages of technological development.

Even the simpler horizontal conception of technology transfer is increasingly complex in relation to low carbon technologies, as the traditional north–south direction of these transfer flows is constantly changing. There are now plenty of examples of south–south low carbon technology transfer as well as examples of south–north transfer. For a more in-depth discussion see Brewer (2008). But what is more complex still is the fact that low carbon technology transfer often has to deal simultaneously with horizontal and vertical transfer. This brings with it a wide range of challenges. Technologies at earlier stages of development are often subject to higher risks and uncertainties. These risks and uncertainties span a range of levels, including but not limited to: investment perspectives – working with new, unfamiliar models to fund new, untested technologies; end-user perspectives – adopting, working with and maintaining new unfamiliar technologies; policy perspectives – incentivizing the development and uptake of non-conventional technologies within a policy space populated by a complex range of different incentives; and technology developer perspectives – working with new technologies in uncertain funding/investment environments, for example dealing with the widely referred to 'valley of death'. The valley of death, as illustrated in Figure 8.3, refers to the widely observed situation where, while public funding is available for early stage innovation and private sector funding is available once technologies become proven, limited funding is available for the critical middle stages of the innovation process (the stage where technologies are demonstrated and revised) leading to many promising low carbon innovations not reaching the commercially viable stage. This list is far from exhaustive but begins to illustrate the complexities of attempting to incentivize the rapid uptake of low carbon technologies that may not yet be commercially viable but are desirable for the purposes of delivering a global public good.

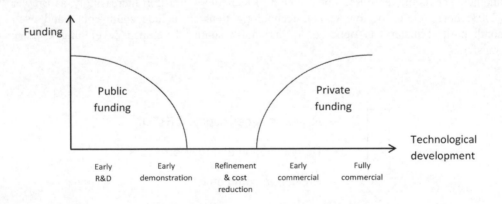

Figure 8.3 The technology 'valley of death' between public and private funding availability

Many promising low carbon technologies might not reach commercial maturity due to a gap in available funding for the middle stages of the innovation process where technologies are demonstrated and revised.

The international policy context

The significance of technology transfer as a means to respond to climate change is reflected in its prominent place within international policy. Several articles under the UNFCCC and Kyoto Protocol assert developed nations' commitments to supporting and financing the transfer of low carbon technologies to developing nations (e.g. Articles 4.3 and 4.5 of the UNFCCC and Articles 2.1 (a, iv) and 11.2 (b) of the Kyoto Protocol). Article 4.5 of the UNFCCC is the most cited article in support of the use of low carbon technologies in developing countries through technology transfer. Here, developed countries:

> shall take all practical steps to promote, facilitate and finance, as appropriate, the transfer of, or access to, environmentally sound technologies and know-how to other Parties, particularly developing country Parties, to enable them to implement provisions of the Convention.
>
> (UNFCCC 1992, Article 4.5: 11)

This promise of access to new technologies was seen as an important incentive for developing nations coming on board with these international policy platforms at their inception in the early 1990s, not least because they recognize the fact that technology ownership is directly correlated with economic wealth and that this ownership has traditionally been weighted in favour of developed countries (Khor, 2008). Low carbon technology transfer is also supported under a range of other multi- and bi-lateral initiatives, including the activities of donor organizations (e.g. DfID), intergovernmental organizations (e.g. the World Bank) and NGOs (e.g. Practical Action, Light Up the World, Barefoot College).

Despite this attention within international policy, low carbon technology transfer has long been viewed as a key area where policy has failed to deliver. For example, the CDM is one of the main policy mechanisms under the Kyoto Protocol credited with delivering low carbon technology transfer – although notably this wasn't what the CDM was designed to deliver. Nevertheless, at the time of its creation, some hoped that industrialized countries would meet some of their emissions through the transfer of new, clean technologies to developing countries through the CDM (Grubb *et al.*, 2001; Ravindranath and Sathaye, 2002). But to date around 83 per cent of cumulative investment has gone to the BRICs (Byrne *et al.*, 2012b) and only around 0.2 per cent of certified emissions reductions are expected to come from LDCs (De Lopez *et al.*, 2009). Of this investment 75 per cent has gone to just five technologies (hydro, methane avoidance, wind, biomass energy and landfill gas), only one of which, wind, could be considered 'new', and even that is a fairly well established, commercially viable technology these days (Byrne *et al.*, 2012b).

Some commentators would argue that this failure to deliver low carbon technology transfer is simply a matter of needing increased financial commitments, or single policies such as a fund to buy up Intellectual Property Rights for low carbon energy technologies and make them freely available (e.g. see various country submissions to the UNFCCC process). Careful research of empirical evidence in this field has, however, yielded a far more complex picture which stresses the need to build new **innovation capacities** in developing countries and to better align low carbon technologies with the **specific contexts** within which they might be adopted. The remainder of this chapter focuses on unpacking these complexities and presents the key conceptual building blocks necessary to understanding how policy might be more effective in this field.

Knowledge vs. hardware, know-how vs. know-why and the centrality of innovation capacities

The first core conceptual issue necessary to understand how policy might more successfully foster low carbon technology transfer and uptake in developing countries is the fact that technology is not simply hardware, but also knowledge. An excellent heuristic for thinking this through is Bell (1990)'s seminal illustration detailed in Figure 8.4. Here the technology suppliers on the left can supply more than just hardware, services and designs – these are only one potential flow of technology, Flow A in Figure 8.4. They can also importantly supply knowledge in the form of the skills and knowledge necessary to operate and maintain new technology, the 'know-how' – Flow B. Flow A and B together contribute to the creation of new production capacities amongst the technology importing firm (or communities at the local level, or country at the aggregate level). The relationship between developing human skills in technological know-how, as well as experience, which has traced the 'staying power' of technology through the training of local staff to operate and maintain the technology is duly noted by some (Renewables, 2004). This new production capacity is important if we want firms, households and countries in the developing world to be able to operate around newer, lower carbon or climate resilient technologies. But it is not sufficient in itself to underpin a broader and sustained process of technological change and development along low carbon, climate resilient pathways. Vital to the latter is Flow C in Figure 8.4 – 'know-why' – the knowledge, expertise and experience that underpinned the development of the

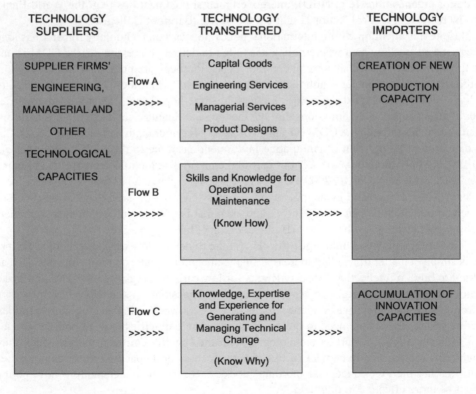

Figure 8.4 The technological content of international technology transfer
Source: Adapted from Bell (1990)

technology that is being transferred in the first place. Knowing why that technology works, not just how, and having the tacit knowledge (knowledge developed by doing) of the related processes that underpinned its design, development and commercialization (vertical transfer) is fundamental to developing new **innovation capacities**.

Innovation capacities can be broadly defined as the capacity to adopt, adapt, develop, deploy and operate low carbon technologies effectively (this definition expands on an earlier definition in Ockwell *et al.*, 2009). Vitally, to be sustainable over time, before firms or organizations can adopt new technologies (i.e. becoming recipients of Flows A and B in Figure 8.4), they first need to have a certain level of existing innovation capacities. This is sometimes referred to as 'absorptive capacity' – the capacity to absorb new technologies. As stressed by the United Nations Convention on Trade and Development (UNCTAD) 'unless the LDCs adopt policies to stimulate technological catch-up with the rest of the world, they will continue to fall behind other countries technologically and face deepening marginalisation in the global economy' (UNCTAD, 2007: I). Furthermore, thinking at an aggregate level, innovation capacities are also the key building block for low carbon development – underpinning broader, sustained lower carbon, climate resilient socio-technical development pathways.

There are three important points of clarification necessary here. First we need to clarify what we mean by innovation. Second we need to flag the fact that these innovation capacities will only be effective if they form part of broader innovation systems. Third, we need to understand who we mean by an innovator. We address each of these points in turn below.

Box 8.2 discusses the Intellectual Property Rights controversy.

Box 8.2 The Intellectual Property Rights (IPRs) controversy

One issue in which the tension between industrialized and developing countries manifests itself is in the area of Intellectual Property Rights (IPRs). The general thrust of the debate is as follows:

- Many developing countries suggest that access to new technologies is paramount in their efforts to address climate change and that strong IPRs can hinder this access. They advocate for international policy levers such as: a fund to buy cutting edge technology, obligatory licensing and active government engagement (e.g. to facilitate transfer at non-market rates).
- Many developed countries indicate that strong IPRs are key in order to elicit foreign direct investment and stress domestic actions to create a thriving market (e.g. a feed-in tariff, strong legal regimes, etc.).
- Evidence on the ground tells a different story, increasingly pointing to the complex, nuanced nature of the issue – harkening policy makers to assess their particular context (which technology, geographic setting, pivotal actors, etc.).
- Research in India for example noted that in the case of photovoltaics and hybrid vehicles, access to the technologies was happening but that many Indian firms felt that IP was slowing down the rate of access (through spending time identifying and negotiating with partners, acquiring the necessary funds and personnel, etc.).

Source: Ockwell *et al.*, 2010

What do we mean by 'innovation'?

Some commentators, when faced with the idea of developing 'innovation capacities' in developing countries, particularly LDCs, tend to react by arguing that the idea is impractical

– these countries, they say, have far more basic technological, economic, political and social issues they need to deal with before the idea of innovation becomes relevant. At present, they argue, it is enough for these countries to adopt existing technologies from elsewhere. This reaction is, however, based on a misunderstanding of what innovation is. Two categorizations are useful here in better understanding what constitutes innovation. The first comes from the OECD's Oslo manual (emphasized by Bell, 2007), which defines innovation thus:

1   **Innovations 'new to the world':** Firm[3] first to introduce innovation for all markets and industries, domestic and international.
2   **Innovations 'new to the market':** Firm first to introduce innovation in its particular market.
3   **Innovations 'new to the firm':** Firm introduces product, process or method new to that firm, or significantly improved by it, even if it has already been implemented by other firms.
4   **Non-innovations:** Include purchase of identical models of equipment, or minor extensions and updates to existing equipment or software.

Many people simply see innovation as category 1 – brand new inventions, new to the world. But it is equally innovative if a firm (farm, household, etc.) is the first to introduce something to their market (or region, village, farm etc.). The term social innovation also tries to capture this more nuanced view, through recognizing new ways of organizing or doing things through social dimensions. Furthermore, it is still innovative if a firm, farm or household introduces a new technology (including new processes and techniques) for the first time in its own everyday practices. Arguably it is these second two categories of innovation that are both far more common throughout the world and far more relevant in a developing country context.

We might also usefully categorize innovation in terms of 'radical', 'incremental' and 'adaptive' innovations. Radical innovation would conform to category 1 above. Incremental innovation refers to gradual changes to hardware, processes, management practices and design, among other aspects, which slowly improve the efficiency, value and so on of the overall activity. This is by far the most common process of innovation and is regularly observed as underpinning the development of technological advances within developing country firms. Adaptive innovation is also an important process, particularly where technologies are to be adopted in new, developing country contexts. This refers to the adaption of existing technologies (processes, designs etc.) to perform in new social, physical, market (and so on) contexts – the discussion of context specificity below unpacks these different contexts in more depth.

The notion of environmental technological 'leapfrogging' is relevant here to capture the rapidly changing dynamics and to question common assumptions (e.g. that 'radical' innovations are solely in the domain of industrialized nations). This is the idea that developing countries can skip certain 'dirty' stages associated with development, at a macro level through development pathways; through skipping stages of industrial development; and/or through the use of lower carbon technologies. As an example of the latter, for those places that currently do not have access to electricity (either through a stand-alone system or through the grid), people can look at low carbon options (e.g. solar home systems, micro hydro) to gain access to electricity, thus skipping over dirtier options such as diesel generators to provide electricity or grid extension where the electricity base is from fossil fuels. As an example of industrial development leapfrogging one can look to the case of wind power manufacturing where, within an extremely short time period, some Chinese and Indian firms have become world leaders (see Sauter and Watson, 2008 for further discussion).

Innovation systems

The second key point to bear in mind when thinking about innovation capacities is that these capacities develop, and are maintained and nurtured, within the context of broader innovation systems. There is no single accepted definition of what constitutes an innovation system, but they include the full array of public and private institutions, actors and practices that interact to produce environments conducive to the uptake of and innovation around technologies (in the broadest sense of the word – including goods, services, management practices, designs, etc.). So this would include policy makers, universities, R&D facilities, firms concerned with parts manufacture, import–export firms, engineers, designers, and so on. In this way it can be seen that this idea of innovation systems is very closely aligned with the idea of innovation capacities.

As Byrne *et al.* (2012a) point out, however, innovation systems operate at different scales to innovation capacities. Innovation capacity could attend to a national scale (the capacity of a nation to innovate). Equally innovation capacity could apply to the scale of an individual firm (although the range of potential innovations would be narrower than at a national scale). Or it could apply at the scale of an individual who might have capacity to innovate in the form of creative skills, technical knowledge, ability to take risks, and so on. The important distinction between innovation capacities and innovation systems relates to the fact that in order to innovate, and certainly if innovation is to underpin more widespread changes in socio-technical practices (see below for discussion of the idea of socio-technical perspectives on development), the available skills, knowledge, institutions, and so on that, on aggregate, constitute innovation capacities, need to connect and coordinate with one another – eventually attending to increasingly coherent systems.

Who is an innovator?

The concept of who is 'doing' innovation is also evolving. In the past, as noted by Charles Leadbeater (2005), innovation was often thought of as being done by 'special people in special places' – be they scientists, engineers, or technical experts, working in R&D labs, often far removed from the people using these technologies. Emerging approaches (e.g. ideas like co-creation or the bazaar model), however, recognize the importance that all players – including those involved in a technology's development, production *and* use – have on technology innovation and uptake. A key distinction in these frameworks is that an individual or small team works on equal footing with others (e.g. key stakeholders, other researchers/developers, etc.) in the development of an innovation. In this vein, Douthwaite (2002) espouses the notion of learning selection. People are exposed to a technology, they first learn to understand the technology, draw conclusions (on possible overall improvements, how it can be adapted to their particular situation), and then undertake actions. In learning selection, these actions are not done in isolation. In other words, in the process of understanding the technology, the end users, researchers, technicians, and so on work together and thus share their own experiences and conclusions with others, who can in turn incorporate these thoughts into their own 'experience' with the technology (Douthwaite, 2002: 47–8, 53). These alternative approaches are also emerging within low carbon energy discussions.

The need to move beyond hardware financing

Clearly, then, developing innovation capacities around low carbon technologies and ensuring these capacities are coordinated to form coherent innovation systems has a central role to play in fostering the transfer and uptake of low carbon technologies in developing countries. This shift of emphasis towards a need for building innovation systems and an understanding of technology transfer not simply as hardware flows but also qualitatively different knowledge flows helps us to begin to understand why 'hardware financing' policy approaches, such as the CDM, have been ineffective (for a more in depth discussion see Byrne *et al.*, 2012b). Under the CDM technology investments have been accrued by those developing countries that already have an existing degree of innovation capacities and coordinated innovation systems – the most advanced example being China, which has also accrued the most investment under the CDM. Countries, such as those in Sub-Saharan Africa, which lack existing innovation capacities/systems have, not surprisingly, accrued little benefit from these hardware-financing type policy incentives.

Context-specific space and socio-technical 'fit'

An important additional consideration for successful technology transfer is for technologies to either fit with, or be adapted to (via adaptive innovation processes) the specific contexts where they are to be used. For example, in industrial complexes with high intensity energy demands and highly centralized power systems it might be more appropriate to explore lower carbon fossil energy or biomass-based options for energy supply, whereas in rural areas with limited capacity for grid connection, distributed renewable energy options such as solar home systems combined with energy-efficient end use technologies like Light Emitting Diode (LED) lighting might be more appropriate. This diversity of energy options also yields the co-benefit of diversifying national energy portfolios and hence increasing energy security. Greater renewable capacity and increased energy efficiency also increases energy security by reducing reliance on fossil imports (UNEP, 2000; Biswas *et al.*, 2001). These are just a few examples of the difference in technology fit to context-specific considerations. These could equally be thought of in relation to a range of other spatial levels, for example the characteristics of different countries (e.g. different consideration faced by BRICS vs. LDCs vs. SIDS) or the differing needs of households versus firms and industries.

Importantly, these context-specificities also apply across different social and cultural spaces. This is a concept that is well captured by the literature on socio-technical transitions (see, for example, Rip and Kemp, 1998; Geels, 2002; Smith *et al.* 2010). A socio-technical approach recognizes that technologies are embedded interdependently in existing social practices and reflect knowledge of these practices as well as knowledge of technical principles (see Byrne *et al.* 2012b, upon which the following draws, for a more in-depth discussion of the relevance of socio-technical transitions thinking to climate technology transfer). A firm or farm might be the locus of innovation and technological learning (UNCTAD, 2007), but they are embedded within a broader framework of institutions that define and are defined by these processes. The spatial development of towns and cities, the nature of transport infrastructure and the institutional norms governing travel, for example, have all developed around the use of the internal combustion engine, and continue to influence and constrain the direction and nature of current innovations in transport modes and efficiency. An important hypothesis that flows from this perspective is that technologies will be widely adopted not simply because they successfully harness technical principles but also if their form and function are 'aligned' with dominant social practices, or offer opportunities to realize new practices that are attractive in particular social and geographical settings. This has important implications for the kinds of low carbon technologies that are likely to be adopted and work effectively within the specific contexts of different developing countries and locales therein.

This concept is particularly acute in a world where policy makers, practitioners and academics attempt to apply 'lessons learned' to different places and struggle when these experiences fail to translate into successes (either in practice or in theory) elsewhere. For instance, it is important to understand that 'new' technologies often tend to be based upon technology already in place, and so it is often easier for firms to conduct R&D and invest in ways in which to tweak older technologies, rather than support the transition to a new form of different technology. This dynamic is important to consider regarding the uptake of renewable energy technologies, for example, as their global large-scale adoption would, in many cases require a major paradigm shift from fossil fuel energy sources to these alternatives. Therefore, this 'entrenchment' or 'socio-technological lock-in' means that, aside from the vested interests worldwide in maintaining the fossil fuel industry, it is often easier for a company, government, or village, to use 'cleaner' fossil fuels, which enable the use of the existing infrastructure in place, rather than installing an entirely new technology, such as solar, wind or small-hydro power. This is, however, dependent upon the nature of existing infrastructure. As noted above in the concept of leapfrogging, in many rural areas of developing countries where fossil-based infrastructure is lacking (e.g. electricity grid access), the infrastructural investments required to pursue fossil-based technologies can be higher than the costs of distributed renewable energy options.

Pro-poor, needs-based approaches

Closely aligned with the idea of context-specific considerations is the need to maintain a critical view of the extent to which existing approaches to encouraging low carbon technology transfer serve the needs of poor countries, or people. The example of the CDM above, for instance, emphasizes the failure of this particular mechanism to deliver benefits to LDCs. It could be further asked whether CDM investments in the BRICs are necessarily benefiting poor people therein, remembering that a huge proportion of the world's poor live in these countries (Sumner, 2011).

Many scholars point to the direct relationship between access to energy and the reduction of poverty in developing nations (Forsyth, 1999; Juma and Yee-Cheong, 2005; Modi *et al.*, 2005). Indeed, energy is central to meeting all of the MDGs (UNDP, 2007) and is a pivotal focus for the United Nations in their Sustainable Energy For All (SE4All) initiative, which aims for universal energy access by 2030.[4] For example, studies demonstrate that poorer people (especially women) are often burdened with the task of finding conventional energy sources, such as fuel wood (which can take up to several hours per day), and so they are left with little or no available time; they argue that low carbon technology adoption – through freeing up time – can help to improve the socio-economic situation of poorer people (Biswas *et al.*, 2001). But, increasing evidence purports that efforts to increase the uptake of low carbon technologies in order to reduce GHG emissions have trumped those aimed at serving the most vulnerable populations. For example, as noted by Byrne *et al.* (2012b), and echoed by Lederer (2009), the bulk of CDM projects target large-scale, centralized energy options, versus smaller scale, decentralized options, which can be more amenable to addressing the needs of the poor. Domestic policies are also being questioned. As one example, some claim that a blanket subsidy for fossil fuels (e.g. cheaper gas) ends up benefiting the wealthy more than the poor. For instance, in India, subsidies on the price of electricity (and fertilizer) have often been criticized as helping wealthy agrobusiness rather than family farms, which often do not have electricity connections (Vedavalli, 2007). Some also have concerns in India with that government's feed-in tariff law aimed at encouraging the use of photovoltaics, as it favours large-scale solar farms, which only wealthy investors have the necessary capital to pursue, rather than smaller, decentralized options (Mallett *et al.*, 2009)[5]. As another example, while an army of consultants conduct studies highlighting the financial and energy savings that can accrue over time with many low carbon options (for instance, once a solar home system or wind turbine is purchased, the majority of expenses are for maintaining and operating the system, which are often substantially less than the capital and installation costs), many people in developing countries live in financially precarious positions, not having the funds available for these upfront costs. Many traditional lenders (conventional banks) in developing countries have shied away from investing in renewable due to risk, and so other agencies such as private firms, international organizations, foreign aid agencies and multilateral banks have been active in this area (for further discussion of these experiences see Ockwell and Mallett, 2012, and Mallett, 2012). In addition, micro-credit institutions are also increasingly expressing interest in this area, such as organizations targeting rural energy options including Grameen Shakti in Bangladesh, which has made some impressive inroads regarding the diffusion of low carbon technologies in developing countries (e.g. as of the end of 2010, more than half a million solar home systems had been installed)[6]. These efforts are encouraging, but paying particular attention to socio-technical 'fit' is also important. This is because previous efforts for micro-credit institutions to provide lending for renewables have been mismatched due to differing experiences and requirements (e.g. for large-scale renewable options, large amounts of credit are required rather than the small amounts of funds lent in these schemes; some lending requirements (weekly payments and membership fees) are still too stringent for many potential low carbon technology users, etc.) (Rodrigues and Matajs, 2005; UNDESA, 2005; Pramana, 2006, personal communication[7]). Nevertheless, these alternative funding options appear to be more amenable to smaller-scale, decentralized options.

Understanding the particular context is key. Research examining solar water heaters in Mexico City, for example, highlighted that people would only make a five- or six-year investment on a house or a car, not a water heating device (Mallett, 2009). Some conventional studies on renewables categorize this challenge as an economic trait, noting that those with less disposable income have higher discount rates (i.e. money they have today is worth significantly more than money they will have tomorrow) (Philibert, 2006). But this facet is also intrinsically linked with socio-cultural aspects, which are often neglected when promoting these environmental advantages. Targeted actions aimed at addressing this concern (e.g. providing a grant or concessional loan to help with upfront costs) may not be as effective as envisioned; people may not want to invest in a technology if they are unsure where they will be living in five or more years. Calls for a re-think of low carbon technology transfer or cooperation in the developing world are growing as the gulf between what many decision makers want (rapid, large-scale deployment) and what communities want (poverty alleviation, appropriate technologies to suit their needs) deepens.

Promising new policy approaches?

Designing new policy approaches for delivering low carbon technology transfer that are able to address all of the issues raised above is clearly no easy task. Policy is required that can both build innovation capacities and at the same time respond to the socio-technical, context-specific needs of different actors in different places. Nevertheless, some promising strands of new policy thinking and practice are beginning to emerge.

Engaging local stakeholders

One implication of the discussion above regarding context-specificities is a need for policy approaches to understand and respond to the needs, desires and existing cultural practices of local stakeholders whose engagement is critical to the uptake of new low carbon technologies. Some strands of emerging work on low carbon technology transfer are beginning to speak to this need for new institutional approaches that facilitate deeper engagement with developing country stakeholders. Forsyth (2005b, 2012), for example, provides evidence from Southeast Asia suggesting cross-sector partnerships (i.e. partnerships between local communities and investors/developers/governments) can bring about effective technology transfer and benefits at the local level by considering local development needs (sometimes referred to as the 'development dividend') concurrently with low carbon mitigation – through fostering community discussion and active participation in the project. Echoing, to some extent, Forsyth's emphasis on the benefits of cross-sector partnerships, Lovett *et al.*'s (2012) assessment of existing technology financing mechanisms concludes that neither finance nor technology access are the real limiting factors to broader uptake of low carbon technologies; instead, it is a lack of 'enabling environments', which, they suggest, might be fostered via a new approach characterized by 'multi-stakeholder partnerships'.

Low carbon innovation centres

Another promising emerging policy idea is that of 'climate innovation centres' in developing countries (Sagar *et al.*, 2009; Sagar, 2010). This is currently being trialled via an initiative by the Information for Development programme (InfoDev) and DfID in Kenya and India. A version is also under discussion as part of the proposed Technology Mechanism under the UNFCCC. The 'Technology Mechanism' is a new proposed approach to delivering the transfer of low carbon technologies (technologies of relevance to climate mitigation *and* adaptation) to developing countries, aiming to address the perceived failure of past efforts under the UNFCCC to achieve technology transfer. The Mechanism comprises of two components – the first is a Technology Executive Committee (TEC) which consists of government officials from industrialized and developing countries. The Committee is to undertake a series of actions to do with the development and transfer of these technologies (e.g. assessing and recommending policies and programmes, seeking cooperation with relevant players, etc.). The second component is a Climate Technology Centre and Network (CTCN). The CTC is to be hosted by an organization and is expected to foster a network of other organizations and initiatives to provide advice and support and collaboration related to the development and transfer of these technologies, of which low carbon innovation will be a part. At the time of writing a number of bids have been submitted in which to serve as the CTC host.[8]

Negotiators are building on the Durban Platform, where they agreed to the 'development of a new protocol, another legal instrument or agreed outcome with legal force' (Carpenter, 2012: 14) pertaining to all Parties, not just developing countries – set to be finalised by 2015 and to come into force by 2020. While too early to tell at the time of writing, some encouraging dimensions are manifesting themselves, demonstrating strong potential for the aspirations of developing countries to build innovative capacity alongside reducing carbon emissions and resiliency. For example, the fact that the language in the Conference of the Parties decisions regarding this topic has shifted from 'technology transfer' to 'technology development and transfer' is particularly telling. That being said, there are some who point to the fact that China and India are delaying talks on any such globally binding climate change treaty, arguing for a Kyoto Protocol type of deal, where only developed countries were accountable to reduce GHG emissions (having caused the 'problem').[9] But, we suggest that these emerging policy ideas warrant a closer look, aimed at better reflecting the goals of developing nations, to dovetail within the broader post 2020 discussions.

If developed and implemented effectively there is potential for these centre-based approaches to play a key role in building innovation capacities in developing countries in ways that hardware financing policy approaches have failed to do. This would, however, require carefully tailored policy based on grounded empirical analysis, such as that currently under development in Kenya (see Ockwell, 2012). Without this there is a danger such centres could fall prey to the failures of previous moves towards centres for science and innovation in developing countries, which historically failed to deliver needs-driven, capacity-building opportunities (Leach and Waldman, 2009).

Conclusion

This chapter has covered a lot of ground to discuss the role of low carbon innovation and technology transfer for low carbon development. To summarize, while low carbon technology transfer is considered a key commitment within the international climate change discussions, the majority view is that conventional mechanisms (from international schemes such as the CDM, to domestic policy levers) – looking at the issue at a broad scale, have failed to deliver. As investment and capacity tends to be concentrated in a few places (namely the BRICs) and firms (generally large scale multinational enterprises from both developed and emerging economies), and people (urban elite), there are increasing calls to revisit this issue – to make it more pro poor, more amenable to local needs and better linked with long term objectives. We argue that the current approach to low carbon technology transfer within the international climate discussions, which focuses on one-off, piecemeal actions, such as financing for hardware or equipment is inadequate. One reason for this is the failure to link technology transfer and uptake discussions with low carbon innovation. Here, we remind readers of the importance of innovative capacity, or the ability to contend with change through understanding the technology. Another dimension often neglected is that of context and socio-technical fit; recognizing that each situation is different. This chapter moved from understanding the unique characteristics of low carbon technologies (the goal being a public good, the urgency of the issue and the fact that these technologies are often at different stages of maturity), through to introducing the socio-technical nature of technological and low carbon development, as well as the imperative for policy to engage with building innovation capacities and systems in developing countries, moving away from a singular emphasis on hardware financing. In addition, we want to highlight the complex, dynamic nature of the process, as rhetoric tends to be stalled in the past (envisioning a world where Northern actors transfer technologies to the South), far removed from the reality where south–south cooperation is becoming more commonplace, Southern players are becoming global leaders on low carbon technologies (Brazil's efforts on hydro and ethanol, and the Indian and Chinese wind turbine firms Suzlon and Goldwind are only a few cases in point), and also where South–North partnerships and/or acquisitions are growing (e.g. Indian and Chinese firms have been particularly adept at purchasing high stakes in firms from

Northern countries, but in addition to the BRICs, countries 'beyond the BRICs' are also increasingly playing a role. For example, Malaysia's Petronas recently offered US$5.5 billion to acquire Progress Energy of Calgary, Alberta, Canada, to build liquefied natural gas terminals to export natural gas to Asia.[10] We end by flagging up two promising approaches for achieving low carbon development – those encouraging local engagement and low carbon innovation centres. Finally, we summarize a number of key points arising from the chapter and encourage readers to consult the resources listed in the further reading below.

Key messages from this chapter are:

*   Technology must be understood as consisting of qualitatively different flows of knowledge, as opposed to simply hardware.
*   Critical to sustained development drawing on low carbon technologies is the development of innovation capacities and innovation systems in developing countries. Innovation capacities can be understood as the capacities to adopt, adapt, develop, deploy and operate low carbon technologies effectively in developing countries. This rests on an understanding of innovation as including incremental and adaptive innovation as perhaps more relevant than radical innovation. Without innovation capacities and systems developing countries are unlikely to secure widespread transfer and uptake of low carbon technologies.
*   Low carbon technologies will only be widely transferred and adopted if they attend to the context-specific, socio-technical characteristics of local countries, firms, communities, etc.
*   Careful attention is required to assess the extent to which low carbon technology transfer delivers against the needs of poor people.

References

Able-Thomas, U. (1996) Models of renewable energy technology transfer to developing countries. In: Sayigh, A. A. (ed.) *Renewable Energy, Energy Efficiency and the Environment*. New York: Pergamon Press, pp. 1104–7.

Bell, M. (1990) *Continuing Industrialisation, Climate Change and International Technology Transfer*. Brighton: University of Sussex, SPRU.

Bell, M. (2007) Technological learning and the development of production and innovative capacities in the industry and infrastructure sectors of the Least Developed Countries: what roles for ODA? UNCTAD The Least Developed Countries Report 2007 Background Paper. Brighton: University of Sussex, SPRU.

Biswas, W. K., Bryce, P. and Diesendorf, M. (2001) Model for empowering rural poor through renewable energy in Bangladesh. *Environmental Science and Policy*, 4(6), 333–44.

Brewer, T. (2008) Climate change technology transfer: a new paradigm and policy agenda. *Climate Policy*, 8, 516–26.

Byrne, R., Schoots, K., de Coninck, H., Ockwell, D. and Watson, J. (2012a) Innovating for climate-compatible development: What every climate-technology policymaker should know about innovation in developing countries, Policy Brief, Sussex Energy Group, SPRU and Energy Research Centre of the Netherlands, June.

Byrne, R., Smith, A., Watson, J. and Ockwell, D. (2012b) Energy pathways in low carbon development: the need to go beyond technology transfer. In: Ockwell, D. and Mallett, A. (eds) *Low Carbon Technology Transfer: from Rhetoric to Reality*. Abingdon: Routledge.

Carpenter, C. (2012) Taking stock of Durban: review of key outcomes and the road ahead. New York: United Nations Development Programme (UNDP), April.

Clayton, A., Spinardi, G. and Williams, R. 1999. *Policies for Cleaner Technologies*. London: Earthscan.

De Lopez, T., Ponlok, T., Iyadomi, K., Santos, S. and McIntosh, B. (2009) Clean Development Mechanism and Least Developed Countries: changing the rules for greater participation. *The Journal of Environment and Development*, 18, 436–52.

Douthwaite, B. (2002) *Enabling Innovation*. London: Zed.

Forsyth, T. (1999) *International Investment and Climate Change: Energy Technologies for Developing Countries*. London: Earthscan.

Forsyth, T. (2005) Enhancing climate technology transfer through greater public-private cooperation: lessons from Thailand and the Philippines. *Natural Resources Forum*, 29, 165–76.

Forsyth, T. (2005) Partnerships for technology transfer. Briefing Paper. C. H. Sustainable Development Programme. London: Royal Institute of International Affairs, pp. 1–11.

Forsyth, T. (2012) Reducing the cost of technology transfer through community partnerships. In: Ockwell, D. and Mallett, A. (eds) *Low Carbon Technology Transfer: from Rhetoric to Reality*. Abingdon: Routledge.

Geels, F. (2002) Technological transitions as evolutionary reconfiguration processes: a multi-level perspective and a case-study. *Research Policy*, 31, 1257–74.

Grubb, M., Vrolijk, C. and Brack, D. (2001) *The Kyoto Protocol. A Guide and Assessment.* London: The Royal Institute of International Affairs.

Harvey, I. (2008) Intellectual Property Rights: the catalyst to deliver low carbon technologies. breaking the climate deadlock, Briefing Paper. London: Ian Harvey and the Climate Group.

Intergovernmental Panel on Climate Change (IPCC) (2007) Working Group III contribution to the Intergovernmental Panel on Climate Change Fourth Assessment Report. Climate Change 2007: Mitigation of Climate Change. Geneva: IPCC.

Juma, C. and Yee-Cheong, L. (eds) (2005) Innovation: applying knowledge in development. Task Force on Science, Technology and Innovation, United Nations Millennium Project. New York: United Nations.

Khor, M. (2008) Access to technology, IPRs and climate change. Day One Session, European Patent Forum.

Lall, S. (1995) Science and technology in the new global environment: implications for developing countries. Geneva: United Nations.

Leach, M. and Waldman, L. (2009) Centres of excellence? Questions of capacity for innovation, sustainability, development. STEPS Working Paper 23. Brighton: STEPS Centre.

Leadbeater, C. (2005) Charles Leadbeater on nnovation. TED Talks. Available at: http://www.ted.com/talks/charles_leadbeater_on_innovation.html (accessed 31 October 2012).

Lederer, M. (2009) *Reforming Carbon Governance – the Clean Development Mechanism (CDM) from an Emerging Economy Perspective. Governance in Areas of Limited Statehood*. London: LSE, University of Potsdam.

Lee, B., Iliev, I. and Preston, F. (2009) Who owns our low carbon future? Intellectual property and energy technologies. A Chatham House Report. London: Royal Institute of International Affairs.

Lovett, J., Hofman, P. S., Morsink, K. and Clancy, O. (2012) Technology transfer and global markets. In: Ockwell, D. and Mallett, A. (eds) *Low Carbon Technology Transfer: from Rhetoric to Reality*. Abingdon: Routledge.

Mallett, A. (2009) Technology adoption, cooperation and trade and competitiveness policies: re-examining the uptake of Renewable Energy Technologies (RETs) in urban Latin America using systemic approaches, unpublished PhD thesis. London: London School of Economics and Political Science (LSE).

Mallett, A. (2012) Technology cooperation for sustainable energy – a review of pathways. In: Lund, P. (ed.) Wiley Interdisciplinary reviews on energy and the environment (WIREs). It is accessible online: http://wires.wiley.com/WileyCDA/WiresIssue/wisId-WENE.html?pageType=early

Mallett, A., Ockwell, D., Pal, P., Haum, R., Kumar, A., Abbi, Y., Watson, J., Sethi, G. and MacKerron, G. (2009) UK–India collaboration to overcome barriers to the transfer of low carbon energy technologies: Phase II. Brighton: SPRU, United Kingdom Department of Energy and Climate Change (DECC).

Modi, V., McDade, S., Lallement, D. and Saghir, J. (2005) Energy services for the Millennium Development Goals. Energy Sector Management Assistance Programme, United Nations Development Programme. New York: UN Millennium Project and World Bank.

Mowery, D. C., Nelson, R. R. and Martin, B. R. (2010) Technology policy and global warming: why new policy models are needed (or why putting new wine in old bottles won't work). *Research Policy*, 39, 1011–23.

Ockwell, D., Watson, J., MacKerron, G., Pal, P. and Yamin, F. (2006) UK-India Collaboration to Identify the Barriers to the Transfer of Low Carbon Energy Technology. London: Report by the Sussex Energy Group (SPRU, University of Sussex), TERI and IDS for the UK Department for Environment, Food and Rural Affairs.

Ockwell, D. G. (2012) Pro-poor, low carbon development: improving low carbon energy access and development benefits in Least Developed Countries (LDCs). STEPS Centre, Brighton. Available at: http://steps-centre.org/project/low_carbon_development (accessed 31 October 2012).

Ockwell, D. G., Watson, J., Verbeken, A., Mallett, A. and MacKerron, G. (2009) A blueprint for post-2012 technology transfer to developing countries. Sussex Energy Group Policy Briefing Note. Brighton: Sussex Energy Group.

Ockwell, D. G., Haum, R., Mallett, A. and Watson, J. (2010) Intellectual property rights and low carbon technology transfer: conflicting discourses of diffusion and development. *Global Environmental Change* 20, 729–38.

Organisation for Economic Co-operation and Development (OECD) (2002) Frascati Manual. Proposed standards for surveys on research and experimental development (R&D). Paris: OECD.

Philibert, C. (2006) *Barriers to Technology Diffusion: the Case of Solar Thermal Technologies (IEA)*. Paris: OECD, IEA, 29.

Pietrobelli, C. (2000) Technology transfer in developing countries. In: Schroeer, D. and Micro Elena (eds) *Technology Transfer*. Aldershot: Ashgate.

Ravindranath, N. H. and Sathaye, J. (2002) *Climate Change and Developing Countries*. Dordrecht: Kluwer Academic Publishers.

Renewables (2004) Conference report for Renewables 2004. Renewables 2004, International Conference for Renewable Energies.

Rip, A. and Kemp, R. (1998) Technological change. In: Rayner, S. and Malone, E. (eds) *Human Choices and Climate Change. Vol. 2: Resources and Technology*. Columbus, OH: Battelle.

Rodrigues, D. and Matajs, R. (2005) Brazil finds its place in the sun: solar water heating and sustainable energy. Vitae Civilis and the Blue Moon Fund, Sao Lourenço da Serra, Brazil.

Sagar, A. (2010) Climate Innovation Centres: a new way to foster climate technologies in the developing world? An infoDev publication in collaboration with UNIDO and DfID. Available at: www.infodev.org (accessed 31 October 2012).

Sagar, A. D., Bremner, C. and Grubb, M. (2009) Climate Innovation Centres: a partnership approach to meeting energy and climate challenges. *Natural Resources Forum*, 33, 274–84.

Sauter, R. and Watson, J. (2008) *Technology Leapfrogging: a Review of the Evidence*. Sussex Energy Group, Brighton: SPRU, pp. 1–30.

Smith, A., Voß, J. and Grin, J. (2010) Innovation studies and sustainability transitions: the allure of the multi-level perspective and its challenges. *Research Policy*, 39, 435–48.

Stern, N. (2006) Stern Review on the economics of climate change. London: HM Treasury.

Sumner, A. (2011) Where do the poor live? An update. Brighton: IDS.

United Nations Conference on Trade and Development (UNCTAD) (2007) The Least Developed Country report 2007. Geneva: United Nations.

United Nations Department of Economic and Social Affairs (UNDESA) (2005) Increasing global renewable energy market share: recent trends and perspectives – final report. Prepared for Beijing International Renewable Energy Conference 2005. New York: United Nations.

United Nations Development Programme (UNDP) (2007) Energizing the Least Developed Countries to achieve the Millennium Development Goals: the challenges and opportunities of globalization. New York: United Nations.

United Nations Environment Programme (UNEP)/Division of Technology, I. a. E. (2000) *Natural Selection: Evolving Choices for Renewable Energy Technology and Policy*. Paris: UNEP.

United Nations Framework Convention on Climate Change (UNFCCC) (1992) New York: United Nations, pp. 1–33.

Vedavalli, R. (2007) *Energy for Development – Twenty-first Century Challenges of Reform and Liberalization Developing Countries*. London: Anthem Press.

World Bank (2010) Innovation Policy – a guide for developing countries. Washington, DC: The World Bank.

Wustenhagen, R., Wolsink, M. and Burer, M. (2007) Social acceptance of renewable energy innovations: introduction to the concept. *Energy Policy*, 35, 5, 2683–91.

Further reading

Bell, M. (2009) Innovation capabilities and directions of development. STEPS Working Paper 33. Brighton: STEPS Centre.

Brewer, T. (2008) Climate change technology transfer: a new paradigm and policy agenda. *Climate Policy*, 8, 516–26.

Forsyth, T. (2007) Promoting the 'development dividend' of climate technology transfer: can cross-sector partnerships help? *World Development*, 35(10), 1684–98.

Ockwell, D. and Mallett, A. (eds) (2012) *Low Carbon Technology Transfer: From Rhetoric to Reality*. Abingdon: Routledge.

Notes

1   It is important to note that these issues are highly relevant to discussions regarding climate resilient technologies, or adaptation technologies, but, as per the scope of this chapter, we will be focusing on low carbon or mitigation technologies.

2   Defined as a good which is non-rivalrous and non-excludable.

3   While true that the majority of low carbon technologies are 'owned' by the private sector (Harvey, 2008; Lee *et al.* 2008), for a number of developing countries, other key sources of innovation are public universities and research institutes, NGOs, community groups, households and farms. For example, a 2010 World Bank study, notes that for many developing countries, R&D spending and performance, one proxy used to help 'measure' innovation comes mainly from the government directly or through higher education institutes, many of which are public.

4   See http://www.sustainableenergyforall.org/.

5   Also, for further details on the specifics of these policies please see Mallett *et al.* (2009).

6   See http://www.gshakti.org/index.php?option=com_content&view=article&id=57&Itemid=77.

7   Personal communication, October 2006, V. Pramana, World Bank expert, based on his experience with the Commercializing Renewable Energy in India (CREI) project.

8   See http://unfccc.int.ttclear/jsp/TEC.jsp and http://unfccc.int.ttclear/jsp/CTCN.jsp.

9   See for instance http://www.hindustantimes.com/India-news/NewDelhi/India-seeks-Kyoto-type-agreement-after-2020/Article1-848592.aspx.

10   Pending approval from the Canadian government http://www.theglobeandmail.com/globe-investor/malaysia-makes-big-bet-on-natural-gas-from-canada/article4376077/.

Part 6

Key issues for low carbon development in policy and practice

Editorial for Part 6

Key issues for low carbon development in policy and practice

Frauke Urban and Johan Nordensvärd

Part 6 elaborates the key issues for low carbon development in policy and practice and presents cross-cutting issues such as low carbon energy, forestry, agriculture and transportation. Part 6 also addresses the emerging concept of climate compatible development.

Overview of Part 6

Chapter 9 addresses the key issue of providing energy access to households in developing countries, particularly the rural poor who often have limited access to modern energy services and depend mainly on traditional biomass for cooking and heating. The chapter introduces the issues surrounding energy poverty and details the link between energy access and development. The chapter then goes on to outline the three main types of energy delivery models required to sustainably deliver a range of energy services, including well known case studies. While increasing energy access to reduce energy poverty must remain the priority of energy delivery models in developing countries, it can often be achieved through the utilization of low carbon energy resources. As well as resulting in reduced carbon emissions, low carbon energy delivery models have numerous other benefits such as increasing energy security of a country and providing a range of livelihood benefits, particularly in rural areas.

Chapter 10 discusses how to revolutionize the electricity sector by making it compatible with an increasing share of renewable energy infrastructure. Large-scale renewable energy will be a key strategy for low carbon economies. However, it is challenging for many electricity grids to absorb the variable and decentralized power generated by renewable energy resources such as wind and the sun. This chapter explores those challenges. The chapter also discusses the emerging options and best practices for effectively using these new sources of energy to reduce greenhouse gas emissions. Grid operators are already implementing solutions such as investing in updated electricity infrastructure, reforming electricity markets, investing in storage and using smart grid technologies.

Chapter 11 elaborates the link between forests and low carbon development. Forest vegetation and soils directly contribute to climate change mitigation by absorbing carbon dioxide. Depletion of forests leads to losses of carbon sinks and greenhouse gas emissions due to changes in land use, such as for agriculture. Concerns about climate change and other negative impacts of forest loss have led to the emergence of various policies and mechanisms to integrate the forestry sector in low carbon development strategies. Despite existing opportunities, creating these synergies involves key technical, socio-economic and political challenges. This chapter takes a sectoral perspective focusing on the contribution of forests to low carbon development. The different forestry-related low carbon development practices and policies to achieve are then explored as well as the key structural barriers to achieve effective emission reduction and to make them compatible with environmental integrity and socio-economic justice.

Chapter 12 discusses the link between agriculture and low carbon development. 'Low carbon' in agriculture goes beyond carbon and includes mitigation of GHGs other than carbon dioxide, including nitrous oxide and methane. Changes in land use and different management practices in crop and livestock production are major contributors to the GHG emissions leading to climate change. Fossil fuel-induced emissions due to energy use and transport for food products are also sources of GHG emissions in agriculture. Mitigation in this sector can be achieved not only through various improved techniques but also through the introduction of new policies and programmes that support low carbon agricultural development. Emission reduction will depend on how solutions are appropriate to contextual needs, the creation of synergies with other low carbon development sectors and effective control of agricultural production.

Chapter 13 elaborates key issues related to transportation and low carbon development. Decarbonizing transport is a key element of low carbon development, but emissions from transport are amongst the most intransigent and are expected to rise significantly in the coming decades. Most policies regarding low carbon transport follow a dominant economistic paradigm, exploring the options of either behavioural change to reduce demand for transport or technological change to increase the efficiency of its energy use. However, there is much evidence that this will not be successful. A shift from 'transport' towards socio-technical systems, situated practices of mobility and smart mobility innovation is thus advocated. The chapter focuses on urban transport to elaborate the role of transportation for low carbon development.

Chapter 14 explores the case of climate compatible development. Low carbon development addresses the interface between climate change mitigation and development. However, for people and communities affected by climate change, adapting to climatic impacts is crucial. It is therefore necessary to consider mitigation, adaptation and development as interlinked challenges that have to be addressed together, rather than addressing them as separate challenges. This chapter therefore introduces the concept of climate compatible development, which brings together mitigation, adaptation and development and offers opportunities for producing 'triple wins' to deliver lower emissions development that is resilient to current and future climatic impacts.

9 Low carbon energy and energy access in developing countries

Ewan Bloomfield and Annabel Yadoo

With additions on concepts of energy and development and the hydraulic ram pump programme by Frauke Urban.

This chapter addresses the important issue of providing energy to households in developing countries, particularly the rural poor who often have limited access to modern energy services and depend mainly on traditional biomass for cooking and heating.[1] The chapter introduces the issues surrounding energy poverty and details the link between energy access and development. It provides an outline of the range of energy services and minimum standards that are required to allow people to work themselves out of poverty. The chapter then goes on to outline the three main types of energy delivery models required to sustainably deliver a range of energy services, including well known case studies. While increasing energy access to reduce energy poverty must remain the priority of energy delivery models in developing countries, it can often be achieved through the utilization of low carbon energy resources. As well as resulting in reduced carbon emissions, low carbon energy delivery models have numerous other benefits such as increasing energy security of a country and providing a range of livelihood benefits, particularly in rural areas.

Introduction to energy poverty

While the United Nations' International Year of Sustainable Energy for All (SE4A) in 2012 has the goal to provide access to modern energy services to everyone in the world by 2030, energy access remains low or non-existent for billions of the world's population at the moment. Worldwide, over 1.3 billion people lack access to electricity and 2.7 billion people use traditional biomass, such as fuel wood, for cooking (IEA, 2011). Over 95 per cent of these people live in rural areas of South Asia and Sub-Saharan Africa; worldwide 84 per cent of people who lack access to electricity in their homes live in rural areas (IEA, 2011). The IEA predicts that at the current pace of change, over 1 billion people will still lack access to electricity in 2030 and the number cooking with traditional biomass will remain unchanged (IEA, 2011).

Energy is a central theme for development in general and low carbon development specifically. The lack of access to modern energy services detracts from people's standard of health, education, food security, gender equality and ability to earn a living (DfID, 2002; GNESD, 2007). Furthermore, energy poverty undermines the achievement of the MDGs, hindering the reduction of poverty:

Universal energy access is a key priority on the global development agenda. It is a foundation for all the Millennium Development Goals... Without energy services, the poor are cut off from basic amenities. They are forced to live and work in unhealthy, polluted conditions. Furthermore, energy poverty directly affects the viability of forests, soils and rangelands. In short, it is an obstacle to the Millennium Development Goals

(Ban Ki-moon, United Nations Secretary General, New York, 21 September 2010).

The UN aspires to achieve universal energy access by 2030. Energy practitioners (government, private sector and civil society actors) face the challenge of delivering access to modern energy services, particularly where energy users live in poverty and are situated in very remote locations that lack adequate infrastructure. Awareness about climatic change and the notion of energy security for future generations is also rising up the global agenda.

This chapter addresses the important issue of providing energy to people in developing countries, particularly the rural poor who do not have access to modern energy and depend mainly on traditional biomass for cooking and heating. The chapter introduces the issues surrounding energy poverty and details the link between energy access and development. It also provides an outline of the range of energy services and minimum standards that are required to allow people to work themselves out of poverty. The chapter then goes on to outline the three main types of energy delivery models required to sustainably deliver a range of energy services, including well known case studies. While increasing energy access to reduce energy poverty must remain the priority of energy delivery models in developing countries, it can often be achieved through the utilization of low carbon energy resources. As well as resulting in reduced carbon emissions, low carbon energy delivery models have numerous other benefits such as increasing energy security of a country and providing a range of livelihood benefits, particularly in rural areas. Low carbon energy, particularly renewable energy, is crucial for achieving low carbon development, reducing poverty and increasing energy access in poor countries. Box 9.1 explains some of the key terms that are used in this chapter and the section on 'Energy access and modern energy services' explores what is meant by access to energy and modern energy services.

Box 9.1 Definitions of key concepts and terms

Modern energy forms: Modern energy refers to non-traditional energy forms, which are more convenient and easy to handle, such as electricity as well as gaseous and liquid fuels such as natural gas and ethanol.

Modern energy services: These encompass lighting, cooking, water pumping, transportation, heating, cooling and the powering of electrical equipment for a variety of different purposes, amongst them communications, entertainment, education, healthcare, income generation and improved comfort.

Modern energy access: 'Reliable and affordable access to clean cooking facilities, a first connection to electricity and then an increasing level of electricity consumption over time to reach the regional average' (IEA, 2011: 3).

Traditional energy forms: These include solid fuels, which are less convenient and easy to handle, such as fuel wood, dung and agricultural residues. Traditional energy forms are often of poorer quality and associated with higher economic, health and environmental costs than their modern counterparts.

Energy poverty: A state in which a user of energy does not have access to a minimum level of a range of clean and affordable energy services that allow them to meet all their needs. This minimum level of energy has been defined by a set of minimum energy standards as described below.

Minimum energy standards: These are a set of minimum levels of a range of energy services including lighting, cooking, water and space heating, and so on, which have been defined as being required to allow an individual or household to raise itself out of energy poverty, described as achieving Total Energy Access. These standards are outlined in Table 9.1.

Energy security: A situation whereby an individual or households has access a range of clean, affordable and reliable energy services in the quantities and at the time that they are needed.

Energy delivery model: The system that transposes energy from its original source (e.g. water, sunlight, fuel wood) to a range of energy services (e.g. heating, lighting, cooling) that meet the needs of end consumers, typically households, institutions (including schools, hospitals and community centres) and businesses. An energy delivery model includes a number of processes and activities. These processes range from the design and provision of appropriate technologies and financial systems, to the ownership, management and maintenance components that ensure the energy is affordable and can be supplied indefinitely.

Energy access and modern energy services

Energy access

However, there is not yet a universally accepted definition of what energy access entails[2] and assumptions concerning user needs and the efficiencies of various technologies differ from one publication to the next. In addition non-household-related energy needs, for example access for businesses or community services, are often excluded from energy assessments (Practical Action, 2010). The IEA defines modern energy access in terms of 'reliable and affordable access to clean cooking facilities, a first connection to electricity and then an increasing level of electricity consumption over time to reach the regional average' (IEA, 2011: 3). In this context low carbon cooking facilities denote 'biogas systems, liquefied petroleum gas (LPG) stoves and advanced biomass cookstoves that have considerably lower emissions and higher efficiencies than traditional three-stone fires for cooking' (IEA, 2011: 3).

Minimum electricity consumption levels based on the types of appliances – fans, mobile telephones, light bulbs, and so on – that could be operated within its limit are defined as 250 kWh/year for rural households and 500 kWh/year for urban households, and consumption levels are expected to reach the regional average within five years (by 2030 consumption is expected to be 800 kWh/year/capita) (IEA, 2011: 3). It is of interest to note that in comparison in the UK typical annual household energy consumption has been estimated at 3300 kWh (Ofgem, 2011).

Practical Action, in consultation with other leading energy experts and institutions, has developed nine minimum standards, which focus purely on energy access at the household level. If a household meets all of these standards, they are then considered to have access to modern energy services. Practical Action's definition of Total Energy Access, outlined in Table 9.1, diverts from the IEA's approach by framing the standards in terms of the energy service provided – for example, lighting, cooking and heating – as opposed to the medium through which it is delivered (such as clean cooking facilities and electricity). It is important to note that in most developing countries these energy services are typically obtained through a range of energy resources, both high and low carbon (Practical Action, 2012).

Table 9.1 Practical Action's definition of Total Energy Access

Energy service	Minimum standard
Lighting	300 lumen for a minimum of 4 h per night at household level
Cooking and water heating	– 1 kg fuel wood or 0.3 kg charcoal or 0.04 kg LPG or 0.2 l of kerosene or ethanol per person per day, taking less than 30 min per household per day to obtain – Minimum efficiency of improved solid fuel stove to be 40% greater than a three-stone fire in terms of fuel use – Annual mean concentrations of particulate matter ($PM_{2.5}$) <10 mg/m^2 in households, with interim goal of 15 mg/m^2, 25 mg/m^2 and 35 mg/m^2
Space heating	Minimum daytime indoor air temperature of 18°C
Cooling	– Households can extend life of perishable products by a minimum of 50% over that allowed by ambient storage – Maximum apparent indoor air temperate of 30°C
Informations and communications	– People can communicate electronic information from their household – People can access electronic media relevant to their lives in their households

Source: Amended from Practical Action, 2012

Modern energy services

As highlighted in Table 9.1 modern energy services include activities such as lighting, cooking, water pumping, transportation, heating, cooling and the powering of electrical equipment for a variety of different purposes, amongst them communications, entertainment, education, healthcare, income generation and improved comfort. Traditional, or non-modern, energy forms, such as fuel wood, dung and agricultural residues, could also provide some of these services, but they are often of poorer quality and associated with higher economic, health and environmental costs. For cooking, the use of an energy-efficient biomass stove, generically known as an improved cooking stove, reduces wood consumption and the production of unhealthy emissions when compared with cooking over a traditional three-stone fire.[3] Many traditional cooking fuels can be regarded as being low carbon when they are managed, such as crop residues and wood or charcoal from managed wood plots, while more modern cooking fuels, such as LPG and kerosene, are typically high carbon. For lighting, energy from an electrically powered light bulb is better quality and often cheaper, with a reduced fire risk and fewer emissions, than lighting provided by candles, and can often come from a low carbon source such as solar photovoltaics or a micro hydro installation.

As noted by Ban Ki-moon in 2010, access to modern energy services is the 'foundation for all the Millennium Development Goals' and plays a significant role in increasing economic and human development. Table 9.2 sets out the contribution of modern energy services to the MDGs, particularly those related to healthcare, education, food security, poverty reduction, gender equality and environmental sustainability. Analysis has shown that the greatest incremental benefit from modern energy services is received by those who are currently at the lowest levels of human development (IEA, 2004).

Table 9.2 Modern energy services and the Millennium Development Goals

Water pumping	Water disinfection	Cooking and water heating	Crop drying/cooling	Lighting and powering electrical equipment	Ambient heating/cooling	Transportation
Clean water for drinking and washing improves hygiene (MDG 4, 5)	Health improves as gastro-intestinal infections are reduced (MDG 4, 5)	Modern forms cooking (for example, gas and efficient biomass stoves) can reduce the amount of smoke inhaled and improve the health of women and children (MDG 4, 5)	Preserving produce through the non-harvest season helps farmers feed their families throughout the year and sell produce at times when they fetch a higher price (MDG 1)	Health improves due to the higher retention of professional staff, refrigeration of vaccines, improved lighting and the use of other electrical equipment (MDG 4, 5, 6)	Greater comfort (MDG 1)	Improved communications (MDG 1, 2, 8)
Women and children spend less time fetching water, more can attend school (MDG 2, 3)		Women can spend less time and travel less distance to fetch fuel, personal safety can improve (MDG 3, 5, 6)		Education improves due to the higher retention of professional staff, improved lighting for home study, computers and other learning aids (MDG 2, 4)	Health benefits in colder climates (MDG 4, 5)	Improved healthcare, education and income generation possibilities due to easier access to neighbouring communities and markets (MDG 1, 4, 5)
Irrigation can increase the volumes and diversity of produce, improving incomes and local diets (MDG 1, 4, 5)		Reduced deforestation and associated degradation (soil erosion, landslides, desertification, decreased biodiversity and fewer carbon sinks) (MDG 7)		New or improved income generating possibilities, local production of 'value-added' goods and small-scale industry (MDG 1)		Increased ability for healthcare and education professionals to reach the community (MDG 2, 4, 5, 6)

Cultivation during the dry season can fetch higher prices if produce is sold and save households money if consumed (MDG 1)

Greater comfort, ease and entertainment in the home, security from street lighting (MDG 3)

Improved communications with potential impact on income (MDG 1, 2, 8)

Notes: MDG 1 – End poverty and hunger; MDG 2 – Universal education; MDG 3 – Gender equality; MDG 4 – Child health; MDG 5 – Maternal health; MDG 6 – Combat HIV/AIDS; MDG 7 – Environmental sustainability; MDG 8 – Global Partnership. All energy services can contribute to MDG 7 if low carbon sources are used sustainably

Source: Yadoo, 2011.

Energy and development

Concepts of energy and development

Energy is a central theme for low carbon development. Energy is a vital commodity and is closely intertwined with development. Energy is needed for basic human needs: for cooking, heating, lighting, boiling water and for other household-based activities. Energy is also required to sustain and expand economic processes like agriculture, electricity production, industries, services and transport. It is commonly suggested that energy access is closely linked with development and economic growth (e.g. WHO, 2006; UNDP & WHO, 2009, IEA, 2010) and that alleviating energy poverty is a prerequisite to fulfil the MDGs (DfID, 2002; WHO, 2006; IEA, 2010). Correlations between household income as well as national income and energy access show that there is a link between rising income levels and rising energy access.[4] This has been observed in the form of electricity access and access to modern fuels (World Bank, 2012). This means that countries with higher incomes also tend to have higher electricity access rates. An example is electricity access in Asia: the low income country Cambodia had an electrification rate of 24 per cent in 2011, the middle income country Mongolia had an electrification rate of 67 per cent in 2011 and the high income country Singapore had an electrification rate of 100 per cent in 2011 (World Bank, 2012).

Various concepts describe the relationship between energy and development, most importantly the *Energy Ladder*, *Fuel Switching* and the *Environmental Kuznets Curve* (EKC). These concepts will be discussed below.

The Energy Ladder is a stylized concept which assumes that with increasing incomes, households will be able to switch from traditional biomass use to energy carriers that are cleaner, more efficient and easier to handle, such as charcoal and then progress on to more advanced energy carriers such as natural gas, biogas and electricity (Barnes and Floor, 1996; Holdren and Smith, 2000; Masera *et al.*, 2000; Martins, 2005; Van Ruijven *et al.*, 2008). This is linked to Fuel Switching, which is used to describe a similar process where households switch from a fuel that is often inefficient or unhealthy, to a fuel that is described as being more modern and cleaner such as switching from charcoal to kerosene or LPG (World Bank, 2003). In real life, Fuel Switching and the Energy Ladder are far less discrete, and linear Fuel Switching is contested by leading academics (e.g. Masera *et al.*, 2000). Often various energy carriers are used alongside each other, such as electricity for lighting and charcoal for cooking. Multiple cooking strategies have also been observed (Masera *et al.*, 2000).

The Environmental Kuznets Curve (EKC) is a contentious concept that makes a correlation between environmental pollution and economic development and follows the shape of an inverted U-curve. The hypothesis of the EKC is first that environmental pollution is at a low level when countries have low income and development levels; second, it increases and peaks when mid levels of incomes and development are reached; and third, pollution levels decrease again when income and development levels increase (Beckerman, 1992; Van Ruijven *et al.*, 2008). The EKC is closely related to the decoupling of economic growth from energy use and emissions, which is fiercely debated. See Chapter 1 for a more detailed discussion about decoupling, the EKC and its role for achieving low carbon development. (Van Ruijven *et al.*, 2008; Urban, 2010).

Overcoming energy poverty and improving development

To try and overcome the wide disparity in access to energy between the developed and developing worlds, resulting in extensive energy poverty, a wide range of organizations have been focusing on developing appropriate and sustainable energy delivery systems, including multilateral and bilateral donors such as the European Commission, the German Federal Ministry for Economic Development Cooperation (BMZ), UNDP and USAID, as well as NGOs, such as Christian Aid and Practical Action, and private sector companies, such as Bosch and Siemens Hausgeräte (BSH) and Unilever, which have more recently begun to include social enterprises that have both social as well as financial goals, and often work in collaboration with donors and NGOs, such as Envirofit and Tough Stuff.

The development benefits of increased access to modern energy services have long been recognized; the debate has now returned to what exactly constitutes a modern energy service. The United Nations Industrial Development Organization (UNIDO) defines a modern energy service as one that uses less primary energy, is more affordable and healthy, and offers a higher quality of service to the user in terms of light, heat, and so on, and ultimately allows the target population to enter a sustainable technological path of development (UNIDO, 2010).

The main aim of energy delivery programmes has been to increase the access to a range of energy services for households and institutions, such as cooking, lighting and space heating. However, it is increasingly recognized, for example within UNDP's Energy and Employment report 2012 (UNDP, 2012), and the Poor People's Energy Outlook 2012 (Practical Action, 2012), that energy access should not be considered the end goal of an intervention. Stimulation of a much wider range of development impacts is required, including the productive uses of energy in order to increase livelihoods as well as health, educational and capacity building services.

These energy delivery models involve the design, implementation and financing of systems that are aimed at increasing energy access of the poor in developing countries. The technologies that are used vary widely from more traditional fossil fuel-based generators and power plants, to low carbon solar photovoltaic, hydro and biogas systems, as well as biomass gasifiers, which combine traditional wood fuel resources with more modern, efficient and clean burning technologies.

Energy delivery systems need to be designed to specifically meet a range of needs, such as electricity for refrigeration of vaccines, dairy produce or preserving foods, carpentry workshops, agro-processing centres, computer centres at schools incorporating adult evening classes, which have much wider income producing and social benefits. Sometimes the energy production systems themselves are able to provide a range of additional benefits beyond just the supply of energy, such as biogas digesters, which produce high quality organic fertilizers as a by-product, and biomass gasifiers that produce biochar, which can also significantly increase the fertility of soils for food production. Energy access projects should not only eliminate energy poverty, but also allow poor, rural households to work their own way out of poverty. This can often be carried out through the use of low carbon energy resources, however, they are not always the most appropriate solutions, due to higher capital investment needs and potential complications around ownership, management or maintenance, and reducing energy poverty needs to take priority over ensuring the energy comes from a low carbon source.

Delivering energy for poverty reduction

As people use energy in a variety of forms to meet a range of services, it needs to be packaged, processed and delivered. This requires a variety of processes and a range of technologies, as well as financing, and management and maintenance systems. The energy itself has come from a range of sources, and whilst it has more traditionally come from fossil fuels, such as diesel and natural gas, it may have also been supplied through renewable, low carbon, resources as well, including hydro and bioenergy sources. As the focus gradually moves towards low carbon development, a range of renewable energy sources are being increasingly accessed in developing countries including small solar systems, wind, biogas, biofuels, micro hydro and agricultural waste products.

The systems that deliver the energy from the original resources to the provision of a range of energy services that meet the needs of the end consumers, typically households, institutions (including schools, hospitals and community centres) and businesses, is described as an energy delivery model. The processes range from the design and provision of the appropriate technologies, to the full spectrum of financial systems required, as well as the ownership, management and maintenance components that ensure the energy is affordable and can be supplied indefinitely.

Although the term energy delivery models has been used quite freely in the past to describe a range of methods of delivering energy, there has been no widely accepted agreement of how they should be defined. To try and address this, the authors, together with several other organizations, have identified the three key areas of an energy delivery model as the implementation process, the supporting services and the enabling environment, each of which can help contribute to – or conversely, can help undermine – the successful delivery of a range of energy services (Bellanca *et al.*, 2013), which are outlined in the following sections. This is further detailed within an online delivery model tool (http://practicalaction.org/energy-delivery-model).

Implementation process

The implementation process lies at the heart of an energy delivery model and is carried out by a range of market actors that carry out a range of commercial activities. The implementation process spans the access to the energy resources, including a range of low carbon resources, through to their conversion and processing, their distribution strategies and their delivery to the final end users. It includes the governance, management and ownership structures of the delivery processes, as well as the technologies involved, and the use of financing structures. The implementation process is typically carried out by private sector market actors, but often with some level of support from government and civil society actors, such as the Kenyan Ceramic Jiko (KCJ), which is currently produced by private sector stove producers but received support in its development from a number of organizations as well as government departments (Bellanca *et al.*, 2013).

Supporting services

The supporting services include the additional services that are required to directly support the market actors within the implementation process, to enhance the sustainability of a delivery model, including training and capacity building, as well as financial support services such as micro-finance. The range of services that can potentially add value is huge and includes input supplies, market information, financial and transport services, quality assurance including monitoring and accreditation, technical expertise and business advice, as well as support for product development and diversification. It is important to note that the supporting services will play a significant role in shifting towards low carbon energy resources, through the provision of appropriate and affordable technologies, capacity building and training, support on the initial resource assessments and, crucially, on innovative financial services to ensure they are affordable, particularly for the very poor (Bellanca *et al.*, 2013).

Enabling environment

The enabling environment consists of the regulations and incentives that directly impact an energy delivery model at the national, regional and international level. It is typically beyond the control of the market actors themselves but is amenable to change through concerted international processes such as lobbying and policy entrepreneurship. It includes the policy decisions made by government, including those on infrastructure development, economic policies and laws, trading and quality standards, rights of access to natural resources including land and rivers, most of which are of particular relevance to low carbon energy options, such as supportive policies and the elimination of fossil fuel subsidies.

An aspect of the enabling environment that is particularly important for ensuring the sustainable supply of energy services for the very poor is the full understanding of the socio-cultural context of the household and community end users. This includes their social and cultural norms, the establishment of energy-related practices and preferences, and traditional decision-making structures. Essentially if a technology or its financial and/or management systems are not accepted by the end users they will not function effectively in the long term – this has been the downfall of a great number of energy delivery models. The full inclusion of the views of the end users is also extremely important for scaling up renewable energy, such as with bioenergy, which has traditionally been viewed as a fuel of the very poor, and only with the development of new improved stoves such as Envirofit, Stovetec and wood gasifier stoves, is it starting to be viewed as a potentially modern fuel of the future (Bellanca *et al.*, 2013).

Low carbon energy access: on-grid, mini-grid and off-grid

This section discusses some of the options for implementing on-grid, mini-grid and off-grid energy and the role that low carbon energy can play. Energy has been described by the IEA (IEA, 2011) and others as generally being delivered through three main categories of models: on-grid, mini-grid and off-grid, which are simply defined below. It is important to note that the term grid is not synonymous with the delivery of electricity, and can also be used for the delivery of heat, natural gas and, in rare cases, mechanical power, such as for agricultural processing (although these are rarely delivered through on-grid in developing countries). Heat and mechanical power are often the dominant energy services for households in developing countries, particularly in rural areas, and even if electricity can be provided through new innovative delivery models, the delivery of heat and mechanical power will continue to be important. Box 9.2 provides an overview of the differences between on-grid, mini-grid and off-grid energy systems.

Box 9.2 Definition of on-grid, mini-grid and off-grid energy systems

On-grid: Energy that is delivered through a fully integrated system from its production to its delivery through a grid system typically at a national scale (or even regional scale).

Mini-grid: Energy that is delivered through a grid system to households and community centres, but which is self-contained within a particular area such as village or town and not connected to other regions.

Off-grid: An energy system that is centred on a single household or institution such as solar home system, LPG or biomass stove or individual wind turbine.

Energy experts can learn a lot about the sustainable delivery of energy by looking at well-known examples of energy delivery models, to gain a clear understanding of why some have succeeded whilst others have failed. The following section highlights three well known international energy delivery model programmes, from the rural electrification on-grid programme in China – which has a history of achieving rural electrification through hydropower – to the mini-grid Small Enterprise Management micro hydro programme in Peru, and finally the off-grid hydraulic ram pump programme in the Philippines. All three case studies are examples that highlight the role of hydropower to some extent.

The delivery of energy has always been achieved through a mixture of fossil fuels as well as a range of renewable energy sources; on-grid energy in developing countries is typically supplied through fossil fuel power plants and large hydro facilities (although increasingly geothermal, wind and concentrated solar are being developed); mini-grid energy has typically been delivered with diesel, but a wide range of renewable energy sources are increasingly being implemented, from micro hydro to biogas, wood gasifiers, wind and solar photovoltaics, often within hybrid systems, such as a number of new diesel, solar photovoltaics and biomass gasifier systems in Cambodia (Williamson, 2012); off-grid energy has typically been supplied in urban areas through fossil fuels, predominantly LPG and kerosene, and through biomass in rural areas. However, a range of renewable energy off-grid delivery systems are being implemented in developing countries, including pico hydro,[5] wind, solar PV, biomass rocket and gasifier stoves, biogas and pure plant oil stove and lamps.

On-grid energy delivery

This section first describes on-grid energy delivery systems and then discusses a case study. Energy is generally delivered through centralized energy generation and distribution systems at a district or national scale, typically serving many thousands of households, institutions and businesses. The energy being delivered is usually electricity or gas, but occasionally also hot water through district distribution grids, with typical capacity being in the megawatt to gigawatt scale.

On a national scale the usual technologies include both fossil fuel- and renewable energy-based systems, including large-scale boiler combustion using fossil and biomass fuels; nuclear and geothermal power stations; large riverine dam and hydro facilities; wind farms; solar photovoltaics and concentrated solar photovoltaics; and large-scale bio-digesters. Some examples of small-scale low carbon energy systems, based on micro hydro, solar and biomass gasification technologies that directly feed into the grid are being developed, and such systems can be supported through policy instruments such as feed-in tariffs, and so on. Figure 9.1 gives an overview of an on-grid energy delivery model (Bellanca *et al.*, 2013).

Case Study 1 rural electrification programme, China

Today, China has an electrification rate of 99 per cent, which is far higher than other countries with similar income levels (national average per capita income of about US$1000), and has had particular success in electrifying rural areas through more than three decades of investments in low carbon energy, mainly small hydropower, and linking energy access to rural development and improving agricultural productivity. China thus provides a very useful case study for understanding the limits of on-grid energy delivery.

Despite the rapid process of urbanization within the country due to its fast industrialization over the last two decades, the World Bank currently estimates that approximately 55

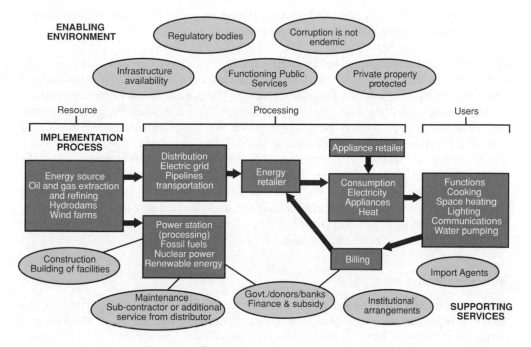

Figure 9.1 Schematic diagram of an on-grid energy delivery model
Source: Bellanca *et al.*, 2013

per cent of the Chinese population still lives in rural areas (World Bank, 2011). The high rural electrification rate (around 96%) is due to the favourable policies and programmes that Chinese government has historically made in favour of energy access for rural population and their strategic development. The government of China considers energy access to be a public service, and therefore has provided for its continuous financial and political support.

The Chinese Rural Electrification can be summarized in three stages (Jiahua *et al.*, 2006):

1   From 1950 until the end of 1970s, the driving force for rural electrification and particularly for small hydro was the development of agriculture. Rural electrification was slow, yet impressive and the progress was made under strict central planning with the investments and implementation led by the local governments and the counties.

2   From the late 1970s to the late 1990s, the Chinese government promoted rural industrialization, and emphasized the development of rural electrification by designing and implementing appropriate strategies and policies to suit local conditions and interests, particularly for hydropower. This included strategies such as 'the one who invests owns and operates', annual subsidies to the implementation of small hydropower plants, plus special loans and other financing to meet their objectives (Jiahua, 2006: 16).

3   The 21st century brought large-scale consolidation and upgrading of rural grids. The driving forces during this period were institutional reform, boosting electricity demand,

integration of rural and non-rural electricity markets, fuel substitution to contribute to environmental protection and improvement of the quality of rural life.

The significant achievements in rural electrification in China have been due to the clear role of the state in the provision of energy electrification services and a strong institutional arrangement with clear roles for the involved actors. The present Chinese government plans are to have the rural population fully electrified by 2015, and it has been implementing large-scale rural electrification programmes since the early 2000s, such as the China Township Electrification Program launched in 2001 and completed in 2005. This was a scheme to provide renewable electricity to 1.3 million people in 1000 townships in the Chinese provinces of Gansu, Hunan, Inner Mongolia, Shaanxi, Sichuan, Yunnan, Xinjiang, Qinghai and Tibet. Presently this programme is being succeeded by the similar but larger 'China Village Electrification Program', bringing renewable electricity to 3.5 million households in 10,000 villages by 2010 (Jiahau, 2006). China is one of the examples of countries with explicit mandates for renewable energy for rural electrification.[6]

Mini-grid energy delivery

Energy is delivered through localized, small- or medium-scale power sources, typically less than 3 MW in size (although usually much smaller), supplying a local distribution grid connected to domestic, business and institutional customers in a locality that is not connected to the national grid. The energy source is often fossil fuels, particularly for multi-functional platforms (MFP[7]), or small-scale renewables, including micro hydro, solar, wind, biomass, biofuels, and possibly geothermal. Hybrid systems are becoming increasingly common, such as diesel and pure plant oil generators. The technology used is often generators that use one, or a combination of, diesel, biodiesel and pure plant oil, as well as micro stations, such as bio-digesters; biomass boilers; gasifiers; solar; hydro dams or run of river systems; wind turbines, as well as community mechanical power systems, such as grain mills and water pumping facilities. Figure 9.2 outlines the various parts of a mini-grid energy delivery model including aspects of the implementing process, the supporting service and enabling environment.

Case Study 2 Mini-grid micro hydro community management model, Peru

The mini-grid micro hydro management model, which was initiated by Practical Action in the late 1990s in Peru, is often cited as one of the most successful examples of sustainable mini-grid energy delivery models through empowering isolated communities to design, construct and manage their own energy systems in a sustainable way (Sanches 1999). It was initially piloted in the village of Conchán, in the Northern Andes of Peru and it has since been implemented, adapted and employed in numerous other villages both in Peru, and other countries including Kenya, Mozambique and Malawi.

The principal objective of the model is the efficient management of small-scale mini-grid electricity schemes, particularly micro hydro, including all the physical elements related to the generation and distribution of electricity: energy resources, civil infrastructure, electro-mechanical equipment and electricity transmission (when needed), distribution networks and household connections. The model introduces the concept of entrepreneurial management, which seeks to promote the financial management of the system free from external interference, both from within the community or outside, involving a team for operating,

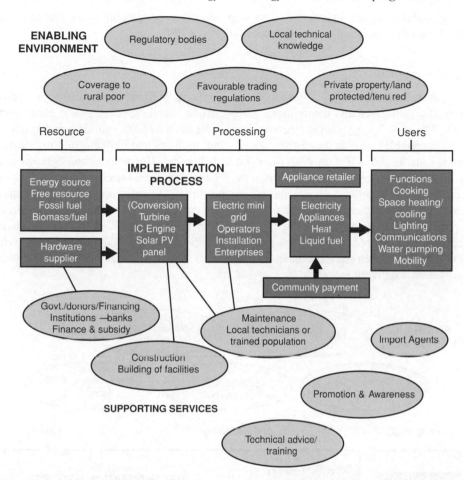

Figure 9.2 Schematic diagram of a micro-grid based energy delivery model
Source: Bellanca *et al.*, 2013

maintaining and managing the system. Management refers to all the activities involved in sustainably operating, maintaining and administrating such mini-grid electrical systems to ensure they operate as a functioning business.

To ensure the financial sustainability of the systems the energy users pay a monthly sum, and the rules on payment collection and the use of this money are established at the beginning. The amount to be paid is defined and agreed upon and fixed in the contracts to ensure that everyone adheres to it. The contract also outlines rules on resolving disputes as well as incorporating relevant local laws where necessary.

As well as delivering energy to individual households for their various needs, this mini-grid energy delivery system also promotes the use of energy for income generation activities through providing a range of local services such as internet and computer access, and the transformation of products, such as jam production from excess fruit, thereby promoting community development. The system also ensures the active participation of the local population in all areas from planning of the management system and in decision-making about the operation, maintenance and management of the scheme. In this way, the end users have full responsibility for the scheme and ownership, which has been an important part of ensuring the long-term operation of the schemes (Sanchez, 1999).

Off-grid energy delivery

Energy is delivered through off-grid systems supplying individual consumers, including households, businesses and institutions, which include hospitals, schools, and community centres. The main energy sources include fossil fuels such as LPG cylinders and kerosene bottles; renewables such as pico hydro, solar, wind, biomass and biofuels, and hybrid fuel systems, such as stoves that use both firewood and charcoal. The main technologies include home heating and cooking systems, such as stoves that can use a variety of fuels, including charcoal, firewood, pellets, ethanol and pure plant oil (PPO); solar water heaters; biomass boilers; and home systems. Generators that produce electricity and run on diesel, biodiesel and pure plant oil; solar home systems; solar lamps; solar fridges; single wind turbine; batteries; and household mechanic power systems, such as water treadle pumps and individual grain milling systems are also included. Figure 9.3 gives a schematic outline of a typical off-grid energy delivery model.

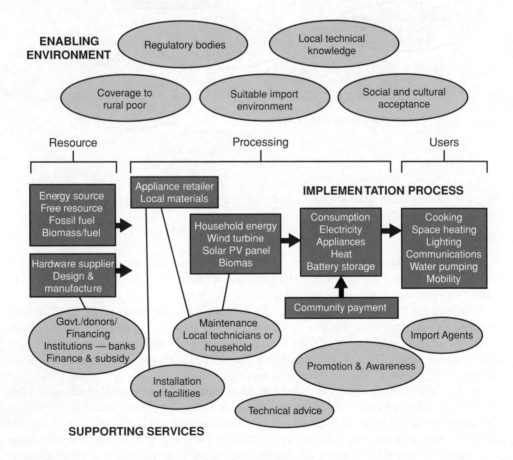

Figure 9.3 Schematic diagram of an off-grid based energy delivery model

Source: Bellanca *et al.*, 2013

Case Study 3 Off-grid hydraulic ram pump programme in the Philippines

Low carbon energy, such as hydropower, wind and solar energy can be useful for providing energy access to individual households in areas where there is no grid. An example of an off-grid low carbon energy access model is the hydraulic ram pump programme in the Philippines. Hydraulic ram pumps are pumps that use the energy within moving water – mechanical energy – to deliver water to remote areas for drinking, hygiene and sanitation, irrigation for agriculture and livestock farming (Ashden Awards, 2007a and 2007b).

The Alternative Indigenous Development Foundation (AID Foundation) in the Philippines won an Ashden Awards in 2007 for their ram pump programme, which enables villagers who live in the hillsides of the Philippines to gain easy, long-lasting and sustainable access to fresh water. Before the pumps, hillside villagers had to collect water from rivers and springs in the valleys, making long and difficult trips up and down steep slopes and sometimes travelling long distances.

The ram pump delivery system works by using a source of water that is located above the pump, and pumping the water up to 200 m vertically and up to over a kilometre horizontally to where it is specifically needed. This low carbon energy system makes use of an innovative mechanical power technology to improve access to water supply and irrigation for households and agricultures in a changing climate, potentially replacing diesel generators to pump the water and thereby avoiding carbon emissions. The pump is manufactured, maintained and installed locally based on locally available products and expertise. The AID Foundation has installed about 100 hydraulic ram pumps in about 70 communities in the Philippines and estimates that up to 10,000 further installations could be made in the future (Ashden Awards, 2007a and 2007b).

Conclusion

This chapter has provided a very brief introduction to the pressing issue of energy poverty in developing countries, as well as what is meant by energy access and the range of energy services and minimum standards that are believed to be required for someone to be able to rise out of poverty. While the benefits of increasing low carbon energy production in developing countries are clear, from providing a range of livelihood benefits to increasing energy security, it is generally recognized that low carbon energy needs to play a vital role in reducing energy poverty to achieve low carbon development.

Energy is supplied to households through energy delivery models, which consist of three main areas: the implementation process, the supporting services and enabling environment; and at three scales: on-grid, mini-grid and off-grid. Although low carbon energy sources are important for all three scales of delivery models, they are particularly important for both mini-grid and off-grid energy delivery models, which are often installed in remote areas where energy poverty is particularly acute.

On-grid energy delivery has historically received the most support from governments and donors, but has been unable to meet the needs of the very poor and those in remote areas. Considering the UN's SE4All initiative, which commits to providing universal energy access (access to electricity and clean cooking facilities to everyone in every country) by 2030, mini-grid and off-grid energy delivery models will become increasingly important. This is of particular importance from a low carbon agenda as the UN estimates that about two-thirds of the rural population in developing countries could get access to electricity through decentralized renewable energy, such as from wind, solar and small hydro (IEA, 2010), and cooking fuel from sustainably managed and efficiently burned bioenergy.

References

Ashden Awards (2007a) Technical report AID Foundation: lLocal manufacture and installation of hydraulic ram pumps, for village water supply. Available at: http://www.ashden.org/files/reports/AIDFI_2007_technical_report.pdf (accessed 1 November 2012).

Ashden Awards (2007b) AID Foundation, Philippines: Ram pumps bring running water to hillside villages. Available at: http://www.ashden.org/winners/aidfoundation (accessed 1 November 2012).

Barnes, D. F. and Floor, W. M. (1996) Rural energy in developing countries: a challenge for economic development. *Annual Review of Energy and the Environment* 21(1), 497–530.

Beckerman, W. (1992) Economic growth and the environment: whose growth? Whose environment? *World Development*, 20(4), 481–96.

Bellanca, R., Bloomfield, E., Rai, K., Vianello, M., *et al.* (2013) *Delivering Energy for Development*. Rugby: Practical Action Publishing.

BMJ (2011) Environmentalists seek to set research agenda on indoor air pollution (342). Available at: http://dx.doi.org/10.1136/bmj.d3062 (accessed 4 November 2012).

Department for International Development (DfID) (2002) Energy for the poor: underpinning the Millennium Development Goals. London: DFID.

Global Network on Energy for Sustainable Development (GNESD) (2007) Reaching the Millennium Development Goals and beyond: access to modern forms of energy as a prerequisite. Roskilde: GNESD.

Holdren, J. P. and Smith, K. R. (2000) Energy, the environment and health. world energy assessment, energy and the challenge of sustainability. New York: UNDP.

International Energy Agency (IEA) (2004) *World Energy Outlook*. Paris: OECD.

IEA (2010) Energy poverty: How to make modern energy access universal? Special early excerpt of the World Energy Outlook 2010 for the UN General Assembly on the Millennium Development Goals. IEA, Paris. Available at: http://www.iea.org/weo/docs/weo2010/weo2010_poverty.pdf (accessed 1 November 2012).

IEA (2011) *World Energy Outlook*. Paris: OECD.

Martins, J. (2005) the impact of the use of energy sources on the quality of life of poor communities. *Social Indicators Research* 72(3), 373–402.

Masera, O. R., Saatkamp, B. D. and Kammen, D. M. (2000) From linear fuel switching to multiple cooking strategies: a critique and alternative to the energy ladder model. *World Development* 28(12), 2083–103.

Nygaard, I. (2010) Institutional options for rural energy access: exploring the concept of the multi-functional platform in West Africa. *Energy Policy*, 38, 1192–201

Office of Gas and Electricity Markets (Ofgem) (2011) Typical domestic energy consumption figures. Factsheet 96. Available at http://www.ofgem.gov.uk/Media/FactSheets/Documents1/domestic%20energy%20consump%20 fig%20FS.pdf (accessed 4 November 2012).

Pan, J., Li, M., Wu, X., Wan, L., *et al.* (2006) Rural electrification in China 1950–2004: historical processes and key driving forces, program on energy and sustainable development. Stanford, CA: Stanford University.

Practical Action (2010) *Poor People's Energy Outlook 2010*. Rugby: Practical Action Publishing.

Practical Action (2012) *Poor People's Energy Outlook 2012*. Rugby: Practical Action Publishing.

Williamson (2012) REEEP funds clean energy in rural Cambodia, Ethiopia and Tanzania. Renewable Energy Focus. Available at: http://www.renewableenergyfocus.com/view/24157/reeep-funds-clean-energy-in-rural-cambodia-ethiopia-and-tanzania/ (accessed 1 November 2012).

Sanchez, T. (1999) *Small Hydro as an Energy Option for Rural Areas of Perú*, ITDG Latin America. Rugby: Practical Action Publishing.

United Nations Development Programme (UNDP) (2012) Integrating energy access and employment creation to accelerate progress on the MDGs in Sub-Saharan Africa. Available at: http://www.undp.org/content/dam/undp/library/Poverty%20Reduction/MDG%20Strategies/Energy AccessAfrica_Web.pdf (accessed 1 November 2012).

UNDP and World Health Organization (WHO) (2009) The energy access situation in developing countries – a review focusing on least developed countries and Sub-Saharan Africa. Available at: http://content.undp.org/go/cms-service/stream/asset/?asset_id=2205620 (accessed 1 November 2012).

United Nations Industrial Development Organization (UNIDO) (2010) Measuring energy access – supporting a global target. Colombo: The Earth Institute, University of Colombia.

Urban, F. (2010) Pro-poor low carbon development and the role of growth. *International Journal of Green Economics* 4 (1), 82–93.

Van Ruijven, B., Urban, F., Benders, R. M. J., Moll, H. C, Van der Sluijs, J., De Vries, B. and Van Vuuren, D. P. (2008) Modeling energy and development: an evaluation of models and concepts. *World Development* 36(12), 2801–21.

World Bank (2003) Household fuel and energy use in developing countries – a multi-country study, ESMAP. New York: World Bank.

World Bank (2012) World Bank data. Available at: http://data.worldbank.org (accessed 1 November 2012).

WHO (2006) Indoor air pollution. Fuel for life: household energy and health. Available at: http://www.who.int/indoorair/publications/fuelforlife/en/index.html (accessed 1 November 2012).

Yadoo, A. (2011) Delivery models for decentralised rural electrification: case studies in Nepal, Peru and Kenya. PhD thesis. Cambridge: Centre for Sustainable Development, Engineering Department at the University of Cambridge.

Further reading

Bellanca, R., Bloomfield, E., Rai, K., Vianello, M. *et al.* (2012) *Delivering Energy for Development*. Rugby: Practical Action Publishing.

Casillas, C. and Kammen, D. (2010) The energy-poverty-climate nexus. *Science* 26, 330(6008), 1181–2.

Masera, O. R., Saatkamp, B. D. and Kammen, D. M. (2000) From linear fuel switching to multiple cooking strategies: a critique and alternative to the energy ladder model. *World Development* 28(12), 2083–103.

Practical Action (2012) *Poor People's Energy Outlook 2012*. Rugby: Practical Action Publishing.

Quadrelli, R. and Peterson, S. (2007) The energy-climate challenge: recent trends in CO_2 emissions from fuel combustion. *Energy Policy* 35(11), 5938–52.

Notes

1 This chapter draws heavily from chapters 1 and 2 of *Delivering Energy for Development*, to be published by Practical Action Publishing in late 2012.

2 Similarly, the UN's definition of universal energy access also creates cause for confusion. It is unclear whether universal energy access means that all of a household's energy needs (cooking and electricity needs) must be met in order for the goal to be achieved. The UN aims to launch specific targets that should provide greater clarification soon.

   There is also disagreement as to whether universal energy access means that all households in a village or city have access to modern energy or whether this is limited to a certain share of households (typically 10%) or whether it might even mean that only one building in a village or city neighbourhood has access to modern energy such as electricity.

3 The World Health Organization estimates that 1.9 million people, primarily women and children, die prematurely each year from exposure to indoor smoke from these cooking practices (BMJ, 2011).

4 While a clear trend can be seen there are always exceptions. An exception is, for example, China, which is a middle income country, but has an electrification rate of almost 100 per cent. This is due to consolidated government efforts over several decades for rural electrification.

5 Pico hydro refers to small-scale hydro power plants, which produce water power of less than 5 kW.

6   It should be noted that although the majority of China has been electrified through the extension of on-grid delivery systems, there have also been mini-grid and off-grid systems installed for very remote settlements and households.

7   A multi-functional platform is defined as a technical and organizational system for increasing access to a range of energy services in an isolated area, often consisting of a small diesel engine turning one or several types of milling machinery as well as generating electricity (Nygaard, 2010).

10 Revolutionizing the electricity sector

Renewable energy and low carbon grid infrastructure

Letha Tawney

Large-scale renewable energy will be a key strategy for low carbon economies. However, it is challenging for many electricity grids (the transmission and distribution systems) to absorb the variable and decentralized power generated by renewable energy resources such as wind and the sun. This chapter explores those challenges.

It also discusses the emerging options and best practices for effectively using these new sources of energy to reduce GHG emissions. Grid operators are already implementing solutions such as investing in updated electricity infrastructure, reforming electricity markets, investing in energy storage and using smart grid technologies.

Introduction

Large-scale integration of variable renewable energy (energy from sources such as the sun and wind, which may be unavailable at night or during bad weather – see Box 10.1 for details) into the electricity system will be required to have a 50 per cent chance of limiting global warming to less than 2°C by stabilizing GHG (CO_{2eq}) concentrations at 450 ppm.[1] Models from the IEA suggest that in order to reach the 450 ppm target, variable renewables will likely make up 24 per cent of global electricity generation by 2035 (Diczfalusy *et al.*, 2010). Additionally, if other low carbon solutions, such as nuclear power and carbon capture and storage are slow to come online, renewables will have to take up some of the slack to keep the 450 ppm goal within reach. The IEA's models are not alone in heavily relying on large-scale deployment of variable renewable power to avoid dangerous climate change. The IPCC special report on renewable energy sources surveyed the current literature and models and found that solar and wind power alone are likely to account for between 16.3 and 60.8 per cent of electricity generation in 2050 (Edenhofer *et al.*, 2011).

Variable renewables already make up a significant proportion of power generated in local grids around the world. Whether three wind turbines providing 31 per cent of the electricity for the Galapagos Island of San Cristobal or 9600 MW of wind turbines providing 8.5 per cent of the power for the state of Texas, grids are coping with variable renewables today and grid operators are learning quickly (Fideicomiso Mercantil Proyecto Eólico San Cristóbal, 2008; Electric Reliability Council of Texas, Inc., 2012). Grid operators in Portugal for example have already managed to increase variable renewable generation from 2 per cent to over 15 per cent of the country's electricity generation from 2004 to 2009 (US Energy Information Administration, 2012).

Low carbon development depends on the electricity system meeting two goals: GHG abatement and limiting costs to the economy – either consumers or public budgets. While low carbon policy often encourages deployment of variable renewable energy, it can give short shrift to how those power supplies reach consumers through the grid and how this in turn impacts the abatement and cost goals.

Costs for variable renewable technologies have been steadily declining, and parity with fossil fuel options is arriving for the most mature options (Bloomberg New Energy Finance, 2011; Bazilian *et al.*, 2012). While this is welcome news from the deployment perspective, the cost of integrating these resources into the grid may still be significant. Similarly, deployment alone does not guarantee that emissions throughout the electricity system decline. There is certainly not a one to one displacement effect, whereby a kilowatt hour (kWh) of electricity produced by a solar panel means a coal-fired power plant explicitly burned less fuel. How the grid is operated and how the electricity market is arranged have a significant impact on whether increased deployment of variable renewable energy decreases GHG emissions in the electricity sector broadly.

In order to meet the dual goals of low carbon development – inexpensive electricity that has lower GHG emissions –grid operations and policy are crucial. There are several options to explore to support large-scale variable renewables and low carbon development within the existing grid. There are also some who argue that the traditional model of the grid is too constraining altogether. In the end, low carbon development will require fundamental changes in not just how power is generated, but how it is managed and delivered. Box 10.1 discusses the key definitions relevant for this chapter.

Box 10.1 Definitions of key concepts and terms

Variable or intermittent renewables: These power sources only generate electricity when the sun is shining, the wind is blowing, and so on. They 'ramp' up and down with weather changes, providing variable output. These include solar photovoltaic, solar thermal without storage, wind, tidal, wave and run-of-river hydro. This is in contrast to reservoir-based hydropower, ocean thermal, geothermal or biomass options, which generate power steadily and on demand.

Grid: The way electricity is transmitted from generators to consumers. Transmission typically refers to high-volume, long-distance power lines while distribution is the low-volume, local system that delivers power to homes and businesses. Figure 10.1 shows a schematic example of an electric grid.

Grid operator: The organization responsible for constantly and precisely balancing electricity demand with supply on a discrete portion of the grid. They may also be called the balancing authority or the system operator. They may be a part of a vertically integrated utility that has a regional monopoly or span a geographic region that includes many utilities and independent power producers.

Smart grid: The integration of information technology capabilities throughout the grid to improve visibility, flexibility and responsiveness. Smart meters are one element, providing detailed information and, potentially, control to the grid operator and the consumer simultaneously.

Reserve power: Extra generation capacity available to address several contingencies, such as an unexpected drop in supply or increase in demand. Spinning reserves are immediately available to serve demand. Operating reserves include spinning reserves, but also generators that can come on to the grid within a specified time. A key question for variable renewable energy is how it changes best practice for reserve power availability. This is broadly called 'backup power' in renewables discussions.

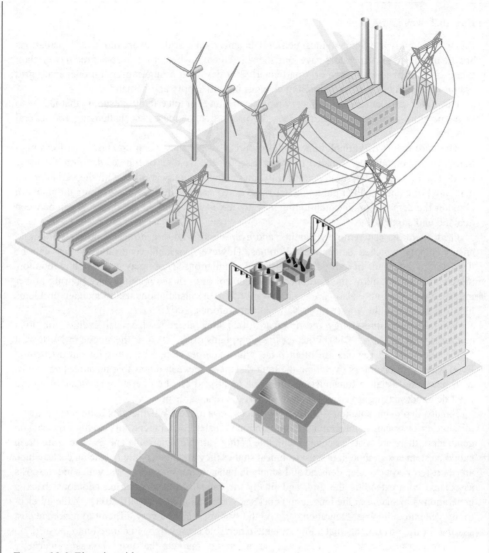

Figure 10.1 Electric grid
Source: NREL, 2010[2]

Distributed generation: Small and medium size renewables installations that provide power locally but may also be connected to the grid. For example, rooftop solar power is distributed generation while an 80-turbine wind farm is 'utility-scale' or centralized generation.

Box 10.2 elaborates the key issues that are important for revolutionizing the grid with regard to renewable energy and low carbon energy.

Box 10.2 Key issues

Electricity supply and demand must be finely balanced on a grid at every moment. Fluctuations are the norm and grid operators have long managed them – whether it is a coal-fired power plant going offline for maintenance or a particularly hot day with a large air-conditioner load, grid operators are accustomed to addressing changes in both supply and demand.

However, variable renewable energy represents a level of uncertainty in supply that is new to grid operators and accommodating it as the proportion increases is challenging for several reasons.

The very nature of variable renewable resources is that they ramp up and down from high output to low output over a matter of hours based on the weather or time of day rather than by the dictate of the grid operator. Additionally, this variability may conflict with the variability in demand. For example, solar photovoltaics ramp down as the sun sets in the evening but in warm climates the demand for air-conditioning may not have tapered off yet, leading to a gap between demand and supply.

Grid operators can remotely monitor and even control large centralized power stations to ensure supply matches demand at all times. However, variable renewable energy can be deployed in thousands of individual, distributed installations. These may not have any monitoring electronics that allow the grid operator to control or even see how they are pouring power into the grid. They may also lack the hardware that large installations use to manage problems like low voltage in the grid (Sandia National Laboratories, 2007).

Variable renewable energy resources are often long distances from large cities, or 'load centres' (Tawney *et al.*, 2011). Whether the high plains of the USA or the steppe in Northwest China, the windiest regions are often rural, with underdeveloped transmission infrastructure. Even when grid operators overcome the long distances between renewable resources and cities with new long-distance transmission lines, the local grid can be operating at capacity during peak demand, making it very difficult to import the renewable power.

Finally, deploying solutions for these challenges costs money. Whether it is building new transmission infrastructure, integrating monitoring and safety equipment, or paying for backup generation, there are costs associated with integrating variable renewable energy. These are often called 'system costs', though in most technical studies they are divided into balancing costs, which are short-term costs to keep demand and supply in balance, transmission costs, which are the costs associated with extending the grid, and finally the capital costs of ensuring additional backup generation is available in the long-term (EnerNex Corporation and NREL, 2011). While all electricity generators impose integration costs on the system, it can be very difficult to negotiate cost sharing for the investments that allow variable renewable energy to be integrated into the grid.

There can also be savings. For example, in energy markets that use wholesale electricity auctions, variable renewables reduce the peak wholesale power price and as a result, can reduce costs to consumers (Philibert, 2011).

Discussion

Grid operators have several options when considering how to best manage the new variability in supply that large-scale deployment creates. The first option is to reduce the variability and uncertainty associated with variable renewable energy itself. There are several strategies to do this, including improving forecasting of variable resources. The second strategy is to reduce variability in demand so that any demand peaks that conflict with troughs in variable renewable energy production are limited. Finally, grid operators can consider their reserve power requirements, both on an hourly basis and over the long term, to determine how that should change to balance the increased supply variability.

Grid operators are primarily concerned with delivering reliable power to customers. Outages or even variances (brown-outs) have a dramatic economic impact including damaging machinery and electronics in businesses and have safety implications for a population. Their secondary concern is typically to keep costs as low as is reasonable. Grid operators are rarely profit-making enterprises and when they may be (such as when they are part of a vertically integrated utility), a regulator often sets their acceptable rate of return to ensure their monopoly power – controlling the infrastructure – does not hurt customers of the power system. These incentives and institutional structures tend to create a risk-averse, conservative culture where change is slow and deliberate. Introducing large-scale variable renewable energy into this system requires difficult technical, process and institutional changes.

Reducing variability and uncertainty

Improved weather forecasting as it relates to the renewable resource (e.g. sunshine, wind speeds, rain) is a crucial first step to reducing the uncertainty in the supply forecast that grid operators use to plan over the coming 24 to 72-h period. Renewable energy project developers typically have characterized the resource over a year in order to decide what equipment to use, how to locate the equipment on the site and whether the project can generate enough power to be economically profitable. However, grid operators need a much finer grain forecast of exactly how much power will be reliably generated in the coming day or so in order to ensure enough supply is available across the system. Wind generation forecasts have been rapidly improving in countries with high wind penetration. In Germany, root mean squared error for wind power forecasting, a common measure of error in predictions, has decreased from 10 per cent in 2001, to 4.7 per cent in 2009 (Corfee *et al.*, 2011).

This improved forecasting is particularly useful if the electricity wholesale or bulk market, in a deregulated electricity system, operates hourly or even 5-minute increments – called 'gate close times'.[3] A grid operator will ask for bids from generators for supply in the coming 24 hours. A wind farm will review their weather forecast, maintenance schedule and other factors and commit to a supply schedule that has very little uncertainty. When the 24-hour period begins, some grid operators operate hourly or 5-minute markets for additional demand. A wind operator in those markets, who had to be conservative in his commitment over a 24-hour period, knows with much more certainty how much power will be available in the next hour and can sell that extra into the market as the opportunity arises. A study of the State of Minnesota found that using hourly markets would reduce the need for backup generation by 10 per cent, while utilizing markets on the 5-min timescale would lead to a 20 per cent smaller need. This would in turn reduce the costs of integrating wind power (Van Hulle and Hassan, 2009).

The second approach to reducing uncertainty and variability is to spread the variable renewable energy generation across a larger geographic area. This can be within a single balancing area managed by a single grid operator, or grid operators can integrate with neighbouring balancing areas more effectively so they can trade excess power across an even wider area. The Nordic power market, including Denmark, Finland, Norway and Sweden, coordinates day-ahead, intra-day and intra-hour trading. This allows Norwegian and Swedish hydropower to balance Danish wind power through significant cross-border trade and is credited with supporting the very significant wind power penetration Denmark has achieved (Chandler, 2010). An analysis of the requirements of integrating up to 10 per cent wind and solar power in the western USA found that running the region as five balancing areas rather than the 106 balancing areas roughly used today could save US$2 billion in operating costs through reduced variation in supply and the option to pool reserve power (discussed below) (GE Energy, 2010).

Managing demand

A third strategy to manage the new variability in supply is to smooth out the variability in demand so that any gaps that emerge between the two are smaller overall. Going beyond promoting energy efficiency measures like fluorescent light bulbs and actively changing demand in real time is called demand response (Wight *et al.*, 2011). There are several reasons to do demand response besides the need to accommodate variable renewable energy, particularly to avoid adding expensive 'peak' capacity. Peak demand happens very rarely, often only a few days a year. To accommodate it, generators have typically built 'peaker plants' – fossil fuelled power generation, often flexible natural gas plants, that runs just a few hours a year at a very high cost (Shively and Ferrare, 2008). Efforts to reduce peak demand and the need for expensive peak capacity can thus be very cost effective.

Smart meters and other information technology enabling monitoring and management of the grid and demand are key to expanding demand response in consumers' homes and offices (Levy *et al.*, 2011). Many grid operators have already arranged for demand response with very large industrial users, who will shut down some of their production to reduce electricity use during peak demand periods (Wight *et al.*, 2011). Smart meters would allow this same model, in a more sophisticated way, to be deployed in consumer's homes and businesses, turning down electric hot water heaters or turning off air conditioning, during times of peak demand.

Demand response can also mean shifting demand to times when it better matches the profile of the variable renewable energy supply (Milligan and Kirby, 2010). This is already common practice in order to make better use of generation that cannot be easily turned down at night when demand typically falls. Many utilities already use 'time of day' pricing to encourage consumers to shift demand voluntarily (Torriti *et al.*, 2010; Wight *et al.*, 2011). In these cases, consumer appliances such as dishwashers and clothes dryers have a delay feature so they will run overnight while demand and thus prices are very low. In regions where the wind blows strongest overnight, for example, this sort of demand shifting can be an effective way to both reduce peaks and make better use of the variable renewable resource.

Increasing flexible supply

Finally, grid operators can back up the variable renewable energy power with other power options that are available on demand. These options have different GHG and cost implications, depending on the fuel used, the technology choice and the electricity market structure for 'ancillary services' such as reserve power.

The first option is accessing power that was stored when the variable renewable energy resource was producing more than the grid needed to meet demand. Storage can take many forms and as a result can have a wide range of costs. For grid operators, stored power appears as just another form of flexible supply, but the efficiency of finding ways to use variable renewable energy when it is needed as opposed to only when it is available is economically and environmentally attractive. Already grid operators use pumped hydro, where water is pumped uphill into a reservoir by excess wind power and run back downhill through hydro turbines to generate power, to convert excess variable renewable power into power that is available on demand. In the northwest of the USA, the grid operator is experimenting with storage in consumers' homes for excess wind generation. In this case, excess wind energy is used to heat hot water tanks for use as home hot water later and ceramic blocks that provide space heat over a few hours (Wald, 2011a). On a larger scale, solar thermal plants can use some of the heat they collect from the sun to melt salt or other media that will store the heat over a matter of hours. Then, when the sun is not providing enough heat, they can tap the stored heat to generate power (Staley *et al.*, 2009).

There are on-going efforts to find economic storage options including batteries, flywheels and a variety of ways to store heat or generate hydrogen. One idea that has gained significant attention is integrating the decarbonization of transportation with deploying large-scale variable renewable energy. In the case of shifting to a largely electric car fleet, there is the potential to access the batteries in cars that are plugged in as distributed storage (Milligan and Kirby, 2010). Excess supply could be used to charge cars and when demand exceeded supply, car batteries could be tapped to provide power to the grid. This integration would require a significant strengthening of the distribution infrastructure and potentially technologies like smart meters. These would also play into demand response, where car charging could be eliminated or decreased during peak demand and shifted to night-time hours instead.

Finally grid operators would look to their reserve power requirements to address the remaining gap between supply and demand. When grid operators estimate demand and plan supply, they always plan for a certain supply surplus to deal with uncertainty. A coal plant might have to shutdown for maintenance unexpectedly or there might be an error in the demand forecast. This extra is the 'reserve power'. Some of it is available immediately and some of it is available in a matter of minutes or hours. Grid operators have requirements for reserve power from their regulators to maintain system reliability and have developed sophisticated systems to estimate, manage and pay for this capacity. Variable renewable energy changes the shape of the supply curve and as a result, the way the gap between supply and demand evolves over time – both on a daily basis and a seasonal basis. This introduces complexity to the reserve power estimates. There is likely a need for larger proportions of reserve generation even after the other strategies have been deployed. For example, preliminary estimates by CALISO, the California grid operator, suggest that if the State of California reaches its 33 per cent renewable target by 2020 while only maintaining its current reserve margin, there will be a maximum shortage of 20 min ramping capacity of 1456 MW (CALISO, 2012). The grid operator will face shortfall of power that is available in a 20-minute window to address declines in variable renewable power. Keeping 1456 MW of reserve power available will likely mean burning fossil fuels with their GHG emissions and costs, even though the power may never be used.

As variable renewable energy changes the dynamics of deregulated electricity markets in particular, these sorts of shortfalls could potentially grow rather than decline. Because renewable energy has no fuel costs, it can often underbid fossil fuel power on a wholesale power market, making it harder and harder for fossil fuel power plants to estimate how much power they will sell at what price over their lifetimes.[4] As they run more often as reserve power, the economics of building fossil fuel plants gets worse and new plants may not be built. On one hand, this is the explicit goal of decarbonizing the power sector. However, in the end the needed reserve capacity may not be available to balance variable renewable energy, unless the way reserve power is paid for is changed. Changing how reserve power is paid for would in turn have cost implications for consumers and could be viewed as a windfall profit or subsidy to fossil fuel power plants. Similarly, fossil fuel reserve capacity would make reducing GHGs harder, which is why carbon-free storage is so critical to ensuring variable renewable power truly displaces GHG-emitting fossil fuel power.

Box 10.3 discusses a critique of the issues presented earlier and some of the challenges.

Box 10.3 Critique

Distributed generation (DG) is often suggested as an alternative to the large-scale grid expansion needed to connect to remote renewable energy resources. DG has experienced rapid growth in recent years, particularly in Germany (Pew Environment Group, 2012). It could be further enabled by the transition to a smart grid, which would in part resolve the way grid operators are blind to how DG is interacting with the grid today. While DG is often thought of as including only residence- or business-scale generation, it may also include community-level generation that connects into the distribution network rather than to high voltage transmission lines. Since 2003, the average size of American power plants has decreased from 493 MW to 171 MW (Fox-Penner, 2010). This size trend is making community-level generation more economic but is unlikely to benefit very small, residence-scale generation. In 2010, a small scale photovoltaics array in the US could produce electricity at about $0.34/kWh, while a community-scale photovoltaics facility could produce electricity at $0.17/kWh.

These medium-scale distributed generators are likely to play an important role in the future electricity sector, however, even they still have several disadvantages that suggest they will be unable to dominate in the near term, if ever. While PV prices are dropping and may reach retail grid parity in parts of the US and several other markets globally by 2015 (Bazilian *et al.*, 2012), other technologies, such as wind and solar thermal power are difficult to downscale. In the US, utility-scale solar photovoltaics is still significantly less expensive than smaller systems (Barbose *et al.*, 2011). Finally, the most abundant wind and solar resources are often in sparsely populated areas, making it often more efficient to build centralized generation capacity far away from population centres. While DG, from the very small scale to community scale, clearly has a role to play, it will not negate the need for grid expansion to meet the low carbon goals.

Conclusion

Perhaps the most significant challenge in incorporating variable renewable energy into grids around the world is the definition of best practice. There is significant variety in how grids are managed, how flexible they can be today, how effectively they can access capital to invest in upgraded hardware and how easily they can reform their markets to accommodate renewable energy. In Northwest China, combined heat and power (CHP) generators were built without the technical capacity to curtail electricity when producing heat. In the winter, when wind power is at its peak, the CHP generators are also pumping out electricity and the wind power is more controllable than the CHP generators, so is taken off the grid (Tawney *et al.*, 2011). Even how the variable renewables interact with other supplies is different from region to region. In Brazil wind is best in the dry season, nicely offsetting lower reservoir hydro output, but the northwest of the USA high hydro production coincides with high wind production in the spring and creates far too much supply for the grid operator to manage (Wald, 2011b; Spatuzza, 2012). Transmission bottlenecks, market configuration, environmental regulations and myriad other nuances of each grid make it easier or harder to implement the strategies outlined above.

This heterogeneity has two immediate impacts. First, it makes learning between grid operators difficult. There are efforts at cooperation, such as Thai grid operators hosting their peers from Tanzania to discuss how to replicate the Thai very small power producer programme to increase supplies of renewables (Weischer *et al.*, 2011). However, codifying best practice broadly will remain difficult.

The second challenge is determining the reasonable cost for absorbing variable renewable energy. While many renewable energy generation technologies are reaching cost competitiveness with fossil fuel generators, these costs of integration have to be accounted for in some way as well. Estimating and allocating he costs of extending transmission, investing in more robust management tools, and increasing the reserve power needed can be highly contentious.

An extensive review of the implications increasing the proportion of wind power in the eastern USA suggested the cost of integrating up to 20 per cent wind ranged from $3.10/MWh to $5.13/MWh, depending on how the wind generators were spread around the grid area (EnerNex Corporation and NREL, 2011). This cost did not include the cost of extending transmission to the wind farms. A review of integration studies by the IEA Wind Implementing Agreement documented balancing cost estimates at 20 per cent wind power penetration from $1/MWh to $7/MWh, though the studies were not perfectly comparable with one another (Chandler, 2011). How effectively the grid operator had deployed improved wind forecasting, implemented market reforms, and how variable renewable energy could be taken offline when it was over-producing all had a significant impact on the balancing costs in models. How these measures would interact with each other in a real system would be much more complex.

This is an important issue because grid operators and utilities that need to make investments in order to integrate variable renewable energy may need to seek permission to raise costs to consumers and their regulators will be faced with difficult questions about what is reasonable, what may be a net cost savings, and whether the strategy proposed is really the least-cost, highest reliability option.

However, variable renewable energy is not only about added costs for consumers. Particularly in deregulated electricity markets, there are very complex changes in pricing because variable renewable energy producers can offer power prices that benefit from zero fuel costs and often an additional premium per kWh. At times of peak demand, as discussed above, variable renewable energy can keep the peak price down for the whole market. One study estimated that if all the power in Germany were purchased for an hour at this reduced rate, generators would lose €2.6 billion in revenue they would have otherwise earned (Sensfuß *et al.*, 2008). This is savings to consumers and is part of the concerns about whether the fossil fuel generators needed to provide reserve power may eventually leave the market altogether. The same effect has been modelled or documented in other deregulated markets (Philibert, 2011).

In the end, grid operators will muddle through. Some will be very innovative, be supported by progressive regulators, and find ways to cooperate with both renewable and fossil fuel generators. Others will be hampered by cost-sensitive regulators, by highly constrained technical systems or political debates, and by their own capacities to learn and adapt. Keeping the cost of decarbonization to a minimum will require that grid operators are supported in their efforts to invest while simultaneously always pushed to find cost-effective solutions. Perhaps even more important, deployment of renewable energy alone will be insufficient to decarbonize the power sector. Ensuring that grid operators are successfully absorbing the new resources and finding new ways to limit the role of fossil fuel power while meeting their reliability requirements will be central to how much GHG benefit societies actually accrue from renewable energy deployment.

References

Barbose, G., Darghouth, N., Wiser, R. and Seel, J. (2011) Tracking the sun IV: a historical summary of the installed cost of photovoltaics in the United States from 1998 to 2010. Lawrence Berkeley National Laboratory. Available at: http://eetd.lbl.gov/ea/ems/reports/lbnl-1516e.pdf (accessed 9 December 2011).

Bazilian, M., Onyeji. I., Liebreich, M., MacGill, I. *et al.* (2012) Reconsidering the economics of photovoltaic power. Bloomberg New Energy Finance. Available at: http://www.bnef.com/WhitePapers/download/82 (accessed 16 May 2012).

Bloomberg New Energy Finance (2011) Onshore wind energy to reach parity with fossil-fuel electricity by 2016. Available at: http://bnef.com/PressReleases/view/172 (accessed 27 November 2011).

Chandler, H. (2010) System integration aspects of variable renewable power generation. In: *Projected Costs of Generating Electricity*. Paris: IEA.

Chandler, H. (2011) *Harnessing Variable Renewables: a Guide to the Balancing Challenge*. IEA, Paris.

Corfee, K., Korinek, D. and Hewicker, C. (2011) European renewable distributed generation infrastructure study – lessons learned from electricity markets in Germany and Spain. KEMA, Inc. Available at: http://www.energy.ca.gov/2011publications/CEC-400-2011-011/CEC-400-2011-011.pdf (accessed 29 February 2012).

Diczfalusy, B. Taylor, P., Cazzola, P., Cuenot, F. *et al.* (2010) *Energy Technology Perspectives 2010*. IEA, Paris. Available at: http://www.iea.org/techno/etp/index.asp (accessed 8 June 2011).

Edenhofer, O., Pich-Madruga, R., Sokona, Y. and Seyboth, K. (2011) IPCC special report on renewable energy sources and climate change mitigation – summary for policymakers. IPCC, Cambridge and New York. Available at: http://srren.ipcc-wg3.de/report/IPCC_SRREN_SPM (accessed 15 July 2011).

Electric Reliability Council of Texas, Inc. (2012) ERCOT quick facts. Electric Reliability Council of Texas, Inc. Available at: http://www.ercot.com/content/news/presentations/2012/ERCOT%20Quick%20Facts%20-%20Jan%202012.pdf (accessed 29 February 2012).

EnerNex Corporation and NREL (2011) Eastern wind integration and transmission study. National Renewable Energy Laboratory. Knoxville, TN: US Department of Energy.

Fideicomiso Mercantil Proyecto Eólico San Cristóbal (2008) Galapagos wind – latest news. Available at: http://www.galapagoswind.org/ (accessed 1 March 2012).

Fox-Penner, P. (2010) *Smart Power: Climate Change, The Smart Grid, and the Future of Electric Utilities*. Washington, DC: Island Press.

GE Energy (2010) Western wind and solar integration study. National Renewable Energy Laboratory. New York: US Department of Energy.

Van Hulle, F. and Hassan, G. (2009) Grid integration. European Wind Energy Association. Available at: http://www.wind-energy-the-facts.org/documents/download/Chapter2.pdf (accessed 29 February 2012).

Levy, R., Kiliccote, S. and Goldman, C. (2011) Demand response. Available at: http://www.naruc.org/Policy/Ferc/LBNL-Webinar5-DRWeb.pdf (accessed 1 June 2012).

Milligan, M. and Kirby, B. (2010) Utilizing load response for wind and solar integration and power system reliability. National Renewable Energy Laboratory, US Department of Energy. Available at: http://www.nrel.gov/docs/fy10osti/48247.pdf (accessed 1 June 2012).

National Renewable Energy Laboratory (2010) Energy analysis fact sheet (NREL/FS-6A2-45653). Solar Power and the Electric Grid by Craig Turchi. Golden, CO: National Renewable Energy Laboratory.

Pew Environment Group (2012) Who's winning the clean energy race? 2011 edition. Pew Charitable Trusts, Washington, DC.. Available at: http://www.pewtrusts.org/uploadedFiles/wwwpewtrustsorg/Reports/Clean_Energy/Clean%20Energy%20Race%20Report%202012.pdf (accessed 17 April 2012).

Philibert, C. (2011) Renewable energy policy and climate policy interactions. In: *Climate and Electricity Annual*. Paris: IEA, pp. 35–42.

Sandia National Laboratories (2007) Solar energy grid integration systems 'SEGIS'. US Department of Energy. Available at: http://www1.eere.energy.gov/solar/pdfs/segis_concept_paper.pdf (accessed 31 May 2012).

Sensfuß, F., Ragwitz, M. and Genoese, M. (2008) The merit-order effect: a detailed analysis of the price effect of renewable electricity generation on spot market prices in Germany. *Energy Policy*, 36(8), 3076–84.

Shively, B. and Ferrare, J. (2008) *Understanding Today's Electricity Business*. Energy Dynamics, San Francisco, CA.

Spatuzza, A. (2012) Higher prices and successful bids show mature industry. *Wind Power Monthly*, 28(2), 29.

Staley, B. C., Goodward, J., Rigdon, C. and MacBride, A. (2009) *Juice from Concentrate: Reducing Emissions with Concentrating Solar Thermal Power*. Washington, DC: World Resources Institute.

Tawney, L., Greenspan Bell, R. and Ziegler, M.S. (2011) High wire act: electricity transmission infrastructure and its impact on the renewable energy market. World Resources Institute, Washington, DC. Available at: http://www.wri.org/publication/high-wire-act (accessed 20 April 2011).

Torriti, J., Hassan, M. and Leach, M. (2010) Demand response experience in Europe: policies, programmes and implementation. *Energy*, 35(4), 1575–83.

US Energy Information Administration (2012) International energy statistics. Available at: http://www.eia.gov/cfapps/ipdbproject/iedindex3.cfm?tid=2&pid=alltypes&aid=12&cid=PO,SP,&syid=2004&eyid=2009&unit=BKWH (accessed 29 February 2012).

Wald, M. L. (2011a) As wind energy use grows, utilities seek to stabilize power grid. *The New York Times*. Available at: http://www.nytimes.com/2011/11/05/business/energy-environment/as-wind-energy-use-grows-utilities-seek-to-stabilize-power-grid.html (accessed 14 November 2011).

Wald, M. L. (2011b) Bonneville Power ordered to change wind rules. *The New York Times*. Available at: http://www.nytimes.com/2011/12/08/business/energy-environment/bonneville-power-ordered-to-change-wind-rules.html (accessed 12 December 2011).

Weischer, L., Wood, D., Ballesteros, A. and Fu-Bertaux, X. (2011) *Grounding Green Power: Bottom-Up Perspectives in Smart Renewable Energy Policies in Developing Countries*. Washington, DC: World Resources Institute.

Wight, D., Daly, C., Kathan, D., Lee, M. *et al.* (2011) Assessment of demand response and advanced metering. Washington, DC: Federal Energy Regulatory Commission (FERC). Available at: http://www.ferc.gov/legal/staff-reports/2010-dr-report.pdf (accessed 1 June 2012).

Further reading

IEA (2011) *Harnessing Variable Renewables: A Guide to the Balancing Challenge*. Paris: IEA.

Tawney, L., Greenspan Bell, R. and Ziegler, M.S. (2011) High wire act: electricity transmission infrastructure and its impact on the renewable energy market. Washington, DC: World Resources Institute. Available at: http://www.wri.org/publication/high-wire-act (accessed 20 April 2011).

Notes

1   GHGs are measured by their concentrations in the atmosphere. They are powerful but scarce, so they are measured as parts per million (ppm) in a volume of atmosphere. For comparability and target setting several GHGs have been defined by their potential to cause warming, as compared to carbon dioxide, CO_{2eq}. Thus ppm CO_{2eq} provides a sense of how much greenhouse gas pollution is in the atmosphere and in turn, a range of likely temperature increases.

2   This image has been reprinted from National Renewable Energy Laboratory (2010) Energy analysis fact sheet (NREL/FS-6A2-45653). Solar Power and the Electric Grid by Craig Turchi.

3   A deregulated electricity market is a situation where other generators, beyond the main utility, can sell power. This often done on a 'wholesale' electricity market that operates as an auction.

4   How an electricity market values different kinds of power services is only one part of determining the economics of a power plant. Many risks, such as fuel price volatility also factor into the

decision. Similarly, explicit and implicit subsidies, such as ease of transmission access or support for mining and extraction, change the economics of different options. While many low carbon power sources receive subsidies, the historical and current subsidies for fossil fuels and the way the power system is built around the fossil fuel model make direct economic competition difficult. Underbidding in wholesale markets is just one element of a shifting and complex set of advantages and disadvantages a renewable generator has in the system today.

11 Forestry and low carbon development

Rocio Hiraldo

Forest vegetation and soils directly contribute to climate change mitigation by absorbing carbon dioxide. Depletion of forests leads to losses of carbon sinks and GHG emissions due to changes in land use, namely for agriculture. Concerns about climate change and other negative impacts of forest loss have led to the emergence of various policies and mechanisms to integrate the forestry sector in low carbon development strategies. Despite existing opportunities, creating these synergies involves key technical, socio-economic and political challenges. This chapter takes a sectoral perspective focusing on the contribution of forests to low carbon development. The first section studies the links between forests and climate change; the next section then describes other functions of forests. The third section analyses how particular development pathways relate to forest loss. The different forestry-related low carbon development practices and policies are then explored as well as the key structural barriers to achieve effective emission reduction and to make low carbon development compatible with environmental integrity and socio-economic justice.

Forests and climate change

Forests contribute to climate change mitigation through the absorption of carbon dioxide (CO_2) by vegetation and soils. Thus, the amount of carbon stored by forests decreases with deforestation, forest degradation, peatland burning (anthropogenic drivers) and natural causes such as disasters or unintended fires (Watson *et al.*, 2000: 4). The anthropogenic drivers of forest loss are estimated to contribute to 15 per cent of global CO_2 emissions (Van der Werf *et al.*, 2009). In addition, changes in forest land use to agricultural purposes indirectly lead to emissions of nitrous oxide (N_2O) and methane (CH_4) (see Chapter 12). Taking into account these indirect emissions is important if it is considered that N_2O has a global warming potential (GWP) 310 times bigger than CO_2 and it is the source of 7.9 per cent of total GHG emissions, while CH_4 has a GWP 21 times greater than CO_2 and it is responsible for 14.3 per cent of total GHG emissions (IPCC, 2007: 36).

Box 11.1 explains the key definitions relevant for this chapter.

Box 11.1 Definitions

Deforestation: refers to the direct human-induced conversion of forested land to non-forested land and the long-term reduction of tree canopy cover to below 10–30 per cent (FAO, 2010).

Forest degradation: is typically considered partial deforestation, with more than 10–30 per cent of forest cover remaining (for example, through selective logging) (FAO, 2010).

Forestry-based low carbon development: makes reference to forestry-related actions that reduce GHG emissions and contribute to development. These include a wide range of policies, practices and interventions that, with or without economic compensation, contribute to keeping forests standing and/or increase forest biomass.

Reducing Emissions from Deforestation and Forest Degradation (REDD+): climate change mechanism approved under the UNFCCC that financially rewards governments, communities and private companies for reducing emissions from deforestation, forest degradation and enhancement of carbon stock.

Afforestation: the direct, human-induced conversion of non-forest land to permanent forested land for a period of at least 50 years.

Global Warming Potential (GWP): is a measurement of the impact of a particular gas on 'radiative forcing', that is, the additional heat/energy that is retained in the Earth's ecosystem through the addition of this gas to the atmosphere. The GWP is used to compare the impacts of different greenhouse gases on global warming (Yamin and Depledge, 2004: 78).

It is estimated that although forest loss decreased by 17 per cent during the 1990–2000 period, around 13 million hectares of forest were converted to other uses or lost annually in the last decade, leading to a decrease of 0.8 Gigatonnes (Gt) of carbon per year (Van der Werf *et al.*, 2009; FAO, 2010). Calculating forest loss figures and its related emissions is particularly difficult and data provided usually have a 50 per cent error margin, but current numbers of forest biomass loss are highly alarming even under low estimates (Van der Werf, 2009). While the effects of forest loss on GHG emissions are well known, it is less clear what specific changes in climate are derived from forest loss, including decrease of moisture as well as precipitation, increased ground surface temperature, evaporation and shortening of the wet season (McGuffie *et al.*, 1995).

This chapter takes a sectoral perspective focusing on the contribution of forests to low carbon development. The first section studies the links between forests and climate change; the next section then describes other functions of forests. The third section analyses how particular development pathways relate to forest loss. The different forestry-related low carbon development practices and policies are then explored, as well as the key structural barriers to achieve effective emission reduction and to make low carbon development compatible with environmental integrity and socio-economic justice.

Forests are more than carbon

But forests are not just carbon, they are vital to the existence of life on Earth and they provide resources that are important to society and in turn contribute to the development of local as well as national economies. Forests thus fulfil productive as well as protective functions. The economic profits from productive functions of forests are significant. Wood removals were valued at just over US$100 billion annually in the 2003–2007 period (FAO, 2010: 120).

Furthermore, the value of the trade in non-timber forest products (NTFPs) (for example, pharmaceutical plants, mushrooms, nuts, syrups and cork) has been estimated at US$11 billion (World Bank, 2002: 13–14), but more recent estimates suggest the reported value of NTFPs amounts to about $18.5 billion for 2005, most of them are food products (FAO, 2010).

Forest protective functions include the regulation of the water cycle, climate protection of upstream watersheds, soil formation and conservation, avalanche control, sand dune stabilization, desertification control, coastal protection, nutrient recycling, plant pollination and gene pools for future generations (Nodvin, 2008: 1). In addition, forests contribute to biodiversity conservation, harbouring up to 90 per cent of terrestrial world biodiversity support (CIFOR, 2008: 3). More than 50 per cent of all species live in tropical forests that are under threat from deforestation (Pimm and Raven, 2000), and habitat loss and fragmentation are the leading causes of species endangerment (Joppa and Pfaff, 2010).

Forests resources are vital for the subsistence of rural people living in forested areas. They provide food, energy, employment and an alternative healthcare system based on forest plants (ITTO, 2010: 3). Forest conservation and management are a key source of employment for around 10 million people globally. This number is likely to be higher as a large number of people are involved in the informal timber sector (FAO, 2010). Furthermore, forests are part of the culture and way of living of indigenous communities and they have contributed to forest conservation, due to the fact that forests are sacred elements in certain societies (Kanninen, 2009: 136; Seymour, 2010: 214–15). There are therefore synergies and tensions among the wide variety of interests converging around forest management and development that are worth exploring. The next section discusses the link between forest loss and human action.

Forest loss and human action

Since the 15th century approximately, the focus of forest management has been on forest exploitation rather than on the protective functions of forests. Large-scale natural resource extraction, spread since the Spanish encounter of Latin America in 1492, marked the start of massive forest land conversion. This trend was accelerated significantly after the Industrial Revolution and in the period 1700–1915 there was a 50 per cent decrease in global forest area (Meyer and Turner, 1995). A key challenge in achieving low carbon development is the fact that the development of contemporary societies has been and it is still highly dependent on the industrialization of production, which entails negative environment and climate costs (Mathews, 2011).

Large-scale industrialization of agriculture and livestock has been a key process driving deforestation globally (Mathews, 2011), particularly in the three countries with the highest annual deforestation rates, Brazil, Indonesia and Australia (Seebrook *et al.*, 2006; Pirard and Irland, 2007; Richards *et al.*, 2012). The other two main anthropogenic causes of deforestation are road building, timber extraction and urban growth (Kanninen *et al.*, 2007; McAlpine *et al.*, 2009; FAO, 2010).

All these drivers are embedded in particular interrelated socio-economic, political and cultural systems (Kaimowitz and Angelsen 1998; Seabrook *et al.*, 2006). Economic globalization through the incorporation of a country or region into the expanding world capitalist economy is in fact a major underlying cause of deforestation. Agricultural and timber enterprise integration in the global economy has become a key driver of deforestation in tropical forest countries since the 1990s (Lambin *et al.*, 2001; Rudel, 2007). The entrance of

Tanzania in global timber markets is increasing deforestation rates due to growing demand from Chinese and Indian logging companies (Milledge *et al.*, 2009). More recently, the need to find low carbon energy sources in Annex I countries has led to the expansion of the biofuel industry, which, contradictorily is today a major cause of large-scale deforestation in Indonesia, the Brazilian Amazon (Butler, 2008; Rodrigues, 2008) and the Peruvian Amazon (Gutiérrez-Vélez *et al.*, 2011). Countries with great forest surfaces see them as a national comparative advantage, often selling forested land to outside agricultural and timber companies. That is, forest land is often seen as too valuable to preserve it. Indirectly – low land prices, low wages, high crop prices and currency devaluation are factors of deforestation, as they are incentives for agricultural enterprise expansion in forested-rich countries (Kanninen *et al.*, 2007; Rodrigues, 2008; Richards *et al.*, 2012). As Table 11.1 shows, countries with the greatest amount of deforestation have vast, tropical forests where land is highly productive.

Deforestation rates increase with poor forest governance, including weak law enforcement at the national and subnational level, corruption and inappropriate control of value chains of timber production (involving illegal logging) (Barr *et al.*, 2010). The lack of protected areas is actually an indirect source of forest loss as they can help not only preserve biodiversity, but also avoid deforestation (Joppa and Pfaff, 2010).

While forest communities are often blamed for deforestation and forest degradation (Brockington and Igoe, 2006; Peluso and Vandergeest, 2011; Potete and Ribot, 2011), recent research suggests their impact on deforestation and forest degradation is insignificant even when populations are growing (DeFries *et al.*, 2010; Godar *et al.*, 2012). In fact, national actors who favour forest conversion have historically been more powerful than those who support forest conservation (Sunderlin and Atmadja, 2009).

Table 11.1 Countries with highest deforestation rates

Countries with highest annual deforestation rates in the period 2005–2010	*Number of average deforested hectares/year*	*Countries with the highest annual percentage of forest loss*	*%*
Brazil	2,194,000	Comoros	9.71
Australia	924,000	Togo	5.75
Indonesia	685,000	Nigeria	4.00
Nigeria	410,000	Uganda	2.72
Tanzania	403,000	Pakistan	2.37
Democratic Republic of Congo	311,000	Ghana	2.19

Source: FAO, 2010

Options to achieve low carbon development in the forestry sector

This section discusses options to achieve low carbon development in the forestry sector. Transition to low carbon economies in the forestry sector involves changing both production and consumption systems. A focus on production uses implies reducing pressure on forested land due to timber exploitation, agriculture, mining, infrastructures and urbanization. In high economic growth scenarios this can be a key challenge, especially when central governments do not see forest conservation as a profitable substitute for agriculture or livestock. Solutions can focus on improving forest governance as it enhances control over forest exploitation while avoiding economic losses. Global economic costs of illegal logging were estimated at

$10 or $15 billion in 2002 (World Bank, 2002: 7) and it is estimated that about $5 billion per year is lost due to corruption in uncollected taxes and royalties on legally sanctioned timber harvests. For instance, in Papua New Guinea, lost tax revenues from transfer pricing within the forestry business alone are estimated to be between $9 and $17 million (Sikka and Willmott, 2010: 348–9). Improving governance may also provide development opportunities through the levying of taxes. On the other hand, de-growth advocates suggest that slowing down economic growth rates and industrial resource exploitation, which dominate current global production systems, can contribute to low carbon development in the forestry sector. In fact, the financial crisis led to a decrease in deforestation rates in the Amazon as external demand for exports declined (Schneider *et al.*, 2010).

In highly industrialized and urbanized countries, achieving forestry-related low carbon consumption is likely to be a challenge. For many consumers, especially urban-based middle class consumers, current standards of living are dependent on continued high levels of resource use (Emel and Bridge, 1995: 322). A forestry-based 'low carbon lifestyle' approach (see Chapter 17) may be achieved through consumers' choices to buy food, fuel and other material whose production has involved little large-scale deforestation. This is the case of products which comply with International Forestry Certification systems that ensure sustainable forest management, such as the Forest Stewardship Council (Stupak *et al.*, 2010; Eden, 2011). Carrier (2011) however, warns against the 'fetishisation' of ethical standards as they may make invisible the actual production processes and strengthen consumers' assumptions on product sustainability. In addition, Eden (2011) argues that forest certification standards may represent a poor challenge to current timber production systems that are incompatible with ecological limits.

A 'coexistence with nature approach' (see Chapter 17) to forestry-based low carbon development focuses on reducing consumption of products that involve large-scale deforestation. Shifting consumption from imported food products grown in large-scale agricultural surfaces to local products grown by small farmers, buying second-hand timber products, reducing use of paper and other material whose production has involved large-scale deforestation and high GHG emissions. Achieving low carbon consumption in the forestry sector through this approach also implies providing alternative and more sustainable energy sources for the rural poor, who are highly reliant on firewood and charcoal consumption (CIFOR, 2008: 5–7). This has additional benefits such as the reduction of health problems caused by the emission of hundreds of harmful pollutants during the burning of biomass and coal (Jin *et al.*, 2006).

While the above-mentioned low carbon development options are focused on changing production and consumption patterns related to forest extraction, forest conservation is increasingly being regarded as a key source of low carbon development. Today there are 100,000 protected areas that cover around 13 per cent of the total forest area on Earth (FAO, 2010), but they cost money and other resources, such as time and political capital and, in many cases protected areas have been abandoned and land converted to more profitable uses, including timber exploitation or farming (Joppa and Pffaf, 2010). As a result, new options have been explored to connect the protective functions of forests, *inter alia*, carbon storage, with economic development. For example, payments for ecosystem services (PES) are a voluntary transaction, in which a well-defined environmental service is being 'bought' by at least one buyer, from at least one provider under the condition the service is actually preserved (Wunder, 2005). The potential for achieving climate change mitigation through PES is particularly high and it has been shown that almost 30,000 km^2 – out of 134,301 km^2 – of natural habitat could potentially meet these three purposes at the same time (Wendland,

2010). This number could be even larger if large-scale use-restricting (i.e. avoiding land conversion to agricultural purposes) PES were to be implemented (Pirard, 2011).

While the potential for climate change mitigation might be high, the environmental impacts of PES should not be taken for granted. Since these schemes are voluntary, land stewards can decide whether to participate or not (Wunder, 2009). Moreover, in most cases, when PES enable private sector and central governments from Annex I countries to offset their emissions or environmental damage these impacts are not reduced, rather they are displaced to other countries, also known as leakage (Robertson, 2004; Sullivan, 2010; Pawliczek and Sullivan, 2011).

Box 11.2 critically discusses the commoditization (commodification) of forests. For more discussions on low carbon development and commoditization/commodification of natural resources see Chapter 5.

Box 11.2 Low carbon development and criticisms of the commoditization of forests

The new trend towards payments for environmental conservation has also been criticized from the point of view that it leads to a commoditization of forest resources. Commoditization is understood as interlinked processes whereby production for use is systematically displaced by production for exchange (Prudham, 2008). Emissions trading has created new forms of exchangeable property through which forest carbon has become a commodity that can be bought and sold in global markets (Corbera and Brown, 2010). As with other natural resources, extractive activities undertaken in forests (including hydrocarbon extraction, timber exploitation, mining and forest land clearing for agriculture), forest carbon trading creates new systems of private property. Thus, forest carbon offsets in developing countries are seen as new forms of green capitalism that enable the private sector not only to cost effectively (cheaper labour and land) reduce emissions, but also to make profit through them and continue their polluting activities (Bumpus and Liverman, 2008). They are seen as a 'spatial fix' for private sector profit that only serves to deepen the problematic role of capitalism in environmental management (Peet *et al.*, 2011). The commoditization of forests through climate change mitigation is thus understood as 'green grabs' through which natural resources as well as forest land come into private companies' ownership (Bridge, 2008), often dispossessing local people from their territories and limiting their access to and use of resources (Peluso and Ribot, 2003; Bridge, 2010; Fairhead *et al.*, 2012).

Furthermore, evidence from Latin America, Asia and Africa suggests that the social impacts of previous payment-based ecosystem conservation projects have been poor, especially because PES schemes make the assumption that if communities hold property rights they will benefit from them, while in practice land tenure is contested and it does not ensure local people will get a profit from PES. This is the case for a large number of indigenous peoples whose ownership over land is being threatened by private companies and central governments interested in forest carbon markets (Fenton, 2010). Communities often lack capital, knowledge, expertise, technology and, more importantly, power to negotiate carbon contracts to their own benefits (Corbera and Brown, 2010; Lele *et al.*, 2010; Sullivan, 2010; Larson and Ribot, 2009).

Global forestry-related low carbon development initiatives under the UNFCCC

With the current trend of payment-based environmental conservation, new climate change mechanisms that compensate forest carbon sequestration have emerged. The 1997 Kyoto

Protocol under the UNFCCC led to the emergence of the CDM. By providing certified emissions reductions (CERs), the CDM is intended to help channel private sector investment towards emission reduction projects in developing countries that might not otherwise have taken place (Yamin and Depledge, 2004: 160). CDM allows private companies from Annex I countries to earn CER credits, each equivalent to one tonne of CO_2), that can be traded, sold and used by industrialized countries to meet a part of their emission reduction targets under the Kyoto Protocol. Forestry-related interventions under the CDM interventions include afforestation and reforestation (A/R) projects in non-Annex I countries (UNFCCC, 1997).

With PES, the social as well as environmental effects of CDM A/R projects have been mixed. Often projects that seek primarily to enhance the financial viability of forest plantations typically will focus on industrial mono-species plantations that reduce biodiversity (Spellerberg, 1996) In fact, the wood industry has shown great interest in using the carbon market to justify and help finance new large-scale monoculture plantations for these purposes (Boyd *et al.*, 2007).

The focus on afforestation and reforestation activities implied that forest-rich developing country efforts to avoid or reduce deforestation were not compensated (Santilli *et al.*, 2005) as GHG land use change emissions were deliberately dropped from the Kyoto Protocol (Laurance, 2007). Thus, in 2005 Papua New Guinea and Costa Rica, representing a group of 15 countries, solicited the creation of a global climate change mechanism that would financially reward developing countries for avoiding and/or reducing deforestation (Parker and Mitchell, 2009). This mechanism was formally approved as REDD in the 2007 UNFCCC Conference of Parties (COP) in Bali (UNFCCC, 2007). At COP 15 REDD became REDD+, which goes beyond deforestation and environmental degradation and includes the role of environmental conservation, sustainable management of forests and enhancement of forest carbon stocks (UNFCCC, 2009).

Achieving sustainable forestry-related low carbon development: REDD+ and beyond

The idea of REDD+ payments has received much attention at the global and national policy levels, but its implementation involves various challenges that range from techno-managerial issues such as carbon monitoring, reporting and verification (MRV), the uncertainty involved in baseline calculations for REDD+ (Angelsen, 2009) and forest definitions (Davies *et al.*, 2010) to more structural factors. This section focuses on the latter and discusses key opportunities for sustainable low carbon development through forestry, meaning development processes that reconcile climate change mitigation objectives with ecological integrity, economic development and social justice (Mulugetta and Urban, 2010).

At the national level, REDD+ may be overwhelmed by the profitability of competing activities on forest land (Killeen *et al.*, 2011). For instance, in Indonesia REDD+ financing competes with politically connected agricultural investors on large-scale biofuel and palm oil plantations, resulting in a high uncertainty of the current logging moratorium that emerged through REDD+ (Brockhaus *et al.*, 2011). It is estimated that even if avoided deforestation is compensated at the same price as avoided emissions from fossil fuel use, continued profitability of forest clearing for oil palm bio-energy will do little to halt deforestation (Persson, 2012). For this reason, it has been suggested that at an early stage REDD+ could financially reward governments not only for emission reductions but also for the introduction of policy changes that prevent deforestation (Combes *et al.*, 2011; Karsenty and Ongolo, 2012). However, assumptions on behavioural change generated through economic incentives may ignore critical issues such as conflicts among different ministries, for example, the Ministry of the Environment and Agriculture, corruption and pressure from private enterprises to central governments. This also implies enhancing coordination at the global level, for instance between the biofuel industry and REDD+ programmes. Recent modelling suggests that transnational leakage of forest conservation due to market forces ranges from 42% to 95%, with an average leakage rate of 70% or higher for most countries/regions (Gan and McCarl, 2007). Improved cooperation between the UNFCCC and global environment and human rights conventions such as the Convention on Biological Diversity and the Human Rights Convention can help ensure REDD+ and other PES mechanisms do not come at the expense of biodiversity and social justice (Gardner *et al.*, 2011).

On the one hand, REDD+ monetary benefits have been regarded as an opportunity for poverty reduction when communities lead forest management (Agrawal and Angelsen, 2009) and when payments capitalize with other rural development strategies (e.g. REDD+ payments on local infrastructures, health and education) and integrate the voices and needs of community members (Blom *et al.*, 2010). On the other hand, there are concerns that REDD+ fails to integrate the needs of the rural poor, especially due to the democracy deficits within much of forest exploitation and conservation strategies. Thus, a large number of civil society organizations have positioned against REDD+ (Thompson *et al.*, 2011; Shankland and Hasenclever, 2011).

While economic incentives have become popular as a key strategy towards low carbon development, in many cases payments may not be needed to encourage ecological conservation and reduce poverty. For many years forests have been preserved without economic incentives by local communities (Fairhead and Leach, 1996; CIFOR, 2008) and conservationists (Joppa and Pfaff, 2010; Oldekop, 2010) contributing to climate change mitigation. From this perspective, sustainable forestry-based low carbon development is not so much about a one-size-fits-all approach, but about shifting current development strategies so they do not entail negative environmental as well as climate costs. It is also about ensuring forestry-related climate change mitigation interventions are compatible with biodiversity conservation and do not exacerbate poverty as well as power inequalities. In fact, integrating both conservation and development purposes into a common strategy may actually limit the effectiveness of both objectives (Salafsky, 2011).

Conclusion

This chapter has explored the links between forestry and low carbon development by analysing how the forestry sector intersects with climate change and their ecological, socio-economic and cultural values. It has shown how forest landscape dynamics are embedded within particular social, economic, political and cultural factors shaping development pathways. It has finally proposed different options to achieve low carbon development in the forestry sector and discussed the key challenges to ensuring its compatibility with environmental integrity and social justice issues.

There is not a single path to achieve low carbon development in the forestry sector. REDD+ payments can be seen as part of the solution, but low carbon development in forestry will require work on structural issues to ensure the underlying causes of deforestation and forest degradation are effectively challenged and policies are fair. Under high economic growth scenarios these drivers are less likely to be dealt with, especially because capitalism, in the form of industrial production and consumption, comes at high environmental as well as climate costs (Newell, 2011; Peet *et al.*, 2011). It is also problematic because it shapes green governance, creating new property regimes that exacerbate power inequalities (Mansfield, 2011). Ensuring forestry policies are deliberative and representative will imply engaging local governments and community members in decision-making processes and supporting local democratically elected authorities through financing, capacity building and discretionary powers (Boyd *et al.*, 2007; Ribot *et al.*, 2008; Larson and Ribot, 2009; Phelps *et al.*, 2010). De-growth approaches to development are likely to be more effective in transforming current production and consumption systems so that forestry-related GHG emissions are reduced (Schneider *et al.*, 2010; Kallis, 2011; Peet *et al.*, 2011).

The cross-sectoral nature of forest land allocation and the global dimension of climate change mean coordination among plural institutional objectives as well as decision-making levels will be needed to ensure effectiveness. This should not imply the dominance of certain levels of decision-making over others, but rather should ensure the social as well as environmental costs of forestry-related low carbon development are taken into consideration in policy-making. Understanding forest allocation through a political economy lens can help evidence how forest conservation or conversion comes to be produced and therefore the key structural challenges ahead in bringing about effective transformation in policies so they are environment and climate sound and reduce democracy deficits (Brockhaus *et al.*, 2011; Peet *et al.*, 2011; Tanner and Allouche, 2011). Finally, taking institutional agency as a driver of change by creating awareness among development practitioners as well as policy-makers will play a key role in challenging the status quo towards a more effective and sustainable forestry-related low carbon development (Peet *et al.*, 2011; Potete and Ribot, 2011).

References

Agrawal, A. and Angelsen, A. (2009) Using community forest management to achieve REDD+ goals. In: Angelsen A. (ed.). Realising REDD+ at the national level. National strategy and policy options. Bogor: CIFOR, pp. 1–44.

Angelsen, A. (2009) Introduction, in Angelsen A. (ed.) Realising REDD+ at the national level. National strategy and policy options. Bogor: CIFOR.

Barr, C., Dermawan, A., Purnomo, H. and Komarudin, H. (2010) Financial governance and Indonesia's reforestation fund during the Soeharto and Post-Soeharto periods, 1989–2009: a political economic analysis of lessons for REDD+. Occasional paper 52. Bogor: CIFOR.

Blom, B., Sunderland, T. and Murdiyarso, D. (2010) Getting REDD to work locally: lessons learned from integrated conservation and development projects. *Environmental Science & Policy* 13(2), 164–72.

Boyd, E., Gutierrez, M. and Chang, M. (2007) Small-scale forest carbon projects: adapting CDM to low-income communities. *Global Environmental Change*, 17, 250–9.

Bridge, G. (2008) Global production networks and the extractive sector: governing resource-based development. *Journal of Economic Geography*, 8, 389–419.

Bridge, G. (2010) Resource geographies 1: making carbon economies, old and new. *Progress in Human Geography* 35(6), 820–34.

Brockhaus, M., Obidzinski, K., Dermawan, A., Laumonier, Y. and Luttrell, C. (2012) An overview of forest and land allocation policies in Indonesia: Is the current framework sufficient to meet the needs of REDD+? *Forest Policy and Economics*, 18, 30–7.

Brockington, D. and Igoe, J. (2006) Eviction for conservation. A global overview. *Conservation and Society*, 4(3), 424–70.

Bumpus, A. G. and Liverman, D. M. (2008) Accumulation by decarbonization and the governance of carbon o?sets. *Economic Geography*, 84(2), 127–55.

Butler, R. A. (2008) U.S. biofuels policy drives deforestation in Indonesia, the Amazon. Available at: www.Mongabay.com (accessed 21 November 2012)

Carrier, J. G. (2011) Protecting the environment the natural way: ethical consumption and commodity fetishism, in Brockington, D. and Duffy, R. (eds) *Capitalism and Conservation*. Oxford: Wiley-Blackwell, pp. 203–20.

CIFOR (2008) CIFOR's strategy, 2008–2018. Making a difference for forests and people. Bogor: CIFOR.

Combes, P., Pirard, R. and Combes, J. L. (2011) A methodology to estimate impacts of domestic policies on deforestation: compensated successful efforts for 'avoided deforestation' (REDD). *Ecological Economics*, 68, 680–91.

Corbera, E. and Brown, K. (2010) Offsetting benefits? Analyzing access to forest carbon. *Environment and Planning A*, 42(7), 1739–61.

Davies, C., Nakhooda, S. and Daviet, F. (2010) Getting ready: a review of the World Bank forest carbon partnership facility readiness preparation proposals, WRI Working Paper. Washington DC: World Resource Institute.

Defries, R. S., Rudel, T., Uriarte, M. and Hansen, M. (2010) Deforestation driven by urban population growth and agricultural trade in the twenty-first century. *Nature Geoscience*, 3, 178–81.

Eden, S. (2011) The politics of certification: consumer knowledge, power and global governance in ecolabelling, in Peet, R., Robins P. and Watts M. J (eds) *Global Political Ecology*. New York: Routledge, pp. 169–84.

Emel, J. and Bridge, G. (1995) The Earth as input: resources, in Johnston, R. J., Taylor, P. J. and Watts, M. J. (eds) *Geographies of Global Change. Remapping the World in the Late Twentieth Century*. Oxford: Blackwell, pp. 318–32.

Fairhead, J. and Leach, M. (1996) Rethinking the forest-savannah mosaic: colonial science and its relics in west Africa, in Leach, M. and Mearns, R. (eds) *The Lie of the Land: Challenging Received Wisdom on the African Environment*. London: James Currey, pp. 105–21.

Fairhead, J., Leach, M. and Scoones, I. (2012) Introductory essay: green grabbing: a new appropriation of nature? *Journal of Peasant Studies*, 39(2), 237–61.

Fenton, E. (2010) Realising rights, protecting forests: an alternative vision for reducing deforestation case studies from the Accra Caucus. Available at: http://www.rightsandresources.org/documents/files/doc_1590.pdf (accessed 6 November 2012).

Food and Agriculture Organization (FAO) (2010) Global forest resources assessment. Rome: United Nations.

Gan, J. and McCarl, B. (2007) Measuring transnational leakage of forest conservation. *Ecological Economics*, 64, 423–32.

Gardner, T. A., Burgess, N. D., Aguilar-Amuchastegui, N., Barlow, J., Berenguer, E., Clements, T. *et al.* (2012) A framework for integrating biodiversity concerns into national REDD+ programmes. *Biological Conservation*, 154, 61–71.

Godar, J., Tizado, E. J. and Pokorny, B. (2012) Who is responsible for deforestation in the Amazon? A spatially explicit analysis along the Transamazon Highway in Brazil. *Forest Ecology and Management*, 267, 58–73.

Gutiérrez-Vélez, V. H., DeFries, R., Pinedo-Vasquez, M., Uriarte, M., Padoch, C., Baethgen, W. *et al.* (2011) High-yield oil palm expansion spares land at the expense of forests in the Peruvian Amazon. *Environmental Research Letters*, 6.

IPCC (2007) IPCC fourth assessment report: climate change 2007. Synthesis Report. Geneva: IPCC.

International Tropical Timber Organization (ITTO) and Food and Agriculture Organization (FAO) (2010) ITTO Thematic programme on forest law enforcement, governance and trade. Geneva: International Tropical Timber Organization.

Joppa, L. and Pfaff, A. (2010) Reassessing the forest impacts of protection. The challenge of nonrandom location and a corrective method. *Annals of the New York Academy of Sciences,* 1185, 135–49.

Kaimowitz, D. and Angelsen, A. (1998) Economic models of tropical deforestation: a review. Bogor: CIFOR.

Kallis, G. (2011) In defence of degrowth. *Ecological Economics*, 70, 873–80.

Kanninen, M. (2009) Forests, development cooperation, and climate change – is there room for win-win situations? in Palosuo, E. (ed.) *Rethinking Development in a Carbon-constrained World*. Helsinki: Development Cooperation and Climate Change, Ministry of Foreign Affairs.

Kanninen, M., Murdiyarso, D., Seymour, F., Angelsen, A., Wunder, S. and German, L. (2007) Do trees grow on money? The implications of deforestation research for policies to promote REDD. Bogor: CIFOR.

Karsenty, A. and Ongolo, S. (2012) Can "fragile states" decide to reduce their deforestation? The inappropriate use of the theory of incentives with respect to the REDD mechanism. *Forest Policy and Economics*, 18, 38–45.

Killeen, T. J., Schroth, G., Turner, W., Harvey, C. A., Steininger, M. K., Dragisic, C. and Mittermeier, R. A. (2011) Stabilizing the agricultural frontier: leveraging REDD with biofuels for sustainable development. *Biomass and Bioenergy*, 35(12), 4815–23.

Lambin, E., Turner, B., Geist, H., Agbola, S., Angelsen, A., Bruce, J. *et al.* (2001) The causes of land-use and land-cover change: moving beyond the myths. *Global Environmental Change*, 11, 261–9.

Larson, A. M. and Ribot, J. C. (2009) Lessons from forestry decentralization, in Angelsen A. (ed.). Realising REDD+ at the national level. National strategy and policy options. Bogor: CIFOR, pp. 175–87.

Laurance, W. F. (2007) Have we overstated the tropical biodiversity crisis? *Trends in Ecology & Evolution*, 22(2), 65–70.

Lele, S., Wilshusen, P., Brockington, D., Seidler, R. and Bawa, K. (2010) Beyond exclusion: alternative approaches to biodiversity. Conservation in the developing tropics. *Current Opinion in Environmental Sustainability* 2, 94–100.

Mansfield, B. (2011) 'Modern' industrial fisheries and the crisis of overfishing, in Peet, R., Robins, P. and Watts, M. J. (eds) *Global Political Ecology*. New York: Routledge, pp. 84–99.

Mathews, J. A. (2011) Naturalizing capitalism: the next great transformation. *Futures* 43, 868–79.

McAlpine, C. A., Etter, A., Fearnside, P. M., Seabrook, L. and Laurance, W. F. (2009) Increasing world consumption of beef as a driver of regional and global change: a call for policy action based on evidence from Queensland (Australia), Colombia and Brazil. *Global Environmental Change*, 19(1), 21–33.

McGuffie, K., Henderson-Sellers, A., Zhang, H., Durbidge, T. B. and Pitman, A. J. (1995) Global climate sensitivity to tropical deforestation. *Global and Planetary Change*, 10, 97–128.

Meyer, W. B. and Turner, B. L. (1994) *Changes in Land Use and Land Cover: a Global Perspective*. Cambridge: Cambridge University Press.

Milledge, S. A. H., Gelvas, I. K. and Ahrends, A. (2007) Forestry, governance and national development: lessons learned from a logging boom in southern Tanzania, TRAFFIC East/Southern Africa, Dar Es Salaam.

Mulugetta, Y. and Urban, F. (2010) Deliberating on low-carbon development. *Energy Policy*, 38(12), 7546–9.

Newell, P. (2011) The elephant in the room: capitalism and global environmental change. *Global Environmental Change*, 21, 4–6.

Nodvin, S. C. (2008) *Forest Environmental Services*. Boston, MA: IUCN.

Oldekop, J. A., Bebbington, A. J., Brockington, D. and Preziosi, R. F. (2010) Understanding the lessons and limitations of conservation and development. *Conservation Biology*, 24(2), 461–9.

Parker, C. and Mitchell. A. (2009) *The Little REDD+ Book: a Guide to Governmental and Non-Governmental Proposals for Reducing Emissions From Deforestation and Forest Degradation*. Oxford: Global Canopy Programme.

Pawliczek, J. and Sullivan, S. (2011) Payments for ecosystem services in conservation: performance and prospects. Conservation and concealment in SpeciesBanking.com, USA: an analysis of neoliberal performance in the species offsetting industry. *Environmental Conservation*, 38(4), 1–10.

Peet, R., Robins, P. and Watts, M. J. (2011) Global nature, in Peet, R., Robins, P. and Watts, M. J. (eds) *Global Political Ecology*. New York: Routledge, pp. 1–48.

Peluso, N. L. and Vandergeest P. (2011) The making of national natures, in Peet, R., Robins, P. and Watts, M. J. (eds) *Global Political Ecology*. New York: Routledge, pp. 252–84.

Persson, U. M. (2012) Conserve or convert? Pan-tropical modeling of REDD–bioenergy competition. *Biological Conservation*, 146, 81–8.

Phelps, J., Guerrero, M. C., Dalabajan, D. A., Young, B. and Webb, E. L. (2010) What makes a 'REDD' country? *Global Environmental Change*, 20(2), 322–32.

Pimm, S. and Raven, P. (2000) Biodiversity: extinction by numbers. *Nature*, 403, 843–5.

Pirard, R. and Irland, L. C. (2007) Missing links between timber scarcity and industrial expansion: the lessons from the Indonesian Pulp and Paper sector. *Forest Policy and Economics*, 9(8), 1056–70.

Pirard, R. (2011) Payments for Environmental Services (PES) in the public policy landscape: 'Mandatory' spices in the Indonesian recipe. *Forest Policy and Economics, Special issue on Global Governance*, 18, 23–9.

Potete, A. R. and Ribot, J. (2011) Repertoires of domination: decentralization as process in Botswana and Senegal. *World Development*, 39(3), 439–49.

Prudham, S. (2008) Commodification, in Castree, N., Demeritt, D., Liverman, D. and Rhoades, B. (eds) *A Companion to Environmental Geography*. Chichester: Wiley, pp. 123–42.

Ribot, J. (2009) Authority over forests: empowerment and subordination in Senegal's democratic decentralization. *Development and Change*, 40(1), 105–29.

Ribot, J., Chhatre, A. and Lankina, T. V. (2008) institutional choice and recognition in the formation and consolidation of local democracy, representation, equity and environment, Working Paper Series 35. Washington DC: World Resources Institute.

Richards, P. D., Myers, R. J., Swinton, S. M. and Walker, R. T. (2012) Exchange rates, soybean supply response, and deforestation in South America. *Global Environmental Change*, 22(2), 454–62.

Robertson, M. M. (2008) The neoliberalization of ecosystem services: wetland mitigation banking and problems in environmental governance. *Geoforum*, 35, 361–73.

Rodrigues, E. G. (2008) Agricultural explosion in Brazil: exploring the impacts of the Brazilian agricultural development over the Amazon. *International Journal of Society of Agriculture and Food*, 16(1), 1–12.

Rudel, T. K. (2007) Changing agents of deforestation: from state-initiated to enterprise driven processes, 1970–2000. *Land Use Policy*, 24, 35–41.

Salafsky, N. (2011) Integrating development with conservation. A means to a conservation end, or a mean end to conservation? *Biological Conservation*, 144, 973–8.

Santilli, M., Moutinho, P., Schwartzman, S., Nepstad, D., Curran, L. and Nobre, C. (2005) Tropical deforestation and the Kyoto Protocol: an editorial essay. *Climatic Change*, 71(3), 267–76.

Schneider, F., Kallis, G. and Martinez-Alier, J. (2010) Crisis or opportunity? Economic degrowth for social equity and ecological sustainability. *Journal of Cleaner Production*, 18(6), 511–18.

Seabrook, L., McAlpine, C. and Fensham, R. J. (2006) Cattle, crops and clearing: regional drivers of landscape change in the Brigalow Belt, Queensland, Australia 1840–2004. *Landscape and Urban Planning*, 78, 373–85.

Seymour, F. (2010) Forests, climate change and human rights: managing risks and trade-offs, in Humphreys, S. (ed.) *Human Rights and Climate Change*. Cambridge: Cambridge University Press.

Shankland, A. and Hasenclever, L. (2011) Indigenous peoples and the regulation of REDD+ in Brazil: beyond the war of the worlds? *IDS Bulletin*, 42(3), 80–8.

Sikka, P. and Willmott, H. (2010) The dark side of transfer pricing: its role in tax avoidance and wealth retentiveness. *Critical Perspectives on Accounting*, 21, 342–56.

Spellerberg, I. F. (1996) Plantation forests protect biodiversity? Too much of a generalization to be true. *New Zealand Forestry*, 39, 19–22.

Stupak, I., Lattimore, B., Titus, B. D. and Smith, C. T. (2011) Criteria and indicators for sustainable forest fuel production and harvesting: a review of current standards for sustainable forest management. *Biomass and Bioenergy*, 35, 3287–308.

Sullivan, S. (2010) Ecosystem service commodities. A new imperial ecology? Implications for animist immanent ecologies, with Deleuze and Guattari. *New Formations*, 69(18), 111–28.

Sunderlin, W. D. and Atmadja, S. (2010) Is REDD+ an idea whose time has come, or gone? in

Angelsen, A. (ed.) Realising REDD+ at the national level. National strategy and policy option. Bogor: CIFOR, pp. 45–56.

Tanner, T. and Allouche, J. (2011) Towards a new political economy of climate change and development. *IDS Bulletin*, 42(3), 1–14.

Thompson, M. C., Baruah, M. and Carr, E. R. (2011) Seeing REDD+ as a project of environmental governance. *Environmental Science and Policy*, 14, 100–10.

United Nations Framework Convention on Climate Change (UNFCCC) (1997) Kyoto Protocol. Available at: http://unfccc.int/resource/docs/convkp/kpeng.pdf (accessed 6 November 2012).

UNFCCC (2007) Bali Action Plan. Available at: http://unfccc.int/files/meetings/cop_13/application/pdf/cp_bali_action.pdf (accessed 6 November 2012).

UNFCCC (2009) Copenhagen Accord. Available at: http://unfccc.int/resource/docs/2009/cop15/eng/11a01.pdf (accessed 6 November 2012).

Van der Werf, G. R., Morton, D. C., DeFries, R. S., Olivier, J. G. J., Kasibhatla, P. S., Jackson, R. B. *et al.* (2009) CO_2 emissions from forest loss. *Nature Geosciences*, 2, 737–8.

Watson, R., Noble, I. R., Bolin, B., Ravindranath, N. H., Verardo, D. J. and Dokken, D. J. (2000) *Land use, Land-use Change and Forestry: a Special Report*. Cambridge: Cambridge University Press.

Wendland, K. J., Honza, M., Portela, R., Vitale, B., Rubinoff, S. and Randrianarisoa, J. (2010) Targeting and implementing payments for ecosystem services: opportunities for bundling biodiversity conservation with carbon and water services in Madagascar. *Ecological Economics*, 69, 2093–107.

World Bank (2002) Sustaining forests: a World Bank Strategy. Washington DC: World Bank.

Wunder, S. (2005) *Payments for Environmental Services: Some Nuts and Bolts*, Volume 26. Bogor: CIFOR.

Yamin, F. and Depledge, J. (2004) *The International Climate Change Regime: a Guide to Rules, Institutions and Procedures*. Cambridge: Cambridge University Press.

Further reading

Angelsen, A. (ed.) (2010) Realising REDD+ at the national level. National strategy and policy options. CIFOR, Bogor.

Blom, B., Sunderland, T., Murdiyarso, D. (2010) Getting REDD to work locally: lessons learned from integrated conservation and development projects. *Environmental Science & Policy*, 13(2), 164–72.

Food and Agriculture Organization (FAO) (2010) Global forest resources assessment. Rome: United Nations.

Kanninen, M., Murdiyarso, D., Seymour, F., Angelsen, A., Wunder, S. and German, L. (2007) Do trees grow on money? The implications of deforestation research for policies to promote REDD. Bogor: CIFOR.

12 Agriculture and low carbon development

Rocio Hiraldo

This chapter takes a sectoral perspective by addressing the role of agriculture for low carbon development. 'Low carbon' in agriculture goes beyond carbon and includes mitigation of GHGs other than carbon dioxide, including nitrous oxide and methane. Changes in land use and different management practices in crop and livestock production are major contributors to the GHG emissions leading to climate change. Fossil fuel-induced emissions due to energy use and transport for food products are also sources of GHG emissions in agriculture. Mitigation in this sector can be achieved not only through various improved techniques but also through the introduction of new policies and programmes that support low carbon agricultural development. Emission reduction will depend on how solutions are appropriate to contextual needs, the creation of synergies with other low carbon development sectors and effective control of agricultural production.

Agriculture and climate change

Agriculture, including crop and livestock production, is a vital sector for development not only contributing to food security, but also as a source of revenues for individuals, communities and countries. Agriculture contributes to national economic growth, it constitutes one of the main activities for rural people in the world, employing a large share of the population (FAO, 2009) and it is a key element of local cultures (McMichael, 2011). However, the sector is a source of GHG emissions leading to climate change and therefore changes are needed in the way production takes place.

The first section of the chapter analyses the links between agriculture and climate change. The various management practices and policy options to address climate change mitigation are then explored followed by a discussion on the key challenges and opportunities to achieve sustainable low carbon agricultural development in high, middle and low-income countries.

Box 12.1 elaborates the key definitions relevant to this chapter.

Box 12.1 Definitions

Agricultural lands: lands used for agricultural production, consisting of cropland, managed grassland and permanent crops including agroforestry (the planting of trees around agricultural plantations) and crops used to produce biofuels (Smith *et al.*, 2007).

Land use change emissions: emissions derived from changes in land cover that decrease the amount of carbon stored in vegetation and soils. Agriculture is a major driver of land use change-related emissions since cropland as well as pasture land demands for expansion often lead to carbon sink losses through deforestation (Watson *et al.*, 2000).

Livestock farming: practices related to the production of animal-derived products, including beef, poultry and pig meat as well as milk, cheese and eggs. It is the world's largest user of agricultural land, directly as pastures and indirectly through the production of forage and feed.

Agricultural lands contribute today to the release of 13.5 per cent of global anthropogenic GHGs (IPCC, 2007). The sector is source of highly polluting gases, namely carbon dioxide (CO_2) and also nitrous oxide (N_2O) and methane (CH_4). N_2O and CH_4 have global warming potentials 310 and 21 times greater than CO_2, respectively (Yamin and Depledge, 2004). Agriculture-related emissions from these two gases are significant, contributing about 52 per cent and 84 per cent of global CH_4 and N_2O emissions, respectively (Smith *et al.*, 2008). The main direct and indirect sources of agriculture-related GHG emissions are outlined in table T2.1.

Table 12.1 Direct and indirect sources of GHG emissions in agriculture

Direct drivers of agricultural GHG emissions	*Emission process*
N_2O from nitrogen fertilizers	Formed in the soils at the expense of the nitrogen (N) fertilizers
CH_4 emissions from enteric fermentation	Produced as a by-product of feed digestion by animals, mostly ruminants, either belched or passed out as flatulence
N_2O and CH_4 emissions from manure	N_2O: when manures are recycled back to land to increase soil fertility (Mosier *et al.*, 1998). CH_4: When animal manure is stored in anaerobic (oxygen-deprived) conditions
CO_2, CH_4 and N_2O from burning savannah, forest and crop residues	These gases are released when organic matter is burnt. Carbon sinks in soil and biomass are also lost with fire
CH_4 from rice cultivation	Through fermentation of decomposing organic matter when soils in rice paddies are flooded
Indirect drivers of agricultural GHG emissions	*Emission process*
Land use change (from other uses to agriculture)	Through deforestation and conversion of pasture to cropland
CO_2 from agricultural transport and energy	Through the burning of fossil fuels for on-farm energy use; when food is transported; in the production of fertilizers and in the cooling of agricultural products

Agriculture can also act as a carbon sink as there is carbon uptake into both vegetation and soils in terrestrial ecosystems (Watson *et al.*, 2000). Studies, worldwide, have now shown that significant amounts of soil carbon can be stored in this way, through a range of practices including reduced tillage, water management, removing land from annual cropping and converting to forest, grassland or perennial crops (Lal in Smith *et al.*, 2007). Unfortunately this potential is minimized due to the large release of other GHGs in agricultural lands and the indirect agriculture-related emissions above mentioned (Powlson *et al.*, 2011).

Development and changes in GHG emissions in the agricultural sector

Agriculture has been a key issue in development agendas and governments from both Annex I as well as non-Annex I countries[1] and large- as well as small-scale farmers have invested in agricultural modernization during the 20th century. Agricultural mechanization and new cost-effective technologies have accelerated global crop as well as livestock production substantively. However, these rates went hand in hand with a massive use of inorganic fertilizers, water and soil (Dethier and Effenberg, 2012). Thus, while agricultural development has reduced hunger and improved nutrition, it has also entailed high environmental as well as climate costs (Tilman *et al.*, 2002; EPA, 2006; Smith *et al.*, 2007). In fact, the doubling of global cereal production within the 1960–1995 period has gone hand in hand with a sevenfold increase in global use of nitrogen fertilizer, a fourfold increase in phosphorus fertilizer use (Tilman *et al.*, 2002) and a fourfold increase in global per capita withdrawal of fresh water (Meyer and Turner, 1995) in the same period. Moreover, all livestock categories except sheep have increased in the order of 30 to 600 per cent from 1961 to 2007, implying an increase in the total area of soybeans (the main feed crop in industrial livestock production) of 375 per cent in the same period (Smith *et al.*, 2007). As a consequence, global agricultural CH_4 and N_2O emissions have overall increased by 17 per cent in the 1990–2005 period (EPA, 2006). This rapid pace of production is linked to the expansion of industrial capitalist agriculture, which goes hand in hand with a large and rapid mobilization of inputs as well as natural resources (Emel and Bridge, 1995; Weis, 2010).

Governments, private sector and small producers all over the world are being called to substantially reduce agricultural-related emissions, especially in high income nations. Annex I countries have started taking measures to address this problem and emissions have remained stable or declined in many of them. However, in others such as the USA, Canada, Australia and New Zealand these trends have not been reversed yet and the agricultural sector increased by 18% and 21%, respectively, in 1990 and 2006 (Smith *et al.*, 2007).

In a large number of developing countries demands for agricultural production have been growing within the last two decades with changing lifestyles, government policies to increase food supply and lowering of world trade barriers (Tilman, 2002; Tubiello and Fischer, 2007; Rodrigues, 2008). As conventional agricultural development pathways remain dominant today (McMichael, 2011), these demands have been translated into a 32 per cent increase of agricultural-related emissions in developing countries from 1990 to 2005 (Smith *et al.*, 2007). Crop production is still constrained in many developing countries where different strategies are being discussed to develop agriculture and increase production. With new investments going to this sector the need to involve not only Annex I countries, but also non-Annex I countries in agriculture-related mitigation strategies has been acknowledged (FAO, 2009).

Low carbon[2] development in agriculture

The global GHG mitigation technical potential in agriculture is estimated at 5500–6000 Mt CO_2-eq. per year (Smith *et al.*, 2008). Achieving this large potential will largely depend on the measures taken. Since concerns about the impacts of agriculture on climate change emerged, researchers and policy-makers have been looking for low carbon development pathways focused on reducing emissions, avoiding carbon sink losses and enhancing carbon storage. Options are varied and range from management practices to policy options, from production- to consumption-oriented policies and from high to low growth scenarios. The different possibilities are explored in the following subsections.

Low carbon management options

Agricultural management strategies are varied and affect the amount of agricultural production and therefore potential economic profits gained through it. In agricultural mitigation strategies under a green economy approach (see Chapter 14) the priority will be to deliver maximum output at minimum GHG cost. A wide range of agricultural low carbon management practices that maintain productivity levels while achieving GHG emission reduction are described in Box 12.2.

Box 12.2 Agricultural practices that can reduce GHG emissions while maintaining high production levels

Improved synthetic nutrient use: today, only 30–50 per cent of applied nitrogen fertilizer is taken up by crops, and further increases in N fertilizer application are unlikely to augment yields. In China fertilizer application has increased by 271 per cent from 1977 to 2005, while total grain output increased by only 71 per cent (Kahrl *et al.*, 2010). Nutrient use can be reduced while enhancing crop production by applying fertilizers during periods of greatest crop demand at or near the plant roots and in smaller and more frequent applications (Tilman *et al.*, 2002).

Pest and disease control: crop rotation, breeding and vegetative cover between agricultural crops by reducing or eliminating crop tillage can help improve crop resilience to pests and therefore reduce the use of chemical pesticides that lead to N_2O emissions (Tilman *et al.*, 2002).

Water management: CH_4 emissions can be reduced by avoiding drainage of organic and peaty soils, improving irrigation efficiency and adopting improved irrigation schedules (Karimi *et al.*, 2012). Also, water control in rice paddies can reduce CH_4 emissions by draining the field intermittently or, even better, during the second half of the growing season and increase production (Smith *et al.*, 2008).

Manure management: N_2O and CH_4 emissions can be reduced by changes in livestock buildings, manure storage facilities, manure treatment and grazing management. For example, storing manure in dry conditions rather than in lagoons or tanks reduces CH_4 emissions (Steinfeld, 2006). Also, as CH_4 is released in oxygen-deprived conditions, removing manure from the indoor storage pits reduces methane emissions (De Boer *et al.*, 2011).

Improved feeding practices: CH_4 emissions released during fermentation (see Table 12.1) can be reduced through the improvement of pasture quality and the use of feed additives or supplements like certain oils or oilseeds to the diet and improving pasture quality that decrease the amount of nitrogen in animal feed. However, small livestock producers may lack the necessary capital and knowledge (Smith *et al.*, 2007, 2008).

In addition to the various farming practices, agricultural mitigation can be achieved by reducing fossil fuel-induced emissions released during the process of food production and distribution. Options include improving on-farm energy efficiency, reducing emissions from agricultural transport (i.e. by declining imports) and replacing fossil fuel by renewable energies or residue-based bio-energy. For example in addition, to CO_2, biogas produced through manure can reduce CH_4 emissions from manure by up to 50 per cent (Steinfeld, 2006). Moreover, carbon storage can be enhanced in agricultural lands through a range of available options. For example, reduced- or no-till agriculture, also called conservation agriculture, often results in soil carbon gain since soil disturbance tends to stimulate soil carbon losses (Snyder *et al.*, 2009). Agroforestry can also increase the amount of carbon stored by agricultural soils and vegetation due to the greater efficiency of integrated systems in resource (nutrients, light, and water) capture and utilization than single-species systems (Smith *et al.*, 2007; Ramachandran *et al.*, 2009). Other enhancement of carbon stock options include set-aside, conversion of arable land to grassland or woodland, perennial crops and deep rooting crops, improved rotations and organic farming.

Supporting low carbon development in agriculture: policy options

Transitions to low carbon development in agriculture will require global, regional, national as well as subnational policies that create the necessary conditions to encourage mitigation in agriculture and ensure its effectiveness. Options may include creating regulatory and legal frameworks, macro-economic policies, providing financial and technical support for farmers, monitoring and evaluating the impacts of agricultural-related mitigation policies and sanctioning polluters. They will also vary between high growth and low growth scenarios.

National carbon tax systems can be implemented that include a tax on the emission of GHGs from agricultural production (so-called E-tax). In addition, this could include a so-called N-tax that increases the price for synthetic nitrogen fertilizers. It is estimated that prices should increase threefold for N to achieve the desired emission reduction effects (Neufeldt and Schäfer, 2008). In addition to taxes, cap and trade schemes have been developed, such as the EU trading scheme that targets intensive energy users, including large food companies. This scheme has been widely criticized as being ineffective since too many 'free' permits have been allocated (Garnett, 2008).

Rewarding producers for their contribution to agricultural GHG mitigation through conditional payments for environmental services can enhance transitions to low carbon development. National payments for environmental services (PES) already include schemes for farmers to reduce water pollution from N fertilizer residues programmes in Europe, Japan and the USA (Tilman *et al.*, 2002). In the UK around five million hectares – around 50 per cent of the available farmland – are covered by this scheme (Garnett, 2008).

The effectiveness of such policies should not be taken for granted. Under high growth scenarios, even if taxes are paid and financial rewards exist, emissions may continue growing. For example, a voluntary policy programme in the USA that plans to reduce GHG intensity per dollar of GDP by 18 per cent by 2010 is actually projected to allow GHG emissions to increase by 12 per cent because GDP continues growing (Smith *et al.*, 2007). These figures are from before the financial crisis. In recent years, growth in the USA was negative (2009) or zero (2008), hence the GHG emissions would be lower.

In addition, low carbon development agricultural policies should be followed by appropriate monitoring and evaluation and sanctions when needed. A growing number of farmers in Annex I countries are already voluntarily adopting environmental farm management practices, but only around one-third to half of Annex I member countries are regularly monitoring whether and how these changes are happening (Parris, 2011). In fact, strict rules for fertilizer applications have only been only set out for organic agriculture followed by annual inspections (Garnett, 2008). Appropriate monitoring and evaluation of low carbon regulations in the agricultural sector could help Annex I countries comply with their pledges on emission reduction targets.

In order to comply with regulations, farmers will require sustained technical support to implement low carbon agricultural management practices. Extension services that provide information to farmers on the application of these new techniques such as organic farming, conservation agriculture, agroforestry and their associated benefits are necessary to consolidate low carbon agricultural management (McMichael, 2011). Furthermore, issues concerning equity and social justice should be taken into account so the trade-offs that a low carbon transition implies for low income farmers are considered.

Equilibrium economy options[3] for low carbon development in agriculture

While taxes, PES schemes and sanctions can encourage producers to shift to low carbon agriculture, other options may have a larger potential to reduce emissions, including reducing overproduction (De Fraiture and Wichelns, 2010) and slowing the pace at which food is produced and decreasing agricultural intensity (implying reduced use of synthetic fertilizers, reduced livestock density and less pressure on soils) (Tilman *et al.*, 2002; Del Prado *et al.*, 2012). In fact, decreases in agricultural emissions in Annex I countries since the 1990s have been mostly due to agricultural de-intensification policies in Eastern Europe, the Caucasus and Central Asia (Smith *et al.*, 2007).

Organic agriculture, while it might not achieve the same outputs at the same pace as conventional agriculture, has generated interests in many countries, leading to a rapid increase in land under organic farming globally in recent years. For example, in the EU more than 7.5 million hectares were managed organically by the end of 2008 and four European countries already have more than 10 per cent of their agricultural land under organic production (Willer, 2009). While yields may be lower in the short term under organic production than under conventional agriculture, in the long term they may produce higher yields (Azadi *et al.*, 2011) as it prevents future environmental problems including soil degradation and water pollution that will impact on future food security and increase climatic resilience.

Equilibrium economy options can be highly optimal for high-income countries where soil and water pollution are significant and food insecurity is inexistent. Nearly half of Annex I countries record that nutrient and pesticide concentrations in surface water and groundwater monitoring sites in agricultural areas exceed national drinking water limits for nutrients and pesticides (Parris, 2011). In addition, the equilibrium economy approach to agricultural low carbon development can be appropriate for emerging economies already experiencing agricultural-related environmental problems with sufficient income and technical capacity to invest in low carbon development. For instance, in China water pollution due to agricultural inputs has also started to be a concern. Chemical fertilizer use in this country experienced a 25-fold increase from 1970 to 2008 (Kahrl *et al.*, 2010). However, in practice, taking these decisions can be challenging as agricultural companies may not see the equilibrium economy approach as a profitable option.

Enabling low carbon consumption in globalized food systems

Large-scale producers should supply information on the modes of food production, environmental costs and emissions generated through the process so that consumers can make an informed decision. Implementation of carbon footprint standards and commodity carbon labelling could influence consumer behaviour towards 'low carbon foods'. This can be done by giving information on the emissions generated from farm until food is consumed (also called food miles), including transport, cold storage, packing and other emissions generated during this process. These integrative approaches to sectoral carbon accounting, also called life cycle assessments, are increasingly being used to better estimate agri-food system emissions (Steinfeld, 2006; Fiala, 2008; De Boer *et al*., 2011; Garnett, 2011). In livestock production this may imply accounting emissions not only related to manure management and enteric fermentation but also those due to land use change emissions from forest land clearing to plant soybean, which is used as a livestock feedcrop. Life cycle assessments can be useful to unpack consumer assumptions on sustainability of new agricultural-related low carbon development strategies in Annex I countries (see Box 12.3, which discusses whose responsibility agricultural emissions are). Other options for consumers to reduce food miles include buying food that is produced locally, although emissions generated can be greater if consumers drive to do the shopping (Coley *et al*., 2009).

Box 12.3 Whose responsibility? The case of emission displacement in agricultural mitigation

Non-Annex I country emissions have grown substantially in recent decades (Smith *et al*., 2007) and deforestation for agriculture has also accelerated in the tropics (FAO, 2010). On the one hand, this is led by food security policies and changing lifestyles in developing countries. On the other, lowering trade barriers have substantially increased the presence of companies coming from Annex I countries in the developing world. It is estimated that trade liberalization has increased carbon leakage by 3 per cent (Kuik, 2001). In the case of agriculture this implies that a country can deliver its Kyoto emission target by outsourcing or exporting agricultural production. Since the Kyoto Protocol's accounting methodology is territorial/production-based rather than consumption-based, developing countries carry the responsibility for those emissions generated for food produced in their country but consumed elsewhere (Franks and Hadingham, 2012). Despite increasing global concerns about developing countries' rapidly growing populations, the largest per capita calorie intake rates and meat consumption rates are still found in Annex I countries where population growth rates are not that high (Smith *et al*., 2007). For example, the USA accounts for the world's largest per capita calorie intake consumption rates and it has the fourth largest annual per capita meat consumption rate, with 124 kg of meat (WRI, 2012) compared with the average worldwide at 31 kg per year (Fiala, 2008). Western European countries are also at the top with Denmark and Luxembourg having the highest per capital meat consumption rates and Ireland and Austria having the second and third largest per capital calorie intake rates globally (WRI, 2012). Moreover, national policies encouraging overproduction, as it is the case of the United States, are often the main driver behind large food availability rather than excessive demand by consumers (Guthman, 2011). Ensuring the effectiveness of agricultural-related mitigation strategies in a globalized economy will require international coordination. This implies national carbon accounting systems should find a way to consider not only domestic production and supply issues but also international ones so responsibilities for emissions are shared (Franks and Hadingham, 2012).

Low carbon development in agriculture for developing countries

Developing countries, especially middle income countries are increasingly being called to reduce their emissions, particularly as they contribute to 75 per cent of agricultural GHG emissions (Smith *et al*., 2008). Today, Brazil is the country with the highest deforested annual surface globally and China is now the world's largest producer and consumer of nitrogen fertilizers (Kahrl *et al*., 2010). At the same time it is argued that, as historically low emitters, they should be allowed to wait before entering a transition to low carbon development so that they can first address key problems of hunger and poverty. As a result, most climate change policies in low income countries focus solely on adaptation. The challenge for low income countries of meeting their food security goals is often framed as a problem of producing more food through industrial, input-intensive agriculture (World Bank, 2010) and policy solutions are being oriented towards this approach. For example, in the 2006 Abuja Fertiliser Summit African Union state members adopted a number of resolutions to promote the supply and use of fertilizers by Africa farmers, with the explicit objective of raising the level of fertilizer use from the current average of 8 kg to at least 50 kg per hectare by 2015 (African Union, 2006.

However, less attention has been given to the possible benefits developing countries might obtain from low carbon development transitions in agriculture, including efficiency savings, reduced economic dependency and long-term sustainability (FAO, 2009; Funder *et al.*, 2009). In low-income countries development cooperation can help start up this leapfrogging process as mitigation in agriculture can be financially challenging for these countries (FAO, 2009). Such initiatives can bring substantive development benefits if low income farmers' needs are considered and synergies between mitigation and poverty reduction are created (see Box 12.4). Such an approach has the added value of developing farmers' resilience to the impacts of climate change (VijayaVenkataRaman *et al.*, 2012; Swart and Raes, 2007; Van Vuuren *et al.*, 2011). For example, reducing water pollution through low carbon agriculture can help citizens adapt to future climate change impacts (i.e. water stress) while contributing to long-term food security, as the sector is responsible for 70 per cent of water withdrawals (OECD, 2010). It is equally important to consider how low carbon development strategies in agriculture undermine poverty and citizens' rights. Rural people in different countries across the world are seen their lands grabbed for biofuel production, which not only constitutes a threat to their food security but which can also affect physical security. In Senegal, for instance, people have been killed for defending their lands against claims by an Italo-Senegalese biofuel company. Box 12.4 discusses options for reducing poverty through low carbon development in agriculture.

Box 12.4 Reducing poverty through low carbon development in agriculture: the role of development cooperation in Senegal

In Senegal a development organization called ENDA is helping farmers and their families benefit from low carbon agriculture. Farmer schools have been created to support the application of organic farming. In addition, oil-based energy is being replaced by wind power to pump drip irrigation systems. Not only are emissions mitigated, but also the economic costs of energy use are minimized. Manure and organic residues are being used to fertilize soils and produce domestic biogas to generate energy for cooking and lighting. Farmers are getting support in the commercialization of their organic products. In addition, the organization is enhancing farmers' access to emerging biogas markets in synergy with a national biogas programme. Financial support is provided by international donors and the central government. This kind of projects is a positive example of the ways in which low carbon agriculture can contribute to reducing poverty.

Conclusion

Agricultural production will continue to be vital for human lives and a main source of income for farmers and countries. Current predominant agricultural development pathways have rapidly increased food production, but also GHG emissions and environmental pollution, which are already worrying trends in many parts of the world. A wide range of practices that reduce emissions in agriculture are already known and governments as well as farmers have started taking action.

Annex I countries should be playing a leading role, not only as the largest food consumers and historically high emitters, but also because they are endowed with the financial and technical resources needed for mitigation. Ensuring their emission reduction policies are effective will require appropriate monitoring at the farm level and enforcement mechanisms (e.g. sanctions) where needed. Issues concerning equity and social justice should be integrated so the largest polluters are targeted and appropriately held accountable. High income countries with high levels of water and soil pollution will improve the impacts of their low carbon development strategies if the pace and intensity at which food is being produced is reduced.

In a globalized economy international coordination will be required and international carbon accounting systems are needed in which both producer as well as consumer country responsibilities are shared and GHG emission displacement is avoided. Moreover, creating synergies for mitigation with other sectors including the transport and energy sector will be crucial in order to maximize emission reductions. Appropriate carbon accounting of agricultural production, if provided to consumers, can also help them make informed decisions and therefore contribute to low carbon development in agriculture.

While a global transition to low carbon development is needed, this should not undermine other regional, national and subnational objectives. Mitigation strategies in the agricultural sector within emerging economies, if well integrated with country needs to create employment, reduce poverty and increase growth, can provide substantive development benefits while avoiding future environmental problems and gaining resilience to climate change. Recent work in developing countries is showing low carbon development can be highly beneficial when sustained financial support and skills transfer are provided to farmers (Lybbert and Sumner, 2012). From this perspective, mitigation strategies that adapt to contextual features will be more likely to sustain in the long term, not only from a climate perspective, but also for their compatibility with social welfare and environmental integrity.

References

African Union (2006) Abuja declaration on fertilizer for an African green revolution, Available at: http://www.nepad.org/system/files/Abuja%20Declaration%20on%20Fertilizers%20for%20an%20 African%20Green%20Revolution.pdf (accessed 20 November 2012).

Azadi, H., Schoonbeek, S., Mahmoudi, H., Derudder, B., De Maeyer, P., Witlox, F. (2011) Organic agriculture and sustainable food production system: main potentials. *Agriculture, Ecosystems and Environment*, 144, 92–4.

Coley D., Howard M. and Winter M. (2009) Local food, food miles and carbon emissions: a comparison of farm shop and mass distribution approaches, *Food Policy*, 34(2), 150–5.

De Boer, I. J. M., Cederberg, C., Eady S., Gollnow S., Kristensen T., Macleod M. *et al.* (2011) Greenhouse gas mitigation in animal production: towards an integrated life cycle sustainability assessment. *Current Opinion in Environmental Sustainability*, 3, 423–31.

De Fraiture, C. and Wichelns, D. (2010) Satisfying future water demands for agriculture. *Journal of Agricultural Water Management*, 97, 502–11.

Dethier, J. J. and Effenberger, A. (2012) Agriculture and development: a brief review of the literature. *Economic Systems*, 36(2), 175–205.

Del Prado, A., Chadwick D., Cardenas, L., Misselbrook, T., Scholefield, D. and Merino, P. (2012)

Exploring systems responses to mitigation of GHG in UK dairy farms. *Agriculture, Ecosystems and Environment*, 136, 318–32.

Emel, J. and Bridge, G. (1995) The earth as input: resources, in Johnston, R. J., Taylor, P. J. and Watts, M. J. (eds) *Geographies of Global Change. Remapping the World in the Late Twentieth Century*. Blackwell, Oxford, pp. 318–32.

Environmental Protection Agency (EPA) (2006) Global anthropogenic non-CO_2 greenhouse gas emissions. Washington, DC: United States Environmental Protection Agency.

Food and Agriculture Organization (FAO) (2009) Food security and agriculture mitigation in developing countries: options for capturing synergies. Rome: FAO.

FAO (2010) Global forest resources assessment. Rome: FAO.

Fiala, N. (2008) Meeting the demand: an estimation of potential future greenhouse gas emissions from meat production. *Ecological Economics*, 67, 412–19.

Franks, J. R. and Hadingham, B. (2012) Reducing greenhouse gas emissions from agriculture: avoiding trivial solutions to a global problem. *Land Use Policy*, 29, 727–36.

Funder, M., Fjalland, J., Ravnborg, H. M. and Egelyng, H. (2009) Low Carbon development and poverty alleviation. Options for development cooperation in energy, agriculture and forestry, *DIIS Report*, 20. Copenhagen: Danish Institute for International Studies.

Garnett, T. (2008) Cooking up a storm. Food, greenhouse gas emissions and our changing climate. Food Climate Research Network. Guildford: Centre for Environmental Strategy.

Garnett, T. (2011) Where are the best opportunities for reducing greenhouse gas emissions in the food system (including the food chain)? *Food Policy*, 36, 23–32.

Guthman, J. (2011) Excess consumption or over-production?, in Peet, R., Robins, P. and Watts, M. J. (eds) *Global Political Ecology*. New York: Routledge, 51–66.

IPCC (2007) IPCC Fourth Assessment Report: Climate Change 2007. Synthesis Report. IPCC, Geneva.

Kahrl, F., Li, Y., Su, Y., Tennigkeit, T., Wilkes, A. and Xu, J. (2010) Greenhouse gas emissions from nitrogen fertilizer use in China. *Environmental Science and Policy*, 13, 688–94.

Karimi, P., Qureshi, A. S., Bahramloo, R. and Molden, D. (2012) Reducing carbon emissions through improved irrigation and groundwater management: a case study from Iran. *Agricultural Water Management*, 108, 52–60.

Lybbert, T. J. and Sumner, D. A. (2012) Agricultural technologies for climate change in developing countries: policy options for innovation and technology diffusion. *Food Policy*, 37(1), 114–23.

Kuik, O. (2001) The effect of trade liberalization on carbon leakage under the Kyoto Protocol: experiments with GTAP-E. Paper prepared for the 4th Annual Conference on Global Economic Analysis, 27–29 June. West Lafayette, IN: Purdue University.

McMichael, P. (2011) Food system sustainability: questions of environmental governance in the new world (dis)order. *Global Environmental Change*, 21, 804–12.

Meyer, W. B. and Turner, B. L. (1994) *Changes in Land Use and Land Cover: a Global Perspective*. Cambridge: Cambridge University Press.

Mosier, A. R., Delgado, J. A. and Keller, M. (1998) Methane and nitrous oxide fluxes in an acid oxisol in western Puerto Rico: impact of tillage, liming, and fertilization. *Journal of Soil Biology and Biochemistry*, 30, 2087–98.

Neufeldt, H. and Schäfer, M. (2008) Mitigation strategies for greenhouse gas emissions from agriculture using a regional economic-ecosystem model. *Agriculture, Ecosystems and Environment*, 123, 305–16.

Organisation for Economic Co-operation and Development (OECD) (2010) *Sustainable Management of Water Resources in Agriculture*. Paris: OECD.

Parris, K. (2011) Impact of agriculture on water pollution in OECD countries: recent trends and future prospects. *Water Resources Development*, 27(1), 33–52.

Powlson, D. S., Gregory, P. J., Whalley, W. R., Quinton, J. N., Hopkins, D. W., Whitmore, A. P. *et al.* (2011) Soil management in relation to sustainable agriculture and ecosystem services. *Food Policy*, 36(1), 72–87.

Ramachandran, P. K., Nair, V. D., Kumar, B. M. and Haile, S. G. (2009) Soil carbon sequestration in tropical agroforestry systems: a feasibility appraisal. *Environmental Science and Policy*, 12(8), 1099–111.

Rodrigues, T., E. (2008) Agricultural explosion in Brazil: exploring the impacts of the Brazilian agricultural development over the Amazon. *International Journal of Society of Agriculture and Food*, 16(1), 1–12.

Smith, P., Martino, D., Cai, Z., Gwary, D., Janzen, H., Kumar, P. *et al.* (2007) Agriculture, in: Metz, B., Davidson, O. R., Bosch, P. R., Dave, R. and Meyer L. A. (eds), *Climate Change 2007: Mitigation. Contribution of Working Group III to the Fourth Assessment Report of the Intergovernmental Panel on Climate Change*. Cambridge: Cambridge University Press.

Smith, P., Martino, D., Cai, Z., Gwary, D., Janzen, H., Kumar, P. *et al.* (2008) Greenhouse gas mitigation in agriculture. *Philosophical Transactions of the Royal Society B*, 363, 789–813.

Snyder, C. S., Bruulsema, T. W., Jensen T. L. and Fixen P. E. (2009) Review of greenhouse gas emissions from crop production systems and fertilizer management effects. *Agriculture, Ecosystems & Environment*, 133(3–4), 247–66.

Steinfeld, H., Gerber, P., Wassenaar, T., Castel, V., Rosales, M. and de Haan, C. (2006) Livestock's long shadow: environmental issues and options. Rome: FAO.

Swart, R. and Raes, F. (2007) Making integration of adaptation and mitigation work: mainstreaming into sustainable development policies? *Climate Policy*, 7, 288–303.

Tilman, D., Cassman, K. G., Matson, P. A., Rosamond, N. and Polasky, S. (2002) Agricultural sustainability and intensive production practices. *Nature*, 418(8), 671–7.

Tubiello, F. N. and Fischer, G. (2007) Reducing climate change impacts on agriculture: global and regional effects of mitigation, 2000–2080. *Technological Forecasting & Social Change*, 74, 1030–56.

Van Vuuren, D. P., Isaac, M., Kundzewicz, Z. W., Arnell, N., Barker, T., Criqui, P. *et al.* (2011) The use of scenarios as the basis for combined assessment of climate change mitigation and adaptation. *Global Environmental Change*, 21, 575–91.

VijayaVenkataRaman, S., Iniyan, S. and Goic, R. (2012) A review of climate change, mitigation and adaptation. *Renewable and Sustainable Energy Reviews*, 16, 878–97.

Watson, R., Noble, I. R., Bolin, B., Ravindranath, N. H., Verardo, D. J. and Dokken, D. J. (2000) *Land use, Land-use Change and Forestry: a Special Report*. Cambridge: Cambridge University Press.

Weis, T. (2010) The accelerating biophysical contradictions of industrial capitalist agriculture. *Journal of Agrarian Change*, 10(3), 315–41.

Willer, H. (2009) *Organic Farming in Europe. a Brief Overview*. Frankfurt and Main: Research Institute of Organic Agriculture.

World Bank (2010) Opportunities and challenges for a converging agenda: country examples, in The Hague Conference on Agriculture, Food Security and Climate Change. The Hague. Washington, DC: World Bank, 1–62.

World Resources Institute (WRI) (2012) World Resources Institute. Available at: http://www.wri.org (accessed 20 November 2012).

Yamin, F. and Depledge, J. (2004) *The International Climate Change Regime: a Guide to Rules, Institutions and Procedures*. Cambridge: Cambridge University Press.

Further reading

De Boer, I. J. M., Cederberg, C., Eady S., Gollnow S., Kristensen T., Macleod M. *et al.* (2011) Greenhouse gas mitigation in animal production: towards an integrated life cycle sustainability assessment. *Current Opinion in Environmental Sustainability*, 3, 423–31.

Garnett, T. (2008) Cooking up a storm. Food, greenhouse gas emissions and our changing climate. Food Climate Research Network. Centre for Environmental Strategy, Guildford.

Smith, P., Martino, D., Cai, Z., Gwary, D., Janzen, H., Kumar, P. *et al.* (2007) Agriculture, in: Metz, B., Davidson, O. R., Bosch, P. R., Dave, R. and Meyer L. A. (eds), *Climate Change 2007:*

Mitigation. Contribution of Working Group III to the Fourth Assessment Report of the Intergovernmental Panel on Climate Change. Cambridge: Cambridge University Press.

Smith, P., Martino, D., Cai, Z., Gwary, D., Janzen, H., Kumar, P. *et al.* (2008) Greenhouse gas mitigation in agriculture. *Philosophical Transactions of the Royal Society B*, 363, 789–813.

Tilman, D., Cassman, K. G., Matson, P. A., Rosamond, N. and Polasky, S. (2002) Agricultural sustainability and intensive production practices. *Nature*, 418(8), 671–7.

Notes

1   Annex I countries are members of the OECD and Economies in Transition (EITs), whereas non-Annex I countries are mostly developing countries (Yamin and Depledge, 2004: 24).

2   'Low carbon' in agriculture goes beyond carbon and includes other GHG emissions, including N_2O and CH_4.

3   See Chapter 16 by Urban *et al.*

13 Transportation and low carbon development

David Tyfield

Decarbonizing transport is a key element of low carbon development, but emissions from transport are amongst the most intransigent and are expected to rise significantly in the coming decades. Most policies regarding low carbon transport follow a dominant economistic paradigm, exploring the options of either behavioural change to reduce demand for transport or technological change to increase the efficiency of its energy use. However, there is much evidence that this will not be successful. A shift from 'transport' towards socio-technical systems, situated practices of mobility and smart mobility innovation is thus advocated. The chapter focuses on urban transport to elaborate the role of transportation for low carbon development.

Introduction

Transport carbon emissions' continued growth

This chapter will discuss the role of transportation for low carbon development, with a focus on urban transport.

Transport is a key element of low carbon development. GHG emissions from transport represented about 22 per cent of total emissions in 2009 (IEA, 2011). These emissions are expected to rise significantly in the coming decades (Figure 13.1).

Energy demand for transport is expected to more than double from 2000 to 2050 (Stern, 2006; Banister, 2009). The majority of these emissions are due to road transport, which in turn is dominated by cars (Figure 13.2).

From 1990–2009, total global transport emissions rose 42.5 per cent, while road transport emissions rose 48.3 per cent (IEA, 2011). These rises occurred across the world: in the EU, from 0.8 to 1.0 Gt CO_2 per annum, and the US, from 1.4 to 1.7 Gt CO_2 per annum (Schwanen *et al.*, 2011). These trends will likely continue in the global North. While the financial crisis of 2007–8 precipitated a collapse in car sales and a crisis in the car industry, especially in the USA, the most recent figures reveal a recovery in the car market (*Financial Times*, 2012).

Moreover, significant growth of transport emissions in large and fast-developing countries such as China and India is expected. China is already the world's largest car market, since 2009. Yet transport accounts for only about 7 per cent of total emissions, as against 25.5 per cent for the EU or 31.1 per cent for the USA (IEA, 2011). Similarly, transport emissions *per capita* are around only 0.3 tonnes CO_2 in China compared with 2 tonnes in the EU and over 5 tonnes in the USA (Sentance, 2009). This represents the comparatively low number of cars *per capita* in China, and commensurate room for growth of the car market (see Figures 13.3 and 13.4).

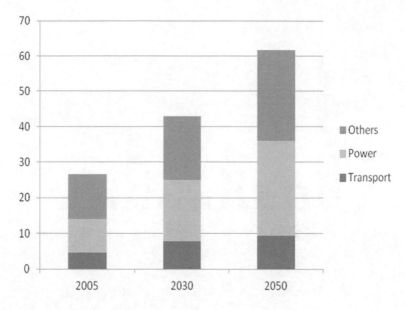

Figure 13.1 Expected growth in GHG emissions (Gt CO_2)
Source: IEA, 2009

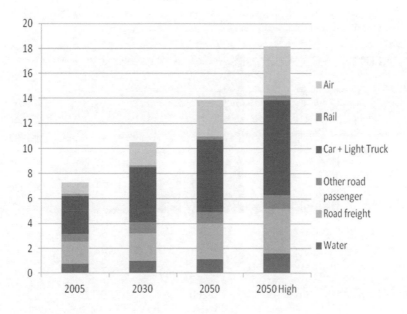

Figure 13.2 Expected growth of transport emissions by mode (Gt CO_2)
Source: IEA, 2008

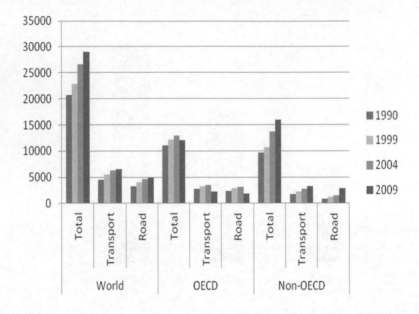

Figure 13.3 Total GHG emissions (Mt CO₂)
Source: IEA, 2001, 2006, 2011

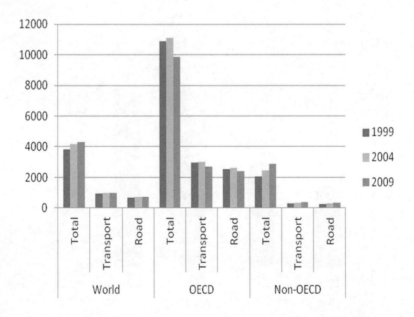

Figure 13.4 GHG emissions per capita (kg CO₂/capita)
Source: IEA, 2001, 2006, 2011

Low carbon transport as a 'test case'

Even from a brief consideration of current trends, therefore, it is clear that decarbonization of transport is a massive challenge. Indeed, low carbon transport is arguably a 'test case' for low carbon development, in two respects: regarding actual decarbonization; and, inseparably, regarding the need to reconceptualize what 'low carbon development' involves, without which timely transition simply will not happen.

First, it is unfortunately the case that currently the 'modes... experiencing the most growth are also the most polluting' (Chapman, 2007: 357). Furthermore, transport, and the emissions it generates, is not just a matter of particular forms of vehicle and their more or less efficient use of fuel in getting from A to B. Think about what you depend on every time you get in a car or take a journey by public transport. Think about what the *experience* of modern travel involves. Urban mobility is today dominated by a system of automobility (Paterson, 2007; Dennis and Urry, 2009). This system presupposes powerful car industries, cheap and abundant oil, massive road-building, suburbs and parking spaces, consumer credit and innumerable cultural connections with personal freedom ('the open road'), rites of passage, expectations of personal and comfortable mobility etc. Transforming these *socio-technical mobility systems* to low carbon, therefore, involves not just new technologies but also profound social, political, economic and cultural change. To approach these changes, however, we must also effect a similar transformation in our understanding.

Box 13.1 elaborates the key concepts and terms relevant for this chapter.

Box 13.1 Definitions of key concepts and terms

Disruptive innovation refers to 'cheaper, easier-to-use alternatives... often produced by non-traditional players that target previously ignored customers' (Willis *et al.*, 2007: 4) and/or use in novel contexts. It is *not* therefore a radical step up in technological capabilities but often involves *lower* functionality at first. Digital cameras provide a classic example. Initially offering photos of poorer quality than film, they nevertheless opened new possibilities of instant, fun and endless photography and instant sharing by short message service (SMS) and email. As the technology improved, they completely disrupted the camera market.

Electric vehicles (EVs) includes all vehicles using electricity-based propulsion, as opposed to internal combustion engines (ICEs) burning fossil fuels. There is a range of these, including hybrid electric vehicles (pairing an ICE with a battery), battery EVs, plug-in hybrids and fuel cell vehicles.

Market failure/public good argument: if someone asks for the time, you will gladly tell them. If someone asks for your watch, however, you are unlikely to hand it over. The 'time' is importantly different in that is easily appropriated (non-excludable) and may be used by one person without reducing its availability to others (non-rival). Goods such as these are called 'public goods' in economics. Other important examples include public infrastructures (e.g. highways and traffic lights), air quality and the idea of a low carbon technology. The characteristics of public goods mean that markets fail to produce them at socially optimal levels because the incentive of private gain is blunted. In these instances, a public authority (e.g. the state) is usually needed to provide the public good.

Box 13.2 discusses the key issues for transport and low carbon development.

Box 13.2 Key issues for transport and low carbon development

'Mobility systems' vs. 'transport technologies': thinking in terms of low carbon 'transport' focuses attention on specific technologies of getting from A to B. This is misleading as it leaves out of view the socio-technical systems in which these technologies can be used, and the social practices of and need for mobility. For example, the steam engine was invented in ancient Greece. Only in the context of numerous other social conditions did it become a viable form of mass transport, e.g. high socio-economic demand for rapid, long-distance travel; ready availability of finance and labour to construct a rail network; cheap and abundant steel and coal; and major social projects of nation-/empire-building.

Coordination: making transport low carbon involves extremely challenging problems of coordination of multiple parties. For instance, introduction of EVs involves the simultaneous construction of a charging infrastructure, business models for reliable billing and transformation of the electricity grid to accommodate extra loads from mass charging of batteries. This also involves coordination with innovation in issues not directly related to transport, such as decarbonization of electricity.

Government 'Catch 22': markets are failing to produce the 'public goods' of low carbon transportation systems, not least because of the problems of coordination (above). It is beyond the capacity of single private businesses seeking their own profitability to coordinate all the elements of a low carbon transport system. Typically, this would mean government has a key role to play. However, in the absence of a clear emergent alternative to the dominant automobility system, governments struggle to commit to a particular set of new technologies and/or a vision of future mobility upon which to base policies.

Discussion

In this section, we consider the standard approach to transportation and its failings: both practical, regarding failure of transitions to emerge; and conceptual, regarding understanding the problem. We then consider an alternative approach that highlights the full scale of the challenge. Key here is the distinction between transport technologies and socio-technical mobility systems.

Standard approaches to transportation – practical and conceptual failings

Two pillars of transport policy: market failure and technology vs. behaviour change

The standard approach within transport studies (e.g. Sentance, 2009; Stern, 2006) remains fairly positivist methodologically and focuses predominantly on issues of orthodox economic theory and technological and/or infrastructural engineering. It consists of two pillars.

First, low carbon transport is understood as a 'double market failure' (Sentance, 2009) (see Box 13.1). The first of these concerns how environmental costs are not priced into the transport decisions. 'Rational' individuals will not consider the environmental harm caused by their transport decisions. This results in a degraded environment for all. The second market failure concerns innovation of low carbon transport technologies. Private companies cannot take the risk of building charging infrastructures for electric vehicles, for instance, since too few EV drivers may be prepared to pay for them. Yet car companies will not produce EVs until there are such charging stations, since buyers will demand these before they buy an EV. The goal of policy is thus to rectify these market failures; for example, pricing carbon emissions and/or providing intellectual property rights or state-subsidized projects respectively.

The second pillar concerns the two different approaches by which it is understood that transport emissions may be reduced. First, total demand for transport can be reduced through 'behaviour change', with people opting for less, or less polluting means of, transport, such as walking or cycling. Alternatively, the efficiency of energy use (and consequent emissions) can be improved through technical change. These two prongs are potentially complementary. The problem is that neither, alone or together, seems to offer any chance of realizing deep reductions in emissions.

Transport policy tends to admit as much regarding behaviour change. For instance, consider shifting short journeys from cars to bicycles. As Sentance (2009) rightly notes, journeys of 5 miles or less constitute just 19 per cent of current car emissions, which in turn are 40 per cent of total transport emissions. Even if half of these current journeys shifted over to bicycle – an improbably high percentage given current trends – this would still reduce total transport emissions by only 4 per cent.

Transport policy thus tends to focus on technological change, stimulated by market-based fixes to rectify the dual market failures (from pillar 1). Since urban transport around the world is utterly (and increasingly) dominated by the car, the technological focus is to replace fossil fuels in road vehicles. One high-profile and successful example is the shift to bioethanol, made from sugar cane, in Brazil (Augusta da Costa *et al.*, 2010). Governments around the world are also mandating (low) percentages of biofuels in petrol mixes, but these have proven highly controversial. Unlike Brazilian sugar cane, much of this biofuel is made from corn and so depletes grain stocks for human food. Brazilian bioethanol is thus arguably an exception rather than paradigm example (see Chapter 20).

Electric vehicles as technological fix

A more general policy focus is the substitution of fossil fuel with electricity (see Box 13.1). Yet EV mobility is also notably failing to emerge due to several significant problems. First, major car companies have shown little interest in EVs, which would involve changes in their business models and core innovation capacities. This may now be changing: most automotive giants announcing projects in recent years (e.g. Nissan's Leaf, General Motor's (GM's) Volt, Citroen's C1). China's car companies, notably BYD, are also particularly focused on developing EVs. However, as recently as 2009, 80 per cent of global automotive patents remained concentrated in improving ICEs (Oltra and St Jean, 2009).

Second, and of greater importance, is the poor consumer demand for EVs, which suggests that they will likely remain marginal for some time. EVs are more expensive than competing ICE cars due to the cost of the battery, and are 'likely always' to be so (RAEng, 2010). Up-front costs may be recouped when set against the higher (and growing) cost of petrol, but over 10 years or more. These calculations must also reckon with the ongoing improvement in the efficiency of ICEs, likely to be considerable in the coming decades (e.g. King Review, 2008; RAEng, 2010). EVs thus may serve a small, 'green' consumer elite in the global North, including as a second car for short-distance urban driving. As a supplement rather than replacement of existing cars, this will further limit their impact on overall emission reductions.

EVs also remain uncompetitive regarding distances they can travel without refuelling and the ease of recharging – both major conditions for consumer demand. There are numerous ingenious schemes for recharging, including battery lease and swap stations, rapid off-road recharging, recharging at public car parks or private domestic plug-ins. None of these, however, currently could feasibly rival the ease and speed of the ICE (RAEng, 2010). Domestic charging plugs, for instance, depend on private garages that are not always found in the West's low-rise suburbs, let alone the crowded, high-rise mega-cities of the global South. Conversely, the asset value of a battery lease and swap infrastructure in the UK has been estimated at a prohibitive £200 billion, or 100 times greater than the UK's entire railway rolling stock (RAEng, 2010).

Finally, replacing an ICE with an electric motor will have no decarbonizing effect unless the source of that electricity is itself low carbon. Indeed, in countries with very high-carbon electricity grids, such as China's coal-dominated power sector, EVs may be even more polluting in terms of GHGs than conventional ICEs (e.g. iCET, 2011). Gains are likely to be slim even with other less polluting forms of fossil fuels, such as gas, as in the UK (RAEng, 2010).

Market failure? The Catch 22 of government

According to the dominant framing in terms of 'market failure', these obstacles to the technological fix of EVs should be familiar and straightforward for policy: government should step in to furnish these public goods. Certainly, the state has a key role to play. But low carbon urban transport graphically illustrates a pervasive 'Catch 22' for government, which applies to much low carbon transition per se, but is inescapable for low carbon transport.

On the one hand, mass uptake of EVs would involve a massive (set of) infrastructure project(s). This includes construction of charging infrastructures but also major upgrading of electricity grids to 'smart grids', which must be able to cope with the changes in the extent, timing, surges, etc. of demand for electricity. To keep this low carbon, this must also avoid making the grid *more* carbon intensive through construction of more fossil fuel power stations. This would need major public leadership and involve unprecedented collaboration across government departments and with numerous other stakeholders. Even international agreement may be needed; for instance, on standards for charging plugs, voltages, safety, etc. This in turn demands a clear government vision and commitment, visible in both policies and public finances.

Yet, on the other hand, such a clear vision is exceptionally difficult to formulate for low carbon (urban) mobility. Existing technologies are not capable of delivering the necessary emission reductions and no single trajectory of an emergent socio-technical system is apparent. Governments may therefore commit to building necessary infrastructures, but *which* infrastructures are these? In the UK, for instance, smart grids that current policy envisions constructing would not be adequate for the mass uptake of EVs (RAEng, 2010), therefore threatening the construction of new infrastructures that would quickly become unfit for purpose. In short, the coordination problems of low carbon EV mobility are much more complex than the 'market failure' perspective allows. Continuing policy dominance of this paradigm is thus a major problem for realizing low carbon transport.

Socio-technical systems for transportation

Low carbon transport niches

While standard policy focuses on transport technologies, a more informative way to think about low carbon transport is in terms of *socio-technical mobility systems* (see Box 13.3 for a critique of the standard transportation policy). From this perspective, low carbon transport becomes a matter of thorough-going transition from the current high-carbon 'system of automobility' to future low carbon systems. The key question thus becomes 'how does or can such a system transition emerge?', and the empirical focus becomes specific 'niches' of promising low carbon sociotechnical practices. This, in turn, immediately opens up a whole new vista on potentially significant initiatives. For instance, in recent work Geels (2012; Geels *et al.*, 2011) suggests there are six types of niche that currently are attempting to transform the system of automobility:

1   The most obvious is the new green propulsion technologies discussed above.
2   Going beyond technology, however, there exists a growing plethora of 'cultural and socio-spatial niches' (Geels, 2012: 5) including: projects in sustainable urban planning; 'compact cities' and 'smart growth'; multiple car sharing platforms, enabled through the internet and social media; and public bike-sharing schemes (e.g. in London, Paris, Hangzhou, etc.).
3   Similarly, 'new practices and initiatives' (Geels, 2012: 5) are emerging to manage transport demand more effectively, including 'workplace travel plans, public transport information . . . , travel awareness campaigns, teleworking . . . and home shopping, . . . and urban cycling initiatives'.
4   There are also a number of niches that use information and communication technologies; in particular, the management of traffic through intelligent transport systems (ITSs), such as variable speed limits, and the substitution for physical travel through internet-based contact, as in home teleworking, e-commerce or tele-conferencing;
5   Public transport is also being transformed, often as high-profile examples of the other types of niche. Buses are often used to test new green technologies, such as electric engines or liquefied natural gas, while urban redesign and intelligent transport systems are being used in various cities to speed up bus transport through designated bus lanes or prioritized traffic lights. Various innovations also attempt to make bus transport more attractive, for example by 'subsidised flat fare schemes, real-time passenger information systems, pre-paid ticketing to speed up boarding and improved closed-circuit television (CCTV) to ensure personal safety' (Chapman, 2007: 363) or by making personal car transport more difficult through congestion charges, etc.
6   Finally, various niches are also attempting to encourage the low(er)-carbon option of public transport by transforming intermodality, as in train-taxi schemes (offering reduced taxi fares), bus- and/or bike-rail integration schemes, park and ride, tickets valid across all modes of public transport, etc.

From niches to system transition?

The very existence of these niches greatly broadens the purview on the possibilities for low carbon transport beyond the standard perspective. The key question, however, is whether or not these niches seem likely to engender bigger transformation at the 'higher' level of entire mobility systems. Unfortunately, there is significant evidence that this is not currently the case. First, as regards these niches themselves, each of them presently appears to have limited impact. These comparative weaknesses and failures, however, are indicative of some broader structural 'lock-ins' (Unruh, 2000) that embed that domination of the ICE-based automobility system. These include:

- the major economic role of car industries in many societies (especially the US, Germany and China) and the associated strength of their political lobbies and governmental support;
- the built environment and urban geography, which often privileges cars and renders other modes dangerous, inconvenient and/or more expensive;
- a widespread cultural preference for private property and hence personal ownership of one's means of transport, together with a prioritization of minimal journey times and strong affective associations with the privacy, comfort and autonomy of the car (Urry, 2011; Geels, 2012);
- the supreme social and economic importance of unfettered access to personal mobility in an age of intense individualization and globalization, characterized by the 'space of flows' (Castells, 1997), both for that individual herself and for the orderly 'going on' of the chaos of global market societies (Urry, 2011).

Crucially for low carbon development, this prioritization of the car is equally marked in many developing countries (Sakamoto *et al.*, 2010):

- the car industry and road-building programmes are often understood as irreplaceable drivers of economic growth;
- transport policies are formulated by and for the relatively rich and prioritize the private car ownership to which they have access;
- increasing prosperity, easy credit and business incentives for employees all facilitate the growth of the car.

A bleak outlook?

For these reasons, therefore, the conclusion seems more or less inescapable that, given current trends and policies, mobility *will not be decarbonized* to a sufficient extent up to 2050, but will remain dominated by ICE automobility (and high carbon aviation). A systems analysis thus, first, does us the uncomfortable service of providing a realistic assessment forcing us to confront the real scale of the challenges ahead. Conversely, the standard approach, with its limited analytical repertoire of 'technology' or 'behaviour' and its associated Panglossian faith in technological and market-based solutions, resembles the proverbial drunkard searching for his keys underneath the streetlamp because this is all it can see.

Furthermore, an effective decarbonization of transport is simply the first step. As *socio*technical, mobility systems (and innovation thereof) also have irreducible qualitative and normative dimensions. A key set of questions thus arises regarding who gains and loses from low carbon innovation (Stirling, 2009), including:

- explicit consideration of the balance between competing values, such as efficiently coordinated travel vs. privacy or private vs. public good;
- equity of access to cheap, rapid, low carbon transport and distribution of gains for business inter- and intra-nationally;
- multiple, geographically appropriate transport options.

A systems approach, however, is not just the purveyor of indigestible truths. By focusing on sociotechnical systems and the niches that may come to introduce significant discontinuities, we also have the possibility of conceiving how a low carbon transport transition may be possible.

Box 13.3 provides a critique of the standard transportation policy, its role for low carbon transport and alternative opportunities.

Box 13.3 Critique of the standard transportation policy

From transport technologies to socio-technical mobility systems

The dominant framing of transport policy, in terms of market failure and either technological or behaviour change, offers little guidance to the construction of low carbon transport. Even with foreseeable improvement in existing transport technologies, they offer no blueprint or techno-logical fix. There are major conceptual inadequacies with this mainstream approach, however, and confronting these offers more helpful and hopeful analyses. The most important of these focuses on the inadequate conception of what can, and indeed must, be changed, namely *sociotechnical systems of mobility*. This terminology highlights three major flaws.

First, the standard policy perspective completely ignores how innovation is always a process that is simultaneously and inseparably both technological and *sociocultural*. Social factors – such as established habitual practices, norms, social networks, regulations and institutional struc-tures – condition the ways in which technologies are taken up or not and the specific qualitative directions in which they are altered in that process (e.g. MacKenzie and Wacjman, 1999).

Second, once established, the use of technologies is always embedded in complex sociotech-nical *systems*. Focusing on technologies alone, therefore, offers little explanatory understanding of how and why they dominate at any given time. Taken together, therefore, policy that intends to utterly transform the technological basis of mobility in order to cut drastically the associated emissions is precisely concerned with the transition in sociotechnical systems. This involves understanding what must be done from *within* one such system of mobility in order to incubate the emergence of another. This systemic perspective, however, is notably absent in standard approaches.

Third, the standard approach takes as given, or beyond its analytical remit, the demands, purposes, use and nature of current transport. The social function served by 'transport', however, is not primarily to get from A to B but rather *mobility* for various, socially specific and change-able purposes. Of particular importance here are demands of personal co-presence – being physically together with others, for work, personal responsibilities or leisure – and the advan-tages and/or pleasures of mobility for its own sake – consider the 'Sunday drive', the road trip or the hike over distant hills.

This perspective is evident in a growing body of work at the intersection of innovation stud-ies, evolutionary economics, science and technology studies, sociology and economic geography. Amongst the most informative of theoretical frameworks is the multi-level perspec-tive (MLP) of Frank Geels (2005, 2011) and colleagues (e.g. Elzen *et al.*, 2004; Van Bree *et al.*, 2010). The MLP itself, however, has several conceptual weaknesses (see Smith *et al.*, 2010 for a review). First, change in sociotechnical systems is actually achieved by changing the *practices* of using technologies (Shove and Walker 2007; Büscher *et al.*, 2011). Moreover, these practices and the associated processes of change are rarely the result of deliberate and intentional decision alone. Yet a lot of research presumes just such intentional decision-making. Conversely, attend-ing to practice, which may be embodied, habitual or enculturated, tackles this cognitivist bias in research. Second, as situated human practices, mobility systems also have irreducible normative dimensions that demand concerted attention (Stirling, 2009).

Box 13.4 provides a case study from China, with a focus on electric bikes. This case study has been chosen because China is currently the largest emitter of GHGs, it has a rapidly growing transport sector and, despite growing car ownership of fossil fuel-driven cars, China has a well-established market for electric bikes. This case study is therefore relevant for studying the rapidly changing developments in low carbon transport.

Box 13.4 Case study

From a sociotechnical systems perspectives, a key question for low carbon mobility is 'how can and will (auto)mobility be socially *redefined*?' Chinese electric bikes present one possible case study in that what are currently called 'bikes' may develop to a point where the established conceptual boundaries between 'cars' and 'bikes' are blurred.

The Chinese government, at both national and local level, is increasingly focusing efforts on the supposedly singular technological opening of EVs. EVs have been identified as one of seven 'key strategic emerging industries' for the next five years. One hundred billion yuan (US\$15.7 billion) of support over the next 10 years has been announced, with a view to getting 500,000 EVs on China's roads by 2015, and five million by 2020. EVs are subject to 0 per cent sales tax and receive consumer subsidies of up to 60,000 yuan (US\$9400) from central government, which is doubled by some city-based programmes. This policy focus has been matched by the striking emphasis of Chinese car companies, in comparison with those domiciled elsewhere, on developing EVs.

There are several good reasons for this focus. But EVs also come with significant problems, including their failure to address questions of congestion and the coal-intensity of the electricity grid. The most important problem, as regards innovation and systems transition, however, is the almost complete lack of consumer demand for EVs, despite the significant state subsidies for their purchase.

Conversely, a striking success story in China, namely electric bikes (E2W, for electric two-wheelers) offers a different possible route to low carbon mobility and *future* EVs, but as a 'disruptive innovation' (see Box 13.1). China is already the undoubted leader in E2Ws, with approximately 120 million on the road by the year 2009/10. The appeal of this transport is as a low-cost, speedy (maximum speeds can reach 40–50 km/h) and nimble form of transport, able to weave through congested streets and onto and off pavements.

The real promise of E2Ws, however, is that they could redefine the very concept of the 'car'. This is in striking contrast to the EV efforts of Chinese car companies, which are simply – and unsuccessfully – trying to change the engine in otherwise conventional vehicles. Conversely, E2W companies are taking advantages of the opportunities for considerable experimentation and radical redesign of the 'car' offered by an electric drive train; for instance, as 'E3Ws' (i.e. electric three-wheelers). This may, in turn, increasingly come together with seemingly isolated changes, whether increasing the levels of ICTs and digital technologies integrated into their design or the development of innovative vehicle-sharing schemes.

There are, of course, important objections to E2Ws too. These include the penalties and even outright bans that several Chinese cities have placed on them, and the potentially negative environmental effects of the disposal of lead-acid batteries (ADB, 2009). The biggest objection, however, is that E2Ws are likely to replace only bikes, not cars, and thus *increase* energy inefficiencies and demand. Certainly, this is possible, and indeed even likely insofar as electric 'bikes' and 'cars' are understood as simply replacements for existing technologies. But such understanding is not written in stone and there are significant economic incentives for disruptive Chinese companies and consumers to challenge these established definitions with new visions of vehicles and vehicle use. These new E2Ws or E3Ws, then, would not so much replace cars as render the very category outdated, obstructive and obsolete.

Conclusion

What can be done regarding a low carbon transport transition and on a global scale, including in developing countries? We have explored how current low carbon technology policies are not only inadequate for the expedited emergence of low carbon mobility systems but also occlude this failing and rule out alternative and more insightful perspectives. There is limited potential for breaking the high carbon system of automobility in the next few crucial years. A significant shift towards low carbon transport thus demands some unsettling or disintegration of the currently dominant system.

Using the MLP systems framework (see Box 13.3), there are two ways in which this may be conceived. First, there is the possibility of 'landscape' shocks from issues external to the system itself but with significant repercussions for it. For instance, massive increases in oil price, whether from 'peak oil' or a geopolitical event, could produce a rapid rebalancing in the economics of EVs vs. ICE cars. For instance, petrol price rises of 50 per cent since 2008 in the UK correlate with 'peak car'; the first evidence of annual *reductions* in total miles driven. For these to unsettle dominant systems, however, they must also be translated into a palpable collective sense of crisis rather than simply triggering stabilizing mechanisms – as happened for the car industry following the financial turmoil of 2007/8, for instance, with government bail-outs of major car companies. Second, the various niches could themselves grow and coalesce in novel combinations that offer possibilities that are simply more attractive to consumers than the car (or flight or...).

Both of these disruptions, in fact, may well be crucial, suggesting that it is highly unlikely that the route to a low carbon transport system is going to be linear and smooth. In any case, this perspective suggests that low carbon transport policy should be focused on two goals: the medium-term task of building up niches that continue to challenge the various lock-ins of current mobility systems (cars, road freight, aviation); while also attending as much as possible to the urgency of actions entailed by long lead times and infrastructure legacies. This medium-term perspective is crucial given that the incumbent dominant sociotechnical *system* is unfit for purpose, but there is as yet no alternative system taking shape. Policy should therefore be formulated with the flexibility to accommodate, and then expedite, the emergence of an alternative in the coming decades.

Visions of future low carbon mobility systems are needed, however, to frame policy as a whole. One particularly promising vision is 'smart mobility'. Amongst the biggest transformations in car innovation is its increasing incorporation of digital technologies and its shift from a predominantly mechanical to electronic technology. This is already transforming the mobility practices associated with cars but also has the potential for much greater changes in the very concept of the 'car' by enabling diverse user experiments in mobility. In conjunction with new social media, digitized vehicles could transform the coordination of co-presence – with both journey-end acquaintances, transforming *which* journeys are made, and/or shared and trusted modes of (low carbon) transport, transforming *how* we travel. This, in turn, could transform the nature of mobility systems. For instance, consider a world in which it may be cheaper, easier, more sociable, more relaxed *and* lower carbon to bike to a rendezvous with some unforeseeable EV car share that is arranged in real time by social networking tools. The EV car share then ferries you to a motorway 'stop', where you pick up a reliably available public e-bike for the final section of your journey.

Finally, the potentially synergistic positive feedbacks between innovation in social media and digitised vehicles may also open up both the policy Catch 22 of government coordination without a coherent vision and the structural lock-in of the automobility system. As regards the former, the bottom-up experiments in low carbon mobility may help mitigate the need for an *ex ante* policy vision. The inseparability of innovation and use of mobility technologies means that new possibilities of coordinating mobility per se (as in the EV car share example above) also open up new possibilities for coordinating systems *innovation*. Gaps may therefore open up allowing new low carbon mobility systems to emerge that are not dependent upon major prior commitments from government.

Similarly, as regards the latter, growing active participation in low carbon mobility experiments – perhaps to the point at which the aggregate and emergent effects of these hitherto insignificant niches takes on critical mass – may well contribute to a constructive and pervasive sense of crisis. This, in turn, would be the basis for emergence of a *collective* will to action, including as regards a breakthrough in the 'acceptance and investment' needed for further embedding of low carbon and smart mobilities (Büscher *et al.*, 2011). At this point, political will for just such major public investment may thus become unstoppable.

Smart mobility is thus emphatically *not* just to propose a different technofix, but rather to open up possibilities for broader sociotechnical change. This includes transformation of the social definition, and so prospects, of the EV. While apparently not imminent, therefore, continuing development of diverse low carbon niches (such as Chinese e-bikes (see Box 13.4) or Brazilian biofuels (see Chapter 20)) may well come together – and possibly quite suddenly – into the systemic change that is needed for low carbon development.

References

Asian Development Bank (ADB) (2009) Electric bikes in the People's Republic of China: impact on the environment and prospects for growth. Mandaluyong City: ADB.

Augusta da Costa, A., Pereira Junior, N. and Gomes Aranda, D. (2010) The situation of biofuels in Brazil: new generation technologies. *Renewable and Sustainable Energy Reviews*, 14, 3041–9.

Banister, D. (2009) Getting in the right lane. Low carbon European transport beyond 2050. Paper. Oxford: Transport Studies Unit, Oxford University.

Büscher, M., Coulton, P., Efstratiou, C., Gellersen, H. and Hemment, D. (2011) Connected, computed, collective: smart mobilities, in Grieco, M. and Urry, J. (eds) *Mobilities: New Perspectives on Transport and Society*, Farnham: Ashgate, pp. 135–58.

Castells, M. (1997) *The Rise of the Network Society*. Oxford: Blackwell.

Chapman, L. (2007) Transport and climate change: a review. *Journal of Transport Geography*, 15, 354–67.

Dennis, K. and Urry, J. (2009) *After the Car*. Cambridge: Polity.

Elzen, B., Geels, F. and Green, K. (eds) (2004) *System Innovation and the Transition to Sustainability: Theory, Evidence and Policy*. Cheltenham: Edward Elgar.

Financial Times (2012) US car market rebounds sharply, 4 January.

Geels, F. (2005) The dynamics of transitions in socio-technical systems: a multi-level analysis of the transition pathway from horse-drawn carriages to automobiles (1860–1930). *Technological Analysis and Strategic Management*, 17(4), 445–76.

Geels, F. (2011) The multi-level perspective on sustainability transitions: responses to seven criticisms. *Environmental Innovation and Societal Transitions*, 1(1), 24–40.

Geels, F. (2012) A socio-technical analysis of low carbon transitions: introducing the multi-level perspective into transport studies. *Journal of Transport Geography* 24, 471–82.

Geels, F., Kemp, R., Dudley, G. and Lyons, G. (eds) (2011) *Automobility in Transition? A Socio-Technical Analysis of Sustainable Transport*. London: Routledge.

iCET (2011) Electric vehicles in the context of sustainable development in China. UN Commission on Sustainable Development, Nineteenth Session, Background Paper 9, 2–13 May, New York.

International Energy Agency (IEA) (2001) *CO₂ Emissions from Fuel Combustion 1971–1999*. Paris: IEA.

IEA (2006) *CO₂ Emissions from Fuel Combustion 1971–2004*. Paris: IEA.

IEA (2008) *Energy Technology Perspectives*. Paris: IEA.

IEA (2009) *Transport, Energy and CO₂*. Paris: IEA.

IEA (2011) *CO₂ Emissions from Fuel Combustion*. Paris: IEA.

King Review (2008) The King review of low carbon cars. Part II: recommendations for action. Norwich: HMSO.

MacKenzie, D. and Wacjman, J. (eds) (1999) *The Social Shaping of Technology*, 2nd edn. Buckingham: Open University Press.

Oltra, V. and Saint Jean, M. (2009) Variety of technological trajectories in low emission vehicles (LEVs): a patent data analysis. *Journal of Cleaner Production*, 17(2), 201–13.

Paterson, M. (2007) *Automobile Politics: Ecology and Cultural Political Economy*. Cambridge: Cambridge University Press.

Royal Academy of Engineering (RAEng) (2010) *Electric Vehicles: Charged with Potential*. London: RAEng.

Sakamoto, K., Dalkmann, H. and Palmer, D. (2010) *A Paradigm Shift towards Sustainable Low carbon Transport: Financing the Vision ASAP*. New York: ITDP.

Schwanen, T., Banister, D. and Anable, J. (2011) Scientific research about climate change mitigation in transport: a critical review. *Transportation Research Part A*, 45, 993–1006.

Shove, E. and Walker, G. (2007) CAUTION! Transitions ahead: politics, practice, and sustainable transition management. *Environment and Planning A*, 39, 763–70.

Sentance, A. (2009) Developing transport infrastructure for the low carbon society. *Oxford Review of Economic Policy*, 25(3), 391–410.

Smith, A., Voss, J.-P. and Grin, J. (2010) Innovation studies and sustainability transitions: the allure of the multi-level perspective and its challenges. *Research Policy*, 39, 435–48.

Stern, N. (2006) *The Economics of Climate Change: the Stern Review*. Cambridge: Cambridge University Press.

Stirling, A. (2009) Direction, distribution and diversity! Pluralising progress in innovation, sustainability and development. STEPS Working Paper 32. Brighton: STEPS Centre.

Unruh, G. (2000) Escaping carbon lock-in. *Energy Policy*, 28, 817–30.

Urry, J. (2011) *Climate Change and Society*. Cambridge: Polity.

Van Bree, B., Verbong, G. P. J. and Kramer, G. J. (2010) A multi-level perspective on the introduction of hydrogen and battery-electric vehicles. *Technological Forecasting & Social Change*, 77, 529–40.

Willis, R., Wilsdon, J. and Webb, M. (2007) *The Disrupters*. London: NESTA.

Further reading

Büscher, M., Coulton, P., Efstratiou, C., Gellersen, H. and Hemment, D. (2011) Connected, computed, collective: smart mobilities, in Grieco, M. and Urry, J. (eds) *Mobilities: New Perspectives on Transport and Society*. Farnham: Ashgate, pp. 135–58.

Dennis, K. and Urry, J. (2009) *After the Car*. Cambridge: Polity.

Geels, F. (2012) A socio-technical analysis of low carbon transitions: introducing the multi-level perspective into transport studies. *Journal of Transport Geography*, 24, 471–82.

Royal Academy of Engineering (RAEng) (2010) *Electric Vehicles: Charged with Potential*. London: RAEng.

14 Triple win? The case of climate compatible development

Frauke Urban

Low carbon development addresses the interface between climate change mitigation and development. However, for people and communities affected by climate change, adapting to climatic impacts is crucial. It is therefore necessary to consider mitigation, adaptation and development as interlinked challenges that have to be addressed together, rather than addressing them as separate challenges. This chapter therefore introduces the concept of climate compatible development, which brings together mitigation, adaptation and development, and offers opportunities for producing 'triple wins' to deliver lower emissions development that is resilient to current and future climatic impacts.

Introduction

In the international UN climate change negotiations and the plans of many organizations and governments, climate change adaptation and mitigation are often treated as two separate issues. However, in real life, adaptation and mitigation cannot be treated separately, but pose interrelated challenges to people, communities and countries affected by climate change.

The chapter therefore elaborates this theme by addressing climate compatible development (CCD). 'Climate compatible development' is development that minimises the harm caused by climate impacts, while maximising the many human development opportunities presented by a low emissions, more resilient, future. CCD is at the core of a 'triple win' strategy that combines climate change adaptation, mitigation and development to tackle climate change while increasing the opportunities for human development (Hagemann *et al.*, 2012). This chapter explores what climate compatible development is and, by doing so, the chapter discusses the linkages between climate change adaptation, mitigation and development at the conceptual and the practical level. The chapter also elaborates the role low carbon development plays for CCD and some of the opportunities and challenges faced by this new approach.

While the benefits and challenges of addressing climate change adaptation and mitigation in an integrated way have been studied since the early 2000s (e.g. Dang *et al.*, 2003; Becken, 2005; Klein *et al.*, 2005, 2007; Roy, 2009; Falloon and Betts, 2010), an explicit development perspective has often been missing from the debate. This changed when the concept of CCD emerged in 2010.

Similarly to low carbon development, the concept of CCD was first developed by the development aid industry and its donors, particularly the Climate and Development Knowledge Network (CDKN),[1] which is funded by DfID and the Dutch Ministry of Foreign

Affairs. CCD was developed by donor agencies such as CDKN as a response to the imme-diate needs of developing countries to address climate change while at the same time promoting development. It has to be noted here that CCD is not an academic concept *per se* and it has been developed rather as a normative concept by practitioners, policy-makers and later on also by academics (e.g. see Hagemann *et al.*, 2012). Its origins within the develop-ment aid industry mean that its main purpose from the beginning was to help developing country governments to promote development in a changing climate and to access funding for achieving this. Since its beginnings, the concept of CCD has been taken up by regional, national and local governments and NGOs in several developing countries, for example in Bangladesh, Ghana, Honduras, Malawi, Mozambique, Nepal, Pakistan and the Caribbean.

The following sections define what CCD is and how it developed. This is followed by presenting some practical approaches to CCD. The chapter will then explore a critique of the concept, before concluding the discussion.

First, Box 14.1 provides an overview of key definitions relevant for this chapter.

Box 14.1 Definitions

Box 14.1 presents some definitions of key concepts in the field of climate compatible develop-ment (see also Hagemann *et al.*, 2012).[2]

Climate compatible development (CCD) is 'development that minimises the harm caused by climate impacts, while maximising the many human development opportunities presented by a low emissions, more resilient, future' (Mitchell and Maxwell, 2010: 1). CCD brings together mitigation, adaptation and development.

Mitigation is defined as 'an anthropogenic intervention to reduce the anthropogenic forcing of the climate system; it includes strategies to reduce greenhouse gas sources and emissions and enhancing greenhouse gas sinks' (IPCC, 2001: 379).

Adaptation is defined as 'adjustment in natural or human systems in response to actual or expected climatic stimuli or their effects, which moderates harm or exploits beneficial opportu-nities' (Smith *et al.*, 2001: 881).

Low carbon development addresses climate change *mitigation* and development. It is defined as a development model that is based on climate-friendly low carbon energy and follows princi-ples of sustainable development, makes a contribution to avoiding dangerous climate change and adopts patterns of low carbon consumption and production (Skea and and Nishioka, 2008). It includes switching from fossil fuels to low carbon energy, promoting low carbon technology innovation and business models, protecting and promoting natural carbon sinks such as forests and wetlands, and formulating policies that promote low carbon practices and behaviours (DfID, 2009).

Climate resilient development addresses climate change *adaptation* and development. It is defined as 'development processes that safeguard development from climate impacts' (Mitchell and Maxwell, 2010: 1).

Triple win addresses the fact that CCD aims to achieve mitigation, adaptation and development. Reducing emissions, adapting to climatic impacts and achieving development are strategies that can result in three potentially beneficial or 'win' situations.

Co-benefits are the interlinkages between mitigation and adaptation. Co-benefits can be, for example the mitigation aspects of urban green belts, which sequester carbon, but were predom-inantly planted to increase water retention in soils to overcome periods of water stress and thereby help adapting to a changing climate. Co-benefits do not include development aspects.

Discussion

This section discusses the linkages between climate change adaptation, mitigation and development at the conceptual and the practical level. The chapter also elaborates the role low carbon development plays for CCD.

CCD is at the interface between mitigation and development – commonly referred to as low carbon development – and adaptation and development – commonly referred to as climate resilient development. Often CCD is also referred to as low carbon climate resilient development, which is basically the same concept with a different name. This is indicated in Figure 14.1.

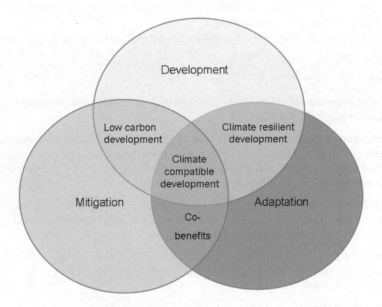

Figure 14.1 Climate compatible development diagram
Source: Adapted from Mitchell and Maxwell, 2010

The next section outlines the differences and similarities between climate change mitigation and adaptation, followed by a section outlining the differences and similarities between low carbon development and climate resilient development, which is followed by a discussion about climate compatible development and its aims.

Climate change mitigation and adaptation: differences and similarities

To understand what CCD is, it is first necessary to understand the differences and similarities between climate change mitigation and adaptation. This is outlined in this section.

Mitigation aims for the reduction of GHG emissions emitted by human activity, for example from the combustion of fossil fuels, and the enhancement of carbon sinks (IPCC, 2001). Mitigation happens mainly at the national and global scale, for the global benefit. It predominantly focuses on sectoral approaches, such as reducing the emissions from the energy sector or the transport sector. It therefore targets the main emitters measured in absolute terms, such as the USA, the EU, Russia, Japan, but also emerging emitters such as China and India. Its approach to reducing emissions and thereby achieving results is often based on key technologies such as renewable energy and CCS. A reduction in emissions is therefore measurable and the goal is clearly defined, which can potentially lead to a global benefit.

An example of mitigation is the target of the EU to reduce its greenhouse gas emissions by 60–80 per cent by 2050 compared with 1990 levels (EC, 2007). This reduction in emissions is likely to have a global benefit as it will reduce the overall level of atmospheric emissions.

Adaptation aims for a response to climatic impacts that reduces its adverse affects (Smith *et al.*, 2001). Opposite to mitigation, adaptation often pursues a local or national scale, for the local or national benefit. It often uses a cross-sectoral approach that addresses the economy-wide or nation-wide adaptation needs, particularly for the most vulnerable people, communities and countries. In the case of climate change, the most vulnerable countries are the LDCs, the Small Island Developing States and the African countries. There are various approaches that can focus on climatic impacts perspectives, vulnerability perspectives, disaster risk reduction or development perspectives. The time frame is often short to medium term as climate change is already posing a problem in many countries today and solutions need to be found immediately. Compared to mitigation, the results are more difficult to measure.

An example is the adaptation needs in Bangladesh, where floods, tropical storms and sea-level rise pose a serious challenge. Adapting to these impacts requires a variety of responses and approaches and has primary benefits at a local and national level. While the outcomes of the adaptation process can make a significant positive impact, they are more difficult to measure and quantify as sometimes they can only be measured in terms of potentially avoided impacts, such as avoided loss of lives, avoided illnesses and avoided destruction of homes and livelihoods.

Table 14.1 indicates the differences and similarities between mitigation and adaptation. These differences refer to scale, benefit, actors, outcomes, priority, approach and time perspective. These differences provide some evidence as to why it is so difficult to link adaptation and mitigation and why governments, multilateral organizations, NGOs and researchers have been slow in addressing adaptation and mitigation as an integrated challenge.

Table 14.1 The differences and similarities between mitigation and adaptation

	Mitigation	*Adaptation*
Scale	Global	Local to national
Benefit	Global	Local to national
Actors	Sectoral (e.g. energy, transport, forestry)	Cross-sectoral
Outcomes	Measurable	Difficult to measure
Priority	The largest emitters	The most vulnerable
Approaches	Narrow: technical approach/ techno-centric	Broad: from vulnerability to impacts perspective
Time perspective	Longer term	Short to medium term

Source: Adapted from Urban and Naess, 2011

Low carbon development and climate resilient development: differences and similarities

To understand what CCD is, it is first necessary to understand the differences and similarities between low carbon development and climate resilient development. These are outlined in this section.

While mitigation and adaptation are very different, there are more similarities between low carbon development and climate resilient development. Low carbon development addresses mitigation and development, while climate resilient development addresses adaptation and development (Hagemann *et al.*, 2012). While climate change mitigation is often seen as a vehicle for emission reductions in developed countries in the far future, low carbon development addresses very tangible issues relevant for both developed and developing countries in the short- and medium-term future. An example is the need to mitigate emissions in the EU vs. the need to introduce widespread rural electrification in Africa that can be supported by renewable energy.

On the other side of the spectrum is climate change adaptation, which focuses on adapting to local climatic impacts, predominantly in developing countries, which are the most affected by climate change. Climate resilient development brings in the development perspective and addresses issues that are relevant beyond the local level for both developed and developing countries. In fact several developed countries have started to pursue strategies to increase their resilience to climatic changes; for example, the UK is interested in increasing the resilience of its water sector due to increased risk of droughts in parts of the country.

Low carbon development focuses on the global, national and local scale and benefits, and often works cross-sectorally. Due to the development focus, its outcomes are more difficult to measure than more straightforward emission reductions. The focus is emitters with development needs, which can be any developing country, but also developed countries. Its approach is broad in comparison to mitigation as it aims for mitigation and development and thereby considers a range of social, economic and environmental challenges and opportunities. Low carbon development delivers benefits for the long term, but also for the medium term and sometimes even the short term.

For example, access to renewable energy for poor people in developing countries means both that emissions can be avoided in the long term in comparison to using fossil fuels, but for the short and medium term it means that poor people will be able to get access to energy and thereby improve their living conditions.

Climate resilient development focuses on the local and national scale with sometimes regional or even global implications. For example, if Bangladesh increases its resilience to current and future climatic risks involving floods, tropical storms and sea-level rise and incorporates responses to climate change in its development strategies, there is a reduced risk for climate-induced migration to other countries, particularly neighbouring countries, which in turn has a positive effect on the overall stability of the region. Climate resilient development also works at the cross-sectoral level, remains rather difficult to measure, has a short- to medium-term time perspective and prioritizes the most vulnerable. At the same time, the example from reducing drought risks in the UK shows that even developed countries are interested in increasing their resilience to climate change, beyond targeting only the vulnerable areas or sectors, depending on the climatic impacts. Table 14.2 shows the differences and similarities between low carbon development and climate resilient development.

Table 14.2 The differences and similarities between low carbon development and climate resilient development

	Low carbon development	*Climate resilient development*
Scale	Global to local	Local to national
Benefit	Global to local	Local to national, with global implications
Actors	Cross-sectoral, but still limited to a few approaches	Cross-sectoral
Outcomes	More difficult to measure	Difficult to measure
Priority	Emitters with development needs	The most vulnerable
Approaches	More broad: mitigation for achieving development needs (co-benefits)	More narrow: climate risk management and vulnerability perspectives
Time perspective	Medium term	Short to medium term

Source: Adapted from Urban and Naess, 2011

These rather conceptual discussions on low carbon development and climate resilient development are based on recent research findings. Some research outcomes on climate resilient development are discussed for example by Alam *et al.* (2011) and Sperling *et al.* (2008). Some research outcomes on low carbon development are discussed for example by Urban (2009), Ockwell and Mallett (2012) and many other publications by the authors of this book and their respective institutions.

Bringing low carbon development and climate resilient development together: CCD

CCD brings all the above-mentioned concepts together and has the aim of delivering a 'triple win' strategy by reducing emissions, adapting to climatic impacts and achieving development. The text below highlights some of the key issues, explains how CCD works in practice and provides a critique of CCD.

While adaptation and mitigation are strongly compartmentalized areas of research, policy and practice, in real life adaptation and mitigation are interlinked challenges and the two are difficult to separate. Therefore, people and communities affected by climate change often do not treat adaptation and mitigation as separate issues.

CCD is a concept that combines adaptation, mitigation and development. This has the advantage that climate change is approached and tackled as a holistic problem, not as a problem that is compartmentalized or piecemealed.

CCD has the potential to combine funding streams from various sources for tackling climate change, it can enable a dialogue between various agencies, institutions and ministries to tackle climate change and it can explore economy-wide or nation-wide responses to climate change that are for the national, regional and even global benefit, and go beyond targeting only the most vulnerable or only the largest emitters. CCD can further achieve multiple development goals through strategic planning (Hagemann *et al.*, 2012).

Low carbon development plays a crucial role for achieving CCD, and many low carbon development approaches simultaneously address adaptation or climate resilient development aspects as the examples in Box 14.2 indicate.

Box 14.2 How does climate compatible development work in practice?

While this chapter has so far mainly addressed the conceptual and planning-related aspects of CCD, this box explores two practical examples of CCD, namely the solar-powered pump project for irrigation in Benin and the mangrove restoration programme for coastal protection, livelihoods and carbon storage in Vietnam. These two examples have been chosen for the following reasons. First, they present successful projects/programmes that exemplify how CCD works in practice. Second, they address two different sectors that are important for developing countries, namely the agricultural sector and the forestry sector. There are also benefits for other important activities, such as for access to fresh water for the project in Benin, and improved income-generating activities from fisheries for the programme in Vietnam. Third, they present two different initiatives from two different world regions, namely Sub-Saharan Africa and Southeast Asia, where climate change is a reality in people's daily lives and where social and economic development is a national priority. We will start by discussing the solar-powered pump project in Benin, followed by the mangrove restoration programme in Vietnam.

The solar-powered pump project for irrigation in Benin

Benin is a country in Sub-Saharan Africa, more specifically in West Africa. It is a low income country, with a yearly per capita income of only US$780 in 2011 (compared to US$37,780 in the UK) (World Bank, 2012). The country depends heavily on agriculture; nevertheless climatic impacts have made it more prone to water stress and drought, which makes agriculture difficult especially in the dry season. At the same time, the country receives abundant sunshine, which makes it ideal for using solar panels for electricity or even irrigation. This is why the solar-powered pump project for irrigation in the Kalalé district of rural Benin is useful in promoting solar-powered irrigation for agriculture.

For the project, Stanford University and the Solar Electric Light Fund have worked together to set up an irrigation system for agriculture based on solar photovoltaic systems in Benin. The photovoltaic systems power a pump and a drip-irrigation system that provides regular access to water for the agricultural activities of the villagers. It enables the villagers to grow their agricultural produce, mainly vegetables, for their own use and for selling to local markets, even in the dry season. At the same time the photovoltaic systems provide electricity to local community buildings such as schools and clinics.

The renewable energy systems replace diesel generators for water pumping and electricity generation thereby avoiding carbon emissions. At the same time the photovoltaic systems improve access to water and irrigation for farmers and households in a changing, more drought-prone climate. In addition, they enable famers and the community to make a modest income from selling their agricultural produce on the market and thereby improve their livelihoods (Stanford University, 2008; Solar Electric Light Fund, 2008).[3] Hence, there are mitigation, adaptation and development aspects.

Mangrove restoration programme for coastal protection, livelihoods and carbon storage in Vietnam

Vietnam is a country in Southeast Asia. It is a lower middle income country, with a yearly per capita income of about $1,260 in 2011 (compared to $37,780 in the UK) (World Bank, 2012). While the country has seen increasing economic growth in recent years, about 19 per cent of the rural population still lived below the poverty line in 2008 (World Bank, 2012). UNEP reports that Vietnam has witnessed an increase in temperatures and sea-level rise in the last 50 years, as well as more frequent and severe occurrences of natural disasters, such as tropical storms, floods and droughts (UNEP, 2009). This has severely affected Vietnam's shoreline and increases the vulnerability of the coastal areas and its inhabitants.

To overcome this problem, the Red Cross planted 175 km^2 of mangrove forests to protect the Vietnamese shoreline from extreme weather events such as tropical cyclones and floods. The planting was done by people from local communities who afterwards received the right to harvest crabs, shrimps and mussels from the mangrove area they had planted and thereby benefitted in terms of food security and income generation from the mangrove planting. It is estimated that about 7750 families benefitted from the initiative both in terms of increasing their resilience to climate-related disasters and by increasing their income. At the same time, the costs for planting the mangroves were an estimated seven times cheaper than the costs spent on dyke maintenance in the absence of mangroves (UNEP, 2007). In addition, mangroves play an important part in carbon sequestration, and studies suggest that mangroves even sequester carbon faster than terrestrial forests (Suratman, 2008; Urban *et al.*, 2011). Hence, there are mitigation, adaptation and development aspects to the programme.

These two examples present how CCD can be possible by offering benefits in terms of adaptation, mitigation and development. Nevertheless, there are drawbacks, as none of these projects explicitly mentions CCD. There is also a fine line between the interlinkages of adaptation and mitigation, so-called co-benefits, and CCD. As sometimes the development aspects of projects are difficult to evaluate, measure and quantify, there tends to be uncertainty as to whether co-benefits have been achieved or whether development benefits have been achieved that would justify the labelling of CCD. For example, simply planting mangroves or irrigating a field with photovoltaic systems (PV) does not mean that a development benefit has been or will be achieved.

Box 14.3 provides a critique of CCD.

Box 14.3 Critique

The academic sector has been more sceptical in taking up the concept of CCD. This is partly based on the fact that CCD emerged as a donor-driven initiative rather than a research-driven initiative, the fact that little is known about its actual implementation as most of the projects are in their beginnings and the results will only be visible in a few years and the fact that CCD overlaps with other concepts such as low carbon climate resilient development[4] and climate-smart development.[5]

CCD is a new, predominantly donor-driven concept for policy, planning and practice (Hagemann *et al.*, 2012). While it has ample opportunities for achieving development in a changing climate, there are several drawbacks, which will be discussed here.

The fact that CCD is often donor-driven means that it can create external pressure on developing country governments. Developing country governments might act in line with CCD to receive funding, rather than because it fits the development priorities of their country.

Similarly, not every initiative or project that has benefits for mitigation and adaptation is contributing to CCD. Often the development perspective is missing or the adaptation/mitigation perspective is not much more than an accidental, though beneficial, add-on.

By combining adaptation, mitigation and development, there is the opportunity to treat climate change as a holistic interlinked challenge. However, there is also the risk that it will result in a very complex challenge that can hardly be tackled. This might potentially result in solutions that are 'low quality mitigation', 'low quality adaptation' and maybe even 'low quality development' if the challenge is too complex and the scale of the challenge is too large. Increasing the complexity of the issue can also mean that more human and financial resources are required and more bureaucratic processes might be needed (Hagemann *et al.*, 2012).

CCD can create trade-offs that are undesirable. An example is the development of the biofuel sector, which has been witnessed in many developing and developed countries recently. Investing in biofuels can be beneficial from a low carbon transport perspective, it can provide livelihoods and incomes for those involved and it might in some cases contribute to adapting to a changing climate by growing more climate-resilient crops rather than crops that might be more prone to climatic impacts such as water stress. At the same time, there can be great dangers attached to this as the growing of biofuels has recently been connected to land grabs, particularly in Sub-Saharan Africa (Neville and Dauvergne, 2012; Oxfam, 2012) and the deforestation of tropical rainforest, for example in Indonesia and Malaysia (Knudson, 2009; Whitlow Delano, 2011). The trade-offs of CCD therefore have to be gauged carefully against the benefits.

From an academic point of view, the following critiques apply: as CCD is a new concept, there is so far limited evidence of its opportunities, barriers and implementation at the development practitioner level. There is even less evidence at the academic level as the theoretical, conceptual and implementation basis is underexplored to date. This is, however, quickly changing as recent research suggests (Hagemann *et al.*, 2012).

Since CCD is a new term that addresses the same concept as low carbon climate resilient development, one could argue that it is relabelling an existing concept. This does not have to be negative *per se*, however it risks 'reinventing the wheel' and potentially creating confusion among practitioners, governments and academics. One the other hand, CCD is a term that is practical, short and pragmatic and is widely used around the world.

Conclusion

CCD offers significant opportunities, as it aims to deliver 'triple wins' on climate change adaptation, mitigation and development and has therefore attracted considerable attention from donors, international agencies and developing countries (Kaur and Ayers, 2010).

At the UN level and the research level, adaptation and mitigation are often treated as two separate issues. This has not changed substantially in recent years, despite discussing the integration of adaptation and mitigation in more detail (Klein *et al.*, 2005, 2007). While adaptation and mitigation – and low carbon development and climate resilient development – remain separate at the research and practice level, the CCD agenda is mainly driven by policy ideals and donor agendas, but also the realities of climate change and development on the ground. For those people, communities and countries that are affected by climate change, adaptation and mitigation are interlinked problems and only tackling them in a coherent way will achieve long-term development efforts in the light of climate change (Hagemann *et al.*, 2012).

Nevertheless, as with many emerging concepts, there remain gaps in the understanding of how CCD can best move from concept to practice (Hagemann *et al.*, 2012). CCD requires enhanced cooperation and communication between agencies and institutions, and it requires policy-makers, donors, practitioners and researchers who are able to understand and address the complexities of both low carbon and climate resilient development (Hagemann *et al.*, 2012). CCD may be a newly emerging concept, which has been little tested in reality, and might involve substantial financial and human resources; however, addressing climate change in an integrated, holistic way is the only sensible solution to effectively achieve development in a changing climate.

References

Alam, K., Shamsuddoha, M. D., Tanner, T., Huq, M. J. and Kabir, S. S. (2011) Planning exceptionalism? political economy of climate resilient development in Bangladesh. Available at: http://www.ids.ac.uk/idspublication/planning-exceptionalism-political-economy-of-climate-resilient-development-in-bangladesh (accessed 15 November 2012).

Becken, S. (2005) Harmonising climate change adaptation and mitigation: the case of tourist resorts in Fiji. *Global Environmental Change Part A*, 15(4), 381–93.

Dang, H. H., Michaelowa, A. and Tuan, D. D. (2003) Synergy of adaptation and mitigation strategies in the context of sustainable development: the case of Vietnam. *Climate Policy*, 3(1), 81–96.

Department for International Development (DfID) (2009) Eliminating world poverty: building our common future. DfID White Paper. London: DfID.

European Commission (EC) (2007) A European strategic energy technology plan (SET-plan) – towards a low carbon future. Available at: http://eur-lex.europa.eu/LexUriServ/LexUriServ.do?uri= COM:2007:0723:FIN:EN:HTML (accessed 15 November 2012).

Falloon, P. and Betts, R. (2010) Climate impacts on European agriculture and water management in the context of adaptation and mitigation – the importance of an integrated approach. *Science of the Total Environment*, 408(23), 5667–87.

Hagemann, M., Harvey, B., Urban, F., Naess, L. O., Höhne, N. and Hendel-Blackford, S. (2012) *Planning Climate Compatible Development: the Role of Tools and Methodologies*. London: CDKN.

Intergovernmental Panel on Climate Change (IPCC) (2001) Barriers, opportunities, and market potential of technologies and practices, in Metz, B. (ed.) *Climate Change 2001*. Cambridge: Cambridge University Press.

Kaur, N. and Ayers, J. (2010) Planning climate compatible development: lessons from experience. London: IIED. Available at : http://cdkn.org/wp-content/uploads/2010/12/Planning-CCD.pdf (accessed 15 November 2012).

Klein, R. J. T., Schipper, E. L. F. and Dessai, S. (2005) Integrating mitigation and adaptation into climate and development policy: three research questions. *Environmental Science & Policy*, 8(6), 579–88.

Klein, R. J. T., Huq, S., Denton, F., Downing, T. E., Richels, R. G., Robinson, J. B. and Toth, F. L. (2007) Inter-relationships between adaptation and mitigation, in Parry, M. L., Canziani, O. F., Palutikof, J. P., van der Linden, P. J. and Hanson, C. E. (eds) *Climate Change 2007: Impacts, Adaptation and Vulnerability. Contribution of Working Group II to the Fourth Assessment. Report of the Intergovernmental Panel on Climate Change*. Cambridge: Cambridge University Press, pp. 745–77.

Knudson, T. (2009) The cost of the biofuel boom on Indonesia's forests. *The Guardian*. Available at: http://www.guardian.co.uk/environment/2009/jan/21/network-biofuels (accessed 16 November 2012).

Mitchell, T. and Maxwell, S. (2010) Defining climate compatible development. Available at: http://www.cdkn.org/wp-content/uploads/2011/02/CDKN-CCD-DIGI-MASTER-19NOV.pdf (accessed 15 November 2012).

Neville, K. J. and Dauvergne, P. (2012) Biofuels and the politics of mapmaking. *Political Geography*, 31(5), 279–89.

Ockwell, D. and Mallett, A. (2012) *Low-Carbon Technology Transfer: From Rhetoric to Reality*. Abingdon: Earthscan.

Oxfam (2012) Land grabs. Available at: http://www.oxfam.org.nz/what-we-do/issues/grow/land-grabs (accessed 15 November 2012).

Roy, M. (2009) Planning for sustainable urbanisation in fast growing cities: mitigation and adaptation issues addressed in Dhaka, Bangladesh. *Habitat International*, 33(3), 276–86.

Skea, J. and Nishioka, S. (2008) Policies and practices for a low-carbon society. *Climate Policy, Supplement Modelling Long-Term Scenarios for Low-Carbon Societies*, 8: 5–16.

Smith, J., Schellnhuber, H. J. and Mirza, M. Q. M. (2001) Vulnerability to climate change and reasons for concern: a synthesis, in McCarthy, J. J, Canziani, O. F., Leary, N. A., Dokken, D. J. and White, K. S. (eds) *Climate Change 2001: Impacts, Adaptation, and Vulnerability*. Cambridge: Cambridge University Press.

Solar Electric Light Fund (2008) Benin Solar Irrigation Project Profile. Available at: http://www.stanford.edu/group/solarbenin/references/Benin-Project-Profile.pdf (accessed 15 November 2012).

Sperling, F., Valdivia, C., Quiroz, R., Valdivia, R., Angulo, L., Seimon, A. and Noble, I. (2008) Transitioning to climate resilient development perspectives from communities in Peru. Available at: http://sanrem.missouri.edu/WB-EDP%20115-%20Transitioning%20to%20Climate%20 Resilient%20Development-Peru.pdf (accessed 15 November 2012).

Stanford University (2008) Kalalé Solar Electrification Project. Available at: http://www.stanford.edu/group/solarbenin/project.html (accessed 15 November 2012).

Suratman, M. N. (2008) Carbon sequestration potential of mangroves in Southeast Asia. *Managing Forest Ecosystems*, 17, 1568–319.

United Nations Environment Programme (UNEP) (2007) Environment and disaster risk – emerging perspectives. Available at: http://postconflict.unep.ch/publications/env_vulnerability.pdf (accessed 15 November 2012).

UNEP (2009) Vietnam assessment report on climate change. Available at: http://www.unep.org/pdf/ dtie/VTN_ASS_REP_CC.pdf (accessed 15 November 2012).

Urban, F. (2009) Climate change mitigation revisited: low carbon energy transitions for China and India. *Development Policy Review*, 27(6), 693–715.

Urban, F. and Naess, L. O. (2011) The differences and similarities between mitigation, adaptation, low carbon development and climate resilient development. Brighton: University of Sussex/IDS.

Urban, F., Mitchell, T. and Silva Villanueva, P. (2011) Issues at the interface of disaster risk management and low-carbon development. *Climate and Development*, 3(3), 259–79.

Whitlow Delano, J. (2011) Malaysia: now "green" bio-fuels are destroying the little people of the rainforest. Available at: http://pulitzercenter.org/projects/malaysia-palm-oil-bio-fuel-logging-rainforest-destruction-indigenous-people-batek (accessed 15 November 2012).

World Bank (2012) Country classification according to income groups. Available at: http://data.worldbank.org/about/country-classifications (accessed 16 November 2012).

Further reading

Hagemann, M., Harvey, B., Urban, F., Naess, L. O., Höhne, N. and Hendel-Blackford, S. (2012) *Planning Climate Compatible Development: the Role of Tools and Methodologies*. London: CDKN.

Klein, R. J. T., Schipper, E. L. F. and Dessai, S. (2005) Integrating mitigation and adaptation into climate and development policy: three research questions. *Environmental Science & Policy*, 8(6), 579–88.

Klein, R. J. T., Huq, S., Denton, F., Downing, T. E., Richels, R. G., Robinson, J. B. and Toth, F. L. (2007) Inter-relationships between adaptation and mitigation, in Parry, M. L., Canziani, O. F., Palutikof, J. P., van der Linden, P. J. and Hanson, C. E. (eds) *Climate Change 2007: Impacts, Adaptation and Vulnerability. Contribution of Working Group II to the Fourth Assessment. Report of the Intergovernmental Panel on Climate Change*. Cambridge: Cambridge University Press, pp. 745–77.

Notes

1   For information on CDKN see http://cdkn.org/.
2   It has to be noted that some of these concepts are overlapping or complimentary, which might be confusing when faced with this terminology for the first time.
3   For a short video about the project please see http://www.youtube.com/watch?v=hqxkMxTQcBo, http://www.youtube.com/watch?v=56VzLXnIqEQ.
4   Low carbon climate resilient development is basically another term for CCD and was used before CCD was coined as a term.
5   Climate-smart development aims to increase the resilience to climatic impacts (adaptation), reduce GHG (mitigation), and enhance achievement of development goals. It is often used in relation to climate-smart agriculture, which aims to achieve higher agricultural productivity, increased crop resilience with respect to climatic impacts and higher carbon sequestration.

Part 7

Key issues for low carbon development in low, middle and high income countries: Case studies

Editorial for Part 7

Key issues for low carbon development in low, middle and high income countries: Case studies

Frauke Urban and Johan Nordensvärd

Part 7 discusses how low carbon development is being planned and implemented in various countries in different country income groups. It highlights the key issues for low carbon development in low income, middle income and high income countries by drawing on case studies based on empirical work from Ethiopia, Tanzania, China, Brazil, the USA, Germany and the UK. This editorial provides an overview of the case studies.

Overview of Part 7

Part 7 of this textbook discusses how low carbon development is being planned and implemented in various countries in different country income groups. This part presents case studies from low income, middle income and high income countries. It draws on recent research and empirical case studies from Ethiopia, Tanzania, China, Brazil, the USA, the UK and Germany. There is a fundamental difference between low carbon development in low income, middle income and high income countries. In low income and lower middle income countries, issues of social justice and poverty reduction are key priorities for low carbon development, while for upper middle income and high income countries low carbon innovation and emission reductions are at the heart of implementing low carbon development. Chapter 15 discusses the theoretical and conceptual frameworks necessary for fully exploring the case studies and addresses the challenges and opportunities for low carbon development in low, middle and high income countries. This is followed by the case studies in Chapters 16 to 22. The case studies are briefly introduced below.

Chapter 16 focuses on the challenges and opportunities posed by low carbon development in Ethiopia. Ethiopia is one of the world's least developed countries. Due to marginal emissions and high vulnerability to climate change, it has traditionally focused on adapting to the impacts of climate change rather than focusing on low carbon development. Despite Ethiopia's marginal emissions, the country is committed to become 'climate neutral' (UNEP, 2010: 1). Low carbon development in countries like Ethiopia is not about emission reductions, but about the opportunities and benefits low carbon development can bring for human development. Chapter 16 explores some of these opportunities in relation to energy access, forestry and green growth, and it stresses the need for combining low carbon development with key development priorities related to poverty reduction and economic growth. The chapter also addresses the state and non-state actors driving low carbon development in Ethiopia, their motives and potential trade-offs related to low carbon development.

Chapter 17 focuses on the lessons from Tanzania's solar home system market. Tanzania is an LDC with marginal emissions, but has ambitious aims for low carbon development. Tanzania recently had a breakthrough in its solar home system market. Chapter 17 explores the evolution of the Tanzanian solar home system market, discusses the set of actors, technologies and practices concerned with electricity services using solar photovoltaics (PV) and discusses the lessons that can be learned for the diffusion of sustainable energy technologies in low income countries more generally.

Chapter 18 focuses on middle income countries and discusses the planning and implementation of low carbon development in China, with a specific case study from the wind energy sector. Today, China is the world's largest wind energy manufacturer, has the world's largest wind energy capacity and is a global leader in low carbon development. Chapter 18 discusses some of the reasons why China's wind energy sector has grown significantly in recent years and elaborates the role of various government and industry actors for the Chinese wind energy sector.

Chapter 19 presents a case study from China's low carbon city planning. China hosts currently the world's largest population and more than half of the Chinese population lives in cities. Cities are a main driver for economic growth, wealth and progress, but at the same time they also contribute substantially to GHG emissions, pollution and environmental degradation. Faced by climate change, low carbon city planning is crucial to create climate-friendly, resilient cities. The chapter presents the case of Chinese pilot studies for low carbon cities; it elaborates its policy-making and planning implications and discusses lessons to be learned.

Chapter 20 discusses low carbon development in Brazil. Brazil is the world leader in bioethanol, both in terms of technology and in terms of bioethanol usage. For several decades, Brazil has had programmes and incentives in place to foster the national bioethanol industry, to invest in infrastructure and to make bioethanol commercially viable. Chapter 20 elaborates the current status, policy development and the opportunities and barriers of bioethanol in Brazil, and elaborates how other countries could potentially learn from Brazil's case.

Chapter 21 focuses on low carbon development options in high income countries by using a case study in CCS from the USA. Chapter 21 discusses the latest developments in CCS for energy generation, key policy and the socio-technical dynamics in the USA. The USA depends heavily on coal resources and therefore hails CCS as one of the most promising low carbon technologies of the future. Nevertheless, CCS is heavily debated in the public, media and political circles due to uncertainties that relate to the storage of carbon emissions underground and the time span of the operation as carbon emissions need to be stored for hundreds of years. This raises issues of geographic nature, such as finding adequate and secure storage facilities, and it raises issues of long-term governance, particularly given the fact that energy and climate policies may change from one government administration to the other within just a few years.

Chapter 22 elaborates another case study of a transition to a low carbon economy in high income countries, namely the case of energy efficiency policies in Germany and the UK. The chapter addresses two different approaches to energy efficiency policies for energy and carbon savings in buildings, their success and failures and lessons to be learnt.

These case studies have been chosen to present key issues for low carbon development from high, middle and low income countries, as well as key issues from Africa, Asia, Europe, Latin America and North America. In addition, these case studies have been chosen to present different approaches to low carbon development, which focus on renewable energy, low carbon energy, energy efficiency, biofuels as well as economy-wide examples. Hence, Part 7 of the book and Chapters 15–22 present practical solutions for how low carbon development can be planned and implemented at the global level and in relation to different contexts, with respect to low income, middle income and high income countries.

Reference

United Nations Environment Programme (UNEP) (2010) Climate Neutral Network: Ethiopia. Available at: www.unep.org/climateneutral/Default.aspx?tabid=804 (accessed 15 November 2012).

15 Approaches to low carbon development in low, middle and high income countries

A conceptual framework

Frauke Urban and Johan Nordensvärd

This chapter provides a conceptual framework for low carbon development in low, middle and high income countries, which helps to better understand the case studies presented in the following chapters. This chapter first discusses how low carbon development strategies vary according to different contexts and need to take into account national priorities. The chapter then elaborates different approaches and mechanisms for achieving low carbon development in various contexts.

Introduction

Low carbon development is essential for mitigating the emissions leading to climate change and for enabling development in a carbon constrained world. Low carbon development can bring opportunities and benefits for both developed and developing countries, nevertheless low carbon development can only be implemented when an adequate enabling environment is in place that addresses the key political, economic, social and technological issues. In low income and lower middle income countries, issues of social justice and poverty reduction are the key to low carbon development, while for higher middle income and high income countries low carbon innovation and emission reductions are at the heart of implementing low carbon development.

Differentiating between different contexts, such as country groups, matters for low carbon development as different countries have different needs, priorities, face different challenges and have different solutions, hence understanding these complex differences can help the planning and implementation of low carbon development. It is particularly important to differentiate between low, middle and high income countries as approaches to low carbon development can differ substantially between these country groups.

This chapter provides a conceptual framework for low carbon development in low, middle and high income countries, which aids better understanding of the case studies presented in the following chapters. This chapter first discusses how low carbon development strategies vary according to different contexts and need to take into account the national priorities and capabilities along with considerations of local knowledge. The chapter then elaborates different approaches and mechanisms for achieving low carbon development in various contexts.

Discussion

Differentiating between different contexts for low carbon development: key definitions

Differentiating between different contexts, such as country groups, matters for low carbon development as different countries have different needs and priorities. Differentiating between different contexts within a country, such as between urban and rural, rich and poor, women and men, children and adults, can also help to develop and implement low carbon development approaches that are more in line with people's needs. While recognizing the need to differentiate between different contexts within a country, elaborating this goes beyond the remit of this chapter, hence the following section only briefly discusses different country groupings.

Country groupings according to income are calculated by the World Bank based on each country's Gross National Income (GNI) per capita. The per capita figure is more useful than an aggregate economy-wide figure, as it provides evidence about how well or badly off people are economically in a country, rather than only providing figures about the size of the economy. Nevertheless, the per capita figures are averaged and do not provide information about income distribution in a country and (in)equality. Having a population with more or less similar income can result in the same averaged GNI per capita as having a population with extreme rich and extreme poor, which can average out in terms of the GNI per capita. Other indicators, such as the Gini coefficient, therefore provide evidence about the equality of an economy. For the purpose of this chapter, we will however only refer to GNI per capita and the income classifications by the World Bank. The next section discusses key definitions of country groupings.

A **low income country** is defined by the World Bank as having a GNI per capita of US$1005 or less per year (World Bank, 2012a). An example of a low income country in Africa is Burkina Faso; an example of a low income country in Asia is Nepal; and Haiti is an example of a low income country in Latin America and the Caribbean (World Bank, 2012b). LDCs are often considered to be part of the low income group and therefore a country such as Haiti can be a low income country and an LDC at the same time. LDCs are defined as countries with long-term structural weaknesses, in particular low per capita income, a low human assets index (HAI) and a high economic vulnerability index (EVI) (UN, 2008). The HAI index takes into account health and nutrition as well as education. The EVI index takes into account the risks posed to the economy by shocks, for example when a country depends almost entirely on agriculture, rather than on industry or services (UN, 2008). The LDC category thus goes beyond income levels and takes into account a wider set of development issues.

A **middle income country** is defined by the World Bank as having a GNI per capita between $1006 and $3975 per year for lower middle income countries and $3976 and $12,275 per year for upper middle income countries (World Bank, 2012a). Examples of middle income countries in Africa are, for instance, Ghana on the lower end and South Africa on the higher end; examples of middle income countries in Asia are Laos on the lower end and China on the higher end; and examples of middle income countries in Latin America and the Caribbean are Bolivia on the lower end and Brazil on the higher end (World Bank, 2012b). This group of countries can further be divided into **lower middle income countries** and **upper middle income countries**. The division between lower and upper middle income countries is useful, as often the differences between countries on the lower or upper end are large, for example by comparing Laos to China. Many of the emerging emitters, such as China, India, South Africa, Brazil and Mexico are middle income countries.

A **high income country** is defined by the World Bank as having a GNI per capita of $12,276 or more per year (World Bank, 2012a). High income countries are the countries of the EU, Australia, Canada, Japan, the USA, many Middle Eastern countries such as Israel, Saudia Arabia and the United Arab Emirates, the 'Asian tiger states' of Hong Kong, South Korea and Singapore, and some of the wealthy islands in the Caribbean such as the Bahamas and Trinidad and Tobago. Many high income countries are part of the OECD (World Bank, 2012b).

For climate change purposes, the groupings of other countries beyond their income status is also important, for example the SIDS, which include countries directly threatened by sea-level rise and other climatic impacts, such as the Maldives and Vanuatu. Other important groupings relate to the development status, such as for the LDCs; the emitting status, such as for emerging emitters like China and India; and the regional focus, such as the African countries, which may face different climatic challenges to other world regions. Countries can be presented by various different groupings at the same time, for example Haiti is a low income country, an LDC and a SIDS.

The key definitions of country groupings have been addressed above. The next section discusses different low carbon development strategies and priorities for low, middle and high income countries.

Low carbon development in low, middle and high income countries: different needs, different approaches

Low carbon development strategies vary according to different contexts and need to take into account national priorities and capabilities along with considerations of local knowledge (Urban, 2010a). For example, an LDC and SIDS such as Haiti has fundamentally different aims and challenges in relation to low carbon development to an upper middle income country and emerging emitter such as China. While Haiti focuses more on adaptation to climate change, reducing poverty and increasing access to modern energy and basic services for its population, China focuses more on mitigating emissions while aiming to grow its economic sectors in a lower carbon way and increasing its economic competitiveness. Hence, a one-size-fits-all approach for low carbon development needs to be avoided.

A second important issue is the right to develop: countries with very low emissions need to have the right to develop and to grow their economy. Due to marginal emissions today this will most likely require a certain increase in emissions in the future. Low carbon development means in this case that an increase in emissions is acceptable, although the increase will be lower than the 'business as usual' case (Urban *et al.*, 2011). Some might argue that low carbon development in low income countries is fundamentally unethical, as poor countries should have the right to develop. It is therefore important to keep in mind that poor countries need to achieve economic growth and development first and worry about mitigating their emissions at a much later, more developed stage.

Low carbon development in high income and upper middle income countries is about reducing emissions and expanding the low carbon sectors, while low carbon development in low income and lower middle income countries is mainly about the opportunities it can bring, such as green jobs, access to electricity, low carbon innovation and increased energy security. Another important motivation for low carbon development is to avoid future carbon liability in a world where a price is attached to carbon. Low carbon development for low income and lower middle income countries is about the opportunities and development benefits it can offer, not primarily about reducing emissions, as most of these countries have marginal emissions. However, this situation is likely to change in the future when some of these countries are likely to have higher emissions depending on their fuel and technology choices, economic growth rates and population growth rates (Urban *et al.*, 2011).

Table 15.1 indicates how low carbon development means different approaches for different countries. The table indicates different country groups' mitigation needs, development needs and low carbon development needs, with a focus on LDCs, low income countries, lower and upper middle income countries, high income countries, emerging emitters and SIDS.

In addition to Table 15.1, Figure 15.1 shows graphically how different countries approach low carbon development differently. High income countries are on one side of the extreme, mainly focusing on mitigation and far less on development; emerging emitters and upper middle income countries focus both on mitigation and development needs, whereas lower middle income countries tend to focus more on development and less on mitigation; and low income countries, LDCs and SIDS focus on the other side of the extreme – mainly on development needs and only marginally on mitigation. Local knowledge plays a key role in being able to adapt to climate change and mitigate emissions. However, each approach to low carbon development is equally valid as each country group has its own needs and priorities. Nevertheless the core low carbon development model should still incorporate switching from fossil fuels to low carbon energy, promoting low carbon technology innovation and business models, protecting and promoting natural carbon sinks such as forests and wetlands, and formulating policies that promote low carbon practices and behaviours (DfID, 2009: 58) as well as following principles of sustainable development while avoiding dangerous climate change (Skea and Nishioka, 2008).

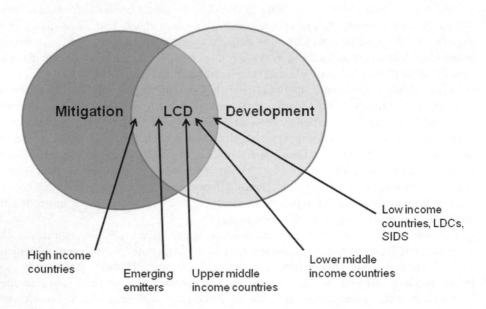

Figure 15.1 The role of mitigation and development for low carbon development in different countries

Table 15.1 Approaches to low carbon development in different countries

Target country	Mitigation needs	Development needs	Low carbon development needs	Country examples
Least developed country (LDC)	Mitigation tends not to be a key concern, but adaptation is an immediate concern Mitigation can be an opportunity, e.g. for increasing energy access with renewable energy, increasing employment and economic growth, safeguarding finite fossil fuel resources	Development is crucial e.g. for economic growth, poverty reduction and social justice	Low carbon development is about the opportunities and benefits it can bring and needs to go along with poverty reduction and social justice. LCD is not about reducing emissions in this country group	Benin, Bhutan, Ethiopia, Democratic Republic of Congo, Haiti, Madagascar, Malawi, Myanmar, Rwanda, Somalia, Uganda
Low income country	Mitigation tends not to be a key concern, but adaptation is an immediate concern Mitigation can be an opportunity, e.g. for increasing energy access with renewable energy, increasing employment and economic growth, safeguarding finite fossil fuel resources	Development is crucial, e.g. for economic growth, poverty reduction and social justice	Low carbon development is about the opportunities and benefits it can bring and needs to go along with poverty reduction and social justice. LCD is not about reducing emissions in this country group	Afghanistan, Bangladesh, Cambodia, Democratic Republic of Congo, Ethiopia, Haiti, Kenya, Malawi, Nepal, Tanzania
Lower middle income country	Mitigation is an increasingly important concern, but often not a priority Mitigation can be an opportunity, e.g. for increasing energy access with renewable energy, increasing employment and economic growth, safeguarding finite fossil fuel resources	Development is crucial, e.g. for economic growth, equal distribution of wealth, poverty reduction and social justice	Low carbon development is about the opportunities and benefits it can bring and needs to go along with poverty reduction and social justice. At the same time mitigation is an important concern and needs to be considered for the country's future	Angola, Bolivia, Fiji, Ghana, Honduras, India, Laos, Sri Lanka, Senegal, Sudan, Tuvalu, Vietnam

Table 15.1 continued

Target country	Mitigation needs	Development needs	Low carbon development needs	Country examples
Upper middle income country	*Countries with high emissions:* cuts in emissions are required in the long term,[a] the emphasis is currently on responding to development needs while reducing or stabilizing emissions	Development is considered important for economic growth, equal distribution of wealth, poverty reduction and social justice	*Countries with high emissions:* Long-term mitigation is required in terms of stabilizing and eventually reducing emissions. This needs to go along with development efforts	High emitters such as Brazil, China, Mexico, South Africa, but also low emitters such as Gabon, Jamaica, the Maldives
	Countries with low emissions: Mitigation is an increasingly important concern, but often not a priority		*Countries with low emissions:* Low carbon development is about the opportunities and benefits it can bring and needs to go along with poverty reduction and social justice. At the same time mitigation is an important concern and needs to be considered for the country's future	
	Mitigation can be an opportunity, e.g. for increasing energy access with renewable energy, increasing employment and economic growth, safeguarding finite fossil fuel resources			
High income country	High and immediate cuts in emissions required	As these countries tend to have high Human Development Indicators, the focus is mainly on equal distribution of wealth, social justice, increasing employment opportunities and reducing debt	Long-term and short-term mitigation is needed and requires significant reductions in emissions	EU and OECD countries

Table 15.1 continued

Target country	Mitigation needs	Development needs	Low carbon development needs	Country examples
Emerging emitters	Cuts in emissions are required in the long term, the emphasis is currently on responding to development needs while reducing or stabilizing emissions	Development is considered important for economic growth, equal distribution of wealth, poverty reduction and social justice	Long-term mitigation is required in terms of stabilizing and eventually reducing emissions. This needs to go along with development efforts	Brazil, China, India, Mexico, South Africa, other rapidly developing countries
Small Island Developing States (SIDS)	Mitigation tends not to be a key concern, but adaptation is an immediate concern Mitigation can be an opportunity, e.g. for increasing energy access with renewable energy, increasing employment and economic growth, safeguarding finite fossil fuel resources	Development is crucial, e.g. for economic growth, poverty reduction and social justice	Low carbon development is about the opportunities and benefits it can bring and needs to go along with poverty reduction and social justice. Low carbon development is not about reducing emissions in this country group	Haiti, Kiribati, Maldives, Micronesia, Vanuatu

Note: ªAs the majority of emissions increase in the future is likely to come from emerging emitters such as China, India and South Africa, some argue that these countries should accept legally binding emission reduction targets in the next few years and their emissions should peak within the next decade.

Different conceptual approaches to low carbon development[1]

The previous section discussed different low carbon development strategies and priorities for low, middle and high income countries. This section elaborates different approaches to low carbon development, which are of a conceptual nature. These different approaches, along with the understanding of each country's special needs for low carbon development, provide a conceptual framework for low carbon development in low, middle and high income countries, which helps to better understand the case studies presented in the following chapters.

In addition to differences in the understanding of and the need for low carbon development in different countries, low carbon development can be planned and implemented differently in different countries, regions or cities. Changes in production such as changes in energy and materials supply or economic growth affect low carbon development. Similarly, changes in consumption such as changes in energy and materials demand, consumption patterns and lifestyles affect low carbon development. Figure 15.2 and Table 15.1 provide

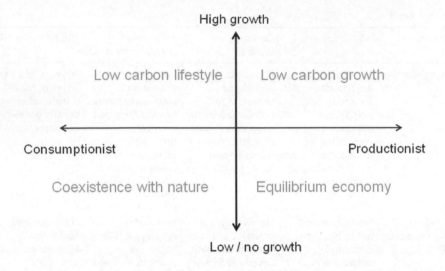

Figure 15.2 Approaches to low carbon development
Source: Amended from Urban, 2010a, 2010b; Urban and Sumner, 2012.[2]

four contrasting interpretations of low carbon development, depending on where policy-makers place themselves on two different dimensions of response: their approach to growth; and their focus on production or consumption-related policy measures (Urban, 2010a, 2010b; Urban and Sumner, 2012).

Figure 15.2 addresses four different approaches to low carbon development (LCD), which here have been named 'low carbon growth', 'low carbon lifestyles', 'equilibrium economy' and 'coexistence with nature'. Each of these approaches is specific in relation to its focus on economic growth and its focus on low carbon changes predominantly in production or consumption.

'Low carbon growth' focuses on the production side of a growing economy and on how goods and services can be produced with lower emissions. It aims at decoupling economic growth from carbon emissions (e.g. halving emissions, but doubling GDP). Its focus is therefore mainly on mitigation, though climate change adaptation also plays a role. Achieving low carbon growth requires technological change and sectoral change (Urban, 2010a, 2010b; Urban and Sumner, 2012).

'Low carbon lifestyles' focus on the consumption side of a growing economy and on the consumer's ability to reduce emissions by consuming climate-friendly products. It implies lifestyle changes and behavioural changes and also leads to a decoupling of carbon emissions (e.g. halving emissions, but doubling GDP). Its focus is therefore equally on mitigation and adaptation. Achieving low carbon lifestyles requires behavioural changes, sectoral change and technological change (Urban, 2010a, 2010b; Urban and Sumner, 2012).

'Equilibrium economy' focuses on the production side of an economy and aims at social development rather than high growth. No decoupling is necessary as growth is neutral or rather low (e.g. halving emissions, but keeping GDP stable), however it implies changes in the production of goods and services. Its focus is therefore mainly on mitigation, though adaptation also plays a role. Achieving an equilibrium economy requires technological change and sectoral change (Urban, 2010a, 2010b; Urban and Sumner, 2012).

'Coexistence with nature' focuses on the consumption side of an economy and aims at social development rather than growth. No decoupling is necessary as growth is neutral or rather low (e.g. halving emissions, but keeping GDP stable), however, it implies lifestyle changes and behavioural changes. Its focus is therefore equally on mitigation and adaptation. Achieving coexistence with nature requires behavioural changes, sectoral change and technological change (Urban, 2010a, 2010b; Urban and Sumner, 2012).

The first two approaches to low carbon development – here labelled 'low carbon growth' and 'low carbon lifestyles' – tend to assume that economic growth is compatible with significant reductions in carbon emissions. The latter two – here labelled 'equilibrium economy' and 'coexistence with nature' – tend to assume it is not. The 'low carbon growth' and 'equilibrium economy' approaches both put the emphasis primarily on reducing the production of carbon through technological changes, for example from inefficient to more efficient technologies, from polluting to less polluting, and/or sectoral changes, for example, from structural changes taking place in the economy. Technological changes refer to changes in technologies, such as switching from fossil fuels to renewable energy. Sectoral changes refer to changes in the sectors of an economy, such as increases in the service sector and decreases in the agricultural or industrial sectors. For example, in China, many inefficient older coal-fired power plants are being replaced with more efficient, less polluting new plants (thus technological changes have happened); and in India, the service economy has been rapidly growing over recent years, while the share of agricultural value added has declined (thus sectoral changes have happened) (Van Ruijven *et al.*, 2008; Urban, 2010a, 2010b; Urban and Sumner, 2012).

The 'low carbon lifestyles' and 'coexistence with nature' approaches tend to focus on reducing demand through lifestyle and behavioural changes as well as through sectoral and technological changes. Behavioural change refers to changes in behaviour and lifestyle: using public transport instead of travelling by car, switching to 'green' electricity instead of fossil fuel-powered electricity, buying local products instead of imported 'air mile products'. However, not all options are equally valid for developing countries (Urban, 2010a; Urban and Sumner, 2012). For example, some behavioural approaches to low carbon development are simply unethical or impossible in poorer developing countries where switching to different types of products or electricity is impossible as many people live below the poverty line and have bigger problems than pondering about consumer choices. In these cases, governments and the private sector tend to have the prime responsibility to create opportunities for low carbon development through technological or sectoral change, such as by providing access to electricity through renewable energy.

Of course, the options presented in Figure 15.2 are not mutually exclusive. Often low carbon development can only be achieved when a mix of various instruments and approaches is implemented. In addition, many policy-makers will favour a mix of production-side and consumption-side approaches to low carbon development (Urban, 2010a; Urban and Sumner, 2012).

Conclusion

Besides the above-mentioned approaches and the UNFCCC mechanisms, there are many other options of how to achieve low carbon development depending on each country's national and local priorities and plans, and the funding and technologies that are available. It is important to have policies and practices in place that are suited for the national circumstances and local needs. As highlighted before, the meaning, scope and scale for low carbon development differ within different groups of countries. Upper and middle income groups in developing countries, particularly in middle income countries, may have consumption patterns that are in some ways similar to developed countries. Reducing excessive consumption and making 'greener' choices can therefore be an important issue. The poor in developing countries have however contributed very little to climate change and their main priority is social and economic development. For poor and vulnerable groups and low income countries, the main issue is how to achieve development in times of climate change. The benefits and opportunities of low carbon development are crucial, such as provision of 'green' jobs, increased access to modern technology and access to electricity, contributions to energy security and improved environmental quality, while emissions reductions are not a concern unless emissions become excessive at some point in the future.

It is therefore important to understand the development needs and the climate change-related needs of each country or region in its own right, rather than using a one-size-fits-all approach for low carbon development. The conceptual framework presented in this chapter can help to understand the differentiated needs of different countries for low carbon development and can aid better understanding of the case studies in the next few chapters.

References

Department for International Development (DfID) (2009) Eliminating world poverty: building our common future. DfID White Paper. London: DfID.

Skea, J. and Nishioka, S. (2008) Policies and practices for a low-carbon society. *Climate Policy, Supplement Modelling Long-Term Scenarios for Low-Carbon Societies*, 8, 5–16.

United Nations (UN) (2008) Handbook on the least developed country category: inclusion, graduation and special support measures. New York: UN Committee for Development Policy. Available at:http://www.un.org/en/development/desa/policy/cdp/cdp_publications/2008cdphandbook.pdf (accessed 15 November 2012).

Urban, F. (2010a) Pro-poor low carbon development and the role of growth. *International Journal of Green Economics*, 4(1), 82–93.

Urban, F. (2010b) The MDGs and beyond: can low carbon development be pro-poor? *IDS Bulletin*, 41(1): 92–9.

Urban, F. and Sumner, A. (2012) Pro-poor low carbon development, in Ockwell, D. and Mallet, A. (eds) *Low Carbon Technology Transfer: From Rhetoric To Reality*. Abingdon: Earthscan.

Urban, F., Watt, R., Ting, M. B., Crawford, G., Wang, Y., Lakew, H. *et al.* (2011) Achieving low carbon development in low and middle income countries – the role of governments, business and civil Society. Final project report. Learning Hub on Adaptation and Low Carbon Development. Brighton: IDS.

Van Ruijven, B., Urban, F., Benders, R. M. J., Moll, H. C, Van der Sluijs, J., De Vries, B. and Van Vuuren, D.P. (2008) Modeling energy and development: an evaluation of models andconcepts. *World Development*, 36(12), 2801–21.

World Bank (2012a) How we classify countries. Available at:http://data.worldbank.org/about/country-classifications (accessed 15 November 2012).

World Bank (2012b) Country and lending groups. Available at: http://data.worldbank.org/about/country-classifications/country-and-lending-groups (accessed 15 November 2012).

Further reading

Skea, J. and Nishioka, S. (2008) Policies and practices for a low-carbon society. *Climate Policy, Supplement Modelling Long-Term Scenarios for Low-Carbon Societies*, 8, 5–16.

Urban, F. (2010a) Pro-poor low carbon development and the role of growth. *International Journal of Green Economics*, 4(1), 82–93.

Notes

1 Parts of the section on 'Different conceptual approaches to low carbon development' has been published in amended form by Inderscience Publishers in Urban (2010a).
2 A similar figure has been published in amended form by Inderscience Publishers in Urban (2010a).

16 Poverty reduction and economic growth in a carbon constrained world

The case of Ethiopia

Frauke Urban, Marie Blanche Ting and Hilawe Lakew

This chapter focuses on the opportunities and challenges posed by low carbon development in Ethiopia. Ethiopia is one of the world's least developed countries. Due to marginal emissions and high vulnerability to climate change, it has traditionally focused on adapting to the impacts of climate change rather than focusing on low carbon development. Low carbon development in countries like Ethiopia is not about emission reductions, but about the opportunities and benefits low carbon development can bring for human development. This chapter, which is based on fieldwork, explores some of these opportunities and stresses the need for combining low carbon development with key development priorities related to poverty reduction and economic growth. The chapter also addresses the state and non-state actors driving low carbon development in Ethiopia, their motives and potential trade-offs related to low carbon development.

Introduction

Ethiopia is engaged with today's low carbon development agenda, but its motivations, approaches and perspectives are quite different from those of other countries, particularly high income and middle income countries. This is due to Ethiopia's development status and income level, its carbon emissions status as a marginal emitter, its governance and political economy situation and its priority low carbon development issues.

Ethiopia has been chosen for this empirical case study on low carbon development in low income countries for the following reasons: it is a low income country with very low carbon emissions and high vulnerability to climate change; nevertheless its government actively strives for low carbon development to achieve development benefits. Only a small number of low income countries are striving for low carbon development, Ethiopia is therefore an exemplary case for other low income countries, particularly African low income countries.

Ethiopia is one of the world's LDCs and is a low income country (World Bank, 2012). The GNI per capita was only US$400 in 2011, compared to a GNI per capita of $37,780 in the UK in 2011 (World Bank, 2012). Ethiopia hosted a population of 85 million people in 2011, of whom more than 85 per cent live in rural areas (World Bank, 2012). Only 5 per cent of the rural population has access to electricity (CSA, 2012) and 15 per cent of the total population, while the majority of the population depends on traditional biofuels such as fuel wood and agricultural residues (IEA, 2012).

Ethiopia has one of the world's lowest emissions: it contributes less than 0.05 per cent of global emissions (UNEP, 2010). In comparison, developed countries are reported to be responsible for about 75 per cent of the historic or accumulated emissions leading to climate change according to the WRI (WRI, 2005). Ethiopia therefore has no historic responsibility for climate change; it has negligible GHG emissions today, however, it needs to develop in a carbon constrained world. Based on its low emissions, the country is already a low carbon society and has had low carbon development for centuries, however involuntarily. Low carbon development activities and policies today therefore need to ensure that the country will be better off in the future and that it will tap into the benefits that low carbon technologies and finance can bring, such as in relation to energy access.

While Ethiopia is not a net contributor to climate change, it is very vulnerable to climate change. The country is largely dependent on agriculture, forestry and fisheries. Recent climate change impacts have resulted in droughts and periodic flooding in some parts of the country, which has had negative effects on food production and water supply (IPCC, 2007). Climate change also poses a challenge to health due to the risk of increased spread of vector- and water-borne diseases, especially in areas with inadequate health infrastructure (UNEP, 2010). It is reported that water scarcity is a serious problem in Ethiopia, which is exacerbated by climate change and may result in 'economic, social and political instability, declining biodiversity that might be irreversible; acceleration of desertification and adverse impact on ecosystems' (UNEP, 2010: 1). As the large majority of the country's electricity is generated from hydropower, the water scarcity has 'affected the water volume in reservoirs leading to power shortages and rationing' (UNEP, 2010: 1; Urban *et al.*, 2011).

Despite not being a net contributor to climate change, Ethiopia aims to become carbon neutral. It has signed the UNFCCC, the Kyoto Protocol and has other national low carbon policies in place. Ethiopia supported UNEP's Billion Tree Campaign, 'contributing more trees than any other nation – over one billion – towards the global target of planting seven billion trees by 2009' (UNEP, 2010: 1). The Ethiopian government is actively promoting low carbon development. This includes introducing a new energy policy that promotes renewable energy and launching large-scale solar and wind energy projects which supply the rural poor with access to electricity. Ethiopia has ambitious Nationally Appropriate Mitigation Actions (NAMAs), which were presented as a response to the Copenhagen Accord: the country aims to rapidly expand its hydropower development with 10 new large hydropower projects and a capacity of 5.5 Gigawatts (GW) to be completed by 2015, in addition an additional 11 hydropower projects are currently under investigation, 7 large wind parks should be completed by 2012, 6 geothermal projects should be built by 2018 (some of them with Chinese funding), 2 new biofuel and bioelectricity projects should be built by 2015 and there are a wide range of other low carbon activities in various sectors of the economy (UNFCCC, 2010; Urban *et al.*, 2011).

Hence, low carbon development in Ethiopia is not at all about cutting emissions. Instead, low carbon development in Ethiopia is about the opportunities and benefits low carbon development can bring for human development. This includes, for example, access to modern energy through low carbon energy and incorporating key development priorities related to poverty reduction, economic growth and human development into low carbon development policies and initiatives.

This chapter explores some of the opportunities and challenges posed by low carbon development in Ethiopia, based on fieldwork conducted in Ethiopia. The chapter stresses the need for combining low carbon development with key development priorities related to poverty reduction and economic growth. This chapter first defines key concepts and terms in Box 16.1, the chapter then elaborates the case study approach and its results. This is followed by a critique of low carbon development in a low income country like Ethiopia, and the chapter concludes with some recommendations for low carbon development in Ethiopia.

Box 16.1 Definitions of key concepts and terms relevant for this chapter

Poverty reduction: poverty reduction is defined as any process that reduces poverty levels (ICT4D, 2011). The causes of poverty are plentiful and can range from environmental factors such as a lack of natural resources or the occurrence of natural disasters to a range of political, social and economic factors such as poor governance, corruption, political instability, conflict and war, unequal distribution of resources, etc. Poverty reduction is therefore a complex process that requires several strategies such as improved access to funding, human capital and technologies, as well as encouraging good governance, equal distribution of resources and services – such as education, employment, health care and energy access – and encouraging development.

Economic growth: economic growth is defined as an increase in GDP (GDAE, 2011). While economic growth is often used as a proxy of the rate of national income generation of a country, it does not provide information about distributional effects, such as who benefits from economic growth and differences between various groups or regions in the country.

Carbon constrained: global climate change is considered one of the greatest threats to development efforts. The IPCC's Fourth Assessment Report indicates that global GHG emissions leading to climate change must be reduced by 80 per cent in 2030 compared to 2000 levels to avoid irreversible and 'dangerous climate change', defined as a global temperature rise above 2°Celsius (IPCC, 2007). Stabilizing GHG concentrations (CO_2 equivalent) at 450 ppm is estimated to achieve a 50 per cent chance of limiting a global temperature rise to below 2°Celsius (IEA, 2010). Hence, the global carbon budget is constrained. A carbon constrained world basically means that carbon emissions cannot rise endlessly, but that a cap in emissions is required to avoid dangerous climate change.

Nationally Appropriate Mitigation Actions (NAMAs): the purpose of NAMAs is to outline national mitigation options that are in line with domestic policies and that are developed in 'the context of sustainable development, supported and enabled by technology, financing and capacity building, in a measurable, reportable and verifiable manner' (IEA/OECD, 2009 :7).

The next section elaborates the case study from Ethiopia, starting first with the conceptual framework and the methodology, followed by the case study findings.

Case study: Ethiopia

Conceptual framework and methodology

This chapter is based on a case study of today's low carbon development efforts in Ethiopia. The chapter has the objective of indicating the opportunities and barriers for low carbon development in low income countries such as Ethiopia. The case study further identifies the key government, business and civil society actors engaged in low carbon development in Ethiopia, their motives and how they influence each other. Hence, it assesses the political economy of low carbon development in Ethiopia. The chapter is based on a project that was funded by the DfID, and involved detailed empirical research, including fieldwork in Ethiopia.

This research was based on the following key research questions:

•   What are the policies, strategies and initiatives in place to promote fair and equitable low carbon development in Ethiopia and how are they being implemented (e.g. in relation to low carbon energy, energy efficiency, forestry, land use etc)?

- What are successful low carbon development initiatives and why?
- What are the co-benefits of low carbon development such as economic growth and poverty reduction?
- Are there any trade-offs (e.g. competition between land for biofuels and food production, high reliance on hydropower threatens stable electricity supply due to a changing climate)?

The methodological approach consisted of three main steps:

1   The first step was a literature review in which the current status of low carbon development in Ethiopia was identified as well as key policies and key initiatives.
2   The second step was to conduct in-depth expert interviews with key actors from government, industry, research organizations and NGOs to assess their roles in planning and promoting fair and equitable low carbon development and the motives that drive low carbon development in Ethiopia. The interviewees were selected based on their expertise in low carbon development or specific aspects of it. The interview questions were semi-structured, qualitative, open questions.
3   The third step related to the motives that drive low carbon development in Ethiopia, particularly climate change mitigation, poverty reduction, economic growth and energy security. This required a motive scoring to rank the importance of each motive. A 'motive' is defined as a dominant theme or central idea. One actor can have many motives and all are equally valid or equally plausible (Urban *et al.*, 2011).

The next section provides a brief overview of the potential for low carbon development in Ethiopia.

Case study findings: a brief overview of low carbon development potential in Ethiopia

The case study findings suggest there is considerable potential today for low carbon development in Ethiopia. The Ethiopian government has ambitious plans to be a middle income country by 2025 and it aims to be carbon neutral around the same time. This is despite the fact that Ethiopia has one of the world's lowest emissions: the country has very low carbon emissions at 0.08 metric tonnes per capita on average compared to other low income countries of 0.28 metric tons per capita on average (IEA, 2012). The majority of Ethiopia's carbon emissions are from agriculture and deforestation for creating agricultural land and for fuel wood consumption (EPA, 2010). This is reported to account for more than 80 per cent of total emissions (NMSA, 2001). In addition, Ethiopia relies heavily on hydro-electricity, which is susceptible to rainfall patterns. There are already cases where the GDP of the country has been affected due to severe drought periods, such as in 2002 and 2003. Hence, the need to diversify away from hydropower and use other low carbon energy options is important. Solar energy could be a suitable alternative as the country has high solar radiation potential (5.20 kWh/m^2) particularly in the northern parts, as well as having abundant wind and geothermal energy resources in the Rift Valley Zone. Hence, low carbon development could be an opportunity for Ethiopia to increase energy security and energy access, promote environmental sustainability and contribute to poverty reduction and economic growth (Ting and Lakew, 2011; Urban *et al.*, 2011).

   To understand low carbon development approaches in Ethiopia and to understand whether they will help the country to overcome poverty and achieve development in the future, it is important to assess both the opportunities and the barriers, as well as the motives or driving forces and the trade-offs of low carbon development. This is presented in the sections below.

Opportunities for low carbon development in Ethiopia

This section first discusses the opportunities to promote fair and equitable low carbon development in Ethiopia, followed by a discussion about its barriers in the next section. The opportunities show the ambitions of the government of Ethiopia to promote fair and equitable low carbon development to increase poverty reduction and economic growth, energy access and energy security as well as environmental sustainability.

Ethiopia has a set of low carbon development policies and initiatives in place, which are mostly linked to poverty reduction and low carbon growth. Ethiopia's Sustainable Development and Poverty Reduction Programme (SDPRP) for the period of 2002 to 2005 envisaged the country's growth via accelerating private sector activity, maintaining rural growth throughout, and subsequently creating employment and income as well as strengthening public institutions to deliver services. The SDPRP has specific indicators that are directly linked to the MDGs. The most relevant targets of the programme for low carbon development are linked to energy access, food security, poverty reduction and reducing social inequality (PASDEP II, 2009; Ting and Lakew, 2011; Urban *et al.*, 2011).

In 2001 the Ministry of Water Resources (MWR) published its initial communication on climate change to the UNFCCC. In this report it was clearly stated that Ethiopia's global contribution to GHG emissions is negligible. However, the country is concerned with environmental sustainability both in the context of the global and national situation. The dual benefits between sustainable economic development and climate change mitigation were therefore acknowledged. Key sectors identified by the government for low carbon development are the energy, land use, forestry, agriculture and waste sectors.

The following low carbon development plans and initiatives were reported to the UNFCCC (NMSA, 2001):

- Promotion of renewable energy, particularly hydro, solar, wind, biomass and geothermal energy, with the benefit of increasing energy access for the population. This could be a substantial benefit for the Ethiopian people as only 5 per cent of the rural population currently has access to electricity (CSA, 2012) and 15 per cent of the total population. Renewable energy can operate as on-grid, off-grid or mini-grid systems to supply the population with electricity for lighting, cooking, heating, charging mobile phones, refrigeration, etc. It can replace the predominant use of traditional biofuels such as fuel wood and agricultural residues by cleaner, less polluting, more efficient and easier to handle modern energy and thereby also reduce negative side-effects such as indoor air pollution and associated health impacts (see Chapter 9).
- Improving and promoting energy efficiency through large-scale dissemination of improved biomass and charcoal stoves.
- Promoting the use of fuels with low carbon content, such as gasohol (a blend of gasoline with ethanol).
- Improving forest management practices, protection/preservation of existing forests from deforestation and initiating new afforestation and reforestation programmes.
- Increased livestock productivity through improved nutrition, promoting the use of manure management system facilities, and improvement of livestock management.
- Integrated waste management systems (Ting and Lakew, 2011; Urban *et al.*, 2011).

These objectives can be directly linked to other strategies of the government, such as the 2007 Biofuel Development and Utilisation Strategy of Ethiopia, the Plan for Accelerated and Sustained Development to End Poverty (PASDEP I) for 2005–2010 and the Growth and Transformation Plan (GTP and PASDEP II) for 2011–2015. The overall objective of the Growth and Transformation Plan is achieving rapid and equitable economic growth in order to eradicate poverty (MoFED, 2010; Ting and Lakew, 2011). Environment and climate change considerations are a part of the Growth and Transformation Plan. Ethiopia plans to build a low carbon and climate resilient economy by addressing adaptation to climate change and mitigation of GHG emissions. Emission reduction is not a central concern due to the country's marginal emissions, but rather a benefit that comes with the introduction of renewable energy options for increasing energy access. Thus, the central priority for the country is economic development and poverty reduction. However, the effects of climate change are understood to limit these ambitions if not properly managed and low carbon development is only possible if access to financing and low carbon technologies is available (Ting and Lakew, 2011; Urban *et al.*, 2011,).

In line with these objectives, Ethiopia has issued the Climate Resilient Green Economy Plan (CRGE) in late 2011, which is in line with Ethiopia's NAMAs and focuses on low carbon agriculture through improved land use management and livestock management; low carbon energy supply, particularly hydropower; a bill for a feed-in tariff for renewable electricity, which is to be passed as legislation at a later stage; rolling out improved cooking stoves for households; low carbon buildings; participating in REDD+; low carbon transport, particularly biofuels, the introduction of mass transport in urban areas such as Addis Ababa, the construction of national railways for freight and passenger transportation and introducing a lower carbon industry, particularly for cement manufacturing (GGGI, 2010, Lockwood and Urban, 2012).

Barriers to low carbon development implementation in Ethiopia

The section above discussed the opportunities for low carbon development in Ethiopia, while this section discusses the barriers to low carbon development. The barriers show where current gaps are and where improvements need to be made in the future to implement low carbon development.

Barriers to low carbon development in Ethiopia are reported to be a lack of appropriate regulatory frameworks and incentives as well as a high level of bureaucracy. This is particularly a challenge for the private sector. However, there is strong political will as low carbon development is driven by the government in Ethiopia.

Interviewees mentioned that the current approach to low carbon development is centralized, top-down and predominantly government-led. A positive step forward is the introduction of a bill for a feed-in-tariff for renewable energy, which could become legislation in the future. This could stimulate long-term financial stability for investors and increase the share of renewable energy in the energy portfolio.

The main policy consideration in relation to scaling up low carbon development is to mainstream low carbon development into national development plans to incorporate it in the wider context of poverty reduction and economic growth. Scaling up low carbon development in Ethiopia will require increased participation from government, businesses and NGOs, and requires capacity building, as well as further access to low carbon technologies and funding, such as from donors. A key issue here is the high upfront costs for renewable energy due to high installation costs, whereas the operation and maintenance costs will be lower than for conventional energy. However, higher upfront costs might result in higher taxes or energy costs for citizens, which might hit the poorest the hardest (Ting and Lakew, 2011; Urban *et al.*, 2011).

Actors that drive low carbon development in Ethiopia and their reasons for pursuing the low carbon development agenda

After discussing the opportunities and barriers to low carbon development in Ethiopia, this section discusses who is actually driving low carbon development, followed by a brief discussion about the key motives for low carbon development. Both the actors and the motives are important for understanding why a low income country like Ethiopia is interested in low carbon development and who pushes this agenda forward.

Government

Ethiopia is a centralist state; hence the government plays an important role in planning and implementing low carbon development. In Ethiopia, the government has the role to formulate low carbon policies, create an enabling environment, mainstream low carbon development into development programmes and engage other actors such as the business sector. The government and its State-Owned Enterprises (SOEs) are further often the main investor and contractor for large infrastructure projects, such as large hydropower plants, nevertheless it has to be acknowledged that in recent years the occurrence of foreign investors – notably the Chinese – has increased. Key government ministries involved with planning and implementing low carbon development in Ethiopia are the Ministry of Transport (MOT), Ministry of Water and Energy (MWE), Ministry of Industry (MOI), Ministry of Agriculture (MOA) and the Environmental Protection Authority (EPA).

Foreign government organizations, such as donors, have advisory roles at a strategic level. In consultation with the government of Ethiopia they support low carbon development programmes. Key donors driving forward low carbon development in Ethiopia include DfID, Deutsche Gesellschaft für Internationale Zusammenarbeit (GIZ), UNDP, United Nations Economic Commission for Africa (UNECA), the Norwegian government and the South Korean government. They are playing a high-level advisory role showing their commitment to supporting low carbon development in Ethiopia (Ting and Lakew, 2011; Urban *et al.*, 2011).

In terms of the motives that drive low carbon development, empirical research reveals that the main concern for pursuing low carbon development among national and foreign government organizations is economic growth, followed by concern about poverty reduction. Energy security and particularly climate change mitigation are motives that are reported to be of less concern.

Private sector

Ultimately, it is the private sector that plays the key role in low carbon technology development and deployment, particularly in the energy sector, industries, transport and waste management. Hence, the private sector is important for low carbon development and in Ethiopia firms of all sizes play a role. It is the role of businesses and industry to implement low carbon development, for example by developing and deploying renewable energy technologies, provided there is an enabling environment to operate in. This is especially the case in relation to regulations and practices such as the proposed feed-in tariff and subsidies for renewable energy. Key industries relevant for the private sector are energy, forestry and agriculture (Ting and Lakew, 2011; Urban *et al.*, 2011).

In terms of the motives that drive low carbon development, the empirical research reveals that the main concerns for pursuing low carbon development among the private sector are economic growth and energy security, followed by concern about poverty reduction. Climate change mitigation is considered a motive that is of marginal concern.

Civil society

NGOs and civil society organizations, such as research organizations and charities, aim to raise awareness and information about climate change and low carbon development issues, contribute to capacity building, provide technical and financial support and fill gaps in implementation that are not being addressed by the private sector.

In addition, research organizations and academia also play a role by conducting research and teaching in the field of low carbon development. Also of importance is the R&D of low carbon technologies by technical universities and research centres (Ting and Lakew, 2011; Urban *et al.*, 2011,).

In terms of the motives that drive low carbon development, the empirical research reveals that the main concerns for pursuing low carbon development among NGOs are poverty reduction, economic growth and energy security. Similar to government agencies and the private sector, climate change mitigation is considered a marginal concern.

What is driving the low carbon development agenda? A reflection about the motives of key actors in Ethiopia

To summarize the information on why different actors pursue low carbon development, it can be concluded that economic growth and poverty reduction play a central role in driving the low carbon development agenda in Ethiopia. Energy security was mentioned as another important motive, as well as climate change mitigation, which was reported, but only as a marginal motive. Some NGOs further report that the low carbon development agenda is an important tool for accessing finance for development from bilateral and multilateral donors. This could be an indication that to some extent the low carbon development agenda is praised and required by donors in Ethiopia and therefore pushed by NGOs and government organizations to obtain funding for wider development activities. Other key motives for pursuing low carbon development are wider development priorities and concerns about social justice. This raises the question of how much the LCD agenda is driven by national government goals and priorities and how much by external pressure from donors. This raises further questions about who benefits from low carbon development and for whom it is being implemented.

There is a distinction between different types of respondents and their perceived motives for driving low carbon development. Representatives of the Ethiopian government and foreign governments that act as donors consider poverty reduction and economic growth as the key drivers of low carbon development. NGOs and the private sector consider poverty reduction and economic growth as well as energy security as three important drivers of low carbon development. However, all respondent groups agree that climate change mitigation is only a marginal concern due to the country's marginal emissions.

Hence, in sum, Ethiopia's approach to low carbon development is driven particularly by considerations about poverty reduction and economic growth, which links into development priorities and concerns about social justice (Ting and Lakew, 2011; Urban *et al.*, 2011).

After elaborating the opportunities and barriers for low carbon development, as well as the key actors and a brief discussion about what drives the low carbon development agenda in Ethiopia, Box 16.2 raises a critique of low carbon development in Ethiopia, with particular emphasis on the trade-offs of low carbon development.

Box 16.2 Critique: the trade-offs of low carbon development in Ethiopia

There are several major trade-offs in relation to low carbon development in Ethiopia. First, the agriculture sector contributes to almost half of Ethiopia's GDP (World Bank, 2012), but it is also the largest contributor of Ethiopia's GHG emissions. The concern is that a reduction of emissions from the agricultural sector might reduce the economic growth generated from the sector and thereby harm development efforts. Agricultural efficiency is also anticipated to be achieved through promotion of large-scale commercial farms, which might have negative impacts in terms of decreasing biodiversity and threatening livelihoods of rural communities that depend on agriculture for a living and cannot afford price competition with large farms. Hence, there is a risk that large industrial farms might be benefitting from low carbon development at the expense of smaller scale farms, which are often owned and operated by relatively poor people who are struggling to make a living.

Second, poverty reduction needs to be at the heart of low carbon development. New fiscal policies need to take into account the needs and priorities of the country's poor. High initial investment in low carbon development sectors might reduce some of the funding available for and needed in other key development sectors, such as education and health. Investments in education and health usually benefit the poor and vulnerable, such as children and women. It would be a shame if low carbon development were to result in reduced funding for these core development sectors. In addition, the costs for high investments in low carbon development sectors, such as in the energy or transport sectors, might be passed on to consumers and citizens. This might mean that citizens and customers might have to pay a higher price in terms of taxes and/or consumer prices. This may have a disproportionate effect on the poor who are already disadvantaged.

Third, a major trade-off is in relation to land development for biofuel production at the expense of land development for food production. As mentioned in Chapter 1, this problem is aggravated as some biofuel crops, such as sweet potato or cassava, are also food crops (Rathmann *et al.*, 2010; Murphy *et al.*, 2011). At the same time, there are allegations that some biofuel operations, including by wealthy corporations, have evicted poor people in developing countries from their lands to gain access to land for growing biofuels. Hence some biofuel developments are reported to be associated with so-called land grabs (Neville and Dauvergne, 2012; Oxfam, 2012). Food security and adequate land resources for food production are therefore crucial factors that need to be safeguarded in Ethiopia and that need to be prioritized over foreign and domestic investments in land for biofuels.

Fourth, another trade-off is in relation to expanding hydropower and thereby increasing the vulnerability to climatic changes in the water sector. Ethiopia, and particularly the capital Addis Ababa, is already experiencing periodic electricity shortages due to water shortages. An increased reliance on hydropower is likely to increase the likelihood of climate-related power cuts, which can cause economic damage. Other energy options, such as wind, solar and geothermal energy, should therefore be promoted and over-reliance on hydropower should be reduced.

To conclude the critique, it is crucial to ensure that low carbon development efforts in

Ethiopia are in line with wider development goals related to poverty reduction, economic growth and social justice. New policies and programmes need to make sure that the poor and vulnerable are not disproportionally affected and that long-term development is sustainable. For the agricultural sector and the overall economy, it needs to be ensured that Ethiopia achieves economic growth and development first and worries about mitigating its emissions at a much later, more developed stage.

Conclusion

This chapter aimed to assess how fair and equitable low carbon development can be achieved today in a low income country such as Ethiopia and what the drivers and motives of low carbon development are. The chapter elaborated the context for low carbon development and the key policies and initiatives in place in Ethiopia. It briefly discussed the role of different actors from governments, business and civil society and their motives for driving low carbon development initiatives in Ethiopia.

Ethiopia has been chosen for this empirical case study on low carbon development as a low income country with very low carbon emissions and high vulnerability to climate change; nevertheless its government actively strives for low carbon development to achieve development benefits. Only a small number of low income countries are striving for low carbon development. Enabling fair and equitable low carbon development in Ethiopia that is based on economic growth and development could therefore make it an example for other low income countries, particularly in Africa. Let's however not forget that the country is already a low carbon society and has had low carbon development for centuries, however involuntarily. Low carbon development activities and policies today therefore need to ensure that the country will be better off in the future and that it will tap into the benefits that low carbon technologies and finance can bring, such as in relation to energy access.

The low carbon development concept is still relatively new to Ethiopia; hence experience with its implementation is only slowly developing. Low carbon development in Ethiopia is mostly driven by the centralist government agencies, thus a top-down approach dominates. In addition, the government is encouraged by donors to pursue a low carbon policy. The engagement of the business sector is still limited, as an enabling environment is still under development. However, the creation of a draft bill for a feed-in tariff for the renewable energy sector might encourage energy firms to invest in low carbon energy. Nevertheless it is important to get access to financial and technological assistance from developed countries in order to pursue low carbon development in Ethiopia. In addition, the government needs to carefully assess the trade-offs of low carbon development in Ethiopia and needs to ensure that low carbon development does not happen at the expense of development, economic growth, poverty reduction and social justice efforts.

The following conclusions have arisen from this chapter: (i) it is advisable to mainstream low carbon development into development policy to ensure it is in line with development needs and poverty reduction efforts; (ii) it is recommended to reduce the trade-offs of low carbon development by promoting those activities that can create opportunities and benefits, particularly for the poor, such as access to off-grid renewable energy, and to restrict other activities that are harmful, such as land development for biofuel production at the expense of food production; (iii) it is advisable to create financial and policy incentives that can foster an enabling environment for firms and stimulate investment in low carbon activities by domestic and foreign investors; and (4) investment in capacity-building is needed to further develop the technical, institutional and financial capacity for low carbon development in Ethiopia. This will need the sustained support of donors for accessing funding and technologies (Urban *et al.*, 2011).

There is a lot to be gained from low carbon development in Ethiopia, however, it needs to be ensured that low carbon development is in line with the country's national development priorities and contributes to poverty reduction, human development, social justice and equitable economic growth.

References

Central Statistical Agency of Ethiopia (CSA) (2012) Welfare monitoring survey, April 27, 2012. Available at: http://www.csa.gov.et/nada3/index.php/catalog (accessed 15 November 2012).

Ethiopian Environmental Protection Authority (EPA) (2011) REDD readiness – Ethiopia, paper presented at Forest Carbon Partnership Facility (FCPF), PC8 meeting. Available at: http://www.forestcarbonpartnership.org/fcp/sites/forestcarbonpartnership.org/files/Documents/PDF/Jan2012/R-PP%20Ethiopia-final%20May%2025-2011.pdf (accessed 16 November 2012)

Global Development and Environment Institute (GDAE) (2011) Encyclopaedia of the earth. Definition of economic growth. Available at: http://www.eoearth.org/article/Economic_growth (accessed 15 November 2012).

Global Green Growth Institute (GGGI) (2011) National Green Growth Plan for Ethiopia. Available at: http://www.gggi.org/opportunity/2011/05/25/ethiopia (accessed 15 November 2012).

Government of Ethiopia (2011) Ethiopia's climate resilient green economy strategy, Addis Ababa. Available at: www.epa.gov.et/Download/Climate/Ethiopia%27s%20Climate-Resilient%20Green%20economy%20strategy.pdf (accessed 15 November 2012).

ICT4D (2011) Definition of poverty alleviation. Available at: http://www.caricomict4d.org/ict-for-development-topics-mainmenu-132/poverty-alleviation-mainmenu-190/68-definition-of-poverty-alleviation.html (accessed 15 November 2012).

International Energy Agency (IEA) (2010) *Energy Technology Perspectives 2010*. Paris: IEA/OECD.

IEA (2012) Energy statistics for Ethiopia. Available at: http://www.iea.org/stats/index.asp (accessed 15 November 2012).

IEA/OECD (2009) Linking mitigation actions in developing countries with mitigation support: a conceptual framework. Available at: http://www.oecd.org/dataoecd/27/24/42474721.pdf (accessed 15 November 2012).

Intergovernmental Panel on Climate Change (IPCC) (2007) Fourth Assessment Report on Climate Change. Available at: http://www.ipcc.ch/ipccreports/assessments-reports.htm (accessed 15 November 2012).

Lockwood, M. and Urban, F. (2012) Low carbon development in low and middle income countries. Summary for the DFID Learning Hub on Adaptation and Low Carbon Development. Brighton: IDS.

Ministry of Finance and Economic Development (MoFED) (2010) Growth and transformation plan, 2010/11–2014/15, Volume 1. Addis Ababa: MoFED.

Murphy, R., Woods, J., Black, M. and McManus, M. (2011) Global developments in the competition for land and biofuels. *Food Policy*, 36(1), 52–61.

National Meteorological Services Agency (NMSA) (2001) Initial communication of Ethiopia to the United Nations Framework Convention on Climate Change (UNFCCC). Addis Ababa: MWR (Ministry of Water Resources).

Neville, K. J. and Dauvergne, P. (2012) Biofuels and the politics of mapmaking. *Political Geography*, 31(5), 279–89.

Oxfam (2012) Land grabs. Available at: http://www.oxfam.org.nz/what-we-do/issues/grow/land-grabs (accessed 15 November 2012).

Plan for Accelerated and Sustained Development to End Poverty (PASDEP II) (2009) Industrial policy direction of Ethiopia: Suggestions for PASDEP II and the next five years, Presented at the GRIPS Forum, Addis Ababa. Available at: http://www.grips.ac.jp/forum/af-growth/ support_ethiopia/document/Nov09doc-direction6.pdf (accessed 16 November 2012)

Rathmann, R., Szklo, A. and Schaeffer, R. (2010) Land use competition for production of food and liquid biofuels: an analysis of the arguments in the current debate. *Renewable Energy*, 35(1), 14–22.

Ting, M. B. and Lakew, H. (2011) Literature review report – low carbon development in Ethiopia. Report for the DFID Learning Hub on Adaptation and Low Carbon Development. Brighton: IDS.

United Nations Environment Programme (UNEP) (2010) Climate Neutral Network: Ethiopia. Available at: http://www.unep.org/climateneutral/Default.aspx?tabid=804 (accessed 15 November 2012).

United Nations Framework Convention on Climate Change (UNFCCC) (2010) Ethiopia's NAMAs. Available at: http://unfccc.int/files/meetings/application/pdf/ethiopiacphaccord_app2.pdf (accessed 15 November 2012).

Urban, F., Watt, R., Ting, M. B., Crawford, G., Wang, Y., Lakew, H. *et al.* (2011) Achieving low carbon development in low and middle income countries – the role of governments, business and civil society. IDS Project Report for the DFID Learning Hub on Adaptation and Low Carbon Development. Brighton: IDS.

World Bank (2012) Data about Ethiopia. Available at: http://data.worldbank.org/ (accessed 15 November 2012).

World Resources Institute (WRI) (2005) Navigating the numbers: greenhouse gas data and international climate policy. Chapter on cumulative emissions. Available at: http://pdf.wri.org/navigating_numbers_chapter6.pdf (accessed 15 November 2012).

Further reading

Government of Ethiopia (2011) Ethiopia's climate resilient green economy strategy, Addis Ababa. Available at: www.epa.gov.et/Download/Climate/Ethiopia%27s%20Climate-Resilient%20Green%20economy%20strategy.pdf (accessed 15 November 2012).

17 Low carbon development in Tanzania

Lessons from its solar home system market

Rob Byrne

This chapter discusses approaches to low carbon development in the low income country Tanzania, with a specific case study from the solar energy sector. Despite multiple efforts over two decades in Tanzania to apply a solar home system (SHS) diffusion 'model' generated in Kenya, it is only in recent years that a Tanzanian SHS market has begun to grow. This chapter attempts to explain the years of failure and this recent success. With international attention increasingly focused on deploying billions of dollars of low carbon technologies in the developing world, there could be important lessons from experiences such as those in the Tanzanian SHS market. So, after analysing the evolution of this market, the chapter highlights lessons for low carbon development more generally.

Introduction

Energy access – including rural electrification – is crucial for development and has been a long-standing objective in developing countries. This is based on the understanding that it can help deliver many benefits, including 'improvements in health, education, and opportunities for entrepreneurship' (Dubash, 2002: 2). For decades, the assumption and practice has been to build centralized generating capacity and transmit the electricity over national grids (Goldemburg *et al.*, 2000: 375). However, despite years of effort, only a small percentage of the rural populations of many developing countries has access to electricity. More recently, photovoltaic (PV) technology has been promoted as a way to achieve widespread rural electrification and pursue low carbon development. Because it is low carbon, PV is aligned with sustainability objectives. Furthermore, PV systems are modular, which is attractive for at least two reasons. First, it is amenable to rural application where power needs are generally small – particularly in households – and grids are weak or non-existent. Second, it is suitable for distribution through retail systems and so aligns with market-based approaches to development. Market-based development approaches – such as the Bottom of the Pyramid[1] (Prahalad and Hammond, 2002) – could provide 'triple win' solutions: the poor gain access to services; private firms increase profits; and society achieves cheaper development than through public sector interventions.

Tanzania has been selected as a case study because it is a low income country and suffers from typical problems such as low electrification rates and restricted energy access. The country has also been selected because there have been efforts to introduce solar energy in Tanzania for decades. Recently, these efforts have resulted in some success, as will be elaborated in this case study. Tanzania could therefore be an example for other low income countries that aim to increase their share of low carbon energy in order to gain development benefits.

Attempts to achieve household rural electrification with household-scale PV systems, or SHSs, have been made in Tanzania since the early 1990s (Byrne, 2011). Much of the early effort was inspired by the success of SHS market growth in Kenya. A model of the Kenyan approach was transferred to Tanzania in the early 1990s but did not appear to work. However, beginning in the early 2000s, the Tanzanian market for SHSs began to grow rapidly. This could be evidence of private sector-led low carbon development. If so, there could be lessons from this experience that translate to other low income countries, and for international policy instruments that seek to increase the diffusion of low carbon technologies via private markets.

This chapter applies a strategic niche management (SNM) conceptual framework to the case of the PV market in Tanzania in order to investigate how the market developed. The main finding is that it was not a simple story of private sector-led development. There was considerable effort by different kinds of actors over many years that generated rich learning about the Tanzanian context. This was shared through increasingly integrated networks of actors sympathetic to the diffusion of PV. Much of this effort took place before the market began to grow, preparing the ground for the later entry of private sector actors. Even then, complementary efforts between private and public sector actors have been important for the continued development of the market. This has implications for the roles that different kinds of actors can play in achieving low carbon development goals and raises questions about international policy instruments that rely on market approaches. Box 17.1 discusses key issues in low carbon technology deployment.

Box 17.1 Key issues in low carbon technology deployment

How to increase the diffusion of low carbon energy technologies in developing countries has become an increasingly important and politically contested issue. International forums, such as the UNFCCC, have seen the issue come close to derailing negotiations, particularly in regard to financing low carbon technologies (Ockwell *et al.*, 2008). Nevertheless, the UNFCCC continues to develop its approach to low carbon 'technology transfer', and international agreement was reached at the Cancún COP on establishing a Technology Mechanism, which was progressed further during the Durban COP in 2011 (UNFCCC, 2012). Part of the mechanism will be a Climate Technology Centre and Network (CTC&N), where the Centre is to be hosted by a consortium led by the UN Environment Programme. In parallel with the UNFCCC approach, DfID, the World Bank infoDev and others are supporting the establishment of Climate Innovation Centres (CICs), the first of which is due to begin operation in Kenya (Njeru, 2012).

There was also progress at the Durban COP on establishing a Green Climate Fund (GCF), although it is not yet operational and how it will link to the Technology Mechanism is not yet decided (UNFCCC, 2012). The GCF would add to a number of finance instruments that aim to assist low carbon technology deployment: the Global Environment Facility, CDM, several Climate Investment Funds, and a long list of bilateral initiatives (see Nakhooda *et al.*, 2011). Estimates for the amount of finance needed to meet the climate challenge in developing countries vary considerably – Stern (2006), for example, gives a range of US$350–400 billion per year – but a large part of it is expected to flow from private sources.

Whatever the levels of finance actually needed, and whatever the precise form of the Technology Mechanism and other initiatives, it is clear from these high stakes that low carbon technology diffusion in developing countries will continue to be a highly political issue. Therefore, understanding how low carbon technologies can be successfully and sustainably diffused, and how they can contribute to development, is critical if the momentum of recent COPs is to be maintained and the engagement of private finance sources is to be secured.

After a brief account of the SNM framework in the next section, the chapter continues with an analytical narrative of the case. The implications of the analysis for low carbon development policy are then discussed in the conclusion.

Conceptual framework

According to the SNM framework, new or novel technologies and practices emerge from experimentation in real settings. Within these spaces, interested actors help to protect new approaches from constraints such as economic viability (Raven, 2005). Experimentation generates learning, builds networks of sympathetic actors and embeds novel socio-technical configurations[2] into the mainstream. SNM refers to such protected spaces as *niches*, while the mainstream consists of *regimes* and the broader context is referred to as the *landscape*. Niches, regimes and landscape are related hierarchically (see Figure 17.1) in a multi-level perspective (MLP) (Geels, 2002). When analysing the evolution of a novel socio-technical configuration, SNM directs us to investigate various interacting processes identified from technological experiments in a social context. These can be summarized as: the quality of learning; the composition and quality of social networks; the evolution of collective socio-technical expectations and visions; and processes of institutionalization (see Box 17.2 for elaboration of these concepts).

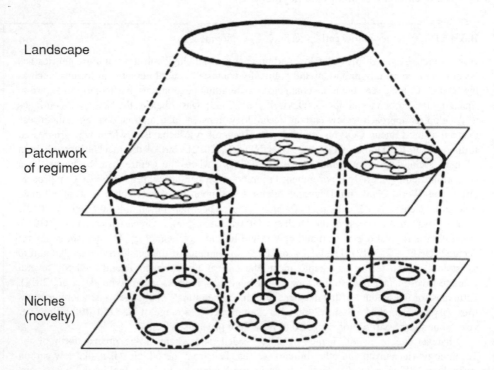

Figure 17.1 The multi-level perspective
Source: Geels, 2002: 1261[3]

Box 17.2 Key strategic niche management (SNM) concepts

Learning

Learning is conceptualized in first- and second-order forms within SNM. First-order learning arises when technologies are tested in practical settings. It is instrumental learning, concerned with the functioning of technologies, not with the assumptions on which their use rests. In contrast, second-order learning arises 'when conceptions about technology, user demands, and regulations are... questioned and explored' (Hoogma *et al.*, 2002: 194).

Actor-networks

Networks of actors are important for attracting resources to experiments, building constituencies of support, and providing multiple sites for experiments from which lessons can be drawn and translated to other contexts (Raven, 2005). Broad networks are more helpful for novel technologies than networks of mainstream actors, who may be more interested in maintaining the status quo (Hoogma *et al.*, 2002).

Expectations and visions

Socio-technical expectations and visions are descriptions of future states of the world in which particular socio-technical configurations perform better than others (Berkhout, 2006). When expectations and visions are shared they guide activity in particular directions – socio-technical trajectories (Geels and Raven, 2006).

Institutionalization

Institutionalization is the process of embedding practices into the routines of actors – whether users or producers, policy-makers and others – and the creation of relevant policies, laws, regulations, etc. (Deuten *et al.*, 1997; Raven, 2005).

Methodology

Following Byrne (2011), a socio-technical expectation is taken here to be a 'target' towards which actors align their activities, while a socio-technical vision specifies the means to achieve the expectation and defines the expectation in greater detail. First-order learning is generated when actors pursue a particular expectation. They hold assumptions that guide their learning, which fills in detail to develop a vision. Second-order learning results in a change to assumptions and a new direction; a new expectation, and new first-order learning to envision it. Figure 17.2 shows these ideas. Actors initially work towards Expectation 1, making progress through first-order learning. Second-order learning changes their assumptions, resulting in Expectation 2. So, first-order learning is recognized when there is activity detailing a particular trajectory; second-order learning is recognized by a change in that trajectory.

Field research was conducted in East Africa from July 2007 to July 2008, supplemented by later interviews in Europe. The research included semi-structured interviews with a wide range of actors involved in PV activities, and the use of various documentary materials.

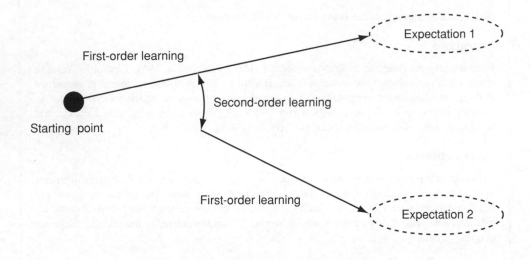

Figure 17.2 Representation of first and second-order learning, and expectations and visions
Source: Byrne, 2011: 37

Case study of PV in Tanzania

This section provides an analytical narrative of the Tanzanian case and draws substantially on Byrne (2011). Here, we examine some of the more relevant aspects of the case to our interest in low carbon development. We begin with a brief account of the Tanzanian context post-independence and the arrival of PV systems into the country. The bulk of the section then focuses on the PV niche during the period from 1992 to the late 2000s.

Post-independence Tanzania

Tanzania achieved independence from Britain in 1961 and, after a short period of pursuing an 'industrialisation by invitation' policy,[4] entered into an African socialist experiment advocated by its president Julius Nyerere in the Arusha Declaration in 1967 (Oman and Wignaraja, 1991). By the end of the 1970s, Tanzania was experiencing political and economic decay (Barkan, 1994), exacerbated by the crippling drain on resources of its unwilling occupation of Uganda following the ousting of Idi Amin (Gordon, 1994). Struggles with the Bretton Woods institutions over financial assistance ensued. In 1985, Nyerere retired and his successor signed an agreement with the International Monetary Fund. The economy began to recover but social programmes were severely damaged (Barkan, 1994). After the ending of the Cold War, the international pressure for political change mounted. Tanzania became a multi-party democracy in 1993 (Gordon, 1994), and has gradually liberalized its economy since.

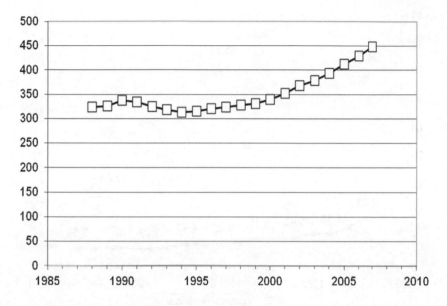

Figure 17.3 Tanzanian GDP per capita 1988–2007 in 2010 US$
Source: African Development Indicators, 2009

However, it remains one of the poorest countries in the world (see Figure 17.3 for GDP per capita) and relies heavily on agriculture for employment (Mueller, 2011). Its electrification rate is estimated to be 14 per cent on average (USDOC, 2011) but much lower in rural areas.

PV technology comes to East Africa

During the late 1970s, PV systems were introduced to Tanzania for powering telecommunications equipment (Mwihava and Towo, 1994) and other applications such as lighting for remote railway stations (Sawe, 1989). In the early 1980s, donors began to fund community-service systems such as for clinics (Roberts and Ratajczak, 1989) and PV-powered vaccine refrigerators (McNelis *et al.*, 1988), while other applications such as community-scale water pumping were also tried (Sawe, 1989). These stimulated a local 'project market' that remains important today (ESD, 2003). An earlier interest in using PV in villages was explored at a workshop in Dar es Salaam in 1977 (UTAFITI, 1978) but little immediate action came of these discussions. The Ministry of Water and Energy later developed some interest in PV (URT, 1992) but never secured resources to implement projects (Sawe, 2008). Certainly, PV systems were expensive, as can be seen from Figure 17.4, which compares international shipped prices of PV modules with some reported prices of systems in Tanzania[5] over the period 1992 to 2008. In any case, the more pressing concern during the 1980s was the issue of wood supply for household energy use (Nkonoki, 1983). Nevertheless, a few international companies set up offices in Dar es Salaam to service the PV project market (Sawe, 1989). Only British Petroleum (BP) expanded (cautiously) beyond this market (Mwihava and

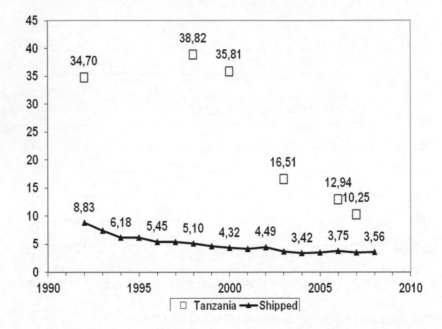

Figure 17.4 International shipped PV prices per watt-peak (Wp) and selected Tanzanian system
prices 1992–2008, 2010 US$

Source: Tanzania: (date, source, system size in Wp) 1992: Kasaizi and Hankins, 1992: 25, 10 Wp system; 1998:
Hifab-TaTEDO, 1998: 54, 50 Wp system; 2003: ESD, 2003: 13, 50 Wp system; 2006, 2007: Felten, 2008b,
average price; Shipped: EIA, 2010, converted to 2010 US$, excluding taxes

Towo, 1994). Outside Dar es Salaam there were very few companies active in PV, and only
occasional PV activities in Tanzania up to the early 1990s.

Birth of a niche: transferring a model from Kenya

A significant event in the development of the PV niche in Tanzania was a 1992 workshop
held in Nairobi and Meru in Kenya (Kimani, 1992). It brought together participants from 10
African countries for an intensive period of practical PV training. Two PV pioneers in the
rapidly growing Kenyan SHS market organized the workshop to disseminate more widely
their knowledge of how this market had developed (Byrne, 2011). The socio-technical vision
they held was one in which they would train a number of technicians in PV using a mix of
classroom-based theory and practical installation over an intensive two-week period.
Following the training, the technicians would then exploit their new skills through entrepreneurial activity that would see a PV market develop. This had worked in Kenya and so they
assumed it would work elsewhere.

An immediate outcome of the 1992 workshop was a project in Tanzania to develop such
a training model at the Karagwe Development Association[6] (KARADEA). The Solar
Enterprise Centre proposed would encompass a set of activities: a solar business; training
courses; development of affordable small systems; installation of demonstration business PV
systems; and a credit scheme (Kasaizi and Hankins, 1992). Despite the project proposers'

common vision for market development, the donors were unconvinced and so funded only the training. The resulting KARADEA Solar Training Facility (KSTF) continued to host training courses in Tanzania up to 2004 (KSTF, 2009). In the process, the implicit expectation-vision that formed was of rural electrification by PV to be achieved via a private market (Byrne, 2011). Many actors, who later became influential in the Tanzanian PV niche, received their training at KSTF where they adopted this expectation-vision and attempted to realize it in their own activities. However, most Tanzanian trainees were unable to continue PV activities once they had returned home. They had no resources to implement projects, there were no nearby PV suppliers, and there was no awareness of PV that could translate into market demand.

Replicating the model: TaTEDO's PV projects

Similar problems emerged during a PV project started in 1999 by the Tanzania Traditional Energy Development and Environment Organisation (TaTEDO). Funded by Hivos and Norad, the project included networking, training, awareness-raising, demonstration systems and market development (Arkesteijn, 2000). Running until 2002, the project covered the regions of Dar es Salaam, Mwanza and Kilimanjaro (Sanga, 2008); selected because of their poor grid infrastructure, potential for renewable energy use and strength of the local cash economy (Arkesteijn, 2000). After internal capacity-building, the project moved into a training phase that borrowed heavily from the KSTF model (Byrne, 2011). The first course took place in Dar es Salaam in May 2000 at the end of which the Tanzania Solar Energy Association[7] (TASEA) was formed (Arkesteijn, 2000). Although the hope had been that those trained by TaTEDO would include PV activities in their organizations, very few were able to do so (Sanga, 2008). Only those who were already involved in PV prior to the course – mostly from PV retailers – continued after the training. Reflecting on this, TaTEDO experienced a degree of second-order learning that resulted in a shifted – if not fundamentally changed – expectation. For the second round of courses, they targeted those either working in PV companies or who demonstrated promising entrepreneurial energies. This was a more successful approach and was continued in a second project that ran until 2005, building both technical and entrepreneurial capacities.

Despite the activities of KSTF and TaTEDO (and others), the market for SHSs did not grow in Tanzania. Nevertheless, we can identify other outcomes. For example, KSTF trained about 175 technicians (KSTF, 2009), while many others were trained in replica courses elsewhere. As mentioned above, some went on to influential positions in Tanzania's PV niche. TaTEDO's projects – inter-regional and integrated – facilitated network-building in the Tanzanian niche, as well as further collectivizing a particular PV expectation, especially through TASEA (Byrne, 2011). And, the delivery of similar training curricula through KSTF and TaTEDO helped to institutionalize technical practices. Without these activities, the subsequent interventions (see below) would have been much more difficult to implement. By the time these interventions began, there was a burgeoning constituency of support for PV in Tanzania, a number of skilled Tanzanians, knowledge of some of the problems in the Tanzanian PV niche and the first links of a private sector supply chain.

New expectations: Umeme Jua enters the niche

The first of the subsequent interventions followed the development in the late 1990s of a relationship between TaTEDO and the Dutch PV manufacturer Free Energy Europe (FEE).

FEE wanted to sell into Tanzania, having already adopted a positive expectation of PV market development from success in Kenya (Byrne, 2011). In 2000, FEE conducted the first PV actor survey in Tanzania and found that, apart from the network in Dar es Salaam, most PV actors in Tanzania were working in isolation. Nevertheless, the views on what was needed to develop the market were highly convergent. An overwhelming response was the need for a central actor who could coordinate information and knowledge exchange. Beyond this, there seemed to be a lack of awareness of PV; difficulty sourcing equipment; lack of standards; taxes were too high; there was not enough training; and there was no finance (Arkesteijn, 2000).

The study informed FEE's 2002 entry into the Tanzanian market (van der Vleuten, 2008). This became *Umeme Jua* – a joint venture between FEE, TaTEDO and Fredka International (a Tanzanian consultancy). Umeme Jua had intended to distribute their modules through the dealer network of a large player, as they had done in Kenya. However, no such player existed in Tanzania and so Umeme Jua identified dealers individually in the regions in which it decided to operate (van der Linden, 2008). As part of this effort, they commissioned market surveys that also helped to articulate a finer description of market demand (EAA *et al.*, 2002a, b, c, d). Steadily, they built a network of dealers and complemented this with a network of technicians who could service the local demand (van der Linden, 2008). Because of the need to train both dealers and technicians, this was a slow and expensive process that is unlikely to have occurred without the significant funding received from the Dutch government (Arkesteijn, 2009). Initially, Umeme Jua used the KSTF training model. However, they realized this was unsuitable for most retailers and so developed a course that could be delivered in repeated short visits to a shop (van der Linden, 2008). The extensive travel required was burdensome but it generated other benefits, including the building of trust with the retailers by cultivating long-term relationships (Arkesteijn, 2009).

Umeme Jua offered incentives to these dealers to sell more modules, including better terms depending on quantities sold and supported by guaranteed delivery (van der Vleuten, 2008). They also demonstrated systems in public locations and advertised on local radio stations (Arkesteijn, 2009). Furthermore, they made extensive use of marketing provided through the Free Energy Foundation, also funded by the Dutch government (van der Vleuten, 2008). They introduced standard systems that reduced the need for long explanations to customers in shops, as well as simplifying design and supply requirements. And, they experimented with micro-financing. A number of these attempts failed but hire purchase was successful (van der Linden, 2008), although it was only open to those with salaried income and so did not extend PV access to the poor. Eventually, 'the numbers [of modules being sold] began to get interesting' (van der Vleuten, 2008). By 2008, Umeme Jua had an annual turnover of about US$1 million, which was estimated to be 50 per cent of the Tanzanian PV market (Sawe, 2008).

A healthy niche? A collectivized expectation, dense networks and market growth

In 2004, the Global Environment Facility (GEF) funded a project through UNDP in the Mwanza Region (URT-UNDP-GEF, 2003). It suffered a long delay before implementation. However, after it had commissioned a survey that helped to articulate the Mwanza market in finer detail (TaTEDO-Fredka, 2001), the delay afforded Umeme Jua an opportunity to influence its final design (van der Linden, 2008). It concentrated on the Mwanza Region for the first three to four years, and was to be replicated in nearby regions (Musa, 2008). While it had been influenced by the Umeme Jua approach, it was not identical. It donated some systems, which were placed in strategic locations as demonstrations, and experimented with productive uses of PV: powering barber shops, providing mobile phone charging services, and others. Furthermore, it included a policy dimension, which involved the development of PV standards in collaboration with the Tanzania Bureau of Standards. It experimented with micro-finance but, as with Umeme Jua, was unsuccessful (Musa, 2008). Nevertheless, the project did achieve its main goal to expand the PV market significantly in the Mwanza Region.

In 2005, a Sida-funded project in cooperation with the Ministry of Energy and Minerals (MEM) got underway, known as the Sida-MEM project. Like the UNDP-GEF project, it suffered a long delay before implementation (Byrne, 2011). Its final design was based on consultations between the incoming project manager, Jeff Felten, and local PV actors such as Umeme Jua (Felten, 2008a). So, as with the UNDP-GEF project, there was interaction and influence among those implementing projects in Tanzania. Although not identical to the other projects, it shared their multi-dimensional market development approach, and included a policy aspect that successfully saw the removal of taxes on PV equipment (Byrne, 2011). It also supported TASEA, paying for a website, annual solar days in Dar es Salaam and a sector magazine – SunENERGY. In terms of stimulating sales of PV modules, the project was highly successful, surpassing its targets in the first two years of operation. According to Sida-MEM figures, the market grew by 57 per cent between 2006 and 2007 to an estimated 285 kWp (Felten, 2008b). If the average size of a system[8] were 20 Wp this would amount to about 14,000 modules. Also according to Sida-MEM, the price per watt-peak of PV in Tanzania fell from US$12.07 in 2006 to US$9.85 in 2007 (Felton, 2008b).

Summary

From our case study, we can see that the early activities of (mainly) donors were useful to build some capabilities relevant to SHSs and connect together local actors who could form a constituency of support for PV technology. However, apart from the relatively consistent commitment to KSTF, donor support was uncoordinated, fragmentary and unfocused. It was also less than coherent in that the guiding expectation was one of PV for rural electrification, including access for the poor, that could somehow be achieved through a private market. Nevertheless, this provided some practical basis on which to build the PV niche as well as to help identify some of the issues that needed addressing.

The entry of Umeme Jua brought a more coherent expectation, if only because it was much simpler. Envisioning and realizing this expectation still required huge effort but this was supported by donor funds and the commitment of those involved in the joint venture, who already held strong positive expectations about PV in the region. The increasing success of the approach helped to collectivize the expectation beyond Umeme Jua to other projects, and something of a self-reinforcing dynamic began to take hold. Problem-solving thus focused on establishing a SHS market for whomever the customers might be: understanding the needs of supply-side actors, and then connecting together and developing the supply chain; understanding the characteristics of demand and raising it; and connecting supply and demand together. In short, we could refer to these activities as descriptive and connective articulation of the market.

One of the main benefits of articulation was to lower risk. The risks for supply-side actors were lowered by the support of other actors: Umeme Jua (who, in turn, were supported by a donor) and the various donor-funded projects. These included risks associated with stocks of components and the sources of supply, as well as prices. They also included the risks associated with finding the market demand and understanding it. Again, these risks were borne by others – mostly donors – in commissioning market surveys and sharing knowledge gained through activities on the ground. For customers, risks were reduced by articulating and demonstrating for them the functionality of PV and how it could meet their electricity needs, as well as making sales and technical support easily available.

Whether the Tanzanian PV niche will develop further and the market continue to grow are both open questions. However, the extent to which a niche has been established and a market has begun to grow, we can say that the analysis here suggests it has been a long-term and resource-intensive endeavour. Moreover, it has required complementary cooperation between both the public and private sectors – international and national – on the many dimensions of a socio-technical trajectory.

Conclusion

We have examined just one case study of low carbon development in this chapter and done so from a particular analytical perspective. Therefore, we need to be careful about drawing lessons for low carbon development more generally. However, this case reveals some of the complexities involved in market development, raising questions about the dominant approaches to the deployment of low carbon technologies, especially in poorer developing countries. Tanzania could therefore be an example for other low income countries that aim for increasing their share of low carbon energy in order to gain development benefits. The following lessons could be drawn from this case study:

First, our analysis suggests there could be problems with the assumptions behind international instruments that seek to promote low carbon technology transfer and the impact this has on development. Second, even if these assumptions were robust where low carbon electrical services are concerned, it is unclear whether they translate to other low carbon energy services. Third, we need to examine whether these dominant approaches are likely to address the needs of the poor, given the emphasis on private sector-led development and all this entails in terms of market demand. And, finally, if we accept the concerns raised in the preceding issues, how do we make progress? Let us explore each of these in turn.

Market and energy system complexities

The case shows the considerable amount of effort involved in developing a market for SHSs; effort over two to three decades. This reflects the complex nature of markets, something that is not so apparent when markets already function in some sense efficiently. In Tanzania, the case demonstrates that an assumption of functioning market systems is unsafe. This is partly attributable to Tanzania's relatively recent emergence from its socialist experiment. There is a weak business culture and many market institutions are still in development. It is likely that many poor developing countries face similar problems, even if they have had more experience with market economies.

Translating to other low carbon energy services

Electricity is in high demand and there are few ways to provide it in the household, particularly in rural areas. Nevertheless, the effort involved in Tanzania to establish some kind of market in PV systems was extensive. If we consider other energy services, there are serious questions as to whether it would be possible to persuade people to change to low carbon technologies. Cooking, for example, is easy to do by burning biomass using simple and cheap technologies. There are likely to be difficult challenges in developing markets for more expensive ways to realize such services.

Addressing the needs of the poor

A simple observation about markets is that they cannot exist without expressed demand. So, people must be able to translate their needs and desires into demand by spending money. For the poor, this is extremely difficult. SHSs in Tanzania are not being bought by the poor and micro-finance experiments have so far failed to provide them with access. The one finance instrument for SHSs that has succeeded in Tanzania has been hire purchase; something only available to salaried employees, not to the poor. If finance is going to work for the poor then there is still a great deal of learning needed to understand how it can be achieved.

How do we make progress?

Our case suggests that the particular expectation adopted by actors guides their problem-solving and so influences what sort of socio-technical trajectory might become established. For low carbon development, this means that we should carefully explore what problems need to be solved. These could be about developing fragile market systems, understanding context-specific energy services and how to address the particular needs of the poor. To do this, we need to be able to experiment in ways that generate learning about the context-specific problems of energy provision systems and associated markets. This requires risk-taking, the bulk of which can only be borne by the public sector. If we want markets to provide longer term solutions then the private sector needs to be deeply and meaningfully involved in these experiments. However, this is not enough. We also need to understand the demand for services and this suggests that our experiments should involve the expected beneficiaries of those services. Where it is not possible for these users to turn needs and desires into market demand – such as is likely the case for the poorest – then we need to consider other forms of service provision; perhaps through community-scale interventions such as in health centres and schools. But, the poor themselves need to be included in the experiments so that learning is focused on their context-specific problems.

It is not clear that the dominant instruments of low carbon technology deployment can address these many challenges. They may well be able to promote the deployment of technologies in some of the developing countries, where market systems are more mature, there are many opportunities for avoiding carbon emissions and market demand is sufficiently large. However, in the poorer developing countries, a different approach might prove necessary. The emerging initiatives such as the Climate Technology Centre and Network, and Climate Innovation Centres, raise the potential to address this need, but they will need to operate in ways that work within local systems, supporting experimentation that helps those systems evolve. If they do this then they are more likely to promote low carbon development, not just low carbon technology deployment.

Box 17.3 provides a critique of the dominant low carbon development instruments.

Box 17.3 Critique of the dominant low carbon development instruments

Although there is frequent reference in discussions of low carbon technology deployment to the need for capacity building, the key instruments in operation to promote technology transfer reflect an understanding of the issue that is narrowly focused on hardware and finance (Byrne *et al.*, 2011). In contrast, the rich literature on innovation demonstrates that the adoption of technology requires a receptive environment; an environment that has the capacity to absorb new technologies (Cohen and Levinthal, 1990). This means the local context must already have some level of knowledge, skills and institutional linkages relevant to the technology being transferred if the transfer is to be successful and the developmental opportunities are to be exploited (Bell and Pavitt, 1993; Bell, 2009). Without this absorptive capacity, finance will not help. Moreover, further adaptation or creation of technology requires innovative capacity if the country concerned is not to be constrained to low-value industrial development pathways (Cimoli *et al.*, 2009).

When we examine the dominant instruments of low carbon technology transfer we find that they have only weak provision for building the local systems that the innovation literature argues are necessary for technology adoption, adaptation and creation (Byrne *et al.*, 2011). If we consider the case of low carbon technologies in particular, this weakness becomes even more acute because they are risky and not yet competitive with high carbon technologies (Ockwell *et al.*, 2010).

Financing the deployment of low carbon hardware is, of course, a necessary part of the solution but it is not sufficient. As our case study shows, particularly in the poorer developing countries, there is much work to be done to develop local systems that can absorb, deliver and use low carbon technologies. But there is even more work to be done to build innovative capacity; something that has not yet taken place in the Tanzanian PV niche. And, finally, the most difficult work is in building these systems of provision to meet the needs of the poor.

References

African Development Indicators (2009) African Development Indicators (ADI) January 2009. ESDS International, (Mimas) University of Manchester.

Arkesteijn, K. (2000) Solar PV actor analysis in selected regions of Tanzania. Report for TaTEDO and Eindhoven University of Technology, Eindhoven, June.

Arkesteijn, K. (2009) Interview with Karlijn Arkesteijn. Former Managing Director of Umeme Jua. Conducted by telephone, 9 January 2009.

Barkan, J. (1994) Divergence and convergence in Kenya and Tanzania: pressures for reform, in Barkan, J. (ed.) *Beyond Capitalism vs. Socialism in Kenya & Tanzania*. Nairobi and Boulder, CO: East African Educational Publishers and Lynne Rienner Publishers, pp. 1–45.

Bell, M. and Pavitt, K. (1993) Technological accumulation and industrial growth: contrasts between developed and developing countries. *Industrial and Corporate Change*, 2(2), 157–210.

Bell, M. (2009) Innovation capabilities and directions of development. STEPS Working Paper 33. Brighton: STEPS Centre.

Berkhout, F. (2006) Normative expectations in systems innovation. *Technology Analysis & Strategic Management*, 18(3/4), 299–311.

Byrne, R. (2011) Learning drivers: rural electrification regime building in Kenya and Tanzania. Doctoral dissertation, SPRU (Science and Technology Policy Research). Brighton: University of Sussex.

Byrne, R., Smith, A., Watson, J. and Ockwell, D. (2011) Energy pathways in low-carbon development: from technology transfer to socio-technical transformation. STEPS Working Paper 46. Brighton: STEPS Centre.

Cimoli, M., Dosi, G. and Stiglitz, J. (eds) (2009) *Industrial Policy and Development: The Political Economy of Capabilities Accumulation*. New York: Oxford University Press.

Cohen, W. and Levinthal, D. (1990) Absorptive capacity: a new perspective on learning and innovation. *Administrative Science Quarterly*, 35, 128–52.

Deuten, J., Rip, A. and Jelsma, J. (1997) Societal embedding and product creation management. *Technology Analysis and Strategic Management*, 9(2), 131–48.

Dubash, N. (2002) Introduction, in Dubash, N. (ed.) *Power Politics: Equity and Environment in Electricity Reform*. Washington, DC: World Resources Institute.

Energy Alternatives Africa (EAA), Tanzania Traditional Energy Development and Environment Organisation (TaTEDO) and Ameco Environmental Services (AES) (2002a) The potential for commercial SHS and small scale PV systems in Dar es Salaam region. Final Report for Umeme Jua, September.

EAA, TaTEDO and AES (2002b) The potential for commercial SHS and small scale PV systems in Mbeya region, Tanzania. Final Report for Umeme Jua, September.

EAA, TaTEDO and AES (2002c) The potential for commercial SHS and small scale PV systems in Morogoro region, Tanzania. Final Report for Umeme Jua, September.

EAA, TaTEDO and AES (2002d) The potential for commercial SHS and small scale PV Systems in Mwanza region, Tanzania. Final Report for Umeme Jua, September.

Energy Information Administration (EIA) (2010) Annual energy review 2009. US Energy Information Administration, Office of Energy Markets and End Use. Washington, DC: US Department of Energy, August.

Energy for Sustainable Development (ESD) (2003) World Bank study on PV market chains in East Africa. Draft Final Copy. Nairobi: Energy for Sustainable Development.

Felten, J. (2008a) Interview with Jeff Felten. Managing Director of Energy for Sustainable Development Africa (Tanzania). Conducted in Dar es Salaam, 23 May 2008.

Felten, J. (2008b) Sida-MEM solar PV project: progress to date. Presentation slides, Energy for Sustainable Development, May.

Geels, F. and Raven, R. (2006) Non-linearity and expectations in niche-development trajectories: ups and downs in Dutch biogas development (1973–2003). *Technology Analysis & Strategic Management*, 18(3/4), 375–92.

Geels, F. (2002) Technological transitions as evolutionary reconfiguration processes: a multi-level perspective and a case-study. *Research Policy*, 31, 1257–74.

Goldemburg, J., Reddy, A., Smith, K. and Williams, R. (2000) Rural energy in developing countries, in UNDP, World Energy Assessment: energy and the challenge of sustainability. New York: United Nations Development Programme.

Gordon, D. (1994) International economic relations, regional cooperation, and foreign policy, in Barkan, J. (ed.) *Beyond Capitalism vs. Socialism in Kenya and Tanzania*. Nairobi and Boulder, CO: East African Educational Publishers and Lynne Rienner Publishers, pp. 235–62.

Hifab-TaTEDO (1998) Tanzania rural energy study. Final Report. Submitted to Sida. Hifab International and TaTEDO, September.

Hoogma, R., Kemp, R., Schot, J. and Truffer, B. (2002) *Experimenting for Sustainable Transport: the Approach of Strategic Niche Management*. London: Spon Press.

Kasaizi, O. and Hankins, M. (1992) The Karagwe Development Association (KARADEA) Solar Enterprise Project: developing a sustainable programme for solar electrification in Tanzania. Project Proposal. Kagera: Karagwe Development Association.

Kimani, M. (ed.) (1992) Regional solar electric training and awareness workshop. Workshop proceedings. Held in Nairobi and Meru, 15–27 March. Washington, DC and Nairobi: African Development Foundation and Muiruri Kimani.

KSTF (2009) KARADEA Solar Training Facility. Available at: http://www.karadea.org/kstf/ (accessed 19 November 2012).

McNelis, B., Derrick, A. and Starr, M. (1988) Solar-powered electricity: a survey of photovoltaic power in developing countries. Intermediate Technology Publications in association with UNESCO, London.

Mueller, B. (2011) The agrarian question in Tanzania: using new evidence to reconcile an old debate. *Review of African Political Economy*, 38(127), 23–42.

Musa, M. (2008) Interview with Mzumbe Musa. Former Manager of KARADEA Solar Training Facility and former Project Coordinator of the UNDP-GEF Project, Mwanza. Conducted in Dar es Salaam, 22 May, and 3 and 6 June 2008.

Mwihava, N. and Towo, A. (1994) A study and assessment of energy projects and their effective utilization in Tanzania. Report to the Tanzania Commission for Science and Technology. Dar es Salaam, March.

Nakhooda, S., Caravani, A., Wenzel, A. and Schalatek, L. (2011) The evolving global climate finance architecture. Climate Finance Fundamentals Brief 2. Overseas Development Institute and Heinrich Böll Stiftung North America, November.

Njeru, G. (2012) New support centre backs Kenyan cleantech. *Green Futures Magazine*, 83. Available at: http://www.forumforthefuture.org/greenfutures/articles/new-support-centre-backs-kenyan-cleantech (accessed 19 November 2012).

Nkonoki, S. (ed.) (1983) Energy for development in Eastern and Southern Africa. Proceedings of the regional workshop in Arusha, Tanzania, Volume 1: Summary Report, 4–13 April 1983.

Ockwell, D., Watson, J., MacKerron, G., Pal, P. and Yamin, F. (2008) Key policy considerations for facilitating low carbon technology transfer to developing countries. *Energy Policy*, 36, 4104–15.

Ockwell, D., Watson, J., Mallett, A., Haum, R., MacKerron, G. and Verbeken, A. (2010) Enhancing developing country access to eco-innovation. The case of technology transfer and climate change in a post-2012 policy framework. OECD Environment Working Papers No. 12. Paris: OECD Publishing.

Oman, C. and Wignaraja, G. (1991) *The Postwar Evolution of Development Thinking*. Part of the series: Economic Choices before the Developing Countries, Griffin K. (general ed.). London and Paris: MacMillan and OECD.

Prahalad, C. and Hammond, A. (2002) Serving the world's poor, profitably. *Harvard Business Review*, 80(9), 48–57.

Raven, R. (2005) Strategic niche management for biomass: a comparative study on the experimental introduction of bioenergy technologies in the Netherlands and Denmark. PhD dissertation. Eindhoven: Technische Universiteit Eindhoven.

Roberts, A. and Ratajczak, A. (1989) The introduction of space technology power systems into developing countries. Report No. NASA TM-102042. Cleveland, OH: NASA-Lewis Research Center.

Sanga, G. (2008) Interview with Godfrey Sanga. Manager of Sustainable Energy Department, TaTEDO. Conducted in Dar es Salaam, 11 April and 17 June 2008.

Sawe, E. (1989) National assessment of new and renewable sources of energy activities in Tanzania. Report for the Renewable Energies Development Project Unit. Ministry of Energy and Minerals, United Republic of Tanzania, Dar es Salaam, February.

Sawe, E. (2008) Interview with Estomih Sawe. Executive Director of TaTEDO (Tanzania Traditional Energy Development and Environment Organisation). Conducted in Dar es Salaam, 7 May, and 10 and 11 June 2008.

Stern, N. (2006) The economics of climate change. Draft report posted online, HM Treasury and Cabinet Office, UK. Available at: http://www.hm-treasury.gov.uk/sternreview_index.htm (accessed 19 November).

Tanzania National Scientific Research Council (UTAFITI) (1978) Workshop on Solar Energy for the Villages of Tanzania. Report of a workshop/seminar held in Dar es Salaam, 11–19 August 1977. Tanzania National Scientific Research Council (UTAFITI), Dar es Salaam.

TaTEDO-Fredka (2001) Awareness raising and development of human resources plan. Tanzania Traditional Energy Development and Environment Organization and Fredka International study for UNDP-GEF PDF-B: Removing barriers to the transformation of the rural PV market in Tanzania, October.

United Nations Framework Convention on Climate Change (UNFCCC) (2012) Report of the Conference of the Parties on its seventeenth session, held in Durban from 28 November to 11

December 2011. FCCC/CP/2011/9/Add.1. United Nations Framework Convention on Climate Change, 15 March.

United Republic of Tanzania (URT) (1992) The Energy Policy of Tanzania. Ministry of Water, Energy and Minerals, United Republic of Tanzania, Dar es Salaam, April.

URT-United Nations Development Programme (UNDP)-Global Environment Facility (GEF) (2003) Transformation of the rural photovoltaic (PV) market in Tanzania. Project Document. United Republic of Tanzania, United Nations Development Programme and Global Environment Facility, February.

US Department of Commerce (USDOC) (2011) Doing Business in Tanzania: 2011 Country Commercial Guide for U.S. Companies. US Department of Commerce.

van der Linden, J. (2008) Interview with Jeroen van der Linden. Former Managing Director of Umeme Jua. Conducted in the Netherlands, 16 September 2008.

van der Plas, R. and Hankins, M. (1998) Solar electricity in Africa: a reality. *Energy Policy*, 26(4), 295–305.

van der Vleuten, F. (2008) Interview with Frank van der Vleuten. Former Marketing Manager of Free Energy Europe. Conducted in Leuden, 17 September 2008.

Further reading

Byrne, R. (2011) Learning drivers: rural electrification regime building in Kenya and Tanzania. Doctoral dissertation, SPRU (Science and Technology Policy Research). Brighton: University of Sussex.

Cimoli, M., Dosi, G. and Stiglitz, J. (eds) (2009) *Industrial Policy and Development: The Political Economy of Capabilities Accumulation*. New York: Oxford University Press.

Ockwell, D. and A. Mallett (eds) (2012) *Low-Carbon Technology Transfer: From Rhetoric to Reality*. London and New York: Routledge.

Notes

1   The Bottom of the Pyramid concept says that companies can make large profits if they can package their products in a form that suits the needs and purchasing power of the poor, who make up the bottom billion of the world's income pyramid.

2   Technologies are considered to exist together with social, cultural and other practices and so are referred to as socio-technical configurations in order to capture this multi-dimensional view.

3   This figure was first published by Elsevier in: Geels, F. (2002) Technological transitions as evolutionary reconfiguration processes: a multi-level perspective and a case-study. *Research Policy*, 31, 1257–74.

4   This policy of 'industrialisation by invitation' was the name given to the strategy to attract foreign investment to set up export industries (Oman and Wignaraja, 1991).

5   Care should be taken with the Tanzanian prices, as these are mostly single estimates of differing systems. However, they serve to demonstrate that system costs have been high, even if they have fallen in recent years, and so would militate against any policy interest in their use.

6   Karagwe is situated in the north-western part of Tanzania, to the west of Lake Victoria.

7   TASEA is now the Tanzania Renewable Energy Association (TAREA).

8   The figure of 20 Wp is chosen based on reports that the most popular modules were 14 Wp amorphous (van der Linden, 2008), as has also been documented in the Kenyan SHS market (van der Plas and Hankins, 1998). The average size is then an estimate to allow for the presence of larger modules. However, the point here is to give an estimate of the number of modules sold rather than to report an exact figure.

18 Ride the wind[1]

Wind energy in China[2]

Frauke Urban, Johan Nordensvärd and Zhou Yuan

This chapter discusses the planning and implementation of low carbon development in the middle income country China, with a specific case study from the wind energy sector. Today China is the world's largest wind energy manufacturer, has the world's largest wind energy capacity and is a global leader in low carbon development. This has been achieved through strong government support and financing for domestic wind energy industries. This chapter discusses the emergence of China's wind energy sector, its current status and key policies. The chapter concludes that China could potentially become a future world leader in low carbon development, at least in the wind energy sector.

Introduction

China is a country of superlatives: it is currently the world's largest emitter of GHG emissions in absolute terms and the world's largest energy consumer in absolute terms, at the same time China is the world leader in renewable energy, most notably in wind energy, solar energy and hydropower. China is leading the renewable energy field in terms of investments, production and installed capacity (IEA, 2012). Reasons for increasing global and Chinese investments in renewable energy are reported to be concerns about economic competitiveness, energy security and climate change (Urban *et al.*, 2012).

This chapter discusses the planning and implementation of low carbon development in the middle income country China by using wind energy as a case study. The case study involved empirical research in China, including interviews with experts. As mentioned in Chapter 15, low carbon development in middle income countries such as China focuses on fostering indigenous innovation and technological trajectories that can mitigate climate change, while ensuring energy security and contributing to economic growth. However, China is not just any middle income country, but it is the most powerful, populous and influential middle income country in the world, which influences the global economy, global politics and the global environment. What China does in terms of emissions, energy use and development trajectory has effects worldwide. In addition, the Chinese wind energy industry experienced rapid growth in recent years and today it is a global leader in terms of investments, production and installed capacity. It is rivalling many of the more established wind energy industries in Europe and the USA (Urban *et al.*, 2012). China's wind energy industry therefore makes a fascinating case study for understanding how a middle income country and emerging emitter such as China is becoming a world leader in a low carbon technology sector. This case study may provide lessons for other middle income countries and emerging emitters such as India, which has a sizeable wind energy industry due to its leading wind firm Suzlon, as well as other middle income countries with emerging wind energy markets.

The wind energy resources in China are reported to be large. China is reported to have a total exploitable wind energy potential of 3000 GW according to the World Energy Council (WEC), of which 750 GW are reported to be situated offshore (Lewis and Wiser, 2007), nevertheless the WEC assumes that only about 250 GW of this offshore potential is economically and technically feasible (Urban *et al.*, 2012). Both the Chinese government and the Chinese wind energy industry play an important role in exploiting the large wind energy potential and developing the world's largest wind energy manufacturing market and the world's largest deployment rates for wind turbines. However, the growth of the Chinese wind energy sector is a relatively new phenomenon. In the early 2000s, the Chinese wind energy sector was still in its infancy and was mainly dominated by foreign firms (Urban *et al.*, 2012).

This chapter therefore elaborates the emergence of China's wind energy sector, its current status and key policies. The chapter examines particularly the role of the government in the wind industry. The chapter concludes that China has a distinct wind energy model that is built on strong links between the government and the wind energy industry. The chapter further concludes that the Chinese wind energy industry may not be a dominant player in overseas markets yet, but it is quickly catching up. China is already today the world leader in wind energy and the renewable energy field in general in terms of investments, production and installed capacity. China could potentially become a future world leader in low carbon development and certainly an example for other middle income countries that aspire to develop their low carbon technology sectors.

The next section will briefly discuss the methodology for this case study, followed by a section that will present the case study findings and the conclusion to the chapter. Box 18.1 below defines wind energy technology and provides an overview of the key components of a wind turbine.

Box 18.1 Definition of wind energy technology

The term wind energy technology mainly refers to wind turbines. A wind turbine is a device that converts wind energy into electricity. It thereby converts kinetic energy into mechanical energy. Wind turbines can range from small turbines, which are usually in the range of kilowatts (kW) to large turbines, which are in the range of megawatts (MW). Smaller wind turbines are usually used on land – on-shore – whereas larger wind turbines are usually used in the sea – off-shore. Very small turbines are sometimes off-grid, meaning that they are not connected to the electricity grid, while larger turbines are mostly connected to the grid. Wind turbines are composed of a tower, blades, rotor and nacelle, which carries the heart of the turbine, such as the generator and the gear box (although some wind turbines have been built without a gear box and operate with a so-called direct drive). The largest turbines built today are in the range of 5–7.5 MW and can have a total height of about 200 metres. For example, one single Enercon E-126 wind turbine can power between 15,000 and 18,000 households that have an average Central European energy consumption, hence an entire small town can be powered by one modern large turbine (Energieblog24, 2012).

Methodological approach: a brief overview

This chapter is based on case study research of the Chinese wind energy sector. Let us first discuss some important conceptual details for this case study.

Wind energy is an important low carbon energy, which plays a crucial role in achieving a transition to low carbon development. The Chinese wind energy sector is composed of wind energy firms, which include large and small firms, state-owned and private firms, national and local firms, lead firms and suppliers of components. These wind energy firms are regulated by policy-makers, such as ministries and authorities at the national and local level. International policies and authorities such as at the UN level also play a role, albeit a minor role. Research institutions and environmental NGOs further influence wind energy policy and wind energy firms by providing expertise and input for national and local plans and policies, as well as influencing through advocacy and lobbying. In China, civil society organizations such as NGOs often face more monitoring and limitations than in other countries, nevertheless a number of international NGOs operate in the environmental sector, such as WWF and Greenpeace.

Let us now briefly present the methodological approach of this empirical case study. This case study discusses the emergence of China's wind energy sector, its current status and key policies relevant for shaping the sector. The methodologies applied for this case study are literature review, policy analysis of key energy, climate and industrial policies, actor mapping and interviews with key actors engaged in the Chinese wind energy sector. The expert interviews were undertaken with key actors from government, wind energy industry, research organizations and NGOs working on Chinese wind energy. The interviews included semi-structured, open questions in which the interviewee had the chance to freely unfold their views. The results of the case study are elaborated in the next section.

Case study findings

The emergence of the Chinese wind energy sector and its current status

The wind energy sector plays an important part for a transition to low carbon development in China. Nevertheless, the emergence of the wind energy sector was very slow in China and it is only recently, with more active engagement of the government, that the sector has grown substantially. This section elaborates the emergence of the Chinese wind energy sector and its current status. This section is meant to provide some insights into how a rather sluggish initial development of a low carbon sector can be boosted to world leadership.

The first wind turbines were installed in China between 1975 and 1985. These were mainly small off-grid wind energy systems that aimed to provide household energy supply in remote areas. Between 1985 and 1995 larger turbines were installed with capacities of 100–300 kW. During this time the first demonstration wind farms were built (Xu *et al.*, 2010; Urban *et al.*, 2012). While only a few of these turbines were built by Chinese manufacturers, access to leading technology was gained through technology transfer, mainly from Denmark, Germany and Spain (Dai, 2011; Urban *et al.*, 2012).

This changed in the late 1990s and the early 2000s when the government promoted the construction of large-scale wind farms and created a Chinese wind power market. In addition, the Chinese government actively promoted indigenous wind energy innovation for turbines of up to 1 MW (Xu *et al.*, 2011; Urban *et al.*, 2012). Nevertheless, the understanding of indigenous innovation is often different in China compared to Western countries such as in Europe or the USA. Western countries usually define indigenous innovation as innovation that is researched and developed within the country's domestic firms, domestic research centres and often this is done within its own national boundaries. This often involves R&D for core technology innovation of wind turbines, such as the gears or the direct drive for turbines without gears. In contrast, Chinese government authorities and wind firms usually consider indigenous innovation as including innovation that can be acquired and licensed from abroad, but then becomes Chinese through ownership, and is then adapted to Chinese conditions. This often involves acquiring foreign licences for core technologies, and then conducting R&D for adapting these technologies to Chinese conditions, such as high altitude, extreme temperatures and low wind speeds.

The Chinese wind energy industry gained momentum in the early 2000s, when the government introduced a so-called local content requirement. The local content requirement meant that there was a quota requiring a certain share of the overall components of the wind turbine to be produced locally. The local content requirement was 50 per cent from 2004 to early 2005 and was then augmented to 70 per cent from mid-2005 to 2009. This meant that 50–70 per cent of all the components of the wind turbine had to be produced in China rather than in other countries (Wang, 2010). This regulation meant that foreign firms still had access to the Chinese market, but their production capacity had to be in China (Urban *et al.*, 2012). While the Chinese wind energy market was mainly dominated by foreign firms until the early 2000s, this changed rapidly once the local content requirement was in place.

> Many domestic firms and joint ventures emerged in the period between 2004 and 2008. Market access was consequently traded for part-Chinese ownership. Within only 5 years, the market share of domestic turbines rose from 25% to more than 60%, while the market share of foreign turbines plummeted from 75% to 40% in 2008.
>
> (Urban *et al.*, 2012: 113; Zhao *et al.*, 2009)

The local content requirements were abolished in 2009, as the Chinese wind energy market had gained considerable power by then. Since then it is able to operate successfully without restricting foreign competition. This is partly due to the fact that many of the leading wind energy firms in China are state-owned enterprises (SOEs) or receive substantial state funding (Liu and Kokko, 2010; Urban *et al.*, 2012).

In more recent years, the international climate change negotiations at the UNFCCC have become one of the drivers of the Chinese wind energy market. Since 2010, the government aims to scale up its wind farms and turbine sizes – including offshore wind turbines – and export Chinese wind energy technology globally (Dai, 2011) (Urban *et al.*, 2012).

Today the wind energy sector in China is in a very strong position. 'China's wind capacity has recently overtaken the US, Germany and Spain and it has now the world's largest installed wind capacity. China achieved an approximate doubling of its installed wind energy capacity in five consecutive years' between 2006 and 2010 (Urban *et al.*, 2012: 113; GWEC, 2011; IEA, 2012). The installed wind energy capacity was about 12 GW in 2008, 25 GW in 2009 and about 45 GW in 2010, which equals a global market share of 50 per cent for new turbines installed in 2010 (WWEA, 2011).[3] China's installed wind capacity made up more than 26 per cent of the global installed capacity in 2011 (GWEC, 2012). China's offshore wind energy capacity even increased by more than 430 per cent in 2010 (WWEA, 2011). China is also the world's largest producer of wind turbines (BTM, 2010; Lema *et al.*, 2011; Urban *et al.*, 2012). This makes China the world leader in wind energy and the renewable energy field in general in terms of investments, production and installed capacity – and this could make China potentially a future world leader in low carbon development.

Figure 18.1 shows the rapid increase in installed wind turbine capacity in China between 2005 and 2010. Hence, wind energy is an important low carbon energy source that can pave the way for low carbon development pathways in China.

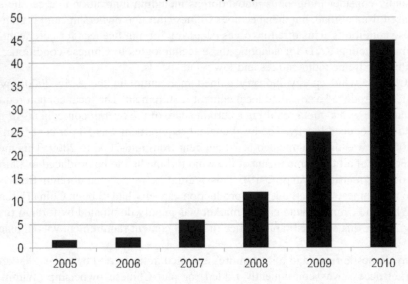

Figure 18.1 Installed wind power capacity in China in GW between 2005 and 2010

Source: Adapted from IEA, 2010; Liu and Kokko, 2010; Urban *et al.*, 2012[4]

The installed wind energy capacity in China has even outpaced government targets, although the growth in installed capacity in 2011 was slower and steadier than the years before. In 2011, more than 62 GW wind energy capacity was installed in China (GWEC, 2012). Due to these substantial growth rates, the new target of the Chinese government is to reach 150 GW installed wind energy capacity by 2020 (GWEC, 2011). Inner Mongolia is especially endowed with high wind resources and is therefore the key to the Chinese wind energy development plans, followed by other provinces such as Hebei, Gansu, Liaoning and Shandong province.

China is currently the world's largest producer in wind turbine manufacturing. However, in 2003, none of the world's top ten turbine manufacturers were Chinese. In 2011, the Chinese firms Sinovel, Goldwind, Guodian United Power and Mingyang Wind Power led the global top ten in wind turbine manufacturing (Clean Tech Investor, 2012; Urban *et al.*, 2012). Sinovel currently ranks second with a global market share of 9 per cent, just behind Danish firm Vestas. Goldwind ranks third with a global market share of almost 9 per cent, Guodian United Power ranks eighth with a global market share of 7 per cent and Mingyang Wind Power ranks tenth with a global market share of 4 per cent. This makes a combined global market share of 29 per cent, which is significantly higher than the combined market share of any other country (BTM, 2010; Lema *et al.*, 2011). Mingyang Wind Power also managed to overtake the German firm Nordex and the Indian firm REpower in 2011, which jointly held the position of tenth largest producers the years before (Clean Tech Investor, 2012).

Key government actors that set the enabling environment for the Chinese wind energy sector and contribute to its success are the National People's Congress, which takes decisions and therefore influences central government, key ministries and planning authorities such as the National Development and Reform Commission (NDRC), the Ministry of Science and Technology (MOST), the Ministry of Environmental Protection (MEP), the Ministry of Finance (MOF), the Ministry of Industry and Information Technology (MIIT), the Ministry of Commerce (MOFCOM), the Ministry of Foreign Affairs (MFA), the State Council, particularly the State-Owned Assets Supervision and Administration Commission of the State Council, and the Energy Bureau.

The section above reviewed how the Chinese wind energy sector emerged throughout the last four decades and how it achieved its rapid growth in recent years. This rapid growth was directly linked to the government's introduction of local content requirements, which resulted in the emergence of a profitable domestic wind energy industry and enabled out-competing foreign competition in China. The next section raises a critique of China's wind energy 'story'.

China's wind energy story – a critique

This chapter has so far discussed the success of the Chinese wind energy sector; however, all that glitters is not gold, hence there are a number of criticisms that need to be addressed at this point.

> The impressive figures and policies supporting China's wind energy development have to be considered with caution. China's rapidly growing economy, its large population and its surging energy demand mean that only 1.2% of China's electricity came from wind power in 2010 (WWEA, 2011). Wind energy policies issued by the central government in Beijing are sometimes only reluctantly implemented by provincial and local governments and authorities. Recent research by Wang *et al.* (2010) shows there are major barriers to China's wind energy development. First, the share of renewable energy in total energy consumption is decreasing, instead of increasing, due to rapid growth of fossil fuel capacity (Wang *et al.*, 2010). Second, the efficiency of wind energy technology tends to be low as often the quality of the technologies is not to the latest standard in China and efficiencies for wind energy technology are generally rather low due to intermittent wind availability and technical limitations. Third, many wind farms are not connected to the grid as this requires high costs and logistic resources. There is a lack of adequate transmission lines and supporting infrastructure (Wang *et al.*, 2010). A part of the installed wind energy capacity is therefore often wasted (Liao *et al.*, 2010; Wang *et al.*, 2010). The WWEA (2010) reports that in 2010 only 31 GW out of the total capacity of 45 GW was connected to the grid; this means that 31% of the installed capacity was standing idle[5].
>
> (Urban *et al.*, 2012: 114)

This could be interpreted as a market failure, particularly in the case where it is not financially viable for businesses to connect installed wind energy technology to the grid or this could be interpreted as a state failure, as wind turbine installations are regulation-driven and provincial government authorities can be reluctant to monitor implementation (Wang *et al.*, 2010; Urban *et al.*, 2012).

State involvement in wind turbine manufacturing

This section deals with state involvement at the provincial and national level and the state's role in Chinese wind turbine manufacturing. The strong involvement of the state players makes China's wind energy model – and its low carbon development model – distinct from other countries (Urban *et al.*, 2012). This is elaborated below.

China currently has 80 turbine manufacturers, approximately 50 rotor blade manufacturers and approximately 100 tower manufacturers (Liu and Kokko, 2010; Urban *et al.*, 2012). Since the local content requirement came into place in 2004, the number of domestic wind technology manufacturers has increased rapidly (Zhao *et al.*, 2009). Leading manufacturers such as Sinovel, Goldwind and Dongfang Electric are SOEs. In fact 84 per cent of Chinese wind equipment manufacturers are state-owned (Liu and Kokko, 2010; Urban *et al.*, 2012). There are three groups of wind equipment manufacturers: the first group of 17 established SOEs includes firms like Sinovel, Goldwind and Dongfang Electric that have been in the sector for some time. These SOEs mainly operate with turbine capacities of about 1 to 2.5 MW, although there is some R&D with 3–6 MW turbines for the offshore market. This group of companies has access to substantial amounts of state funding, is directly 'orchestrated' by the state and has no or only limited responsibility to shareholders (Liu and Kokko, 2010; Urban *et al.*, 2012). It is not unusual for Chinese leading wind firms to acquire technologies and licences from overseas and to amend them for Chinese conditions, such as for high altitudes in Inner Mongolia, for extreme conditions like heat and sand in the Gobi desert and for low wind speeds for areas that are far away from the coast. For example, Goldwind's permanent magnetic direct drive (PMDD) was developed by its German subsidiary Vensys and is today being amended by Goldwind for Chinese conditions.

The second group of wind turbine manufacturers is made of 50 new entrants from the SOE sector. This group belongs partly to established energy or electronics companies and partly to provincial government companies. As these companies are new to the wind power sector and have limited technological skills in this field their strategy is to buy licences from foreign companies that are not based in China, hence technology transfer and cooperation is a key strategy. They mainly operate with smaller wind turbines between 300 and 800 MW. This results in lower utilization rates and lower efficiencies. In addition, many licences come with restrictive clauses, such as restricting export of these turbines. Funding for these firms comes from the state and there is limited responsibility to shareholders (Liu and Kokko, 2010; Urban *et al.*, 2012).

The third group of wind turbine manufacturers are leading foreign firms such as Vestas (Danish), Gamesa (Spanish), GE Wind (US), Suzlon (Indian) and Nordex (German). Many of these foreign firms have set up production plants and R&D centres in China, which is partly a consequence of the local content requirement rules. Another reason is the cheap manufacturing opportunities that China offers. Most of the foreign companies produce turbines below 1.5 MW in China. Larger turbines for the offshore market are mainly produced in the country of origin such as Denmark, Spain, the USA, India and Germany to limit conflict regarding intellectual property rights in China. This enables foreign firms to do the cutting-edge R&D at home rather than in China, while turbines larger than 1.5 MW are mainly imported to China (Liu and Kokko, 2010). It is, nevertheless, the case that the Chinese government is pushing foreign firms more and more to produce larger turbines in China (Urban *et al.*, 2012).

The most crowded space in the Chinese wind energy industry is the turbine manufacturing market below 1.5 MW, where the established and new SOEs are operating as well as foreign firms. While huge wind energy resources remain untapped in China and large turbines are mainly being imported,

> there is concern that the smaller turbine segment of the Chinese wind manufacturing market might be saturated and there might be an overcapacity of companies. The strong engagement of SOEs like Sinovel and Goldwind creates risks that the market might be distorted by state-funded and state-owned firms that are large, have access to abundant funding, can lower prices excessively, are strategically nurtured and protected by the

state and have limited responsibility to shareholders. This might have implications for foreign firms in the long-run, but also for domestic SOEs and provincial firms. SOEs are competing against SOEs which might in the long-run have an effect on the number of firms surviving and the power play between national and provincial actors.

(Urban *et al.*, 2012: 119)

According to some Chinese wind energy experts this market consolidation – the merging of many smaller firms into a few larger firms – is, however, to be expected and shows that the Chinese wind energy market is becoming more mature and stable.

The section above mentioned how the Chinese wind manufacturing industry follows a distinct model, as it has strong domestic firms that are financially and politically supported by the Chinese government, while often acquiring technology and licences from abroad and adjusting them to local conditions and finally the restrictions applied a few years ago to foreign competitors through the local content requirements.

The next section will discuss wind energy policy in China.

Wind energy policy in China

After decades of testing and refining, China's wind energy policy is today well advanced due to the relentless support and regulation of Chinese national and provincial authorities and abundant financing opportunities for wind energy firms. Most of this is based on China's domestic experience, while other policies have been developed based on other countries experiences (e.g. feed-in-tariffs like in Germany). China's wind energy policies can be classified into several categories: (i) national level objectives, such as the 12th Five-Year Plan; (ii) national and regional policies; (iii) Renewable Energy Law; (iv) pricing and competitive bidding policies; (v) tax and localization policies; (vi) other policies and programmes (Urban *et al.*, 2012). Table 18.1 lists the key wind energy policies in China and their details.

Table 18.1 Key wind energy policies in China

Governance level/ type of policy	Date issued	Name of policy	Key aims of policy
National level: objectives	03/2008	The **11th Five-Year Plan** of Renewable Energy Development by NDRC	Sets goals for renewable energy development, including goals for wind power development. Revised the development goal of wind power capacity in 2010 from 5 million KW to 10 million KW by 2012. In addition, the annual capacity of domestic wind power generation should reach 5 million KW and its manufacturing capability of components and parts should reach 8 million KW by 2012
	03/2011	The **12th Five-Year Plan** of China's Economic and Social Development	The installation capacity of wind power should reach 70,000 MW by 2015. The rapid development of wind power will be moderated, and the quality of infrastructure constructions should be improved

Table 18.1 continued

Governance level/ type of policy	Date issued	Name of policy	Key aims of policy
National policies	03/1996	'Ride the Wind Plan' made by NDRC	Encourages indigenous innovation, attracting foreign investment for advanced 300-600 kW turbines. Joint ventures were encouraged (two joint ventures were established respectively in cooperation with MADE in Spain and Nordex in Germany).
	07/2004	'Key Technology for Energy Saving and New Energy' Project by NDRC	The project aimed at large wind power technology and R&D for MW-sized turbines, such as R&D for blades, generators, gearboxes, control systems
	09/2009	Guidelines on Developing Emerging Industries in a Sustainable Way by NDRC	Moderates the rapid growth of the wind energy industry, encourage sustainable growth of firms, restructure the industry, regulate the market and avoid malicious competition
Provincial government policies	04/2006	Long-term Science and Technology Development in Gansu Province (2006–2020), by Gansu Provincial Government. Other provinces have similar policies such as Inner Mongolia, Liaoning, Hebei.	Provincial policy to promote wind energy, solar energy, biomass energy and other technologies. Priority was given to wind power and its equipment manufacturing.
New energy laws	02/2005	Renewable Energy Law by the National People's Congress (NPC)	Encourages the development of renewable energy, including wind energy, solar energy, small hydro, biomass, geothermal. Facilitation of grid integration, creation of special fund to support R&D, encourage product localization/local content requirements, provision of preferential loans with financial discount for some eligible projects
	08/2007	Long-term Renewable Energy Development Plan, by NDRC	Encourages and develops the wind energy market, which aims at spurring technological innovation, encourage product localization/local content requirements, promote market competitiveness. In 2010 and 2020, the wind power's capacity should reach 5 million kW and 30 million kW, respectively
	03/2010	The Committee for Best-Practice Technology in the Wind Power Industry was officially established by the National Energy Administration	Best-practice guidelines for the design of wind farms, wind farm construction, installation, maintenance, grid management technology, machinery equipment and some electrical equipment, etc.

Table 18.1 continued

Governance level/ type of policy	Date issued	Name of policy	Key aims of policy
Wind power pricing policies	09/2003	Wind Power Concession Programme	Ensures grid access for wind power operators. All the electricity generated from wind power will be fed into the grid and purchased by grid providers. The policy establishes a competitive bidding programme where the investor which offers the cheapest price per kWh wins the bid. Other aims of the policy are to include a localization rate/local content requirements for wind power generation equipment
	04/2005	Provisional Measures for the Administration of On-Grid Power Prices by NDRC (on-grid competitive bidding policy)	Renewable energy such as wind power currently does not operate under market conditions. The on-grid price for wind power is either a government-fixed price or a bidding price (see 'Wind Power Concessions Programme' above)
	01/2006	Provisional Measures for Price and Cost Allocation of Renewable Energy by NDRC	The price for wind power is determined by the government according to the lowest bidding price. A price that exceeds the benchmarked on-grid price of local coal-fired power will be deployed on a national scale
Wind power pricing policies	07/2009	Notification of Improving Wind Power On-Grid Price Policy by NDRC	This policy classified the country into four categories of wind energy resources areas with four levels of wind power benchmarked on-grid prices, which are respectively 0.51 yuan, 0.54 yuan, 0.58 yuan and 0.61 yuan per kWh. This offers a better return for wind farm operators than the competitive bidding process did, which often allocated concessions for bidding prices which were under the actual value of generating wind power

Table 18.1 continued

Governance level/ type of policy	Date issued	Name of policy	Key aims of policy
Tax and localization policies/local content requirement policies	02/2000	Guidelines to introduce Local Content Requirements for Wind Power Generating Technology and Equipment by Ministry of Commerce	This policy introduced local content requirements for wind power technology, which was 50% in 2004. This primarily meant that foreign wind power firms had access to the Chinese market, but their production capacity had to be in China. Chinese–foreign joint ventures emerged from this time. The government issued discount loans to locally sourced wind power equipment
	11/2005	Notification of Management Requirements of Wind Power Construction by NDRC	The local content requirements were increased to 70% for wind energy equipment, which meant that 70% of the turbine had to be manufactured in China. Between 2004 and 2008, the market share of domestic turbines rose from 25% to more than 60%, while the market share of foreign turbines plummeted from 75% to 40% in 2008
	11/2009	Abolishment of Local Content Requirements in Local Wind Power Project by NDRC	The 70% local content requirements regulation was abolished as the Chinese domestic wind power industry is well established

Source: NDRC, 2006, 2007a, 2007b; NDC, 2005; Lewis and Wiser, 2007; CCICED, 2009; Zhao *et al.*, 2009; Climate Policy Initiative Tsinghua, 2010; China Dialogue, 2011; Liao *et al.*, 2010; Liu and Kokko, 2010; Wang, 2010; Wang *et al.*, 2010; Xu *et al.*, 2010; Yu and Qu, 2010; Zhou *et al.*, 2011; Urban *et al.*, 2012.

Conclusion

China's wind energy industry makes a fascinating case study for understanding how a middle income country and emerging emitter such as China is becoming a world leader in the low carbon technology sector. Low carbon energy, such as wind energy, is at the heart of low carbon development. This case study may therefore provide lessons for low carbon development in other middle income countries and emerging emitters, particularly for other countries with emerging wind energy markets.

China is an interesting case study for this book for several reasons: first, China is the most powerful, populous and influential middle income country in the world, and influences the global economy, global politics and the global environment. China rivals the Western world, particularly the USA and Europe, in many ways, and provides an example and an option for developing countries and emerging economies all over the world. China can therefore be an example for other countries for how to develop a strong wind energy sector and how to strive for low carbon development. Second, in terms of low carbon development, China is currently the world's largest emitter of GHG emissions in absolute terms and the world's largest energy consumer in absolute terms, at the same time China is the world leader in renewable energy, most notably in wind energy, solar energy and hydropower. Chinese wind power investments, production and installed capacity are larger than that of any other country (IEA, 2012). What China does in terms of emissions, energy use and development trajectory has effects worldwide. Third, the wind industry in China follows a distinct model, such as targeted policies to reduce foreign competition, state-owned wind energy firms as an instrument for developing the domestic wind energy sector, and acquisition of technology and licences from abroad and adapting them to local conditions. These are approaches that seem to be different to the classic arrangements in established wind energy markets in Europe and the USA. Understanding the Chinese model could help other countries build up their own low carbon technology sectors and thereby pursue low carbon development.

This chapter discussed the planning and implementation of low carbon development in the middle income country China by using wind energy as a case study. China's wind energy sector developed rapidly from its modest beginnings in the mid-1970s to being the world's largest player in wind energy. The chapter concludes that the rapid growth of China's wind energy sector follows a distinct wind energy model as mentioned above. This has led to the fact that today China is a global forerunner in striving for low carbon development.

Despite these efforts, it is clear that China faces massive challenges regarding low carbon development, such as being the world's largest emitter of GHG emissions in absolute terms, depending heavily on fossil fuels – mainly coal – and having a rapidly increasing energy demand. Nevertheless, wind energy and other renewable energy technology are rapidly being financed, developed, produced and installed in China with the support of a strong government and capable firms.

While the Chinese wind energy sector still has a way to go to become a dominant player in overseas markets and to develop world-leading cutting edge wind technology, China is already today the world leader in wind energy and the renewable energy field in general in terms of investments, production and installed capacity. China could therefore potentially become a future world leader in low carbon development and already today the country is an example for other middle income countries that aspire to develop their low carbon energy sectors.

References

BTM (2010) World market update 2009. Ringkøbing: BTM Consulting.

China Council for International Cooperation on Environment and Development (CCICED) (2009) China's pathway towards a low carbon economy. Beijing: CCICED.

China Dialogue (2011) China's green revolution. energy, environment and the 12th Five Year Plan. Available at: http://www.chinadialogue.net/UserFiles/File/PDF_ebook001.pdf (accessed 19 November 2012).

Clean Tech Investor (2012) Wind turbine manufacturers – global market shares. Available at: http://www.cleantechinvestor.com/portal/wind-energy/10502-wind-turbine-manufacturers-global-market-shares.html (accessed 19 November 2012).

Climate Policy Initiative Tsinghua (2010) Review of low carbon development in China: 2010 report. Beijing: Tsinghua University.

Dai, Y. (2011) Wind energy in China – an overview. Presentation for the workshop 'Technological trajectories for climate change mitigation in China, India, EU'. Bonn: Tsinghua University.

Energieblog24 (2010) The world's largest wind turbine – the E-126. Available at: http://www.energieblog24.de/e126/ (accessed 19 November 2012).

Global Wind Energy Council (GWEC) (2011) World wind energy report 2010. Brussels: Global Wind Energy Council.

GWEC (2012) World wind energy report 2011. Brussels: Global Wind Energy Council.

International Energy Agency (IEA) (2010) Energy technology perspectives 2010. Paris: IEA/OECD.

IEA (2012) Energy statistics for Ethiopia. Available at: http://www.iea.org/stats/index.asp (accessed 19 November 2012).

Intergovernmental Panel on Climate Change (Lema, R., Berger, A., Schmitz, H. and Hong, S. (2011) Competition and cooperation between Europe and China in the wind power sector. IDS Working paper 377. Available at: http://www.ids.ac.uk/idspublication/competition-and-cooperation-between-europe-and-china-in-the-wind-power-sector (accessed 20 November 2012).

Lewis, J. I. and Wiser, R. H. (2007) Fostering a renewable energy technology industry: an international comparison of wind industry policy support mechanisms. Lawrence Berkeley National Laboratory, LBNL-59116. Available at: http://eetd.lbl.gov/EA/EMP (accessed 19 November 2012).

Liao, C., Jochem, E., Zhang, Y. and Farid, N. R. (2010) Wind power development and policies in China. *Renewable Energy*, 35(9), 1879–86.

Liu, Y. and Kokko, A. (2010) Wind power in China: policy and development. *Energy Policy*, 38(10): 5520–9.

National Development and Reform Commission of China (NDRC) (2006) 11th Five-Year Plan. Available at: http://www.gov.cn/english/special/115y_index.htm (accessed 19 November 2012).

NDRC (2007a) China's national climate change programme. Available at: http://en.ndrc.gov.cn/news-release/P020070604561191006823.pdf (accessed 19 November 2012).

NDRC (2007b) Medium and long-term development plan for renewable energy in China (abbreviated version, English draft). Available at: http://www.martinot.info/China_RE_Plan_to_2020_Sep-2007.pdf (accessed 19 November 2012).

National People's Congress of China (2005) The Renewable Energy Law of the People's Republic of China. Available at: http://www.martinot.info/China_RE_Law_Beijing_Review.pdf (accessed 19 November 2012).

Urban, F., Nordensvärd, J. and Zhou, Y. (2012) Key actors and their motives for wind energy innovation in China. *Innovation and Development*, 2(1), 111–30.

Wang, Q. (2010) Effective policies for renewable energy – the example of China's wind power – lessons for China's photovoltaic power. *Renewable and Sustainable Energy Reviews*, 14(2), 702–12.

Wang, F., Yin, H. and Li, S. (2010) China's renewable energy policy: commitments and challenges. *Energy Policy*, 38, 1872–8.

World Wind Energy Association (WWEA) (2011) Wind Energy International 2011–2012 yearbook. WWEA, Bonn.

Xu, J., He, D. and Zhao, X. (2010) Status and prospects of Chinese wind energy (2010) *Energy*, 35(11): 4439–44.

Yu, X., and Qu, H. (2010) Wind power in China – opportunity goes with challenge. *Renewable and Sustainable Energy Reviews*, 14(8), 2232–7.

Zhao, Z. Y., Hu, C. and Zuo, J. (2009) Performance of wind power industry development in China: a Diamond Model Study. *Renewable Energy*, 34(12), 2883–91.

Zhou, Y., Gu, X., Minshall, T. and Su, J. (2011) *A Policy Dimension Required for Technology Roadmapping: Learning from the Development of Emerging Wind Energy Industry in China*. Portland, MN: PICMET.

Further reading

Climate Policy Initiative Tsinghua (2010) Review of low carbon development in China: 2010 report. Beijing: Tsinghua University.

Liao, C., Jochem, E., Zhang, Y. and Farid, N. R. (2010) Wind power development and policies in China. *Renewable Energy*, 35(9), 1879–86.

Urban, F., Nordensvärd, J. and Zhou, Y. (2012) Key actors and their motives for wind energy innovation in China. *Innovation and Development*, 2(1), 111–30.

Wang, F., Yin, H. and Li, S. (2010) China's renewable energy policy: commitments and challenges. *Energy Policy*, 38, 1872–8.

Xu, J., He, D. and Zhao, X. (2010) Status and prospects of Chinese wind energy, 2010. *Energy*, 35(11): 4439–44.

Notes

1   The title of this chapter is derived from the 'Ride the Wind Plan', which was introduced in 1996 and encouraged indigenous innovation for the first time in the Chinese wind energy sector (see Table 18.1 for more details).

2   Parts of this chapter were published in amended form by Routledge in Urban *et al.* (2012).

3   In 2011, 62 GW of wind energy capacity was installed in China, which equals a global market share of 43 per cent of new turbines installed in 2011 (GWEC, 2011).

4   Figure 18.1 was previously published by Routledge in Urban *et al.* (2012).

5   'While such a large amount of idle-standing capacity might enter the statistics as "installed capacity" and enable firms, provincial and national governments to meet their wind energy targets, it would be economically inefficient. It could therefore be the case that there is a time lag between installing the turbines and connecting them to the grid' (Urban *et al.*, 2012: 114).

19 Low carbon city planning in China

Andreas Oberheitmann and Ruan Xiaodong

Cities are the focal point both for the impacts of climate change and for options for climate change mitigation and adaptation, especially in coastal regions. Hence, low carbon city planning can provide the necessary tools to achieve low carbon development. This chapter uses China as a case study for low carbon city planning. China currently has the world's largest population, of whom more than half live in urban areas, has the world's largest carbon dioxide emissions and is actively engaged in low carbon city planning and piloting to pursue low carbon development. The chapter suggests that developing low carbon cities requires strong government action, close interaction between various city authorities, integration with national policies and developing an appropriate low carbon city strategy in cooperation with relevant stakeholders.

Introduction

Background

Since the Industrial Revolution, cities have become the main driving force for economic development. Owing to growing urban populations and increasing city sizes around the world, cities have become more important than ever. According to statistics, in 1800, urban residents accounted for only 3 per cent of the total world population. Today, more than half of the world's population is living in cities. It is estimated by the UN that by 2030 more than 60 per cent of the world's population will live in cities, among which the urban population in developing countries is likely to increase from 1.9 billion in 2000 to 3.9 billion in 2030 (UN-HABITAT, 2008). Cities highlight a variety of environmental problems such as large resources consumption and impacts on ecological systems (Stern, 2006). With the acceleration of urbanization worldwide, cities, including those in China, are becoming increasingly vulnerable to the impacts of climate change, for example in relation to extreme weather events (IPCC, 2007). Climate research has shown that in the recent half century extreme weather events increased significantly worldwide. For example, in 2008, Shanghai suffered from the biggest heavy rain in the recent century, which ravaged the lives of many residents (Zhai, 2008). In addition, more and more cities are suffering from energy and resource shortages and environmental pollution. More and more cities are suffering from acid rain and their major rivers and lakes are heavily polluted. Water shortage has become a common issue for modern cities, such as Beijing and Paris (*The Guardian*, 2005; *China Daily*, 2012). The main reason for the frequent appearance of urban environmental problems and extensive natural resource use are the unsustainable patterns of production and consumption in cities. Faced by the pressure to tackle global climate change, continued industrialization, rapid economic development, population dynamics and increasing energy consumption, a low carbon economy is urgently required in the world, with the construction of low carbon cities as a vital goal.

This chapter uses China as a case study for low carbon city planning, which is based on empirical research in China. China currently has the world's largest population, of whom more than half live in urban areas, the world's largest carbon dioxide emissions and is actively engaged in low carbon city planning and piloting to pursue low carbon development. The next section will define low carbon cities.

Low carbon city: definitions

There is no fixed definition of a 'low carbon city'. Generally, a low carbon city refers to the model of a city's economic development and is characterized by low carbon energy consumption, low carbon emissions and low carbon technologies (Reed and Wilkinson, 2009). Hence, there are many different definitions of or suggestions for what constitutes a low carbon city. For example, according to the UK's White Paper 'our energy future – creating a low carbon economy' (UK Department of Trade and Industry, 2003), low carbon cities may incorporate the following characteristics:

- A low carbon city is a sustainable upgrade of urban development, which includes improved opportunities for economic growth and social progress, technological progress and industrial innovation.
- A low carbon city requires a new development model that uses less energy, has lower GHG emissions and more socio-economic benefits for its citizens.
- Carbon emission reductions are the main goal of a low carbon city, which requires lower carbon emissions from production and consumption.
- All aspects of urban development should incorporate this new development model including production and consumption patterns, development policies and social culture.

(Gomi *et al.*, 2010; Su *et al.*, 2012)

In this chapter, we define the low carbon city as 'the spatial vector of a low carbon economy'. This implies using low carbon technologies and aiming for low carbon lifestyles that minimize the city's GHG emissions. Options for implementing a low carbon city are for example to switch from fossil fuel-based electricity to renewable-based electricity, to establish green areas in the city and to use low carbon transport modes such as walking, cycling and public transport. Low carbon city planning is the sum of organizational processes of creating and maintaining a roadmap for low carbon city development. Box 19.1 indicates possible planning steps to develop a low carbon city.

The next section provides the case study for China, which is based on empirical research in China. Based on an explanation as to why China has been chosen as a case study and why low carbon city development is important for the country, an overview of the current programme of the National Development and Reform Commission (NDRC) on low carbon pilot regions in China is given. The next section describes the governance structure for the implementation of a low carbon economy in cities in China in terms of the actor constellation and the governmental implementation tools of low carbon city planning and development. The chapter then moves on to discuss two successful examples of low carbon city pilot areas in China, at their current stage: Baoding and Dezhou, followed by a section analysing the current challenges of low carbon city planning and development in China, and, finally the conclusion to the chapter.

Box 19.1 Possible planning steps to develop a low carbon city

1. **Conceptualization of the low carbon city**
    a) Development of a vision for the low carbon city
        *   Low carbon city by 2020
        *   Car-free city by 2020, etc.
    b) Definition of geographic boundary
        *   Inclusion of inner city, suburbs, rural areas, etc.
    c) Definition of sectors to be included
        *   Industry, commerce
        *   Transport
        *   Households, etc.
    d) Definition of technical benchmarks for the low carbon city
        *   t CO_2/m^2; tonnes CO_2/capita; CO_2/produced unit, etc.
        *   Technical benchmarks: best available technology vs. national standard

2. **Planning of the low carbon city**
    a) Establishment of relevant government bodies and responsibilities in different relevant departments on the local level for the planning and implementation of the low carbon city
    b) If necessary, integration with national policies
    c) Designation of architecture bureaus, research centres, construction companies, etc. for the actual planning and implementation on the ground
    d) Development of a strategy for the implementation of the low carbon city concept
        *   Assessment of priorities, definition of steps and milestones for the implementation
        *   Risk assessment
        *   Definition of the time scale for the low carbon city development
        *   Reservation of a government budget for planning, plan enforcement and implementation of the low carbon city concept
        *   Inclusion of private investments
        *   Consultation and communication with the relevant stakeholders (households, enterprises, academia, media, etc.) on the local level
        *   Possibly communication with national stakeholders

3. **Implementation of strategy and enforcement of plans**
    a) Implementation of strategy
        *   Implementation of the low carbon city projects
    b) Enforcement of plans
        *   Monitoring and enforcement of achieving milestones for planning and implementation phases of the low carbon city
        *   Enforcement of time scale for the low carbon city development
        *   Controlling quality of technical implementation and enforcement of achieving benchmarks of the low carbon city
        *   Monitoring of government budget for planning, plan enforcement and implementation of the low carbon city.

Case study China

China as an example for low carbon city planning

China's economy has increased tenfold since 1978, and its focus on economic development at such high growth has led to widespread urbanization. At the same time, China suffers from resource shortage and environmental degradation (Liu and Ren, 2011). High energy consumption and spreading urban areas have negatively affected the environment for at least two decades, and because of the pressure of feeding and housing a population of more than 1.3 billion, the Chinese government is facing even greater pressure to balance economic development and reduce environmental pollution. In 2008, China surpassed the USA as the largest global emitter of GHGs (Liu and Ren, 2011) and at present, China is still the world's largest GHG emitter (Zhang *et al.*, 2011). The significant increase of CO_2 emissions in China accounts for 62 oer cent of the increment in global CO_2 emissions from 2000 to 2010. For comparison, India's incremental emissions are 10 per cent and the emissions in the USA decreased and increments even dropped by 3 per cent (BP, 2011). Against the background of global climate change, China, as the most important emitter in developing countries, is facing an enormous challenge to fulfil its international obligations to reduce its CO_2 emissions, while at the same time addressing its domestic responsibilities to meet the human development needs of hundreds of millions of its people still living in poverty (Liu *et al.*, 2012).

To improve environmental and economic conditions in China, cities are becoming increasingly important. After 30 years of reform and opening up in China, the urban population rose from 172 million in 1978 to 660 million in 2010. In 2010, China had 657 cities, and more than 19,000 small towns (Xinhua Net, 2011). More than half of China's 1.3 billion people live in urban areas. It is expected that due to rapid socio-economic development and expansion of the urban population, China will experience rapid industrialization and urbanization over the next 30 years. Although substantial achievements have been made by China in economic development and environmental protection, China is today facing many serious problems in urban transportation and the urban environment. China has made significant efforts to increase energy efficiency and to promote new and renewable energy. Although some progress has been made, it is still difficult for China to change the trend of high growth in energy consumption and CO_2 emissions within a short time frame. Important economic and ecological indicators of Chinese cities are listed in Box 19.2.

Box 19.2 The importance of cities to China

- 85 per cent of Chinese GDP is generated in cities.
- 90 per cent of the Chinese service industry is located in cities.
- 75 per cent of the total Chinese energy use is consumed in cities.
- It took 120 years in the UK, 40 years in the US, 30 years in Japan, but only 22 years in China to increase the urbanization rate from 20 per cent to 40 per cent.

The development of low carbon cities in a middle income country such as China could be an example for other countries, particularly other middle income countries and emerging emitters that are faced with similar challenges. Against this background, we take China as the case study in this chapter. In the following section, the current programme on low carbon pilot regions by the NDRC will be described.

Overview of the current NDRC programme on low carbon city pilot regions

In 2010 and 2011, the NDRC announced plans to introduce pilot low carbon economic reforms across five provinces (Guangdong, Liaoning, Hubei, Shaanxi and Yunnan) along with eight cities (Tianjin, Chongqing, Shenzhen, Xiamen, Hangzhou, Nanchang, Guiyang and Baoding) (Xinhua Net, 2010; National Development and Reform Commission, 2010;

WWF China, 2010). These 13 low carbon regions are encouraged to develop low carbon production and consumption policies. The main indicators of the NDRC programme are listed in Table 19.1.

Table 19.1 Key statistical indicators of the 13 low carbon regions

Name	Size (in km²)	Location	Climatic region	Population (in million)	GDP (in 2010 ¥)	GDP per capita (in ¥)
Guangdong Province	180,000	South	Hot summer, warm winter zone	79	4.55 trillion	57,561
Liaoning Province	145,900	Northeast	Severe cold zone	43.5	1.75 trillion	42,019
Hubei Province	185,900	Central	Hot summer, cold winter zone	61	1.58 trillion	25,912
Shaanxi Province	156,300	North	Cold zone	35	908.81 billion	25,966
Yunnan Province	383,300	Southwest	Hot summer, warm winter zone	45.5	722 billion	15,868
Tianjin	11,300	North	Cold zone	11	910.89 billion	82,808
Chongqing	82,300	Southwest	Hot summer, cold winter zone	32.35	789 billion	23,218
Shenzhen	1,952	South	Hot summer, warm winter zone	10.36	951.091 billion	91,804
Xiamen	1,565	East	Hot summer, warm winter zone	3.53	0.206 trillion	96,538
Hangzhou	16,596	East	Hot summer, cold winter	8.70	0.595 trillion	86,642
Nanchang	7,402	Central	Hot summer, cold winter zone	4.91	166 billion	18,387
Guiyang	8,046	Southwest	Moderate climate zone	3.92	90.26 billion	24,585
Baoding	22,159	North	Hot summer, cold winter zone	10.89	202 billion	18,549

These regions have been selected as pilot low carbon cities and low carbon provinces for socio-economic reasons. Guangdong, Tianjin, Shenzhen, Xiamen and Hangzhou are part of the eastern costal region, which is relatively wealthy and has a strong economy that relies heavily on coal imports from poorer western regions. Shaanxi, Yunnan, Chongqing and Guiyang are part of the western region, which is poorer, more rural, but has potential for renewable energy development. Liaoning, Hubei, Nanchang and Baoding are part of the northern/central region, which is the 'birthplace' of China's industry and home to China's most emitting industries, but has potential for energy efficiency and low carbon development.

The 'low carbon city' economic reforms across five provinces and eight cities set specific goals for the reduction of energy use and resource intensity. The NDRC programme sets the following targets for 2020:

- energy consumption per unit of GDP should be cut by around 40 per cent compared to 2005;
- carbon dioxide emissions per unit GDP should be cut by around 50 per cent compared to 2005.

As a response to these targets, the 13 regions developed their local low carbon policies based on local characteristics. These policies pay attention to further leveraging China's climate policies and promoting a more coordinated approach to lower energy consumption and energy efficiency. The 13 regions promote new economic, technological and social systems of production and consumption to conserve energy and reduce GHG emissions, compared with the traditional economic system, whilst maintaining momentum for economic and social development.

The NDRC shows China's determination to link its actions against climate change to its national development priorities. In the 11th Five-Year Plan, ambitious targets were introduced for lowering energy consumption per unit of GDP by 20 per cent compared to the 2005 level; raising the proportion of renewable energy (including large-scale hydropower) in the primary energy supply; increasing the forest coverage rate to 20 per cent; and increasing carbon sink capacity by 50 million tonnes compared to the 2005 level by 2010. In addition, the 11th Five-Year Plan made many provincial governments assign energy saving targets to their industries. These targets for energy saving range from 12 per cent in Hainan province and Tibet to 25 per cent in Jilin province (Xinhua Net, 2006).

Each provincial government takes responsibility for the achievement of these objectives. To reduce energy intensity, most provinces have put forward detailed local rules and regulations designed to strengthen energy savings, and have created administrative offices to help implement them.

Furthermore, many provinces and cities in China had taken measures to promote a low carbon economy before 2010/2011. In 2006, Shaanxi, Hebei, Anhui, Henan and Liaoning provinces issued regulations on energy saving (Wang, 2010). With funding from UNDP, Norway and the EU, major efforts are also underway to develop provincial climate change programmes aligned with China's 2007 National Climate Change Programme (Xinhua Net, 2007). Other cities, such as Beijing, Wuxi, Hangzhou, Suzhou, Kunming, Shenzhen and Baoding (see case study in the section on 'Successful low carbon city pilot areas in China'), Dezhou (see case study in the section on 'Successful low carbon city pilot areas in China') and Tangshan, are developing their own low carbon city strategy outside of the NDRC programme.

The next section discusses the governance structure for implementing low carbon cities in China.

Governance structure for implementation of low carbon cities in China

Actor constellation

This section discusses the governance structure for implementing low carbon cities in China and addresses first the actor constellations. The actor constellation is important to understand who plays a role for planning and implementing low carbon cities in China.

As for China, different administrative levels have to be taken into account for the implementation of low carbon cities. The first levels are the national and provincial levels. Basic decisions on politics and measures relating to low carbon cities, such as the renewable energy law, the law on circular economy, etc. have been taken at the national level and transformed into provincial policy.

The second level and, in this context most importantly, is the municipal policy level. Here, the most important actors include city mayors and senior officials as shown in Table 19.2.

The most important driver of building a low carbon city is the political will of the local government. If the mayor of a city is convinced and willing to implement such a project, it can be undertaken more easily in China. A directive from the central government only seems insufficient to provide enough power for a quick and successful implementation. Table 19.2 shows the main tasks and responsibilities of municipal departments to plan and implement low carbon cities in China.

Table 19.2 Main tasks of municipal government departments for low carbon city planning and implementation

Department	Main tasks
Municipal Development and Reform Commission (MDRC)	• Developing economic and social development strategies, including ecological and environmental protection measures • Approving and submitting for approval fixed asset investment projects
Municipal Environmental Protection Bureau (EPB)	• Supervising the exploitation of natural resources • Overseeing ecological environment construction, ecological conservation and recovery of ecological damage
Municipal Science and Technology Commission (MSTC)	• Organizing the formulation and implementation of plans, including annual plans of advanced technology development and industrialization • Municipal earthquake prevention and disaster risk reduction
Municipal Economic and Trade Commission (ETC)	• Involvement of foreign investment
Municipal Construction Commission (MCC)	• Formulating urban and rural development strategies of construction • Fund-raising and use of urban construction funds • Organizing, directing, coordinating and supervising the implementation of important construction projects of the municipality
Urban Planning Bureau (UPB)	• Carrying out and enforcing state urban planning • Providing recommendations for location selection of construction projects
Municipal Transport Bureau (MTB)	• Organizing and formulating medium- and long-term plans on the development of roads, auxiliary facilities and communication industry • Working out annual expenditure plans for funds earmarked for communication

Source: Zhang *et al.*, 2009

Low carbon cities strive to engage citizens in collaborative and transparent decision-making, while being mindful of social equity concerns. To achieve this, different government implementation tools are applied as the next section elaborates.

Governmental implementation tools

The most important governmental implementation tool for the planning and implementation of low carbon cities is the establishment of a designated Task Force (ditan chengshi guihua lingdao xiaozu). This commission, in many cases, includes the following actors:

- Office of the Mayor, being the head of the commission;
- Municipal Environmental Protection Bureau;
- Municipal Development and Reform Commission (MDRC);
- Economic and Trade Commission (ETC);
- Municipal Construction Commission (MCC);
- Urban Planning Bureau (UPB);
- Municipal Transport Bureau (MTB);
- Municipal Science and Technology Commission (MSTC);
- University research institutes and associations, etc.

(Zhang *et al.*, 2009)

For a bottom-up and top-down approach, the main planning and implementation issues should be discussed and decided in a consensual manner. This approach ensures that every major political stakeholder is involved in the decision-making process and after a consensus is reached, the policies and actions can be implemented without large resistance from a single political stakeholder.

Box 19.3 indicates the key issues that need to be addressed by the low carbon task force.

Box 19.3 Key issues for implementing a low carbon city

- Provide safe housing, water, sanitation and food security for all citizens and with priority to the poor in an ecologically sound manner to improve the quality of life and human health.
- Build cities for people, not for cars. Roll back urban sprawl. Minimize loss of rural land by all effective measures, including regional urban and peri-urban ecological planning.
- With low carbon city mapping identifying ecologically sensitive areas, define carrying capacity of regional life support systems, and identify areas where nature, agriculture and built environment should be restored. Also identify those areas where more dense and diverse development should be focused in centres of social and economic vitality.
- Design cities for energy conservation, renewable energy uses and the reduction, re-use and recycling of materials.
- Build cities for safe pedestrian and non-motorized transport use with efficient, convenient and low-cost public transportation. Terminate automobile subsidies, increase taxation on vehicle fuels and cars and spend the revenue on low carbon city projects and public transportation.
- Provide strong economic incentives to businesses for low carbon city building and rebuilding. Tax activities that damage the environment, including those that produce GHGs and other emissions. Develop and enhance government policies that encourage investment in low carbon buildings.
- Provide adequate, accessible education and training programmes, capacity building and local skills development to increase community participation and awareness of low carbon city design and management and of the restoration of the natural environment. Support community initiatives in low carbon buildings.

The next section discusses two examples of successful low carbon city pilots in China.

Successful low carbon city pilot areas in China

Two examples of successful low carbon city pilots at their current stage are described: Baoding and Dezhou.

Baoding

Baoding was chosen as a successful low carbon city for the following reason: Baoding is the base of the low carbon energy industry and low carbon energy equipment industry in China. In 2008, the Ministry of Construction and the WWF jointly chose Shanghai and Baoding in mainland China as two pilot cities for the construction of low carbon cities. In addition, Baoding is one of the first low carbon city pilots selected by the State Council. As a model of China's low carbon cities, Baoding's low carbon development experience plays a significant role in providing an example for other cities.

Baoding is located in the centre of Hebei Province, 140 km south of Beijing. Baoding was approved as a National Development Zone in 1992 and is one of the 53 national level development zones in China. In 2002 the Baoding High-Tech Development Zone began developing a renewable energy industry. In 2003, Baoding was recognized by the National Ministry of Science and Technology (MOST) as the first and only industrial base for development of China's low carbon energy sector (Low Carbon City China Alliance, 2010a).

Baoding's industries related to renewable energy (wind, solar, energy efficiency) are becoming increasingly important in the city's economic structure. In 2007, the renewable energy sector contributed to 12 per cent of GDP, a factor that is expected to increase to 40 per cent by 2050. In the last three years, Baoding's total GDP grew by an average of 14 per cent per year, reaching 1.37 billion RMB in 2007, with the renewable industry being a main driver. In 2006, the Baoding municipal government committed itself to the concept of Baoding as China's Renewable Electricity Valley and decided that the corresponding further development of renewable energy should be the nucleus of Baoding's further development. The area consists of companies and think tanks focusing on wind power, solar photovoltaics, solar thermal energy, biomass energy and energy efficiency. The municipal government also made a development plan for Baoding as China's Renewable Electricity Valley with supporting policies, including tax benefits for companies and investors.

In addition, the strategies in other industries include accelerating the development of modern agriculture and agricultural technology, improving agricultural production scale and intensity level, focusing on the sustainable reconstruction of energy-intensive industries (e.g. electricity and heating, textile and chemical fibre, building materials, etc.), eliminating out-of-date technology, enhancing energy conservation efforts, promoting development of solar photovoltaics, biomass energy use, waste generation, hydropower and other renewable energy, increasing the share of low carbon energy among the total energy consumption, promoting residential energy saving, increasing forest coverage and green vegetation. In 2010, the city banned coal-fired boilers and as a consequence air quality has improved since then. Green space has also increased in recent years and in 2011, 159 residential areas were retrofitted with solar energy facilities (Wong, 2009).

Dezhou

Dezhou was chosen as a successful low carbon city for the following reason: Dezhou Economic Development District became one of the first 13 national photovoltaics demonstration zones. Today, Dezhou has become a leader in the development of low carbon energy industries, especially in the fields of solar thermal and solar electricity. In the past decade, Dezhou has gradually gained a reputation as a solar-powered city. About 80 per cent of residential buildings in the city are equipped with solar water heaters. The application of solar power in Dezhou may help other cities to develop energy-efficient buildings and renewable energy applications.

As one of the successful low carbon city pilots in China, Dezhou is located in the northwest of Shandong Province, China, with a population of 5.6 million people in 2010. Dezhou has become a leader in the development of low carbon energy industries, especially in the fields of solar thermal and solar electricity. In 2009, it was estimated that the city's low carbon energy sector achieved sales revenue of 120 billion RMB and 1.6 billion RMB profit. The city is currently the nation's largest solar thermal R&D and production base, with more than 120 enterprises working in the sector (Low Carbon City China Alliance, 2010b).

At present, Dezhou's solar thermal industry accounts for 16 per cent of the national market, with a total produced surface of over 19 million square metres and a current annual surface growth rate of more than 3 million square metres. Dezhou is currently implementing an energy management and conservation system that focuses on key energy-consuming companies. The city plans to extend this system to all energy-consuming industries as well as to other fields such as transportation, construction and the public sector. It is estimated that the current annual production of solar water heaters and photovoltaics demonstration projects in Dezhou can save up to 640,000 tonnes of standard coal equivalent, representing about 2 billion kWh of electricity and about 1.7 million c tonnes of carbon dioxide.

Dezhou has received many energy-related awards such as 'China Solar City', 'Low carbon energy industrial base', the 'National model city in renewable energy applications in construction', the 'Highest investment in low carbon energy industry city' and 'China's low carbon city'. Dezhou City is characterized by a rapid development of emerging industries in the fields of low carbon energy and bio-technology. In June 2010, Dezhou became a core member municipality of the Low Carbon City China (LCCC) Program. Since then, Dezhou Low Carbon Office has been set up to coordinate and promote low carbon development and low carbon construction work in the city (World Bank, 2012).

Challenges of low carbon city development in China

Despite the positive examples, there are many challenges that China faces with regard to its low carbon city planning and implementation.

As noted before, China is currently the world's largest GHG emitter measured in absolute terms. China has realized the need to reduce its carbon emissions and has made a commitment to reducing carbon emissions intensity by 40–45 per cent in 2020, compared to 2005 levels. The development of low carbon cities is the key to this framework of the 12th Five-Year Plan period (2011–2015) and this action will make its future low carbon cities more sustainable, efficient, more competitive and liveable (Xinhua, 2011). Currently, the low carbon city campaign is carried out comprehensively across the country and more than one hundred cities have set up low carbon city plans. The Chinese Low Carbon City development, however, is also accompanied by many challenges. For China, the challenges are foreseeable, like lacking best practice for policy enforcement and monitoring, lacking adequate financial and technical support for businesses and project developers, low awareness of civil society regarding energy saving and climate change, etc. (Bi *et al.*, 2011). The intellectual work underpinning roadmaps for low carbon cities and climate change mitigation has been presented in many cities, but this is mostly at the policy-making level, and technical capacity for low carbon city development is often lacking (Dai, 2009). The obstacles arise from the fact that traditional development is based on high energy use, mass consumption and rapid depletion of fossil fuel resources, and it seems that this pattern will last for a long time. In addition, the energy structure and industry structure are both linked with the socio-economic structure. Rapid economic growth and a vast population put pressure on China's natural resources and pose considerable challenges to the implementation of low carbon cities. Hence, it is comprehensible that low carbon cities are far from being the final answer to the low carbon future of China and urban planning is just the starting stage of a long-term transition towards low carbon development. In the following section, the main challenges for low carbon city development in China are discussed.

Lack of systematic research

Development of a low carbon city is a complex systematic project. Currently, however, research on the internal driving forces and mechanisms is rarely done and the current low carbon city planning is usually concentrated on a few sectors, such as low carbon buildings, low carbon transport, energy conservation and energy planning. A systematic study of the low carbon city examining the aspects of land use, traffic patterns, industrial development, infrastructure construction and lifestyle is needed. Chinese central government, especially the NDRC, and the governments in the 13 pilot regions need to have a tool (i) to monitor and evaluate the success of the different approaches, and (ii) to make the policies and measures taken in the pilot cities comparable with those implemented in other cities in China. Against this background, the monitoring and evaluation should cover three different dimensions:

- an economic dimension (reduction of CO_2 emissions per GDP, impact on employment, attraction of domestic and foreign investments, etc.);
- an environmental dimension (reduction of CO_2 emissions and other GHG emissions, mitigation, adaptation and resource efficiency aspects, etc.);
- a social dimension (inclusion of public health aspects, migration issues, civil society, etc.).

Lack of innovation

Many cities lack innovation in developing a low carbon city process and fail to establish appropriate development patterns according to the specific character of the city. The copy-cat phenomenon exists in many low carbon cities. In addition, some of the planning and research for the cities is too macroscopic or superficial, and some cities even take 'low carbon' and 'sustainable development' purely as a fashionable label, a case of style over substance. This may not promote, but hinder the development of low carbon cities.

Technical and financial traps

As a new kind of development, low carbon cities have encountered great technical hurdles. Almost all of the cities have been pursuing new methods to tackle carbon emission issues and to balance economy, society, environment and natural resources. Clean energy such as wind energy and solar energy heating systems were taken as the first and final solutions in most cities. Measures such as compact land use, clean transport and waste management are also listed on the plan. However, at the current stage, using those techniques may not necessarily lead to energy-saving results and the costs are still high. Since great financial challenges came up in 2008 due to a downturn in the world economy, more and more cities begin to understand that their low carbon city programmes are constrained by investments, and more and more low carbon city programmes are unprofitable at this stage.

International planning idea conflicts

Some low carbon city projects are the results of cooperation between Chinese and foreign planners, like the Sino-Singapore Tianjin Eco City (SSTEC), the Sino-UK Shanghai Dongtan Low Carbon City, the Sino-Finland Gongqing Digital Low Carbon City, etc. While pursuing a low carbon vision, conflicts often arise between the two sides. The international planners often bring advanced ideas to low carbon cities, however, when national meets international, when traditional meets modern needs, conflicts can occur. A good combination between the new urban pattern and local culture, however, can help to realize low carbon cities in China.

Summary

Increasing urbanization and climate change are two of the greatest global challenges in the 21st century as many regions already face different negative impacts of cities such as growing local pollution, solid and liquid waste and traffic congestion. The growing consumption of fossil fuels in cities leads to increasing CO_2 emissions accelerating climate change. All over the world, not solely in China, the concept of an environmentally friendly low carbon city is promoted.

In China, the most important driver for building a low carbon city is the political will of the local government. This political will has to be increased. Today, the performance of local government leaders is also measured by the success of their environmental policies. This new low carbon policy provides additional incentives for local governments to promote low carbon cities. The chapter suggests that developing low carbon cities requires strong government action, close interaction between various city authorities, integration with national policies and developing an appropriate low carbon city strategy in cooperation with relevant stakeholders.

Technically, the concept of a low carbon city can be achieved through various other means, such as increasing the share of renewable energy meeting the energy demand, improved public transport and an increase in pedestrianization, solutions to decrease urban sprawl and energy conservation systems.

The development of low carbon cities in a middle income country such as China could be an example for other countries, particularly other middle income countries and emerging emitters that are faced with similar challenges.

References

Bi, J., Zhang, R., Wang, H., Liu, M. and Wu, Y. (2011) The benchmarks of carbon emissions and policy implications for China's cities: case of Nanjing. *Energy Policy*, 39(9), 4785–94.

BP (2011) BP statistical review of world energy June 2011. Available at: http://www.bp.com/section-bodycopy.do?categoryId=7500&contentId=7068481 (accessed 19 November 2012).

China Daily (2012) Water shortage in Beijing severe. Available at: http://www.ecns.cn/2012/01-05/5426.shtml (accessed 19 November 2012).

Dai, Y. X. (2009) A study on low carbon city development: concept formation and measurement setting. *Modern Urban Research*, 11, 7–12 (in Chinese).

Gomi, K., Shimada K. and Matsuoka, Y. (2010) A low carbon scenario creation method for a local-scale economy and its application in Kyoto city. *Energy Policy*, 38, 4783–96.

IPCC (2007) Climate change 2007. Synthesis report. Contribution of Working Groups I, II and III to the Fourth Assessment Report of the Intergovernmental Panel on Climate Change. Core writing team, Pachauri, R. K and Reisinger, A. (eds). Geneva: IPCC.

Liu, F. and Ren, J. (2011) On the necessity and governance model of the construction of China's low carbon transportation system. *Energy Procedia*, 5, 1502–7.

Liu, G., Yang, Z., Chen B. and Su, M. A. (2012) Dynamic low carbon scenario analysis in case of Chongqing city. *Procedia Environmental Sciences*, 13, 1189–203.

Low Carbon City China Alliance (2010a) Baoding, Hebei Province. Available at: http://www.low-carboncity.org/index.php?option=com_flexicontent&view=items&cid=45%3Abaoding&id=205%3Alow-carbon-achievements&lang=en (accessed 19 November 2012).

Low Carbon City China Alliance (2010b) Dezhou, Shandong Province. Available at: http://www.low-carboncity.org/index.php?option=com_flexicontent&view=items&cid=15%3Adezhou&id=16%3A background&lang=en (accessed 19 November 2012).

National Development and Reform Commission (2010) Notification of starting pilot work of low carbon province and low carbon city. Available at: http://www.sdpc.gov.cn/zcfb/zcfbtz/2010tz/t20100810_365264.htm (in Chinese) (accessed 19 November 2012).

Reed, R. and Wilkinson, S. (2009) Moving towards a low carbon city: a case study of Melbourne, Australia. London: RICS.

Stern, N. S. (2006) Review of the economics of climate change. Available at: http://webarchive.nationalarchives.gov.uk/ (accessed 19 November 2012).

Su M., Liang, C., Chen, B., Chen, S. and Yang, Z. (2012) Low carbon development patterns: observations of typical Chinese cities. *Energies*, 5, 291–304.

The Guardian (2005) France brings in water rationing after worst drought for 30 years. Available at: http://www.guardian.co.uk/environment/2005/jul/11/weather.france (accessed 19 November 2012)

UK Department of Trade and Industry (2003) Our energy future – creating a low carbon economy. The Stationery Office, Norwich.

UN-HABITAT (2008) Urbanisation: facts and figures. Available at: www.unhabitat.org/mediacentre/documents/backgrounder5.doc (accessed 19 November 2012).

Wang, Y. (2010) Development of low carbon economy in Henan (in Chinese). Available at: http://www.hndrc.org/article-8-2102.aspx (accessed 19 November 2012).

Wong, Y. F. (2009) Baoding City may be icon of low carbon living in China. Available at: http://www.channelnewsasia.com/stories/eastasia/view/439950/1/.html (accessed 19 November 2012)

World Bank (2012) A low carbon path will make Chinese cities more sustainable and liveable. Available at: http://www.worldbank.org/en/news/2012/05/03/a_low_carbon_path_will_make_chinese_cities_more_sustainable_and_livable (accessed 19 November 2012).

WWF China (2010) Low carbon city initiative in China. Available at: http://www.wwfchina.org/english/sub_loca.php?loca=1&sub=96 (accessed 19 November 2012).

Xinhua (2011) Key targets of China's 12th five-year plan. Available at: http://www.Chinadaily.com.cn/xinhua/2011-03-05/content_1938144.html (accessed 19 November 2012).

Xinhua Net (2006) Planning framework of 11th Five-Year Plan (in Chinese). Available at: http://news.xinhuanet.com/ziliao/2006-01/16/content_4057926.htm (accessed 19 November 2012).

Xinhua Net (2007) National Climate Change Programme (in Chinese). Available at: http://news.xinhuanet.com/politics/2007-06/04/content_6196300.htm (accessed 19 November 2012).

Xinhua Net (2010) National Development and Reform Commission launched the pilot of low carbon cities plan. (in Chinese). Available at: http://www.china5e.com/special/show.php?specialid=324 (accessed 19 November 2012).

Xinhua Net (2011) The number of cities in China has reached to 657 (in Chinese). Available at: http://news.xinhuanet.com/local/2011-06/16/c_121545801.htm (accessed 19 November 2012)

Zhai, P. M. (2008) Weather and climate events in August 2008: typhoon, high temperature and heavy rain. Available at: http://www.china.com.cn/news/2008-09/01/content_16368942.htm (accessed 19 November 2012).

Zhang, K., Oberheitmann, A. and Cui, D. (2009) Low carbon economy in the cities in China. Study for InWent. Mimeo.

Zhang, N., Lior, N. and Jin, H. (2011) The energy situation and its sustainable development strategy in China. *Energy*, 36, 3639–49.

Further reading

Bäumler, A., Ijjasz-Vasquez, E. and Mehndiratta, S. (2012) Sustainable low carbon city development in China. Directions in development. New York: World Bank.

Bulkeley, H. and Schröder, H. (2008) Governing climate change post-2012: the role of global cities case-study: Los Angeles. Oxford: Tyndall Center for Climate Change Research.

Phdungsilp, A. (2010) Integrated energy and carbon modelling with a decision support system: policy scenarios for low carbon city development in Bangkok. *Energy Policy*, 38(9), 4808–17.

Zeng, G. S. and Zhang, S. (2011) Literature review of carbon finance and low carbon economy for constructing low carbon society in China. *Low Carbon Economy*, 2, 15–19.

20 From outsider to world leader

Bioethanol in Brazil

Napoleão Dequech Neto and Eva Heiss

This chapter discusses the planning and implementation of low carbon development in the transport sector in the middle income country Brazil, with a specific case study from the bioethanol sector. Brazil is the world leader in sugarcane-based ethanol, both in terms of technology and in terms of bioethanol usage. For more than 80 years, Brazil has had programmes and incentives in place to foster the national bioethanol industry, to invest in infrastructure, as well as technology and to make bioethanol commercially viable. This chapter aims to elaborate the current status, policy development and the opportunities and barriers of bioethanol in Brazil. It also aims to provide some insights about the future of Brazil's bioethanol sector. The chapter elaborates the Brazilian bioethanol experience by using sugar cane-based bioethanol as a case study.

Introduction

Oil is a non-renewable resource, which is being consumed much faster than it can form naturally, and will reach scarcity in the near future. This imbalance between the growing demand for fossil fuel and the decreasing amount of available non-renewable resources, combined with the threat of climate change, results in an urgent need to create an alternative source of fuel for the transport sector.

Ethanol is used as a motor fuel and has demonstrated advantages at the economic, social and environmental level during the last three decades. With the inclusion of ethanol into the national energy matrix, the Brazilian government reduced the dependency on oil imports and the uncertainty surrounding the high volatility of its prices. The domestically produced energy gives the country more sovereignty regarding energy security, while at the same time ethanol strengthens national industry and contributes to economic growth. Also, most environmental assessments of Brazil's bioethanol sustainability and life cycle analysis indicate that bioethanol is beneficial from the perspectives of climate change mitigation and fossil fuel conservation (Blottnitz and Curran, 2006).

Bioethanol has been part of the history of Brazil for more than 80 years. During the 1970s, however, the oil crises combined with less attractive sugar prices in the global market motivated the then totalitarian government to design and implement a more ambitious ethanol programme called Pro-Alcool. This programme resulted in a major mobilization of efforts, for example, in terms of private sector involvement and investments in R&D. Important issues such as the introduction of flex fuel vehicles (FFVs) and the shift from a state-controlled ethanol production to a free market system, contributed to this success story.

The nationwide implementation of biofuels in Brazil is seen as an important example for low carbon development. Biofuels in Brazil contribute to environmental benefits on the production and the consumption side, while at the same time biofuels contribute to avoiding a 'carbon lock-in', which could result in an unsustainable carbon-intensive economy for decades.

The Brazilian bioethanol experience has caught the attention and interest of countries and organizations worldwide and is considered a potential energy alternative under the concept of low carbon development. It is a successful example of how a middle income country such as Brazil can achieve low carbon transport and thereby offer a viable alternative to the dominant fossil fuel-based development paradigm. The Brazilian ethanol experience is an important case study of low carbon development that has been driven mainly by economic and social aspects. This provides evidence that low carbon initiatives are capable of producing sustainable results that go beyond benefits from an environmental perspective.

This chapter will present Brazil's experience in bioethanol as a case study for understanding how a middle income country can achieve low carbon development and transform its transport sector from fossil fuels to low carbon fuels.

Box 20.1 elaborates the key concepts and terms relevant for this chapter.

Box 20.1 Key concepts and terms

Ethanol: A renewable fuel that derives its energy from biomass. Ethanol produced in Brazil is based on sugarcane.

Energy efficiency: Refers to the relation between the output and the input of energy; this means the total amount of fossil fuel energy used for the process, compared to the energy released by the combustion of the ethanol fuel. Sugarcane-based ethanol has a favourable energy efficiency, as more than eight units of energy are produced from each unit of fossil fuel energy consumed.

Flexi-fuel vehicles (FFVs): FFVs are cars that can be powered with pure gasoline, pure ethanol or a blend of both. This automobile is very important for the promotion of ethanol, as costumers are free to choose the fuel they will consume, based on price fluctuations and personal preference.

Hydrous ethanol: Integrates 5.6 per cent of water and is used in automobiles with pure ethanol or flexi-fuel engines.

Anhydrous ethanol: Basically water-free and it is mixed with gasoline prior to its sale. Through the blending of anhydrous ethanol with gasoline, the petroleum consumption is reduced and consumers are provided with a less polluting fuel.

E95: A blending of 95 per cent anhydrous ethanol combined with 5 per cent gasoline.

Planalsucar: Was a governmental programme to develop new varieties of sugarcane crops. The aim was to increase the efficiency of the crop, making it more weather resistant in order to allow growth in new topographic areas.

Lifecycle GHG emissions: The full fuel cycle, accounting for the quantity of emissions arising from all stages of fuel production and use, from feedstock plantation (including direct and indirect land use change) to the final consumer.

GHG balance: The ratio of GHG emitted in producing the biofuel, to the amount emitted in producing and burning of fossil fuel, representing the same end-use energy.

Cogeneration, also known as combined heat and power (CHP): CHP is a self-sufficient energy process that simultaneously generates electricity and heat in one power plant/heat engine. Hence, all the energy (heat and electricity) needed in the sugarcane mills come from bagasse, the fibre left over from the sugarcane stalks.

Sugarcane agro-ecological zoning: A map that determines the vulnerability of the land, the climate risk, the potential for agricultural production and the environmental sustainability of sugarcane crops nationwide.

Learning curve: A concept that, in this case study, represents the increase of efficiency and subsequent decrease of unit costs, with growing experience in technology of sugarcane-based ethanol.

Conceptual framework and methodology

This section elaborates the conceptual framework and the methodology for this case study. Low carbon development, as defined by Skea and Nishioka (2008) (in Urban and Sumner, 2009) is about efforts to stabilize levels of CO_2 and other GHGs, while achieving cuts in global emissions, applying a high level of energy efficiency and utilizing low carbon energy sources. Middle income countries such as Brazil can have great potential to become success-ful in implementing low carbon initiatives since they are able to rely on existing infrastructure, institutional capacity and the necessary willingness from different sectors to invest in new alternatives. In this way, they are able to contribute to the mitigation of danger-ous climate change, while at the same time avoiding a 'carbon lock-in', which would constrain the infrastructure and investments to a carbon-intensive economy for decades (Urban and Sumner, 2009).

An alternative to fossil fuel dependence in the transport sector is biofuel production and usage. Biofuel is derived from biological mass, such as sugarcane, corn and other crops, instead of being derived from petroleum, like gasoline. The environmental benefits can be seen in two areas: production and consumption. The production of this alternative fuel has a low net fossil energy requirement and low lifecycle GHG emissions (IEA, 2011), and the combustion of this fuel in biofuel-powered vehicles also results in fewer emissions than conventional gasoline vehicles (AFDC, 2011). The socio-economic benefits of bioethanol are reported to include a reduction in regional disparities and an increase in individual income, domestic growth, the expansion of production of capital goods and employment creation (Pereira de Carvalho and de Oliveira Carrijo, 2007). The Brazilian bioethanol expe-rience, therefore, is an example of low carbon development, as it embraces a change in production and consumption of fuels for the transport sector, substituting to some extent the utilization of gasoline, while at the same time generating socio-economic benefits.

This chapter provides insights into this experience in form of a case study. The method-ology, including the design, the data collection and the potential limitations of this research are briefly explained below.

The case study's design is exploratory, as it aims to give new perspectives grounded on previous theoretical research in a synthesized matter. The nature of a case study is, as under-lined by Yin (1994), an analysis of the main issues with the study question focusing on the 'How'. Brazil is a case study of *how* a middle income country was able to achieve the current status of world leader in sugarcane-based ethanol, hence being an example for low carbon initiatives worldwide.

The data collection for this research followed two approaches: gathering of primary and secondary data. Primary data were collected from interviews with experts from the Brazilian ethanol sector. Anonymous interviewees provided valuable information, especially with regard to their perspectives about the key aspects of biofuel development in the country, which led to the major findings of the case study in an explanatory manner. The interviews were carried out in a semi-structured method, allowing for elaboration, depending on the flow of the dialogue with the experts.

Secondary data, on the other hand, were collected for historical analysis and technical explanations. This was done through desk-based research using data from available documents and readings, including legislations, policies and literature from agencies and institutions.

Box 20.2 elaborates the key issues of bioethanol development in Brazil, followed by a section discussing the case study findings.

Box 20.2 Key issues of bioethanol development in Brazil

The key issues which led to the success of the Brazilian sugarcane-based ethanol development are:[1]

A well-known crop and technology: Brazil hosts vast available lands with appropriate climatic and geographical conditions to grow sugarcane. This crop has been cultivated in Brazil since 1532 and domestically produced ethanol has been used as mandatory ethanol blending of 5 per cent in fuel since 1931. National public investments in R&D focusing on ethanol fuel development, ethanol running engines and the development of agrarian techniques were key factors in developing the ethanol fuel industry.

Energy security: In 1973, when Brazil was importing 90 per cent of its gasoline, oil barrel prices increased significantly resulting in high expenses on oil imports and fuel shortages. This generated an urgency to find alternative solutions to replace part of the oil demand in Brazil.

The government's role: Government played a crucial role by creating and enforcing the regulations related to the formation of this new market. Some of these regulations helped to enable the environment for the creation of supply and demand of sugarcane-based ethanol. Several incentives were offered for both consumers and producers.

The private sector's role: The private sector played a key role, especially the automotive industry, which invested in R&D for the production of millions of ethanol-running vehicles in the early stages of Pro-Alcool and afterwards in the production of FFVs.

Joint public and private efforts: The combination of efforts by the public and the private sector resulted in actions that accelerated the learning process and added value to the ethanol production. The framework provided by the government to support the ethanol industry was crucial for capacity building and technology development in both sectors.

Existing national demand: In the early 1970s, Brazil already had a well-established car industry with millions of consumers and a reasonable infrastructure (gas stations, roads, etc.). Small investments were necessary for adapting the infrastructure to ethanol.

Ethanol on the political agenda: The strong incentives for the creation of an ethanol market in Brazil had their origins in the governmental programme Pro-Alcool. In spite of experiencing several oscillations during four decades, ethanol was always seen as an important energy source for the national energy matrix and was therefore highlighted in the political agenda. Ethanol blending into gasoline has been used as an 'exhaust valve' for either global sugar price reduction or replacement for high oil prices. During several decades the percentage of ethanol blending changed according to the global and national economic context.

Case study findings

The findings of this case study are presented as four main topics: historical background; Pro-Alcool, the national ethanol programme; the bioethanol learning curve; and the current situation and future perspectives.

Historical background

Five centuries ago, Portuguese sailors arrived in Brazil and introduced sugarcane plantations in the country. The intention was to end the world's monopoly of French sugar that was being produced in the Caribbean Islands (Moreira *et al.*, 1999). Ever since, sugarcane has not only been an integral part of Brazil's agriculture, but also of its social, political and economic history, mainly due to domestic production and the export of sugar. However, the innovative production of sugar from sugar-beet by the French resulted in a decline of sugar exports from Brazil. The focus of investments in R&D for alternative products from sugarcane led the industry to initiate the production of ethanol. In 1931, the government enforced the mandatory blending of 5 per cent of domestically produced ethanol into imported gasoline (Decreto nº 19.717, 1931), and in 1933, the 'Bioethanol and Sugar Institute' (Institute of Sugar and Alcohol, IAA) was created as an attempt to encourage the consumption of both commodities (Martines-Filho *et al.*, 2006). From there on, the production of sugarcane-based ethanol was driven by the fluctuations in sugar and oil prices on the global market.

Due to the oil crisis in 1973 the petroleum prices quadrupled from US$3 to US$12 per barrel[2] (Machado Cavarzan, 2008) and Brazil, as a gasoline importing country, had to face fuel shortages, inflation and account deficits (Martines-Filho *et al.*, 2006). The need for a cheaper liquid fuel, which would replace the import of gasoline, became very strong. Improving the ethanol industry seemed to be the best alternative, and the fall of sugar prices that occurred approximately at the same time on the international market, contributed to the realization that major efforts were needed (Machado Cavarzan, 2008).

The political context contributed to the creation of a national ethanol programme as the ability to rule of the military dictatorship that was in charge of the country between 1974 and 1979 was threatened by the difficult economic situation characterized by the increase in oil prices. The domestic fuel supply for sugarcane-based ethanol was stimulated by implementing market intervention measures such as quotas, marketing guidelines, price setting and subsidized interest rates (Martines-Filho *et al.*, 2006).

Although environmental benefits and low carbon development are nowadays the key drivers for ethanol implementation, the reasons for introducing the programme in 1975 were mainly economic and to some extent political.

Pro-Alcool: ethanol programme

The national ethanol programme Pro-Alcool was launched in 1975 with the main objective of increasing the production of bioethanol fuel for the transport sector (Coelho *et al.*, 2006).

From an economic perspective, the estimated cost of Pro-Alcool is approximately US$7.1 billion, with $4 billion financed by the Brazilian government and the remaining by the private sector. Valuing the volume of bioethanol fuel consumed between 1976 and 2005 at gasoline prices in the world market (adjusted for inflation), this yields an estimate of $195.5 billion in foreign exchange savings, $69.1 billion in avoided imports and $126.4 billion in avoided foreign debt interest (BNDES and CGEE, 2008)

The combination of incentives adopted by Pro-Alcool included:

- establishing higher minimum levels of anhydrous ethanol in gasoline (progressively increased to 25 per cent);
- guaranteeing lower consumer prices for hydrated ethanol relative to gasoline (at the time, fuel prices throughout the entire production chain were determined by the federal government);
- guaranteeing competitive prices to the bioethanol producer, even in the face of more attractive international prices for sugar than for bioethanol (competition subsidy);
- creating credit lines with favourable conditions for mills to increase their production capacity;
- reducing taxes on new cars and on annual registration fees for hydrated bioethanol vehicles;
- making the sale of hydrated bioethanol at gas stations compulsory;
- maintaining strategic reserves to ensure supply out of season.

(BNDES and CGEE, 2008: 149)

The programme went through different phases and there is no consensus on its institutional closure.

First phase: 1975–79

Based on the existing infrastructure from the sugar industry, additional plants for ethanol production were created. Production was not only accomplished, but exceeded target goals (Pereira de Carvalho and de Oliveira Carrijo, 2007). Bioethanol production grew from 580,000 m? to around 3.7 million m?, surpassing the goal established for that year by 15 per cent (BNDES and CGEE, 2008).

Second phase: 1979–85

With the impact of the second oil crisis in 1979, the ethanol production came to a peak during this period. The programme was expanded with a strong emphasis on R&D based on a multi-sectoral approach, including the technological, chemical, agricultural and particularly the automotive and mechanic segments. The manufacture of automobiles powered by hydrated alcohol in the 1980s had meaningful impacts on the use of this fuel, evidenced by an increase from 1.1 per cent to 55.5 per cent in 1979. The percentage of alcohol-powered vehicles rose from 0.5 per cent to 66 per cent in 1986, while the circulation of gasoline-powered vehicles dropped from 89 per cent to 20.9 per cent (Pereira de Carvalho and de Oliveira Carrijo, 2007).

Third phase: 1986 to approximately 2003

Pro-Alcool was affected by increasing inflation, extended domestic and external debt, rising interest rates in the international market and a reduction in the oil price per barrel. The Brazilian state was therefore not able to continue supporting the expansion of the sugarcane industry based on public subsidies. Finally, the drop in the share of alcohol vehicles, the end of government subsidies to the sugarcane sector, the extinction of the IAA and the decrease in ethanol production, among other factors, led to a supply crisis and a reduction in consumer confidence (Pereira de Carvalho and de Oliveira Carrijo, 2007). This phase is also defined as the Brazilian ethanol crisis, or the stagnation period. On the other hand, it is characterized by two key factors that helped to maintain the ethanol industry: the implementation of adequate policies, such as the law increasing the mandatory blending of 20–25 per cent of ethanol and the continuous investments in R&D for technological improvements such as the new development in crop varieties, biological pest control introduction and greater soil selectivity (Martines-Filho *et al.*, 2006).

The end of Pro-Alcool

There is no consensus about the institutional closure of Pro-Alcool. However, 1997 is considered a milestone year as sugarcane prices and all ethanol prices started to be determined by market forces, while the government control has been gradually reduced. At the same time, the 40 per cent tariffs applied on sugar exports were eliminated and market-based prices for anhydrous ethanol took place. A few years later, the deregulation of prices for sugarcane and hydrated ethanol also became effective (Martines-Filho *et al.*, 2006).

The new era without government intervention

In 2003, the production revival of ethanol running cars through the use of FFVs occurred under government supervision and taxation incentives, but without interventions or subsidies.

Bioethanol learning curve

The learning process, with regard to the technology, was crucial to the development of the ethanol industry and to the competitiveness of the fuel, especially in terms of agricultural production, the reduction of production costs, FFV technology and the sustainability of the production process.

Through the implementation of Pro-Alcool, the ethanol industry was experiencing a higher technological growth rate than that of agricultural production. Investments in agricultural technology were necessary to diminish the risk of an uneven growth rate between agriculture and industry. Planalsucar, a governmental programme, addressed this issue by developing new weather-resistant varieties of sugarcane crops, introduced biological pest control and enhanced superior soil selectivity and management. Between 1975 and 2004 sugarcane productivity gradually increased at a growth rate of 2.3 per cent (Martines-Filho *et al.*, 2006).

It was only due to the pricing policy applied by the government that ethanol was made feasible to consumers, as the production costs were not market competitive in the initial phase (Coelho *et al.*, 2006). Over time, due to the increase in agro-industrial yields and economies of scale, unit costs started to fall. When ethanol became more efficient and cost competitive, fuel prices were liberalized, as government subsidies for anhydrous and hydrated ethanol production were no longer needed. Ethanol, compared to gasoline had become economically competitive (Goldemberg *et al.*, 2003). At the same time, the bioethanol industry had matured considerably and is currently subject to private investments rather than government subsidies (Martines-Filho *et al.*, 2006).

FFV technology also passed through significant learning processes, as the automotive industry had to adapt the fleet to the ethanol fuel. União da Indústria de Cana-de-Açúcar

(UNICA) (2009) considers the mandatory blending of gasoline with 20–25 per cent of anhydrous ethanol and the simultaneous expansion of the FFV market essential within the government initiatives towards ethanol expansion. Brazilian FFVs have the advantage of being powered by a whole range of blends of ethanol, up to 100 per cent.

The learning process in industrial ethanol production was important, as a reasonable percentage of the bioethanol mills are energy self-sufficient. In a cogeneration process, the sugarcane bagasse generates the electricity needed for the production of ethanol, meaning that no additional source of external energy has to be included. Fossil fuels are only used indirectly in the ethanol process, as they are limited to the transportation trucks, harvesting machines and the use of fertilizers (Coelho *et al.*, 2006).

Current situation and future perspectives

The recognition of environmental benefits to ethanol production increases the present number of opportunities. For example, the GHG balance is favourable: the avoided emissions regarding the life cycle of gasoline are estimated at 78 per cent when anhydrous ethanol is used as E25 in Brazil. However, improvements are necessary in order to achieve better environmental results. Refining logistics (mainly reducing the use of trucks for ethanol transportation) and increasing surplus electricity production from sugarcane residues are other necessary actions to improve the GHG emission reduction potential (Walter *et al.*, 2009).

At the same time, demand for ethanol fuel consumption tends to increase in Brazil's internal market as well as in other countries. Under these circumstances, the national FFV market is expected to increase production and represent up to 65 per cent of the Brazilian light vehicles fleet by 2015. At the same time, ethanol fuel is being tested in other vehicles such as buses for public transportation, aiming to reduce urban pollution and increasing the transportation energy mix (Moreira *et al.*, 2008).

Further development in Brazil's private sector includes Embraer, a Brazilian aircraft manufacturer, which has also tested ethanol fuel in airplanes (Martines-Filho *et al.*, 2006). The Brazilian giant energy company Petrobras has announced significant investments in the production of cellulosic ethanol fuel aiming to increase ethanol production efficiency without increasing plantation areas. Bioelectricity is another product of sugarcane/ethanol industry development as it transforms the sugarcane bagasse and straw into energy. Sugarcane bagasse is becoming an important primary energy source for generating renewable electricity, and by 2020 could reach a production level comparable with the output of the Itaipu hydropower dam (Leão de Sousa and Carvalho Macedo, 2010). In 2011, the dam generated 92.24 million MW/h (Itaipu, 2012).

As previously mentioned, Brazil's internal demand for ethanol fuel is likely to increase in the coming years. In order to fulfil this demand, national production must increase. The guarantees provided by the government will be crucial to incentivize the increase in ethanol production. Nowadays, ethanol producers take on the entire risk of its production as the fuel distributors will only purchase the amount of fuel they are expecting to sell at that time (Schouchana, 2006).

Based on the latter, ethanol producers in Brazil are now requesting long-term purchase guarantees in order to motivate the ethanol industry. At the same time, ethanol producers also lobby for a more transparent and defined policy regarding ethanol production. Since the state set a free market for ethanol in Brazil, producers feel the necessity for an ethanol regulating policy, providing the necessary incentives (not subsidies) and guarantees as occurs for gasoline. These guarantees are expected to attract new investments to the sector as well as increase the production for existing mills.

On the other hand, the external market supply is also being considered as an opportunity by Brazilian ethanol producers. As an example, the recent targets of biofuel blending adopted by the USA, the EU and Japan have caused optimism regarding the creation of an ethanol global market with reduced barriers. Of particular relevance, the USA announced the end of national ethanol production subsidies and import tariffs that could result in an increase in demand for Brazilian ethanol.

The EU has also established a binding target ensuring that 10 per cent of transport fuel in each member state is provided by biofuels by 2020. This has also been considered as an opportunity by Brazilian bioethanol producers as several National Renewable Energy Action Plans (NREAPs) from EU member countries anticipate the need of significant imports in order to reach the 10 per cent renewable energy share in transport (Atanasiu, 2010). To import this fuel, the EU have set sustainability criteria, as well as certain social and environmental conditions, which have to be met by the producing country, prior to a strong commercial trade agreement among those countries.

This challenge to demonstrate the sustainability of the biofuel-related activities has several initiatives already in place in Brazil, such as the certification process being implemented under the EU's REDDs (Desplechin, 2010). In addition, Brazil also has its own initiatives to ensure ethanol production's sustainability such as the Sugarcane Agro Ecological Zoning. This ecological zoning is being implemented by the Brazilian Agricultural Research Corporation (Embrapa), aiming at defining the appropriate areas to grow crops without causing additional[3] impacts on the environment (Embrapa, 2009).

Box 20.3 presents a critique of bioethanol in Brazil and discusses some of the trade-offs.

Box 20.3 Critique

Food vs. fuel

The so-called food vs. fuel debate is about the trade-offs between the availability of land for energy production and land for food production. Critics focus on the argument that biofuel crops compete with the land needed for food crops. According to UNICA (2011) sugarcane (for ethanol and sugar) covers 2.3 per cent of Brazil's total arable land. It is important to note that this includes both sugar and ethanol production. According to Coelho *et al.* (2006) Brazilian sugarcane-based ethanol has become very productive and weather resistant due to genetic improvements and good agricultural practices, which results in an increase of bioethanol production while the land area stays stable. So far, there is no empirical evidence that ethanol production causes harm to food production in Brazil as food production has increased markedly during the last decades. This debate might however be very different for other countries where less land is available for food production.

Deforestation

Another aspect that has been discussed is the risk of deforestation arising from biofuel crop plantations. Although this is an ongoing debate, some specialists affirm that sugarcane does not put pressure on deforestation in the Amazon, as the crop is not suitable to be produced in this region (Coelho *et al.*, 2006). Sugarcane is mainly produced in the south central/southeastern region where the Amazon and the Pantanal are not located. On the other hand, this is where another Brazilian biome, 'the Cerrado', is located and ecologists affirm that sugarcane plantations are being considered as one of the causes of the Cerrado's deforestation (Franco *et al.*, 2010). At the same time, to supply a possible future global biofuel demand, Brazil's production would have to expand significantly, and this would likely require deforestation and substantial GHG emissions (Eide, 2008).

There is also an additional debate on the possible displacement of other agricultural activities into the rainforest due to sugarcane expansion. Walter *et al.* (2009), however, argue that the theory of ethanol-induced deforestation is not confirmed and requires further investigation. According to UNICA (2010) almost 90 per cent of sugarcane production for ethanol is harvested in south central/southeastern Brazil over 2500 km away from the Amazon and the remainder is grown in northeastern Brazil, about the same distance from the Amazon (see Figure 20.1).

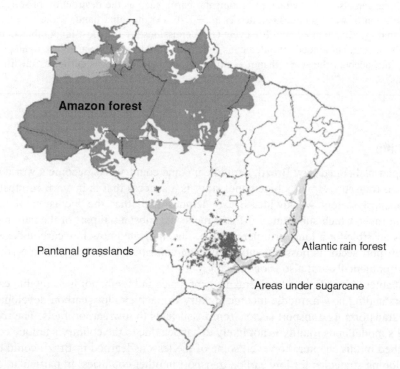

Figure 20.1 Areas under sugarcane cultivation in Brazil
Source: Coelho *et al.*, 2006[4]

Labour conditions

The number of jobs in the sugarcane sector in Brazil is high and is concentrated mainly in the rural areas of the country. According to Coelho *et al.* (2006) 700,000 jobs are created for the 300 million tonnes of sugarcane produced. However, according to Franco *et al.* (2010), the working conditions in the sugarcane plantations are poor and exploitative and are even compared to slave labour. This has caused serious health problems among sugarcane workers during the last decades. Coelho *et al.* (2006), on the other hand, argue that Brazil has recently implemented strict labour laws in the sugarcane sector. They argue that workers in the sugarcane industry are becoming gradually more skilled and better paid. According to primary data, the labour conditions for sugarcane rural workers have improved significantly during the past decade, which might be the result of strict government and civil society control.

GHG emissions and environmental harm

Despite reduced emissions from the combustion of ethanol in vehicles, some experts criticize the final life cycle GHG emissions, as well as the related environmental harm of ethanol. According to Franco *et al.* (2010) the GHG reductions depend on many factors, such as the particular crop, the location, the cultivation methods, land type, as well as production, processing and distribution methods, which do not necessarily mean a real reduction in GHG emissions. As an example, when direct land use change emissions are included in the GHG inventory, sugarcane expansion can promote a carbon debt, becoming an agent to GHG emissions instead of a driver to GHG mitigation (Mello, 2012). At the same time, sugarcane plantations can also cause wider environmental harm, such as the destruction of soil fertility and pollution of water sources (Franco *et al.*, 2010). On the other hand, Walter *et al.* (2008) affirm that the Brazilian ethanol life cycle GHG emissions are the most favourable among all biofuels currently produced. Avoided emissions compared to gasoline are close to 86 per cent, taking into account the way ethanol is utilized in Brazil (and considering a full life cycle analysis).

Conclusion

This chapter elaborated how Brazil, a middle income country, has become a world leader in low carbon transport. Brazil's bioethanol story is a success that is in stark contrast to most other transport sectors worldwide. Brazil demonstrated that the inclusion of clean and renewable fuels, which substitute for fossil fuels as a substantial part of the national energy matrix, is possible for a long term perspective. This indicated how low carbon development in the transport sector is possible and how it can contribute to strengthening a country not only environmentally, but also economically.

The chapter also indicated how Brazil's experience in bioethanol is a suitable case study for understanding how a middle income country can achieve low carbon development and partially transform its transport sector from fossil fuels to low carbon fuels. The replication of Brazil's model in its totality is not likely to happen due to the country's unique conditions as described in this chapter; however, some of the lessons learned in Brazil could be useful for developing strategies for low carbon transport in other countries. In particular, countries that have similar geographic and climatic conditions for sugarcane production, long-term political support and the institutional capacity to provide the required policy framework could be using Brazil's example while respecting their own realities. This chapter also demonstrates that the Brazilian ethanol model does not rely on the global market; its foundations focus on the domestic market supply, which should also be considered as an important factor regarding the programme's sustainability.

In addition, this chapter reveals that some natural and historical key factors were crucial to the implementation of the ethanol programme in Brazil, such as the proper climatic and geographical conditions for sugarcane production, the historical familiarization with sugarcane cultivation as well as the vast land availability found in the country.

On the other hand, during the past decades, ethanol has constantly been included in the agenda of different presidents. This persistence resulted in the strengthening of the institutional capacity to enforce and implement policies and legislation regarding ethanol production and consumption. Several public institutions were designated to support the expansion and improvement of the bioethanol industry.

At the same time, private sector participation contributed to the technological development and adaptation of the transport sector as well as the improvements in R&D in the agricultural development of the sector.

It is also important to highlight the recent government and industry commitment towards solving or clarifying the trade-offs related to bioethanol production, thereby enhancing the opportunities for sustainable low carbon development.

Finally, the chapter shows that low carbon development in the transport sector is neither a distant utopia nor only suitable for high income countries; instead it is a reality in the middle income country of Brazil.

References

Alternative Fuels Data Center (AFDC) (2011) Ethanol emissions, alternative fuels and advanced vehicles data center. Available at: http://www.afdc.energy.gov/afdc/vehicles/emissions_ethanol.html (accessed 19 November 2012).

Atanasiu, B. (2010) The role of bioenergy in the National Renewable Energy Action Plans: a first identification of issues and uncertainties. IEE 08 653 SI2. 529 241. Available at: http://www.ieep.eu/assets/753/bioenergy_in_NREAPs.pdf (accessed 20 November 2012).

Blottnitz, H. and Curran, M. A. (2006) A review of assessments conducted on bio-ethanol as a transportation fuel from a net energy, greenhouse gas, and environmental life cycle perspective. *Journal of Cleaner Production*, 15(7), 607–19.

Brazilian Development Bank (BNDES) and Centro de Gestão e Estudos Estratégicos (CGEE) (2008) Sugarcane-base ethanol, energy for sustainable development, in cooperation with FAO and CEPAL, 1st edition. Rio de Janeiro: BNDES and CGEE.

Coelho, S., Goldemberg, J., Lucon, O. and Guardabassi, P. (2006) Brazilian sugarcane ethanol: lessons learned. *Energy for Sustainable Development*, 10(2), 26–39.

Decreto nº 19.717, 1931. de 20 de Fevereiro de 1931. Available at: http://www2.camara.gov.br/legin/fed/decret/1930-1939/decreto-19717-20-fevereiro-1931-518991-publicacaooriginal-1-pe.html (accessed 19 November 2012).

Desplechin, E. (2010) Certificação do etanol: a visão da indústria brasileira de cana-de-açúcar, ÚNICA Colunas. Available at: http://www.unica.com.br/opiniao/show.asp?msgCode={3CBA204B-8951-446B-8168-EB58391CD6E3} (accessed 19 November 2012).

Eide, A. (2008) The right to food and the impact of liquid biofuels (agrofuels). Rome: FAO.

Embrapa (2009) Sugarcane agroecological zoning, for ethanol and sugar production in Brazil. Available at: http://www.bioetanol.org.br/hotsite/arquivo/editor/file/2o%20Workshop%20Sustentabilidade%20/2nd%20WKS%20Sustainability%20-%20Calso%20Manzato Embrapa%20-%20Ethanol%20Agroecological%20Zoning.pdf (accessed 19 November 2012).

Franco, J., Levidow, L., Fig, D., Goldfarb, L., Hönicke, M. and Mendonça, M. L. (2010) Assumptions in the European Union biofuels policy: frictions with experiences in Germany, Brazil and Mozambique. *Journal of Peasant Studies*, 37(4), 661–98.

Goldemberg, J., Coelho, S., Nastari, P. and Lucon, O. (2003) Ethanol learning curve – the Brazilian experience. *Biomass and Bioenergy*, 26, 301–4.

International Energy Agency (IEA) (2011) Biofuels. Available at: http://www.iea.org/roadmaps/biofuels.asp (accessed 20 November 2012).

Itaipu (2012) Generación. Available at: http://www.itaipu.gov.br/es/energia/generacion (accessed 20 November 2012).

Leão de Sousa, E. and Carvalho Macedo, I. (2010) Ethanol and bioelectricity sugarcane in the future of the energy matrix. Sao Paulo: UNICA – Brazilian Sugarcane Industry Association.

Machado Cavarzan, G. (2008) Economia, discurso e poder: os bastidores políticos do segundo plano nacional de desenvolvimento (II PND). Available at: http://seer.ufrgs.br/aedos/article/view/9817/5616 (accessed 20 November 2012).

Martines-Filho, J., Burnquist, H. and Vian, C. (2006) Bioenergy and the rise of sugarcane-based ethanol in Brazil. *Choices*, 21(2).

Mello, F. (2012) Land use change in sugar cane agrosystem to ethanol production in Brazil. Department of Organismic and Evolutionary Biology, Harvard University, Cambridge, MA. Available at: http://www.hks.harvard.edu/centers/mrcbg/programs/sustsci/people/research-fellows/current-fellows/francisco-mello (accessed 20 November 2012).

Moreira, J. R. and Goldemberg, J. (1999) The alcohol program. *Energy Policy*, 27, 229–45.

Moreira, J. R., Velázquez, S. M., Apolinário, S. M., Melo, E. H. and Elmadjian, P. H. (2008) Projeto BEST – Bioetanol para o transporte sustentável. São Paulo: IEE/CENBIO and Universidade Presbiteriana Mackenzie.

Oilprice.net (2012) Available at: http://www.oil-price.net/ (accessed 20 November 2012).

Pereira de Carvalho, S. and de Oliveira Carrijo, E. L. (2007) A produção de álcool: do PROÁLCOOL ao contexto atual. Goiânia, Brazil.

Schouchana, F. (2006) Formação de estoques de passagem do álcool, Revista Opiniões. Available at: http://www.revistaopinioes.com.br/aa/materia.php?id=258 (accessed 20 November 2012).

União da Indústria de Cana-de-Açúcar (UNICA) (2010) Myths vs. facts. São Paulo: UNICA.

UNICA (2011) Frequently asked questions. Available at: http://english.unica.com.br/FAQ/ (accessed 20 November 2012).

Urban, F. and Sunmer, A. (2009) After 2015: pro-poor low carbon development. IDS Policy Briefing, ISSUE 09. Brighton: Institute of Development Studies at the University of Sussex.

Walter, A., Dolzan, P., Quilodran, O., da Silva, C., Piacente, F. and Segerstedt, A. (2008) A sustainability analysis of the Brazilian ethanol. Supported by UK Embassy, Brazil. London: Defra.

Walter, A., Dolzan, P., Quilodran, O., deOliveira, J., Silva, C., Piacente, F. and Segerstedt, A. (2009) Sustainability assessment of bio-ethanol production in Brazil considering land use change, GHG emissions and socio-economic aspects. *Energy Policy*, 37(10): 5703–16.

Yin, R. (1994) *Case Study Research. Design and Methods*, Second edition. Thousand Oaks, CA: Sage.

Further reading

BNDES and CGEE (2008) Sugarcane-base ethanol, energy for sustainable development, in cooperation with FAO and CEPAL, 1st edition. Rio de Janeiro: BNDES and CGEE.

Goldemberg, J., Coelho, S., Nastari, P. and Lucon, O. (2003) Ethanol learning curve – the Brazilian experience. *Biomass and Bioenergy*, 26, 301–4.

UNICA (2009) Sugarcane industry in Brazil, ethanol, sugar, bioelectricity. São Paulo: UNICA.

Zuurbier, P. and van de Vooren, J. (2008) *Sugarcane Ethanol, Contributions to Climate Change Mitigation and the Environment*. Wageningen: Wageningen Academic Publishers.

Notes

1   According to primary data from interviews with experts.
2   In the first half of 2012 the price per barrel was around US$90–100, with a one-year forecast of $104 per barrel (oilprice.net, 2012).
3   Sugarcane plantations can have negative environmental impacts, such as land use change, water pollution and land degradation (see Box 20.3). The Brazilian government is identifying methods to address these impacts, such as the sugarcane agro-ecological zoning.
4   The figure was first published by Elsevier in Coelho (2006).

21 Carbon capture and storage (CCS) in the USA

Jennie C. Stephens

This chapter reviews the development of carbon capture and storage (CCS) technology in a high income country, namely the USA. The chapter considers the technology, policy and politics, as well as socio-technical dynamics. The USA is among a group of countries with a high carbon energy system heavily dependent on coal, and within these countries many consider CCS as one of the most promising low carbon technologies of the future. CCS is, however, controversial as the technology is debated in the public, media and political circles due to many uncertainties related to costs, the integrity of long-term storage, and how investments in this technology influence investments in and support for other low carbon energy options. This chapter explores the case of CCS development in the USA, revealing perceptions of high potential for low carbon development but various major implementation challenges.

Introduction

As concerns about climate change grow, countries reliant on coal are facing particular challenges with regard to 'low carbon development'. Coal emits more CO_2 per unit of energy than any other fuel, so reconciling coal dependence with the need to reduce CO_2 emissions is a major challenge. Within these countries, carbon capture and storage (CCS) has emerged as a technology with critically important political influence. Visions of 'clean' coal-fired power plants that will not emit CO_2 into the atmosphere have provided powerful motivation for large public and private investments in CCS technology in many of these countries, including the USA (Meadowcroft and Langhelle, 2009). Due to the large scale of CO_2 emission reductions deemed necessary for climate stabilization, some consider CCS a necessary future technology without which society will be unable to mitigate climate change (IEA, 2008). Despite growing interest and investment in CCS, the technology's future remains uncertain due to multiple demonstration and deployment challenges, and the pace of technological development has been slower than many had envisioned five or ten years ago (Bäckstrand *et al.*, 2011).

Understanding CCS development in the USA is important for two reasons: first, the high income country USA has focused its governmental response to climate change on technology rather than policy to a much higher degree than other nations (Stephens, 2009). CCS has been a critical component of this national technological approach, and the USA has invested more money, in absolute terms, in CCS development than any other country in the world (Tjernshaugen, 2008). Second, due to its size, status, and disproportionate contribution to accumulated GHG emissions in the atmosphere, the USA has unique potential for political and technological influence over low carbon development and the future trajectory of global atmospheric CO_2 concentrations (Stephens, 2009).

This chapter will explore the potential of CCS to contribute to low carbon development in the USA by introducing the technology and its current status, by reviewing the USA energy and climate context, by explaining how CCS has changed the politics of coal in the USA, by characterizing the influence of governmental investment in CCS and the changing investment landscape, and by highlighting US technological leadership as well as public concerns and controversy about CCS technology. While CCS has unique potential to contribute to low carbon development, multiple challenges of implementation – including its high cost, its large scale, a lack of regulatory incentives and uncertainty regarding long-term liability, environmental impacts and risks of leakage – are limiting its advancement.

CCS technology and its status

A complete CCS system relies on three sets of technological components: capture, transport and storage (Figure 21.1).

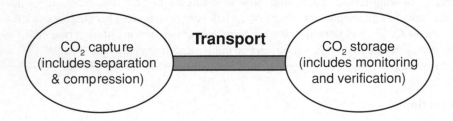

Figure 21.1 CCS system and its technological components: capture, transport, and storage

Technologies that are commercially used in other sectors are currently available for each of these components. CO_2 capture technology, involving separating the CO_2 gas from other gases, is widely used in ammonia production and several other industrial manufacturing processes as well as oil refining and gas processing (IPCC, 2005). CO_2 gas has been transported through pipelines and injected underground for decades, most notably in west Texas where it is used to enhance oil recovery (EOR) of declining-production wells. Millions of tons of CO_2 per year are currently successfully stored underground at several locations, including Sleipner in the North Sea, Weyburn in Saskatchewan, Canada, and In Salah in Algeria (Global CCS Institute, 2011).

Adding CCS to the energy system is projected to be expensive and will involve an energy penalty; that is, capturing, transporting and storing the CO_2 will require additional energy perhaps in the range of 11–40 per cent (House *et al.*, 2009). Estimates of how much it might cost to equip coal-fired power plants with CCS technology vary greatly due to the many uncertainties, complexities and assumptions included; these cost estimates include a range of an increase of 20–90 per cent (IPCC, 2005; Hamilton, 2008; McKinsey, 2008).

Despite growing interest and investment, a fully integrated coal-fired power plant with CCS has not yet been demonstrated (Coninck *et al.*, 2009). There are, however, numerous small-scale projects that focus on demonstrating a limited part of a full CCS system (Global CCS Institute, 2011). Of the 254 CCS projects distributed among 27 countries worldwide (Table 21.1), 20 are actually currently capturing or injecting CO_2 while the others are still in the planning stage.

Table 21.1 Number and type of CCS projects worldwide

Capture projects	65
Storage projects	61
Capture and storage	128
Total	254

Source: NETL 2011 Database

Box 21.1 discusses key terms and concepts relevant for CO_2 capture, transport and storage.

Box 21.1 CO_2 capture, transport and storage

CO_2 capture

CO_2 can be captured from large point sources including power plants and large industrial facilities before it is released to the atmosphere. CO_2 capture technologies associated with power plants can be divided into three categories: (i) post-combustion or 'end-of-pipe' CO_2 capture; (ii) pre-combustion CO_2 capture; and (iii) oxyfuel combustion (IPCC, 2005). Post-combustion CO_2 capture is the type of 'end-of-pipe' technology that could be installed in an existing, conventional coal-fired coal combustion power plants if these facilities were to be retrofitted to capture CO_2. Existing post-combustion capture methods rely primarily on the chemical absorption of the CO_2 in a solvent (amines are most commonly used). Although amine scrubbing for separating CO_2 from dilute gas streams is a widely used process in several industrial applications, amine capture of CO_2 from power plant emissions has yet to be demonstrated in a full-scale commercial power plant, so demonstration projects integrating CO_2 capture technology at operating power plants are needed. Post-combustion capture using chemical absorption is expensive and is estimated to account for up to 80 per cent of some overall predicted costs of a CCS system. The development of advanced methods of post-combustion capture, including membranes and adsorption onto solids, could reduce costs (IEA, 2008).

Pre-combustion CO_2 capture refers to technologies that can separate CO_2 from gaseous fuel before the fuel is burned. The primary currently available pre-combustion capture technology relies on physical absorption of the CO_2 gas onto a solvent. Pre-combustion capture is more efficient and less expensive than post-combustion capture because of the higher percentage of carbon in gaseous fuels before they are burned compared to post-combustion emissions. Pre-combustion CO_2 capture is only relevant for gaseous fuel, so for this technology to be used with coal-fired power plants the coal must be gasified first. With the current suite of capture technologies, therefore, the coal power plant technology known as the integrated gasification combined cycle (IGCC), in which the coal is gasified before being burned, allows CO_2 to be captured at a lower cost than in conventional pulverized coal plants. R&D in pre-combustion capture is currently focusing on developing novel reactor concepts and new adsorption and absorption processes.

Oxyfuel combustion, introducing oxygen instead of air during combustion, is another approach to capturing CO_2 in coal-fired power plants because this produces a relatively pure stream of CO_2 in the emissions. This approach is considered by some to be the best option for retrofitting existing coal power plants; however, the costs of separating oxygen from air to be added to the combustion chamber are high.

Once the CO_2 is separated and captured, the CO_2 needs to be compressed to reduce the volume of the gas to allow for transportation to a storage location. Compressing gas is energy intensive, so this part of the CO_2 capture system adds significantly to the overall operating costs and is also a contributor to the overall energy penalty associated with CCS.

CO_2 transport

After capture, the compressed CO_2 gas needs to be transported to an appropriate storage location. Given the large volumes of CO_2 that would need to be transported, pipelines have been given the most attention. A network of CO_2 pipelines is already in existence in several regions in the USA where CO_2 is used to enhance oil production, so building CO_2 pipelines does not pose technical or safety challenges, although regional siting limitations are possible. CO_2 transportation by ship is also an established technological option that could be important if long distances or challenging geography between sources of CO_2 and storage locations preclude transportation by CO_2 pipeline.

CO_2 storage

Once the CO_2 is captured, injection into naturally occurring geologic formations that provide underground reservoirs is the most promising storage option. Several different types of geologic formations can be used for CO_2 storage, including depleted oil and gas reservoirs, unminable coal seams and deep saline aquifers. Commercial experience injecting CO_2 underground has been established in the oil industry where CO_2 injection is used to enhance oil recovery (EOR); that is, to loosen up residual oil in a well with declining production. This established commercial application of CO_2 injection provides experience as well as early opportunities for deploying CO_2 injection for storage. Storage also includes development of technologies to measure, monitor and verify the location and movement of the CO_2 injected in geologic reservoirs.

US energy and climate context

This section provides some background on the US energy and climate change context that helps to understand the relevance of CCS. Despite a diversity and abundance of energy resources, the USA has been a net importer of energy since the late 1950s when energy consumption began to outpace domestic production. In 2007, imported energy accounted for 29 per cent of all energy consumed in the US (EIA, 2008). Energy consumption is greatest in the industrial sector (about 33 per cent), then transportation (28 per cent), then residential (21 per cent) and finally commercial (17 per cent); consumption has been increasing in all four of these end-use sectors (EIA, 2008). The USA is the largest importer of crude oil and is the third ranking oil-producing country, producing 7.9 per cent of the world total (IEA, 2009).

In 2007, 72 per cent of all electricity generated in the USA was from fossil fuels (coal, petroleum and natural gas), 19 per cent was from nuclear, while renewable energy resources (including hydropower) accounted for 8 per cent (EIA, 2008). Among the fossil fuels, coal dominates, with coal-fired power plants generating almost 50 per cent of all electricity. This major reliance on coal led the USA to pay particular attention to the potential of CCS technology.

The USA has played a conspicuously difficult role in international climate change politics (Sanwal, 2009). At both the international and national level, the USA has been slow to respond to and engage on the climate change issue. A high degree of scepticism about the contribution of human activity to climate changes has been coupled with powerful economic and political interests who want to limit any regulatory or policy change that would incentivize CO_2 emission reductions. This has resulted in deliberate attempts by some US politicians to slow down government action on climate change policy (Dessler and Parson, 2010).

The USA's uncooperative failure to follow through with ratification of the Kyoto Protocol coupled with its failure to develop a domestic climate change policy to reduce GHG emissions demonstrates the divisive and contentious nature of climate change politics in the USA (Boykoff, 2011). And this difficult policy landscape has resulted in the US government focusing on climate mitigation technology rather than climate policy. Given the USA's history of leadership in scientific and technological research, and its human resource and institutional capacity for advancing science and technology, a national focus on climate mitigation technology is not surprising. It is within this context, with a strongly developed scientific and technological research and production base, that the USA took the early lead technologically and politically in many respects with regard to advancing CCS (Coninck, 2008; Tjernshaugen, 2008).

Changing coal politics in the USA: CCS and its low carbon potential

The vision of CCS as a technology that could enable low carbon development while still relying on coal has changed the politics of coal in many places, but its influence in the USA is particularly pronounced (Stephens, 2009). The USA is among the countries in the world that has invested most heavily in CCS (Tjernshaugen, 2008).

Politicians from regions of the country where the coal industry is most influential have been among the most powerful opponents of national climate change legislation (Dessler and Parson, 2010). For coal states and politicians representing those states, however, CCS has provided a potential vision of a carbon constrained future in which the coal industry could still thrive (Feldpausch-Parker *et al.*, 2012). From a political perspective, therefore, the potential of CCS technology has been valuable in contributing to the engagement of critical actors in national climate policy discussions; CCS has enabled some constituents who had been previously reluctant to even acknowledge the challenges of climate change to engage in the climate energy political discourse (Stephens, 2011).

Despite the powerful political influence of coal, public opposition to building new coal-fired power plants has grown rapidly in the past few years. In 2005 over 100 new coal-fired power plants in the USA were in various stages of planning, but cancellations have been frequent and since then only a handful of new plants have actually been built. While economic factors and rising capital costs have clearly contributed to these proposed plant cancellations, some plants have been cancelled in direct response to concerns about CO_2 emissions and the economic and environmental liability of locking-in to a high carbon-emitting power plant.

In this context CCS can be viewed as playing a new moderating role in opposition to coal. A few years ago anti-coal advocates who called for a moratorium on coal-fired power plants may have been considered radical and impractical (Stephens, 2009). Now, some of the same advocates can use CCS as a qualifier to their calls. That is, a position that says 'no new coal plants unless they have CCS' represents a more practical stance. This anti-coal position seems more reasonable (Stephens, 2011). Given the long anticipated time horizon before CCS may be implemented (owing to the need still to demonstrate the technology at scale and also the complicated changes to the regulatory and economic system that would be necessary to create incentives for actual CCS implementation), a call for no new coal plants without CCS is, in the short term, equivalent to a call for no new coal plants (Stephens, 2009).

Government investment in CCS

In considering advancements in CCS, the US government's role is particularly critical due to the technology's large scale and high cost (Torvanger and Meadowcroft, 2011). In addition, unlike other technologies that may have numerous benefits or potential co-benefits which may provide incentives for private firms to invest in technology innovation, there is only one fundamental reason to develop and advance CCS, and that is to reduce CO_2 emissions associated with fossil fuel-based energy production. Given that the economic and regulatory system in the USA has not incorporated a cost to CO_2 emissions, there is limited current value to developing a technology that could avoid CO_2 emissions (Markusson *et al.*, 2012). Some incentive does exist, however, and is derived from a combination of the anticipation of future CO_2 regulation, eagerness to be perceived by the public and investors as being environmentally responsible and prepared for future carbon limitations, and also from a need to be in compliance with carbon regulations in other parts of the world. Nevertheless, the magnitude of investment needed to build a pilot plant and the uncertainty of the financial returns on investing in an unproven technology contribute to the private sector's reluctance to invest in CCS without some government involvement or reassurances (Markusson *et al.*, 2012). Therefore, the level of government interest and investment in this technology plays a huge role in determining its fate.

Box 21.2 elaborates the issue of government support for technology innovation.

Box 21.2 Government support for technology innovation

Technology innovation can be divided into three interconnected phases: R&D, demonstration and deployment (Figure 21.2).

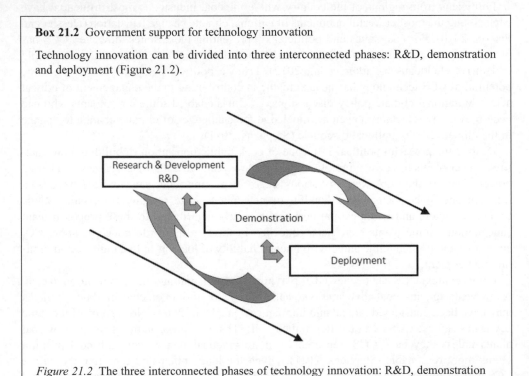

Figure 21.2 The three interconnected phases of technology innovation: R&D, demonstration and deployment

Government support for technology innovation can take various different forms and can be channelled through multiple mechanisms depending on the targeted stage of the innovation process (Gallagher *et al.*, 2006). Government initiatives have different expectations and structures with regard to how the effort will interact with, integrate with, or influence the private sector. For example, at the R&D phase, federal money to support technology research can be allocated for specific R&D institutions (either public or private) or can be awarded through grants to private firms. Similarly at the demonstration phase, government initiatives could provide either full or partial support for pilot projects through grants, tax credits or loans. Federal initiatives to support actual technology adoption at scale, i.e. deployment, include many potential mechanisms including regulations, mandates, subsidies, loans, etc.

Box 21.3 explores the case study of FutureGen, one of the most important CCS projects in the USA. This case study exemplifies the ambivalence the US government has in relation to low carbon development and climate change mitigation.

Box 21.3 FutureGen: an important CCS demonstration project in the USA

FutureGen is one of the most important US CCS projects, and this initiative demonstrates the US government's preference for supporting technology for climate change mitigation rather than policy. FutureGen was initially conceptualized by various US energy experts to be the first near-zero emissions, commercial-scale power plant (275 MW) that would simultaneously demonstrate CCS, hydrogen production and the advanced coal power plant technology known as the integrated gasification combined cycle (IGCC) (DoE, 2004). The FutureGen initiative is a public–private partnership between the US Department of Energy (DoE) and the FutureGen Industrial Alliance, Inc., a non-profit consortium of some of the world's largest coal and energy companies. The project, announced in February 2003, was presented as the flagship programme for the Bush Administration's strategy on clean coal technology development and climate change mitigation. The Bush administration (2001–2009), while expressing opposition to any national regulation designed to reduce CO_2 emissions (Abraham, 2004), consistently demonstrated political support for the development of CCS (NEC, 2006), but the FutureGen CCS project was labelled 'the cornerstone' of the US climate change programme (*Washington Post*, 2008).

Despite almost a decade of planning and political strategizing, FutureGen has not yet been built and the project's design and structure have undergone two major 'restructuring' initiatives. Nevertheless, the project has become widely known and has received significant media attention, thereby facilitating learning about CCS by multiple actors (Markusson *et al.*, 2011). With regard to public acceptance of CCS, FutureGen provides an example of a generally favourable public perception of the technology due in large part to the competitive site selection process that motivated investment in education and outreach by multiple entities, including the US Department of Energy, the FutureGen Alliance and the individual states (Texas and Illinois) who were competing for the project (Markusson *et al.*, 2011).

Changing investment landscape

Given the large-scale infrastructure investments required to develop CCS and the minimal regulatory requirements to incentivize its advancement, both public and private investment has been and will continue to be critical to the technology's advancement. Since 2005, US$25 billion in direct government funding for CCS has been announced worldwide, with

80 per cent of these announcements focused on support for large-scale CCS demonstration projects (Global CCS Institute, 2011). While not all of these announcements have resulted in distribution of public funds, the magnitude of government investment has been large, with the USA, Canada, Australia and Norway among those with the largest public commitments to CCS. Although the global financial crisis has contributed to the cancellation or delay of several projects (Global CCS Institute, 2009), the financial crisis also resulted in some increases of funding in the USA because the 2009 American Recovery and Reinvestment Act committed more than US$3.1 billion to CCS.

Given the high cost and large risks (both financial and environmental) associated with CCS investments, the vast majority of CCS projects around the world have relied on a combination of public and private funding. Quantifying levels of private investment is difficult, but it is clear that levels of private funding are related and to some extent connected to levels of public support. In addition, private sector investment in CCS has been influenced by firms' perceptions of an emerging CCS market, which is influenced by perceptions of the emerging legal and regulatory framework for CCS. In the private sector, the oil and gas industry has dominated private CCS investment due in large part to the strategic opportunity associated with their technical capacity in sub-surface geological engineering.

Public perception and CCS controversy

In considering the potential for CCS to contribute to low carbon development in the USA, public perception of the technology and public controversy must be addressed. Awareness of and understanding about CCS remains limited in the USA, and recognition for the need for communication strategies related to CCS and other emerging energy technologies is growing (Reiner *et al.*, 2006; Reiner, 2008; Stephens *et al.*, 2009). Confidence about the technical feasibility of CCS has been growing, yet like any technology its deployment will be influenced by many social factors including public perception (Markusson *et al.*, 2012).

Although many who work within the CCS community accept the usefulness and necessity of CCS technology, public controversy has the potential to thwart its advancement (Bradbury *et al.*, 2009). Public concern and opposition to CCS can be divided into two categories related to different perceived risks at global and local levels: (i) general opposition to the technology as an end-of-pipe, expensive climate mitigation option that is resource-intensive, promotes the use of fossil fuels, competes with renewable energy sources, and is technologically complex and environmentally risky; and (ii) project-specific opposition among communities that are confronted with planned projects and perceive local risks associated with those projects (Wilson *et al.*, 2003; Bielicki and Stephens, 2008). The environmental community has been divided in their level of support for this technology (Wong-Parodi *et al.*, 2008). Scepticism about the technology's potential to facilitate a transition away from fossil fuels is strong (Greenpeace International, 2008), but there are also environmental organizations that are highly supportive or accepting of CCS (e.g. WWF, Bellona, Natural Resources Defense Council).

The most high-profile public opposition examples have not occurred in the USA, however, but have been associated with several recent proposed CCS projects in Europe including Vattenfall's cancelled and postponed storage projects in Denmark and Germany (NyTeknik, 2009) and the cancelled Barendrecht project in the Netherlands (Feenstra *et al.*, 2010; Van Noorden, 2010). The first public reporting of CO_2 leakage at a CCS storage project occurred in January 2011 in Saskatchewan, Canada, where a farmer alleged that CO_2 from the Weyburn project was degrading his land and killing animals on his property (Weber and Graham, 2011). While representatives of industry and the government moved quickly to reassure the public that the leaking CO_2 was likely from a natural source rather than from the CO_2 storage project, the controversy is not yet over as the community is waiting for an independent investigation that is currently underway. The impact of these public controversies on the future of CCS is not yet clear, but clearly public controversy may limit the potential of CCS to contribute to low carbon development.

Box 21.4 briefly lists the key criticisms of CCS.

Box 21.4 Key criticisms of CCS

- increases costs of energy;
- energy penalty – requires additional energy usage to accomplish;
- detracts investment from developing renewable energy technology;
- subsidizes continued use of fossil fuels;
- end-of-pipe technology so it does not encourage change of behaviour;
- long-term liability – who will be responsible in 50–100 years?
- difficult to imagine a regulatory structure that would effectively monitor, measure and enforce;
- risks of leakage (gradual or sudden leakage) including both environmental risks and health and safety risks;
- unknown ecological impacts of geological storage.

Conclusion – CCS and low carbon development: an uncertain future

Many who are concerned about the challenges of energy and climate change have recognized the valuable potential that CCS has to contribute to low carbon development. Particularly in countries that are heavily reliant on coal for electricity generation, CCS offers a unique technological opportunity to reduce the carbon impact of sustained coal use. Despite this potential, CCS faces major challenges of implementation, including its high cost, the large scale of its deployment, its technological complexity and a lack of regulatory incentives. Other challenges relate to liability (who will be ultimately responsible for ensuring the long-term underground storage of the CO_2?) (Wilson *et al.*, 2007), monitoring and enforcement (how will stored CO_2 be accurately and confidently measured and documented?) (Pollak *et al.*, 2011) and leakage risks (what are the potential environmental, health and safety risks of potential CO_2 leakage?).

A complicated uncertain future for CCS emerges when the strong levels of interest and investment that the technology has received to date are juxtaposed with its multiple challenges. While CCS technology has potential to contribute to a lower carbon future in the USA and beyond, other options, including advancing renewable energy and reducing energy consumption, may be more realistic and practical.

References

Abraham, S. (2004) The Bush Administration's approach to climate change. *Science*, 305(5684), 616–17.

Bäckstrand, K., Meadowcroft, J. and Oppenheimer, M. (2011) The politics and policy of carbon capture and storage: framing an emergent technology. *Global Environmental Change*, 21(2), 275–81.

Bielicki, J. and Stephens, J. C. (2008) Public perception of carbon capture and storage technology workshop report. Energy Technology Innovation Policy Group Workshop Series. Cambridge, MA: Harvard Kennedy School.

Boykoff, M. T. (2011) *The Politics of Climate Change: a Survey*. London and New York: Routledge, Taylor and Francis.

Bradbury, J., Ray, I., Peterson, T., Wade, S., Wong-Parodi, G. and Feldpausch, A. (2009) The role of social factors in shaping public perceptions of CCS: results of multi-state focus group interviews in the US. *Energy Procedia*, 1(1), 4665–72.

Coninck, H. D. (2008) The international race for CO_2 capture and storage: and the winner is…? *FACET Commentary*, 12.

Coninck, H. D., Stephens, J. C. and Metz, B. (2009) Global learning on carbon capture and storage: a call for strong international cooperation on CCS demonstration. *Energy Policy*, 37(6), 2161–5.

Dessler, A. E. and Parson, E. A. (2010) *The Science and Politics of Global Climate Change*. Cambridge: Cambridge University Press.

Department of Energy (DoE) (2004) FutureGen, integrated hydrogen, electric power production and carbon sequestration research initiative. Washington, DC: Department of Energy Office of Fossil Energy.

Energy Information Administration (EIA) (2008) Energy Information Administration. Annual energy review 2007. Washington, DC: Energy Information Administration, US Department of Energy.

Feenstra, C. F. J., Mikunda, T. and Brunsting, S. (2010) What happened in Barendrecht? Case study on the planned onshore carbon dioxide storage in Barendrecht, the Netherlands, ECN and Global CCS Institute. Available at: http://admin.cottoncrc.org.au/files/files/pybx.pdf (accessed 20 November 2012).

Feldpausch-Parker, A. M., Ragland, C., Chuadhry, R., Melnick, L. L., Hall, D. M., Stephens, J. C., Wilson, E. J. and Peterson, T. R. (2012) Spreading the news on carbon capture and storage: a state-level media comparison. *Environmental Communication* (in press). Accepted May 2012.

Gallagher, K. S., Holdren, J. P. and Sagar, A. D. (2006) Energy-technology innovation. *Annual Review of Environment and Resources*, 31, 193–237.

Global CCS Institute (2009) Report 1: status of carbon capture and storage project globally. Strategic analysis of the global status of carbon capture and storage. Canberra: Global CCS Institute.

Global CCS Institute (2011) The global status of CCS 2010. Canberra: Global CCS Institute.

Greenpeace International (2008) False hope, why carbon capture and storage won't save the climate. Amsterdam: Greenpeace International.

Hamilton, M. (2008) How not to build CCS: uncertainty in rising costs and US public policy. Presentation at the MIT Carbon Sequestration Forum IX, 17 September, Cambridge, MA.

House, K. Z., Harvey, C. F., Aziz, M. J. and Schrag, D. P. (2009) The energy penalty of post-combustion CO_2 capture and storage and its implications for retrofitting the US installed base. *Energy and Environmental Science*, 2(2), 193–205.

International Energy Agency (IEA) (2008) CO_2 capture and storage – a key carbon abatement option. Paris: International Energy Agency.

IEA (2009) World energy statistics 2009. Paris: International Energy Agency.

Intergovernmental Panel on Climate Change (IPCC) (2005) IPCC special report on carbon dioxide capture and storage. Cambridge: Cambridge University Press.

Markusson, N., Ishii, A. and Stephens, J. C. (2011) The social and political complexities of learning in CCS demonstration projects. *Global Environmental Change*, 21, 293–302.

Markusson, N., Shackley, S. and Evar, B. (eds) (2012) *The Social Dynamic of Carbon Capture and Storage: Understanding CCS Representations, Governance and Innovation*. Abingdon: Routledge.

McKinsey and Co. (2008) Carbon capture and storage: assessing the economics. Available at: http://assets.wwf.ch/downloads/mckinsey2008.pdf (accessed 20 November 2012).

Meadowcroft, J. and Langhelle, O. (eds) (2009) *Caching the Carbon: the Politics and Policy of Carbon Capture and Storage*. Cheltenham: Edward Elgar.

National Economic Council (NEC) (2006) Advanced energy initiative (report of the National Economic Council). NEC, Washington, DC.

NyTeknik (2009) Protester stoppar danskt CO_2-lager (Protests stop Danish CO_2 storage). Available at: http://www.nyteknik.se/nyheter/energi_miljo/energi/article583207.ece (accessed 20 November 2012).

Pollak, M., Phillips, S. J. and Vajjhala, S. (2011) Carbon capture and storage policy in the United States: a new coalition endeavors to change existing policy. *Global Environmental Change*, 21(2), 313–23.

Reiner, D. (2008) A looming rhetorical gap: a survey of public communications activities for carbon dioxide capture and storage technologies. EPRG Working Paper 0801. European Commission FP6 ACCSEPT Project. Available at: http://www.electricitypolicy.org.uk/pubs/wp/eprg0801.pdf (accessed 20 November 2012).

Reiner, D. M., Curry, T. E., Figueiredo, M. A. D., Herzog, H. J., Ansolabehere, S. D., Itaoka, K., Johnsson, F. and Odenberger, M. (2006) American exceptionalism? Similarities and differences in national attitudes toward energy policy and global warming. *Environmental Science and Technology*, 40(7), 2093–8.

Sanwal, M. (2009) Reflection on the climate negotiations: a Southern perspective. *Climate Policy*, 9(3), 330–3.

Stephens, J. C. (2009) Technology leader, policy laggard: carbon capture and storage (CCS) development for climate mitigation in the US. Political context, in Meadowcroft, J. and Langhelle, O. (eds) *Caching the Carbon: the Politics and Policy of Carbon Capture and Storage*. Cheltenham: Edward Elgar Publishing, p. 320.

Stephens, J. C. (2011) An uncertain future for carbon capture and storage. *Federation of American Scientists*, submitted 17 June 2011.

Stephens, J. C., Bielicki, J. M. and Rand, G. M. (2009) learning about carbon capture and storage: changing stakeholder perceptions with expert information. *Energy Procedia*, 1(1), 4655–63. Proceedings of the 9th International Conference on Greenhouse Gas Control Technologies (GHGT-9), 16–20 November 2008, Washington, DC.

Tjernshaugen, A. (2008) Political commitment to CO_2 capture and storage: evidence from government RD&D budgets. *Mitigation, Adaptation, Strategy Global Change*, 13, 1–21.

Torvanger, A. and Meadowcroft, J. (2011) The political economy of technology support: making decisions about CCS and low carbon energy technologies. *Global Environmental Change*, 21(2), 303–12.

Van Noorden, R. (2010) Buried trouble. *Nature*, 463, 871–3.

Washington Post (2008) The demise of FutureGen. *The Washington Post*, Editorial. 16 February.

Weber, B. and Graham, J. (2011) Land fizzing like soda pop: farmer says CO_2 injected underground is leaking. *The Canadian Free Press*, 11 January.

Wilson, E. J., Friedmann, S. J. and Pollak, M. F. (2007) Research for deployment: incorporating risk, regulation, and liability for carbon capture and sequestration. *Environmental Science and Technology*, 41(17), 5945–52.

Wilson, E. J., Johnson, T. L. and Keith, D. W. (2003) Regulating the ultimate sink: managing the risks of geologic CO_2 storage. *Environmental Science and Technology*, 37(16), 3476–83.

Wong-Parodi, G., Ray, I. and Farrell, A. E. (2008) Environmental non-government organizations' perceptions of geologic sequestration. *Environmental Research Letters*, 3(2).

Further reading

IEA (2012) A policy strategy for CCS. Available at: http://www.iea.org/papers/2012/policy_strategy_for_ccs.pdf: International Energy Agency (accessed 20 November 2012).

IPCC (2005) IPCC special report on carbon dioxide capture and storage. Cambridge: Cambridge University Press.

Markusson, N., Shackley, S. and Evar, B. (eds) (2012) *The Social Dynamic of Carbon Capture and Storage: Understanding CCS Representations, Governance and Innovation*. Abingdon: Routledge.

Meadowcroft, J. and Langhelle, O. (eds) (2009) *Caching the Carbon: the Politics and Policy of Carbon Capture and Storage*. Edward Elgar, Cheltenham.

22 Home energy efficiency policy in Germany and the UK

Jan Rosenow

Energy efficiency has recently experienced a revival as part of the attempts to reduce GHG emissions. However, global energy demand has not fallen so far and is projected to increase even further. There is a need for ambitious energy efficiency policies if energy demand reduction is to play an important role for achieving low carbon development. This chapter looks at the approach taken in Germany and the UK, two high income countries that are internationally recognized for their innovative energy efficiency policies. More specifically, the principal policy instrument targeting energy use in homes in each country is analysed.

Introduction

A path of low carbon development inevitably needs to address two key issues related to energy: The carbon intensity of energy *production* as well as the level of energy *consumption* (Urban, 2010). These are the main two options to reduce the carbon emissions in the energy system which are the focus of national and transnational climate policy. For example, the 2007 EU climate and energy package (European Commission, 2010) sets a reduction target for EU GHG emissions of at least 20 per cent below 1990 levels by 2020 and a reduction of 80 per cent by 2050. Part of the policy package is a binding target to achieve a 20 per cent share of EU energy consumption to come from renewable resources by 2020 (to reduce the carbon intensity of energy production) and an indicative target to reduce primary energy use by 20 per cent by 2020 compared with projected levels, to be achieved by improving energy efficiency (to reduce energy consumption). This chapter focuses on the issue of reducing energy *consumption* through energy efficiency measures in industrialized countries. The issue of energy production is addressed by other chapters in the book (see Chapters 9, 10, 17 and 18).

While discussing some of the key issues around energy efficiency, this chapter looks in more detail at two prominent energy efficiency policies in the household sector as a case study for industrialized, high income countries. The two examples are chosen because they are widely considered as blueprints for successful energy efficiency policies and these countries could therefore provide examples for energy efficiency policies in other high income countries. However, the policy instruments are very distinct in the way they address energy efficiency improvements and show two possible options for tackling energy use in residential buildings. The first example is the Energy Savings Obligations in the United Kingdom (UK), also known as the Supplier Obligation (SO). Today the SO is the most important policy instrument to deliver energy and carbon savings in the residential sector in the UK

(OFGEM, 2005). The second example is the German CO_2 Buildings Rehabilitation Programme (CBRP). In Germany the CBRP is the principal policy instrument to reduce GHG emissions from residential buildings (BMU, 2007). Both policy instruments focus on residential buildings only, a sector that is particularly important for GHG mitigation as will be demonstrated below.

The value of contrasting the two cases is manifold: it shows the very different architecture of the two policy instruments discussed and showcases two prominent examples of energy efficiency policy. The approach of the instruments is very different even though they both focus on residential energy efficiency improvements. This enables the reader to get a better understanding of the potential range of energy efficiency policy instruments. Also, the analysis provides an evaluation of the achieved carbon savings and discusses why the two programmes generate different results. The critical discussion of the contextual factors that need to be considered when drawing conclusions helps the reader to get a better understanding of the difficulties around sound comparative evaluations in this area.

The structure of this chapter is as follows: The chapter starts with an outline of the methodology. This is followed by a section presenting the case study findings for the UK and for Germany including a comparative analysis of the achieved energy and carbon savings as well as a more general comparison of the architecture of the two systems and the actors involved. Finally, the chapter draws some conclusions, highlights areas for future research and makes some recommendations.

Box 22.1 indicates the definitions of key concepts and terms relevant for this chapter.

Box 22.1 Definitions of key concepts and terms

Energy efficiency: Energy efficiency is frequently referred to as the ratio of the useful energy output of a process and the energy input in a process (Patterson, 1996). The higher the energy efficiency of a given technology, the more output one gets from one unit of energy used to run that technology. Hence, energy efficiency focuses on how much energy is consumed *relative* to a service.

Energy conservation: Energy conservation focuses on *total* energy use and is aimed at energy demand reduction (Moezzi, 1998). While energy efficient technologies may be part of that, it also includes *energy sufficiency*, that is, doing without a service altogether and changing consumption *behaviour*. The distinction from energy efficiency is important, particularly when considering issues such as the *rebound effect* (see Box 22.2).

Energy efficiency gap: Even though there are multiple cost-effective energy efficiency technologies, take up remains far below what would be possible. This discrepancy is called the *energy efficiency gap* or the *energy paradox*. This term was first coined by Hirst and Brown (1990).

Methodology

Case selection

The area of energy efficiency policy covers multiple policy instruments across different sectors (domestic, commercial and industrial). It would be a herculean task to cover all of this in one chapter. Hence, only two policy instruments have been chosen for more detailed analysis. The case selection followed a simple logic. First, the focus of the policy instrument should be among the key areas with the highest potential for energy demand reductions.

Second, the countries examined should play an important role in energy efficiency policy. Third, within the countries and the sector chosen the instruments should be the principal policy instrument. With regard to the three conditions the case selection is as following:

1   The sector with the *largest potential for energy efficiency improvements* is the buildings sector: of particular importance for energy demand reduction are residential buildings. Studies indicate that buildings alone (both residential and commercial) contributed about one third to global GHG emissions in 2009, most of which stemmed from residential buildings (UNEP, 2009). The picture looks similar in the UK where almost 30 per cent of carbon emissions come from the energy use in residential buildings (DEFRA, 2010) and Germany where residential buildings contribute about one third to total carbon emissions (BMWi and BMU, 2010). According to the IPCC, energy efficiency in the building sector plays a key role for climate change mitigation policy and can deliver significant reductions of GHG emissions. The IPCC estimates that at least 29 per cent of emissions could be reduced cost effectively in the residential and commercial building sectors by 2020 compared to the projected baseline emissions, the highest reduction potential among all sectors studied in the latest IPCC mitigation report (IPCC, 2007). Unfortunately the IPCC does not list separate estimates for residential and commercial buildings, but the largest proportion of the potential is likely to be within the residential building sector (UNEP, 2009).

2   In terms of the *significance of national energy efficiency policy*, both Germany and the UK are often cited as examples for innovative and ambitious energy efficiency policies. For example, the IEA describes both policy instruments as particularly innovative in its assessment of IEA members' energy efficiency policies (IEA, 2009). Also, the currently debated EU Energy Efficiency Directive proposes that all Member States implement Energy Savings Obligations similar to the British SO. The German CBRP is frequently cited internationally as a blueprint for loan and grant programmes to finance energy efficiency improvements (e.g. UNEP, 2011).

3   The criterion applied to identify the *principal policy instrument* is its contribution to carbon emission reductions in the domestic sector compared to other policy instruments targeting the housing sector; that is, the one with the largest effect on reducing carbon emissions is deemed the principal policy instrument. According to Rosenow (2011), in the UK this policy instrument is the Energy Savings Obligations, the SO. Germany's key policy instrument is the CBRP, a loan and grant scheme run by the bank Kreditanstalt für Wiederaufbau (KfW), the German Reconstruction Loan Corporation.

Because the two policy instruments have a slightly different focus it is useful to define the system boundaries of the analysis.

System boundaries

Both policy instruments target solely energy end use in residential buildings. There are some differences though.

The SO in the UK focuses on heating, warm water provision, electricity use for domestic appliances and lighting. The measures promoted by the programme may increase the energy performance of the building fabric (e.g. through wall insulation), reduce the energy consumption from appliances (e.g. through replacement of inefficient appliances such as fridges with more efficient ones), improve heating systems (e.g. through the installation of an energy efficiency boiler) or reduce electricity consumption from lighting (e.g. through the replacement of incandescent light bulbs with energy efficient light bulbs). While of low significance in terms of the contribution to the overall savings measures may also decarbonize the energy used, for example, by installing solar thermal.

In contrast, the CBRP in Germany has a narrower focus and mainly targets energy use for heating and warm water provision. Measures include insulation (e.g. solid wall insulation), renewal of the heating system (e.g. by replacing stand-alone heating devices) and replacement of windows (e.g. double glazed windows with triple glazed windows). Similar to the SO the CBRP also allows the promotion of micro-renewables such as solar thermal.

To sum up, the SO historically targeted energy use from a wider range of end uses, whereas the CBRP mainly focused on heating and warm water provision.

Analytical approach

The two policy instruments are compared with regard to their carbon and energy savings as well as the financial resources spent. This comparison is undertaken by using annual evaluations of the policy instruments by government departments, government agencies, the regulators and consultants. Note that this can only be an indicative evaluation due to the different methodologies used in the various studies that have been analysed for the purpose of this chapter. The effectiveness of policy instruments aiming at improving the energy efficiency of the building stock may be constrained by barriers to energy efficiency and rebound effects as illustrated in Box 22.2.

Furthermore, the architecture of the two policy instruments is compared based on differences in the key features of those instruments. This comparison is based on document analysis and interviews with experts. A more detailed analysis of the differences between the two policy instruments is provided in Rosenow (2011).

Box 22.2 Key issues

Barriers to energy efficiency: The energy efficiency gap; that is, the fact that cost-effective energy saving opportunities are not exploited, can be explained with obstacles that energy users face – the literature frequently uses the term *barrier* or *market barrier* to explain the low uptake of cost-effective measures.

There have been numerous attempts to develop taxonomies of barriers to energy efficiency (e.g. Brown, 2001; Hirst and Brown, 1990; Sorrell *et al.*, 2004). According to Eyre (1997), the barriers commonly named are:

- imperfect information to energy consumers;
- perverse incentives (e.g. the landlord/tenant barrier);
- limited availability of capital;
- price volatility;
- externalities such as the social and environmental cost of carbon (e.g. the cost of climate change, air pollution, health hazards, etc.) are not sufficiently internalized and reflected in energy prices
- bounded rationality (individuals may not have the cognitive ability to assess the costs and benefits appropriately).

Often energy efficiency programmes only address one or two of these barriers. While it is unlikely that a single policy instrument can incorporate all of the barriers named above, attention needs to be paid to the effect of not addressing them. For example, improving access to capital may help to overcome the lack of financial means of households, but those in the private rented sector are unlikely to be able to benefit from such measures because only the landlord can make decisions for or against energy efficiency measures.

Rebound effect: The rebound effect describes the phenomenon that energy efficiency measures make the consumption of energy services cheaper and hence more attractive to consumers resulting in an increase of total energy demand (Brookes, 1990; Inhaber and Saunders, 1994; Khazzoom, 1980). This phenomenon is called the rebound effect or the *Khazzoom–Brookes Postulate* (Saunders, 1992).

The rebound effect is frequently broken down into three different types: direct, indirect and economy-wide rebound effects.

Direct rebound effects refer to the phenomenon that energy efficiency improvements make it cheaper for consumers to use an energy service and as a result they use more of that service (Greening *et al.*, 2000; Sorrell, 2007). For example, if driving a car uses less fuel due to a more efficient engine people might simply drive their car more and offset some of the energy savings by doing so.

Indirect rebound effects might occur when consumers spend the money they save due to energy efficiency measures on other energy-consuming services. To stick to the previous example, if driving a car becomes cheaper consumers might decide to pay for a flight with the money they saved due to higher fuel efficiency (Barker *et al.*, 2007, Sorrell, 2007).

Economy-wide rebound effects refer to the effects of falling prices for energy services on the economy as a whole. If the cost of energy services decreases, the price of intermediate and final goods in the economy decreases too. This has the effect that more energy-intensive goods become more competitive. Lower cost for energy services might also stimulate economic growth leading to a higher demand for energy services (Barker *et al.*, 2007).

Based on a review of over 500 papers and reports, a study for the UK Energy Research Centre provided estimates of the direct, indirect and economy-wide rebound effects. For household heating, household cooling and personal automotive transport the direct rebound effect is estimated to be less than 30 per cent (Sorrell, 2007).

Case study findings

Energy Savings Obligations in the UK (SO)

In 1994, the UK introduced an obligation on electricity suppliers to deliver a certain amount of energy savings at the customer end, known as the Supplier Obligation (SO). Although the initial obligations were set at a low level and covered only electricity suppliers in the beginning, the instrument became one of the key features of UK energy efficiency policy. In 2000, the SO was extended to both gas and electricity suppliers, which is still the case today (Rosenow, 2012b).

The basic concept of the SO is that the government imposes a savings target on energy companies that has to be achieved at the customer end, that is, not via increasing the efficiency of energy *production* but through the improvement of the efficiency of energy *consumption*. The target may relate to energy consumption or carbon emissions. In the UK, the target is set by the Department of Energy and Climate Change (DECC) for a defined period of time (usually three to four years). The energy regulator, OFGEM, is responsible for administering the SO and enforcing it. It defines individual savings targets for each energy company. The energy companies then contract installers of energy saving measures who carry out the work in homes according to a defined standard and with a certain benchmark

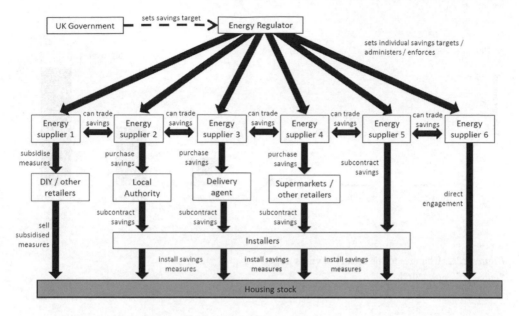

Figure 22.1 Mechanism of the Supplier Obligation in the UK
Source: Rosenow, 2012b

for energy and/or carbon savings. Alternatively, energy companies may choose to work with homeowners directly. In the past, energy companies have for example promoted the use of compact fluorescent lamps (CFLs) via mass mail-outs of free light bulbs, although this is now prohibited. Figure 22.1 summarizes the mechanism of the SO.

While there was a succession of different SO schemes, the basic logic remained the same. The first SO scheme was called Energy Efficiency Standards of Performance (EESoP) and ran from 1994–1998. Its successors, EESoP 2 and EESoP 3, ran from 1998–2000 and 2000–2002, respectively. In 2002 the scheme's name was changed to Energy Efficiency Commitment (EEC). EEC 1 was in place from 2002–2005 and EEC 2 from 2005–2008. EEC was eventually renamed in 2008 as the Carbon Emissions Reduction Target (CERT), which runs from 2008–2012. Figure 22.2 shows the annual energy savings target for the different periods.

It is evident from the data that the ambition of the SO changed significantly over time. The main drivers of this process include climate change policy, rising energy prices, increasing fuel poverty and a number of institutional changes. A detailed analysis of the different drivers and the politics can be found in Rosenow (2012a).[1]

The German CO2-Building Rehabilitation Programme (CBRP)

As outlined above, the CBRP is the most important policy instrument in Germany for reducing carbon emissions of buildings. The CBRP provides low interest loans and grants to households for specified refurbishment measures including energy efficiency. The federal government funds the scheme and enables the bank KfW to issue loans with an interest rate

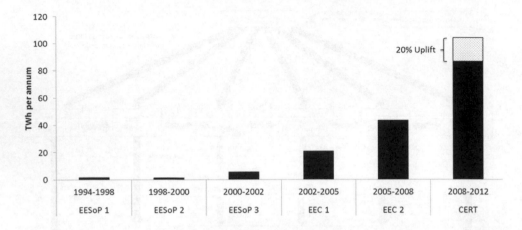

Figure 22.2 Changes to the energy savings target
Source: Rosenow, 2012b

lower than the market rates. In addition, some of the funding provided is used to issue grants. Making use of both federal funding and national as well as international capital markets, KfW offers financial products to finance housing refurbishment. Home owners, housing companies and public bodies can apply for loans and grants at an intermediary bank, which assesses the financial circumstances of the application. The intermediary bank forwards the application to the KfW, which then approves the loan or grant (Rosenow, 2011). Figure 22.3 summarizes the model described above.

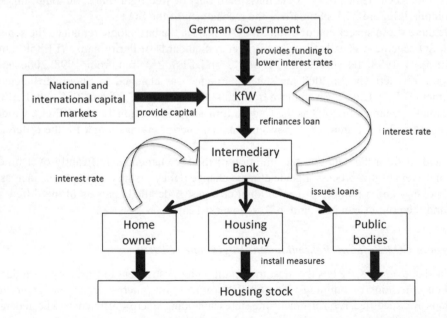

Figure 22.3 Architecture of the CBRP

While the CBRP has been modified over the years since its inception in 2001, the basic principles are still the same. One notable change, however, is the introduction of grants in 2007 (not covered in the graph above), although most of the funding goes into low interest loans.

Comparison

Brief evaluation of policy instruments

This section provides a brief evaluation of the two policy instruments in terms of their effectiveness, that is, the carbon emissions and energy saved compared to the financial resources spent.

A comparison of the data derived is subject to various limitations for a number of reasons: first, the energy and carbon savings accounting methodology differs in the UK and Germany and the figures are not like-for-like. Second, there is no reliable estimate of free rider effects, that is, how many of the energy efficiency improvements initiated by the policy instrument would have happened anyway, and rebound effects in Germany, whereas in the UK free rider effects (called 'deadweight') and rebound effects (called 'comfort taking') are taken into account. Finally, the figures arc based on modelling studies rather than monitoring real energy use and the effects of the policy instruments. Therefore the following remarks have to be taken with a pinch of salt.

Figure 22.4 is based on various evaluations and presents the energy and carbon savings for both programmes.

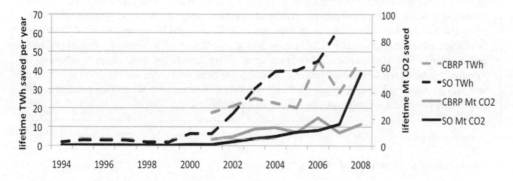

Figure 22.4 CO_2 emissions in Mt lifetime emissions and TWh saved per year in the UK (SO) and Germany (CBRP)

Source: Rosenow, 2011

From 2002 to 2008 about €1.3 billion were spent by energy suppliers as a result of the SO (based on Lees, 2006, 2008). According to the Federal Ministry of Transport, Building and Urban Development (BMVBS, 2010), in the same period federal funding for the CBRP amounted to more than three times as much (about €4.5 billion). In the case of the SO the energy customers paid for the scheme with their bills, while the CBRP funding was based on taxpayers' money. The carbon savings achieved over the same period amount to 109 million tonnes of lifetime CO_2 emissions for the SO and to 91 million tonnes of lifetime CO_2 emissionsfor the CBRP (Rosenow, 2011). The 'dips' that occur in some years in the case of the CBRP are the result of varying funding for the programme from year to year.

Considering that both programmes led to comparable carbon savings, the question remains why the CBRP required significantly more funding. One reason is the different energy efficiency performance of the building stock; dwellings in Germany are much more energy efficient than buildings in the UK, a result of laxer energy performance requirements for new buildings in the past and the older building stock in the UK (BPIE, 2011). Hence energy savings are more costly as the low hanging fruits have already been picked. However, a more detailed analysis would be required in order to answer that question confidently, and there are several factors that need to be considered: the CO_2 emissions from residential energy use per household are broadly similar (around 5 tonnes CO_2 per year) (DEFRA, 2010; Diefenbach, 2008), even though British buildings are less energy efficient. A more moderate climate and less living space per person offset the lower energy efficiency though resulting in similar levels of emissions. Therefore it is difficult to draw quick conclusions without further analysis.

Box 22.3 presents a critique of mainstream energy efficiency policy.

Box 22.3 Critique of mainstream energy efficiency policy

Most energy efficiency programmes are still pursued from a perspective that puts technological efficiency and financial aspects centre stage – they, intentionally or unintentionally, aim at improving nominal efficiency of energy services leading to relative savings. This helped to trigger remarkable technological innovations with regard to efficiency in many areas. However, at an aggregate level enhanced efficiency just does not seem to add up. In order to employ energy efficiency as a means (rather than an end in itself) to reduce carbon emissions on a large scale, a different approach is needed. While it is unlikely that the focus on efficiency as it stands will change significantly in the foreseeable future, there is potential to recalibrate existing policy instruments with an increasing orientation towards achieving total energy savings. Similar thoughts have been explored by others, who also highlighted the need to realign energy efficiency efforts with total energy savings (Wilhite and Nørgård, 2004; Harris *et al.*, 2008). Harris *et al.* (2008) developed the concept of *progressive efficiency*, which proposes that as the scale of energy use or service increases, the level of required efficiency should be higher to make sure total consumption is accounted for. This concept could potentially be applied to buildings, appliances, heating systems, etc.

Comparison of architecture of the policy instruments

While having a similar effect in terms of delivering energy efficiency measures across the housing stock, the two policy instruments are very different with regard to their general architecture.

ACTORS INVOLVED

In both countries the level of ambition is set by a government department, although it is the Department of Energy and Climate Change (DECC) in the UK and the Federal Ministry of Transport, Building and Urban Development (BMVBS) in Germany. The two departments have a very different focus: DECC's main remit is reducing carbon emissions and setting the framework for a low carbon energy system, whereas BMVBS's primary task is the development of infrastructure, although this has a climate change and energy efficiency component.

The CBRP channels funding for energy efficiency retrofits through the bank KfW. The SO, in contrast, utilizes energy suppliers as a vehicle for delivering energy efficiency, a model quite distinct from the German approach. It also relies on the regulator, OFGEM, to administer the scheme. In Germany, the regulator is not involved in the CBRP.

FINANCE

The CRBP is funded out of the public budget and total funding may change every year depending on the overall budgetary considerations. While funds have been projected for three years into the future, those projections are mere statements of what the government would like to spend on the CBRP rather than binding figures. The CBRP was subject to austerity measures in 2010 when the responsible minister announced that funds would be cut by half for the year 2011 (Rosenow, 2011), although additional funds were made available later in the year. The volatility and risk of funding cuts trigger considerable uncertainty in the market leading to a stalling of orders for energy efficiency retrofits.

In Britain the SO is paid for by the energy companies, but energy suppliers are permitted to pass the costs through to households via energy bills. Therefore, the treasury has no involvement in the financial transactions taking place and neither benefits directly from nor contributes to the SO. Hence, even substantial spending cuts, as seen at the moment, cannot affect the SO as it is not based on public expenditure. Taking into account that larger targets and the promotion of more expensive measures increase the total cost of the programme, it comes as no surprise that every household in the UK contributes about £50 to the SO through their annual energy bill. This puts a burden on some households who do not benefit from the SO (for example the fuel-poor living in private rented accommodation). This means that there are limits to how far the costs of the scheme can expand if paid via energy bills.

FOCUS

The SO incentivizes energy suppliers to use the cheapest measures available in order to deliver their obligation. In a competitive market where energy companies compete on price it is assumed that the suppliers will try to minimize the cost of the delivery of the SO. This is probably one of the reasons why micro-generation measures never had a significant share of the SO measures and why most of the activity has been in loft and cavity insulation as well as lighting. In a nutshell, the SO is a scheme that incentivizes the picking of low hanging fruits.[2]

In contrast to the SO, the CBRP focused on packages of measures from the beginning, taking the view that carrying out many measures at once is advantageous. The so called 'whole house approach', where all of the building fabric is upgraded to a higher energy efficiency performance, has played an important role for the calibration of the CBRP. In order to be eligible for support from the CBRP, a defined standard in terms of the buildings energy use compared to the basic energy performance standard for new buildings has to be achieved. However, the CBRP also promotes single measures and combinations of measures, so it is not just about the whole house approach.

Conclusion

The path of low carbon development includes 'using less energy, improving the efficiency with which energy is used' (Urban, 2010: 93). This chapter focused on precisely this issue and presented two high profile case studies in the area of energy efficiency policy.

Both instruments resulted in significant energy and carbon savings over time and it is difficult to judge which instrument is 'more effective'. They both serve as examples of successful energy efficiency policy and will probably continue to do so.

Based on the above a number of recommendations can be made:

Funding: The CBRP was funded by the public budget – there was some volatility in the past in terms of funding levels and there is the risk that the budget may continue to vary in the future. This is unhelpful for the long-term certainty in the energy efficiency market. Similar loan and grant programmes should be designed in a way that is less prone to budgetary changes. The SO is currently focusing on low-cost measures. As discussed above, larger targets and the promotion of more expensive measures increase the premium paid via the energy bill. There are limits to how much consumers are willing and able to pay, and for deep retrofits additional resources will be required. Loan schemes similar to the CBRP might be a sensible option.

Scale: In order to achieve significant refurbishment rates of 2 per cent or more of the building stock every year, the current ambition of both policy instruments does not suffice. Therefore additional instruments, for example building regulations setting minimum standards for existing buildings, are likely to be required to increase the refurbishment activity.

Social equity: Some segments of consumers did not benefit as much as others from the two policy instruments. Particularly poorer households are negatively affected if the energy efficiency of their buildings is not improved and energy prices continue to rise in the future. In order to cover a wider range of households there needs to be additional support, particularly for the private rented sector.

Future policy initiatives for energy efficiency and low carbon development in industrialized, high income countries should draw on the experiences with the two policy instruments and carefully assess their limitations. What is likely to be required is a sensible mix of different policies rather than one silver bullet.

References

Barker, T., Ekins, P. and Foxon, T. (2007) The macro-economic rebound effect and the UK economy. *Energy Policy*, 35, 4935–46.

BMU (2007) Das Integrierte Energie- und Klimaprogramm der Bundesregierung. Available at: http://www.bmu.de/files/pdfs/allgemein/application/pdf/hintergrund_meseberg.pdf (accessed 20 November 2012).

BMVBS (2010) Wohnen und Bauen in Zahlen 2009/2010. Berlin, Bonn: BMVBS.

BMWi and BMU (2010) Energiekonzept für eine umweltschonende, zuverlässige und bezahlbare Energieversorgung. Endfassung. 28 September. Berlin: BMWi.

BPIE (2011) Europe's Buildings under the microscope. A country-by-country review of the energy performance of buildings. Brussels: BPIE.

Brookes, L. (1990) The greenhouse effect: the fallacies in the energy efficiency solution. *Energy Policy*, 18, 199–201.

Brown, M. A. (2001) Market failures and barriers as a basis for clean energy policies. *Energy Policy*, 29, 1197–207.

Department for Environment, Food and Rural Affairs (DEFRA) (2010) Measuring progress: sustainable development indicators 2010. Greenhouse gas emissions. Available at: http://webarchive.nationalarchives.gov.uk/20110223093550/http://defra.gov.uk/sustainable/government/progress/data-resources/documents/02_greenhouse_gas_emissions.xls (accessed 20 November 2012).

Diefenbach, N. (2008) Deutscher Gebäudebestand: Basisdaten und Modellrechnungen bis 2020. Available at: http://www.iwu.de/fileadmin/user_upload/dateien/energie/ake44/IWU-Tagung_17-04-2008_-_Diefenbach_-_Basisdaten.pdf (accessed 20 November 2012).

European Commission (2010) EU energy and climate package. Available at: http://ec.europa.eu/clima/policies/package/index_en.htm (accessed 20 November 2012).

Eyre, N. (1997) Barriers to energy efficiency more than just market failure. *Energy and Environment*, 8, 25–43.

Greening, L. A., Greene, D. L. and Difiglio, C. (2000) Energy efficiency and consumption – the rebound effect – a survey. *Energy Policy*, 28, 389–401.

Harris, J., Diamond, R., Iyer, M., Payne, C., Blumstein, C. and Siderius, H.-P. (2008) Towards a sustainable energy balance: progressive efficiency and the return of energy conservation. *Energy Efficiency*, 1, 175.

Hirst, E. and Brown, M. (1990) Closing the efficiency gap: barriers to the efficient use of energy. *Resources, Conservation and Recycling*, 3, 267–81.

International Energy Agency (IEA) (2009) Implementing energy efficiency policies: are IEA member countries on track? Paris: OECD Publishing.

Inhaber, H. and Saunders, H. (1994) Road to nowhere: energy conservation often backfires and leads to increased consumption. *The Sciences*, 34, 20–5.

Intergovernmental Panel on Climate Change (IPCC) (2007) Climate change 2007. Mitigation of climate change: contribution of Working Group III to the fourth assessment report of the Intergovernmental Panel on Climate Change. Cambridge: Cambridge University Press.

Khazzoom, J. D. (1980) Economic implications of mandated efficiency standards for household appliances. *Energy Journal*, 1, 21–40.

Lees, E. (2006) Evaluation of the energy efficiency commitment 2002–05. Wantage: Eoin Lees Energy.

Lees, E. (2008) Evaluation of the energy efficiency commitment 2005–08. Wantage: Eoin Lees Energy.

Moezzi, M. (1998) The predicament of efficiency. ACEEE 1998 Summer Study on Energy Efficiency in Buildings, 4.273-4.282. Washington, DC: ACEEE.

OFGEM (2005) A review of the energy efficiency commitment 2002–2005. London: OFGEM.

Patterson, M. G. (1996) What is energy efficiency? Concepts, indicators and methodological issues. *Energy Policy*, 24, 377.

Rosenow, J. (2011) Different paths of change: the case of domestic energy efficiency policy in Britain and Germany. ECEEE Summer Study 2011, 2011 Belambra Presqu'île de Giens, France, pp.261–72.

Rosenow, J. (2012a) Energy Savings Obligations in the UK – a history of change. *Energy Policy*, 49, 373–82.

Rosenow, J. (2012b) Understanding policy change: Energy Savings Obligations in the UK. World Sustainable Energy Days 2012, Wels.

Saunders, H. (1992) The Khazzoom–Brookes postulate and neoclassical growth. *Energy Journal*, 13, 131–48.

Sorrell, S. (2007) The rebound effect: an assessment of the evidence for economy-wide energy savings from improved energy efficiency. London: UK Energy Research Centre.

Sorrell, S., O'Malley, E., Schleich, J. and Scott, S. (2004) *The Economics of Energy Efficiency – Barriers to Cost-Effective Investment.* Cheltenham: Edward Elgar Publishing.

United Nations Environment Programme (UNEP) (2009) Buildings and climate change. Summary for decision-makers. Paris: UNEP.

UNEP (2011) Towards a green economy: pathways to sustainable development and poverty education. Available at: www.unep.org/greeneconomy (accessed 20 November 2012).

Urban, F. (2010) The MDGs and beyond: can low carbon development be pro?poor? *IDS bulletin*, 41, 92.

Wilhite, H. and Nørgård, J. S. (2004) Equating efficiency with reduction: a self-deception in energy policy. *Energy and Environment*, 15, 991–1009.

Further reading

Eyre, N. (1997) Barriers to energy efficiency more than just market failure. *Energy and Environment*, 8, 25–43.

Jaffe, A. B. and Stavins, R. N. (1994) The energy-efficiency gap. What does it mean? *Energy Policy*, 22, 804–10.

Moezzi, M. (1998) The predicament of efficiency. ACEEE 1998 Summer Study on Energy Efficiency in Buildings, 4.273-4.282. Washington, DC: ACEEE.

Wilhite, H. and Nørgård, J. S. (2004) Equating efficiency with reduction: a self-deception in energy policy. *Energy and Environment*, 15, 991–1009.

Notes

1   Parts of this section were amended from a paper first published by Elsevier: Rosenow (2012a).
2   By 'low hanging fruits' the cheapest options for improving energy efficiency are meant.

Final thoughts

Frauke Urban and Johan Nordensvärd

Global climate change is one of the greatest challenges of our times. It is not a distant vision of a troubled future, but very much a reality of today that requires urgent action.

Former UN-Secretary General and President of the Global Humanitarian Forum Kofi Annan mentioned a few years ago that 'Today, millions of people are already suffering because of climate change' (Annan, 2009: i). The UN Secretary-General Ban Ki-moon confirmed recently at a trip to the small Pacific nation Kiribati that 'climate change is not about tomorrow. It is lapping at our feet – quite literally in Kiribati and elsewhere' (Ban, 2011: 1). Ban further said 'I have watched the high tide impacting those villages. The high tide shows it is high time to act.' He also addressed the current development model and suggested that something is 'seriously wrong with our current model of economic development' (Ban, 2011: 1).

In line with these thoughts, the book *Low Carbon Development: Key Issues* stresses two key messages: first, it is essential to mitigate GHG emissions now to tackle climate change. Second, enabling development in a carbon constrained world requires a new development model, which focuses less on economic growth and exploiting finite natural resources and instead focuses more on fair and equitable human development within the limits of our planet. Low carbon development is a new development model, which aims to achieve these two goals simultaneously.

Low carbon development can bring opportunities and benefits for both developed and developing countries, nevertheless low carbon development can only be implemented when an adequate enabling environment is in place that addresses the political, economic, social and technological key issues. However, the greatest challenge of all is to overcome the current mindset and to develop alternative, more sustainable and more equitable development models for humankind.

References

Annan, K. (2009) The anatomy of a silent crisis. human impact report – climate change. Geneva: Global Humanitarian Forum.

Ban, K.-M. (2011) Climate change lapping Pacific shores: Ban Ki-moon. TVNZ. Available at: http://tvnz.co.nz/national-news/climate-change-lapping-pacific-shores-ban-ki-moon-4387638 (accessed 20 November 2012).

Index